PERCEPTION
A Cognitive-Stage Approach

McGraw-Hill Series in Psychology

Consulting Editors
Norman Garmezy
Lyle V. Jones

PERCEPTION
A Cognitive-Stage Approach

Second Edition

Ronald H. Forgus
Lake Forest College

Lawrence E. Melamed
Kent State University

McGRAW-HILL BOOK COMPANY

*New York   St. Louis   San Francisco   Auckland   Düsseldorf
Johannesburg   Kuala Lumpur   London   Mexico   Montreal   New Delhi
Panama   Paris   São Paulo   Singapore   Sydney   Tokyo   Toronto*

To
Michael, Sandra, Tristan,
and Kilian Forgus
and Jodi and Douglas Melamed

This book was set in Times Roman by University Graphics, Inc.
The editors were Richard R. Wright and Susan Gamer;
the cover was designed by J. E. O'Connor;
the production supervisor was Charles Hess.
New drawings were done by J & R Services, Inc.
R. R. Donnelley & Sons Company was printer and binder.

PERCEPTION: A COGNITIVE-STAGE APPROACH

234567890DODO79876

Library of Congress Cataloging in Publication Data

Forgus, Ronald H
    Perception : a cognitive-stage approach.

    (McGraw-Hill series in psychology)
    Bibliography: p.
    Includes index.
    1. Perception. I. Melamed. Lawrence E., joint
author. [DNLM: 1. Perception. BF311 F721p]
BF311.F58 1976   153.7   75-25842
ISBN 0-07-021620-7

Contents

Preface

When the first edition of this book was published ten years ago, we found it necessary to include the word *cognitive* in the title. Today this orientation has been justified, since hardly anyone working in perception would deny the tremendous involvement of cognitive processing in perception. In capturing the essence of how cognition is concerned in the acquisition of knowledge, Naomi Weisstein has aptly defined cognitive psychology as "how something out there gets in here, and what happens to it here, and then how it gets out there" (Solso, 1973, p. i).

Weisstein's definition covers the realm of perception as we present it in this book. We broadly define *perception* as the process of information extraction. This definition is of course very general and requires refinement; but refining it in a single definition is virtually impossible. In fact, the entire book deals with the complexities of information extraction in the general process of perception.

In Chapter 1 we present our orientation, which considers perception in the context of human adaptive behavior. In order to deal effectively with their environment, individuals must extract reliable information and act competently. Perception guides this adaptive activity and in so doing becomes intricately tied up with other cognitive processes, such as learning, memory, and thinking. Chapters 1 and 2 also present our theoretical position that perception is not a single act but rather is organized into a set of hierarchically arranged, temporal stages.

In a sense, the rest of the book works out these hierarchical stages. Thus, Chapter 3 deals with detection; Chapters 4 to 6 deal with sensory transduction and psychophysical relationships; and from Chapter 7 to the end we progress up the hierarchy from brightness and unity to figure, form, space, motion, events, and personal dynamics. Throughout this presentation, we attempt to specify and analyze the coding systems or mechanisms that exist for processing the relevant information in each of these areas. We also deal with the knotty problem of how wired-in, innate programs become modified with perceptual learning and sensory-motor experience.

It is evident in this book that we owe a tremendous intellectual debt to those who have influenced us and have led the way in defining the modern domain of perception—the gestalt psychologists and the phenomenologically oriented psychologists, Hebb, Gibson, George Miller, Jerry Bruner, Wendell Garner, Fred Attneave, Julie Hochberg, and the host of modern information processers. Ronald Forgus would also like to express his personal gratitude to two of his teachers, Abe Luchins and the late Robbie MacLeod. Larry Melamed would similarly like to express gratitude to Willard Thurlow and Sheldon Ebenholtz.

This book would never have been completed without the dedicated and conscientious clerical work of Patricia Harlan. She not only typed most of it herself but also supervised a team of other typists when we were fighting a deadline. They include, Patricia Conti, Kim Cook, Sandra Forgus, Frances Hale, and Valerie Younge. Our thanks to all of them, and especially to Mrs. Harlan. We must also express our appreciation to Ted Maciejewski of Downey VA Hospital, Downey, Illinois, for doing the photographs, and Richard Goldman at Kent State. Finally, we want to express our deep gratitude to Claire Michaels, our friend and colleague, for reviewing most of the final draft. True friend and scientist that she is, she was a tough critic.

We express our thanks to authors and publishers who have allowed original work to be reprinted. Individual credit is given where such material is cited.

Ronald H. Forgus
Lawrence E. Melamed

Chapter 1

Perception as an Information-Extraction Process

There are many ways that a book on perception can be organized. We have decided to place the process of perception within the context of man's general need to adapt to his environment so that he can cope effectively with the demands of life.

Definition of Perception

The way the individual gains knowledge about his environment in this quest for adaptive behavior is of prime importance. The gaining of such knowledge necessitates the extraction of information from the vast array of physical energy which stimulates the organism's senses. Only those stimuli which have *cue* value, i.e., which trigger some kind of reactive or adaptive action from the individual, should logically be called information. *For our purposes perception will be defined as the process of information extraction.*

A primary focus of our consideration of information extraction will be a description of the *cognitive structures* (those mechanisms that direct the way cues are processed) involved as people accomplish various perceptual tasks. Later in the book individual differences in the organization of these cognitive structures will also be considered.

A PHYLOGENETIC PERSPECTIVE

It is quite logical to conceive of the perceptual process in lower animals in stimulus-response terms. Thus we could simply write behavioral laws which relate the information contained in the stimulus complex to the nature of the organism's responses. This is, in fact, what has been done with great accuracy and predictability in lower animals by ethologists and animal psychologists. For example, Tinbergen and Perdeck (1950) have shown that the mechanism through which the fledgling herring gull pecks food from its mother's beak is contracted by a very simple, *built-in* reflex system. The releaser stimulus (which invariably gives rise to the built-in pecking response) is a segregated red area against a yellow background.

Similarly, ethologists such as Lorenz (1958) and his co-workers have shown how such adaptive behavior as spawning, imprinting, and aggression (as well as its inhibition) are controlled by instinctive patterns which are chains of reflexive-tropistic reactions. For example, baby salmon swim down to warmer water and away from the hot sun because they have no protective pigment (a *reflex* reaction against the cold of the shallow stream where they were born). When they are older, the production of pigment leads them to seek colder water. Hence they are *attracted* to areas having colder water (a *tropistic* reaction). The term *reflex* refers to an innate reaction from within, whereas the term *tropism* refers to a pull from without. Most adaptive instincts, like spawning in salmon, involve patterns of chain reactions involving both kinds of processes.

It is interesting to note that the ethologists approach perception in much the same way as modern behaviorists like Skinner. That is, they essentially dispose of the problem of perceptual processing by defining the problem as one of response analysis. The present authors believe, however, that, in order to do justice to perception, as such, we must address ourselves to the *nature* of *information processing*.

As we ascend the phylogenetic scale, the nature of perceptual reactions becomes increasingly influenced by learning. In the human infant, for example, the perception of light is determined by *built-in* or *unlearned* programs. Evidence that ability to code specific dimensions results from highly specific reactions (genetic programs) of specialized cortical cells has been obtained by Hubel and Wiesel (1962; 1963; 1968) whose work is analyzed in Chapters 2 and 4. This innate coding ability is necessary for adaptive behavior to begin, but the *programs become modified* with growth, development, experience, and varied sensory stimulation.

Lack of sensory stimulation not only leads to loss of innate connections (i.e., the built-in programs) but also precludes the learning necessary to develop central organizations required for the perception of more complex patterns, such as form (Hebb, 1949). Let us just think, for example, of the highly complex and abstract kinds of information which have to be extracted in such diverse tasks as the aesthetic appreciation of a painting or a great musical composition, the solution of a mathematical problem, or the perception of another human being.

It is this universal involvement of the process of information extraction in man's adaptive behavior which leads us to believe that we must relate perception to the general problem of cognitive or knowledge development if we are to understand fully the nature of the reception, acquisition, assimilation, and utilization of knowledge. Looked at in this way, perception becomes the core process in the acquisition of *cognition* or *knowledge*. We thus conceive of perception as the *superset,* with *learning, memory* and *thinking* as *subsets* subsumed under the perceptual process.

While we shall not deal with the formal dynamics of learning as such, we must, to support our position, go more deeply into the relationship between perception, learning, and thinking. Then we can outline the subtasks or stages involved in various perceptual tasks.

Relationship between Perception, Learning, and Thinking

Our thesis that perception is a superset which subsumes the subsets of learning, memory, and thinking in the total act of information extraction requires elaboration. It gives perception a much broader scope than is usual, and requires further examination between these three cognitive processes. For the present we are simply postulating a relationship between these cognitive events. After we have examined the role of memory in perception, later, we shall conduct a critical evaluation of these relationships.

Perception, learning, and thinking have traditionally been referred to as the cognitive processes since they all deal, to some extent, with the problem of knowledge. *Perception* has been regarded as the process by which an organism receives or extracts certain information about the environment. *Learning* is defined as the process by which this information is acquired through experience and becomes part of the organism's storage of facts in memory. Thus, the results of learning facilitate the further extraction of information since the stored facts become models against which cues are judged. The most complex of these cognitive processes, namely, *thinking,* is an activity that is inferred to be going on when an organism is engaged in solving problems, which also involves the use of models. Our definition of perception links all three processes.

Now, the solution of complex problems requires the use of mediating symbols like language, mathematics, or some other powerful tool. The difficulty of the problem can be determined by the relative ease with which the information required for its solution can be extracted. When an individual can extract the information almost immediately, he has no problem. The problem becomes more and more difficult as the "potential information" becomes less and less available or more and more abstract. The way we extract abstract or more "hidden" information is to learn to use concepts. The greater our conceptual abilities are, the better our general problem-solving abilities are.

A way of summarizing what we have said thus far in this section is to state that, *as the perceptual set is broadened and becomes more complex* and richly patterned with experience, *the individual becomes capable of extracting more information from the environment.* The *process* starts with simple *reflexive* action at birth and grows through maturation and learning to produce more powerful *sets,* which are mediated by concepts; hence *thinking* becomes more expert.

Even though we have differentiated perception, learning, memory, and thinking in the definitions given above, the four cognitive processes are closely interrelated and difficult to separate in practical situations. Thus other individuals may define these terms in a slightly different manner. Our aim is specifically to *emphasize the continuity of the cognitive process.* At the beginning of this process, learning and thinking either are nonexistent or operate at a low level. (In contemporary computer terminology, we may say that the programming is of a *built-in* or *wired-in* nature.) Where information extraction requires more active effort on the part of the organism, learning, memory, and thinking play an increasingly important role. (The basic programming becomes more and more *modified.*) Thus we consider learning and thinking as events or processes which aid in the extraction of information.

Having defined perception as the process of information extraction, it seems clear why we made it the parent construct, for *adaptive behavior originates in perception.* For example, the discrimination of the mother's face, which requires learning in the infant, presupposes a built-in reaction to light, which is perception. (See Fantz, 1961b, discussed in Chapter 12.)

The relationship between learning and thinking in the perceptual process is diagramed in Figure 1-1. Stimuli processing potential information are observed by the organism, which extracts some of the information present, aided by the process called *learning.* This learning modifies the organism so that perception of the same stimuli later also will be modified. For example, John Jones is introduced to Bill Smith, hears his name, and learns other things about him. The next time that John encounters Bill, he *perceives* him somewhat differently than he did on the first occasion. Now he may have positive or negative emotional reactions because of his previous experience with Bill.

In Figure 1-1 it is indicated also that learning may lead to thinking (a manipulation of previously learned aspects); this thinking modifies the organism through the involvement of new learning, which in turn modifies the perception

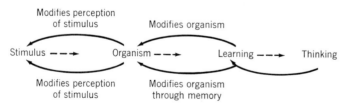

Figure 1-1 The relationship of learning and thinking in the complex process of perception. Stimuli possess potential which is extracted by the organism as learning. This learning is stored as memory and modifies the organism so that later perception of the same stimuli will be different. The process of thinking (resulting from previous learning) also modifies the organism because new learning occurs; thus the perception of stimuli is modified.

of the stimulus situation. These relationships can be illustrated by the change in perception which occurs as we gain insight about the solution of a particular problem through continuing to think about possible approaches. When we find an appropriate solution, the problem is no longer a problem, and all aspects are placed in proper perspective.

Variation from Sensation to Problem Solving   In the past, many authors separated the constructs *sensation* and *perception,* defining sensation as the process containing the physiological or sensory elements out of which the percepts were compounded. The problem of perception is extremely complex, however, and such a limited conceptualization is no longer tenable. This is especially important when we remember that few, if any, pure sensory acts occur after an organism has had a little interaction with the environment. We believe it is more useful to consider perception as a continuing process that varies from events which are of a simple, elementary nature to those of greater complexity which require more active learning and thinking. The simple sensory events are processed by built-in coding programs, while more complex perceptual events require modified programs for effective processing. In that case, sensation, as the beginning of the perceptual process during which *primary* aspects of the stimuli are coded by sensory-perceptive systems, is part of the total perceptual act. Primary aspects refer to brightness, color, and orientation which are processed by the specified built-in programs, while, as we have said, more complex aspects like recognition and identification require modified programs for complete processing.

Now let us look more closely at the interrelationship of learning and thinking in the perceptual process. Some percepts are necessary before we can learn, since we cannot acquire facts until we have first received them. Obviously a blind person cannot perceive or come to know the color of an object. Who would deny that the tools of thinking and learning depend to a large extent on what the individual has previously learned? For example, how could we solve mathematical problems if we had not learned the meaning of signs or symbols, which, in turn, would have been impossible if we had not been able to discriminate, i.e., perceive, differences among the shapes of the symbols? The difference between an addition and a multiplication sign, for instance, involves only a slight rotation, yet you see them to be very different indeed. Or let us take an example from the English language: it requires extremely good visual acuity to discriminate between the words *bear* and *beer,* and yet the distinction is rather significant.

As human adults we take this discriminatory process for granted, but such fine discriminations are not found in lower mammals like rats, unless they have received very special training; in young children their accuracy is questionable. Hebb has suggested that the learning in young animals is of a slow, trial-and-error nature but that in mature animals quick, insightful learning frequently occurs; the insightful learning is possible because of the information which the organism has stored over the years. Similarly, Piaget and his colleagues have indicated that a child is unable to form certain concepts until he has learned to perceive certain relationships among stimuli.[1] Furthermore, Harlow has shown that monkeys, after receiving training in a long series of discrimination problems, are able to solve other problems, which involve totally different stimulus patterns, within a single practice trial (Harlow, 1949). The dependence of higher problem-solving ability on conceptual ability is well established (Piaget & Inhelder, 1951). It is easy to think of many other examples from almost every aspect of human life, but these few instances from the areas of discrimination, concept formation, problem solving, language, and communication emphasize the fact that important aspects of behavior, including social interaction, depend on the integrated action of the cognitive process.

The order of these temporal relationships in the development of this integrated cognitive process has generated much contemporary theoretical controversy. Such controversy centers around Piaget's assertion that the learning of these higher cognitive abilities is a maturational process which requires the previous development of simpler cognitive structures. Moreover, these *stage-dependent* sequences emerge at specific ages. For example, Piaget believes that various cognitive achievements emerge at relatively fixed time periods. Thus, he deduces from his research that the concept of reciprocity (if $A = B$, then $B = A$), a cognitive achievement, does not appear until about age 8. There are others who have shown, however, that enriched experience can speed up the emergence of this cognitive ability to a younger age.

More recent data and their theoretical interpretation suggest that it is not so much *when* these abilities are learned but *what* is learned that determines the kinds of cognitive information that the individual is capable of extracting. For example, Bryant (1974), in a most fascinating book, has demonstrated that children are capable of generating inferences, in perceptual behavior, which are more complicated than those specified by Piaget for particular age periods.

It is known also that learning not only aids thinking ability but can also impede efficient problem-solving behavior. Everyone can recall instances in which the mechanized learning of a certain method or formula for solving a problem interfered with the solution of other problems because the individual finds it difficult to change his mode of attacking the problem. This stereotyped thinking, which is often caused by repetitive previous learning or training, has been called an *Einstellung* or set (Luchins, 1942).

Interrelationship of the Processes

The relationship between the cognitive processes is *by no means unidirectional*. Thus far we have indicated only how some perception must precede learning and how previous percepts and learning affect thinking, but it is also known that the result of thinking modifies future learning and that learning in turn can influence the way we perceive our world. We have only to think about certain social or ethnic stereotypes or the nature of social attitudes to realize the extent to which

---

[1]See, for example, Forgus (1954), Hebb (1949), and Piaget (1950).

learning determines the selectivity of perception. An instance of such constricted perception is the fact that racially prejudiced people are set (stereotyped) to perceive the target race in a specific way, the characteristics being attenuated or not processed. It has also been established that learning improves perceptual discrimination and selection (Forgus, 1955a & 1955b; Eleanor J. Gibson, 1955 & 1969; Hebb, 1949). Further, it has been suggested that efficient learning is improved by the way the individual organizes the problem task; i.e., learning is often dependent on thinking or directional sets. Thus it has been found that learning by principles facilitates retention and transfer (Forgus & Schwartz, 1957; Hilgard, Edgren, & Whipple, 1953; Katona, 1940). These findings have become particularly important in the field of modern education, in which scholars have stressed the importance of learning to develop the problem-solving attitude by directing learning through encouraging the child to understand how to approach a problem task (Bruner, 1961).

INFORMATION-PROCESSING APPROACHES TO PERCEPTION

The way we have described perception implies that the process can be broken down into an *ordered set* of stages, from simple to complex. One basic problem is to specify the relationship between the informational aspects of stimulus energy and the corresponding psychological experience for each stage of this order. This is the problem of *psychophysical correspondence,* which refers to the congruence between the information in physical energy and the corresponding psychological experience, e.g., between wavelengths and color, between space-time relations and motion perceptions, and between spatial relationships and form perception.

Our approach to this problem will emphasize the increasing disparity between experience and the *distal stimulus* (the physical stimulus) as one proceeds to each successive stage in this order. We shall also argue that *within* the more complex tasks (e.g., stimulus recognition of an identity) there is a *temporal* progression of stages (Sternberg 1969a & 1969b) during which successive transformation of proximal stimulation on the sense receptor is accomplished. Detailed experimental investigation of perceptual processes suggests that these increasing transformations often involve an active construction of stimulus information (Neisser, 1967) rather than merely a passive decoding of such information. Thus, perception, particularly in tasks higher in the perceptual order, requires that information be sampled rather than simply resulting from direct stimulation. This conceptualization is illustrated in Figure 1-2. The arrows which point from left to right represent the *inflow* of information from environmental stimulation. The arrows which point from right to left represent the *outflow* of information from the person. The resulting *perceptual experience* is thus viewed as an amalgamation of information from these two sources. Though the base line implies a rough temporal sequence, the details of this temporal sequence are the subject of many current experimental investigations, a number of which will be reviewed in later chapters, especially Chapters 10

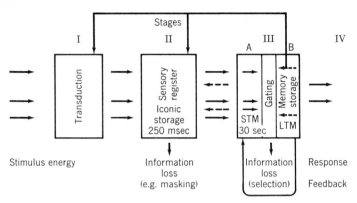

Figure 1-2 An information model of information processing.

and 11. Note that the vertical arrows indicate that information loss or modification is known to occur at two stages: (1) at the level of the sensory register (see Chapter 4) through such phenomena as sensory masking (see Chapter 10), and (2) as a result of the selectivity determined by the cognitive structures of long-term storage.

Notice further that we have specified the approximate maximum dimensions of iconic storage and short-term memory (STM). Long-term memory (LTM) has unlimited time. Furthermore, we specify feedback from LTM and STM. For example, when information is in LTM, it can feed back and help the referral in STM. Before describing in more detail the four stages depicted in Figure 1-2, it is important to clarify the concept of stimulus energy, which starts the inflow of information. The aspect of physical energy which concerns the psychologist can be distinguished from that which is of more general interest to the physicist. When physical scientists or technologists think of physical energy, they conceive of a force which changes the physical structure of a machine or system in some permanent way, or at least for a relatively long period of time. The stimulus contains a variety of higher-order patterns of information, which we shall discuss in later chapters.

When the psychologist thinks of energy, he has in mind certain properties within the stimulus which affect the ongoing behavior of the system only while the energy is present or for short durations thereafter. That is, some characteristics of the energy are directly changing behavior immediately. These characteristics are referred to as *informational aspects of energy;* they prevail only while the stimulus is present, and carry messages to the organism. What is more, the informational aspects are limited: only units which fall within certain limits of the energy scale stimulate the senses informationally. For example, in the case of the visual perception of light, the eye is senstive only to that portion of electromagnetic radiation which falls between the wavelengths of approximately 400 and 700 billionths of a meter. The shorter wavelengths are perceived as violet and blue, and the longer wavelength as red, the other hues (colors) of the visible spectrum falling between these values. The eye is insensitive to the physical energy falling below 400 or above 700. No visual information is extracted outside this range.

Similarly, in the case of auditory perception of pitch, the receptors in the inner ear select only those informational dimensions of physical energies of sound vibration which fall between approximately 15 and 20,000 Hz. Human beings are deaf to basses lower than approximately 10 Hz and trebles higher than approximately 20,000 Hz.

Now, since the senses are differentially sensitive to specific kinds of informational dimensions in the vast array of energy, we must possess special kinds of sensory mechanisms which change the physical dimensions into message units that the nervous system can understand. This takes us to the first stage of the perceptual process.

I Sensory Transduction

The translation of physical information into information messages that the nervous system can use is called sensory transduction.

Most of this information originates in the external environment, but some results from changes in the internal organs. The former are usually called *environmental stimuli,* while the latter are called *state stimuli* (in reference to the state of the organism).

The informational aspects of these stimuli impinge upon the various sense organs, which selectively transduce specific kinds of information. The specific sense organs and the kinds of informational energy they transduce are listed below.

A   The exteroceptors, or distance senses
1   Vision, which transduces light energy.
2   Audition, which transduces sound energy.
B   The proprioceptors, or near senses
3   The *cutaneous* or *skin* senses, which transduce changes in touch (pressure), warmth, cold, and pain stimulation.
4   The chemical sense of *taste,* which transduces change in the chemical composition of liquids stimulating the tongue.
5   The chemical sense of *smell,* which transduces gases reaching the nose. Taste and smell are closely related. The sensation of different flavors within a specific taste (e.g., different flavors within the primary tastes of sweet, sour, salty, and bitter) requires interaction of the senses of taste and smell.
C   The interoceptors, or deep senses
6   The *kinesthetic* sense, which transduces changes in body position and the motion of the muscles, tendons, and joints.
7   The *static* or *vestibular* sense, which transduces changes in bodily balance, rotation, and acceleration.
8   The *organic* sense, which transduces changes related to maintaining the regulation of such organic functions as taking nourishment and water, and sexual activity.

See Lowenstein (1960) for details of the mechanism of transduction.

The listing of the eight senses above should give the reader an idea of the scope of the contact between the organism and the environment. From these eight sources of energy the senses continually receive the stimulus information which the organism uses in its total adaptive behavior.

The transduction stage is the initial one in extracting information from the environment. The limitations in our ability to transduce certain physical dimensions of the stimulus, e.g., those of vision and audition listed above, are imposed at this stage. Following transduction, information must be registered.

II Sensory Register

The concept of sensory register is necessitated by findings which indicate that, following transduction, sensory information is maintained for a brief time interval, on the order of 200 to 300 milliseconds (msec) (0.2 to 0.3 second). Visual input is preserved for this brief, but crucial, period of time. We shall describe the form of this visual persistence later in this section.

Sperling (1960, 1963, & 1967), while not the first to note that visual sensations outlast the stimulus, was the first to examine the role that their brief persistence plays during information processing.

In his first experiment, Sperling (1960) presented rows of letters, three in a row, for exposure durations of 50 msec. The stimulus input, for example, consisted of the following:

TRN
FDR
GZR

Generally, only four or five letters could be reported. However, Sperling used the method of "partial report." In this method, *after* the stimulus was flashed, the subject was instructed to name the letters in a particular row. The subject could name the three letters with perfect accuracy, indicating that (in our example) all nine letters must have registered. This must be so since he had no prior warning about which three of the rows he would have to report back.

The results of Sperling's experiment indicated that the information persists after the stimulus is removed, with most accurate reporting occurring in the very earliest period of its maintenance. This brief storage of the image, which begins to fade at about 250 msec, has been called the *icon* by Neisser (1967). Before we describe the form of iconic storage, we should point out some of its implications for perceptual processing.

Probably the most important advantage of the stage information-processing approach is that it has provided methods by which we can break down the total act of perception into separate time frames and study each frame in detail. The methods used for doing this are reaction time, backward masking, and poststimulus samples. We report on the first two methods in Chapter 10, so we shall here deal with the importance of results from the third method. Note, however, that information in the stimulus usually exists over time, and in limiting oneself to a static time frame, one will miss much information.

Poststimulus sampling requires the subject to report something about the stimulus after it has been removed. Furthermore, the instructions as to what to report are given *after* the stimulus has been removed. In addition to the results of Sperling, Averbach and Coriell (1961) found that the accurate recognition of a *single* letter as a function of the *interstimulus interval* between a sixteen-letter array and an answer which indicates the poststimulus instructions declined gradually for several hundred milliseconds. Then there was a steep drop until it reached the base line of accuracy equivalent to the percentage accuracy for reporting all sixteen letters.

The data suggest that during the early stage of iconic registration all (or nearly all) the stimulus information is presented intact. Additional processing then proceeds from this representation, rather than the actual stimulus itself. The advantage is that it actually "continues" the stimulus for some time after its removal.

In addition to the interstimulus interval, research has also studied the effect of processing duration on accuracy of reporting iconic registration. For example, Mackworth (1963), using a method similar to Sperling, found that the *number of digits* a subject could report accurately increased markedly two to five with exposure time up to 50 msec, then leveled off.

Mackworth's findings were verified and additional refinements were uncovered by Sperling (1967). He presented five letters in a row for varying exposure times up to 200 msec. The exposure was terminated by presenting a visual noise at different times after the stimulus letters were presented to mask the letters. He found that the subject appeared to be processing letters from left to right since the first letter on the left reached its peak at 25 msec, while the second to fifth took progressively longer and did not reach as high a percentage of accuracy.

Thus, processing time influences effectiveness of processing within and transfer from iconic storage. Some parallel processing or transferring must go on, since the accuracy rate for the other letters begins to rise before the first one on the left has reached its peak. These results certainly indicate that part of the reason we have *ordinal* stages in perception is because of processing time, and the variables which influence this processing rate and sequence are quite complex indeed.

A third issue studied by producing a time frame concerns the question of what is stored in iconic registration. Using visual noise to mask, Haber and Standing (1968) and Liss (1968) found that subjects report a *visual impression* of the display but are unable to describe any of its characteristics. If the mask is delayed for a short while, the subject can describe the general layout of the display, name some of the items, and rate the contrast of the lines against the background, but they cannot name forms. Thus the development of the visual image begins prior to or faster than the naming of items.

How about the limitations of iconic storage? During sensory registration we probably have processing at the first two levels of the hierarchy—that is, detection and orientation and probably the transition to level III.

IIIA Short-Term Memory (STM)

If the icon lasts for only about a quarter of a second, it is evident that information from it must be transformed and then transferred to a more permanent storage if it is to have any significant effect on behavior. But here is an interesting problem. Lloyd and Margaret Petersen (1959) asked subjects to remember three letters and 18 seconds later asked them to recall the three letters. Amazingly they could not. Why? In the 18-second interval, they were required to engage in some other mental activity. What is more, it does not matter whether there are three letters or three words in this kind of experiment. If some time elapses after original presentation and before mental activity is introduced, the items are remembered. Then accuracy drops off. The time and the rate at which it drops off do not depend on whether we use letters or words—we get the same findings.

What we described above is short-term memory (STM). It is a memory that has small capacity and a short life (up to 30 seconds if rehearsal is not permitted). It is not too sensitive to the length of the items stored. It is distinguished from long-term memory (LTM) which appears to last forever, although one sometimes has trouble in retrieving information from LTM.

One important way of aiding storage in STM is by rehearsing. Recall what happens when we look up a number in the telephone book. We rehearse and are able to retain it until we dial the number. This rehearsing suggests that a verbal or linguistic code is an important part of short-term memory storage. However, since preverbal children and animals also perceive, visual imagery must also be involved in the coding process of STM.

IIIB Long-Term Memory (LTM)

Recently I experienced a dramatic example of LTM at work. I was driving in my car listening to the radio. I mistakenly heard the announcer say that Vicki Carr was going to sing a song. When it came on, her singing sounded amazingly bass. It took a few seconds to realize that it was Andy Williams—then he sounded quite terrific. That is what LTM is all about. It sends out testing signals to code incoming information which is always coded in the content of LTM programs or sets.

LTM is more than the final deposition of processed perceptual information. A cognitive structure develops in LTM whose organizational properties enable the individual to uncover the information necessary for successful interaction with the environment. As indicated earlier, this information extraction involves reasoning and problem solving.

It is important to reemphasize the bidirectional aspects of the arrows indicating *information flow* in Figure 1-2. Information proceeds sequentially from lower stages to higher ones, but there is also an *outflow* from the central structures involved in the LTM to the lower-level processing stages. While information proceeds in the inflow direction, selective filtering and modification take place. Perception, as we have said, is a process of active construction from available cues, externals as well as internal. At times, outflow messages represent purely physiological inhibition such that the ability of the receptors to respond to the stimulus is reduced or eliminated.

In the determination of the conscious experience, outflow from LTM has many selective effects. These include such phenomena as gating retained from STM. In fact, the position here maintained asserts that most of, if not all, perception is dominated by the *outflow* process.

IV Response

The last paragraph of the preceding section brought us to the fourth stage of the perceptual process. While we study the output stage in terms of the verbalized or other objectified behavioral response, it is surely reasonable to suppose that the behavioral measure is an index of the intervening brain process or experience, although we shall later have to determine the process involved in response organization. It is therefore unnecessary to elaborate further on this stage, other than to say that we know that perception has taken place when a person tells us verbally or through some other behavioral indicator that he has perceived such properties as a gray patch, a red color, a short line, a long distance, an isosceles triangle, a receding surface, a familiar face, a moving musical composition, the solution to a problem, or a hostile act.

The above description of stages in perception will guide our consideration of information extraction in two separate contexts. The first concerns a *taxonomy* of perceptual tasks. In Chapter 2 we shall argue that perceptual tasks can be ordered into a hierarchy from the simplest to the most complex. This hierarchy is cast in the form of the amount and kind of stimulus information extracted as stages I to III.

The second context in which the above stages will be considered concerns a detailed description of the *cognitive activities* which intervene between the presentation of a stimulus and the execution of a response in the various levels of the hierarchy.

Evaluation of Our Perceptual Model

Before concluding this chapter we should point out two important aspects which are not as clear as we might have implied. The first concerns our proposition about the relationship between learning, thinking, and memory in the complex process of perception. We hope that it is clear by now that we believe that these three processes are *not* independent. That is why we say that they are subsets under the superset, perception. It could, of course, be just as logical to postulate that perception is the process where learning, thinking, and memory intersect. It is because we believe that *all* these mutually related processes deal with the processing of information and because we have defined perception as the process of information extraction, that we have adopted the position that perception is the superset.

The other aspect concerns the statement that perception is an active, constructive process. There are theorists who do not believe this. For example, Gibson (1950), discussed in detail later, believes that structure of the physical energy provides the perception without any cognitive mediation. Gestalt psychologists had a similar approach. These theories view the processes as far more passive. The data which we have produced in this chapter plus what we shall elaborate on later lead us to the view that the constructive, active theory is more correct. While most of our examples have referred to vision, similar operations exist in audition (see, for example, Broadbent, 1958).

Historical Context

Anyone who thinks that the questions raised by the problems of investigating the nature of psychophysical correspondence are relatively simple should peruse the rich philosophical and experimental history which is available in excellent sources.[2] A very interesting and novel approach to the analysis of psychophysical correspondence is seen in the creations of J. J. Gibson (1950 & 1966), whose work we shall discuss in many parts of this volume.

Much progress has been made in our understanding of the nature of perception since the time of the theorizing of the early philosophers and scientists. Between the sixteenth century and the early part of the present century some individuals conceived of perception as inborn, while others conceived of it as wholly determined by learning. The former group usually stated that the entire stimulus pattern was capable of being perceived at birth, while the latter thought that it had to be built up gradually through experience. There were also many theorists who believed that perception was an identical copy of the external-stimulus pattern. The Gestalt psychologists (Wertheimer, Köhler, and Koffka) and Egon Brunswik did much to clarify our thinking about perception.

We can thus no longer hold a simple view of perception, and very few psychologists would dichotomize perception as an exclusively unlearned or exclusively learned process.[3] The consensus, rather, seems to be that we begin with unlearned, wired-in programs, which are reflexive and necessary to start the adaptive process going, and then progress to higher-order, modified, or learned programs. Thus it is easier to measure psychophysical correspondence in brightness and color perception than in the perception of such complex forms as the human face, music, or visual illusions. Also, more variation is found in the degree of correspondence among people in the latter cases.

The modern theoretical advances made by such persons as Hebb, Gibson, Bruner, Garner, Neisser, Broadbent, Posner, and Sternberg have given us a clearer perspective on the nature of perceptual operations. (Compare Hebb, 1949; J. J. Gibson, 1950; Bruner, 1957; Garner, 1962; Neisser, 1967; Broadbent, 1958; Sternberg 1969a & 1969b; and Posner, 1969. See also Attneave, 1955, and Sperling, 1967.) The intellectual debt owed by the present authors

---

[2]See, for example, Boring (1942 & 1950) and Murphy (1949).
[3]See, however, Francés (1962), Pratt (1963), and J. G. Taylor (1962). The first reminds us of the debate, the second attempts an integration, while the third gives an extreme learning theory.

to each of the above, as well as others, will become increasingly clear as the reader proceeds through this book. It will be the purpose of the present work to give the reader as authentic a flavor as we can of the cross section of perceptual theorizing and research spanning the range from simple detection to complex identification. This review will not be an eclectic one. We have a point of view which is presented and elaborated throughout. This is not done in order to win "converts" to our position, but more to provide a unifying structure to our consideration of this complex and fascinating subject matter.

PLAN OF THE BOOK

Chapter 2 examines the evidence which suggests that the perceptual task consists of an ordinal sequence of subtasks. The level attained in the hierarchical process depends on the amount and kind of information extracted. Before working out the details of the organization at each level of the perceptual hierarchy, we describe in Chapter 3 the traditional psychophysical measurements, procedures, various psychophysical scaling techniques, and some current innovations in psychophysical methodology. These topics are discussed in terms of their historical development.

Chapters 4, 5, and 6 work out the mechanisms of the earlier stages of sensory transduction and registration and the lowest level in the hierarchy which is detection. Specifically, Chapter 4 deals with the sensory physiology of the visual system. Chapter 5 covers visual psychophysics, while Chapter 6 includes the sensory physiology and psychophysics of the auditory system.

Chapter 7 discusses why brightness constancy should also be considered as resulting primarily from built-in programs. Any contextual problems of brightness and color perception (e.g., seeing a color against backgrounds of different colors) seem to be accounted for by interactions in the stimulus conditions and their effects on the receptors and the brain.

By contrast, we see in Chapter 8 that size and shape constancy can be fully understood only if we consider the mediating influence of cortex.

Chapter 9 begins an examination of how the perception of figure starts to develop and becomes organized. The determination of stable and unstable figures is investigated. The Ganzfeld and the autokinetic effect as special cases of figural instability are discussed. The chapter also includes a discussion of the gestalt laws of perceptual organization.

Chapters 10 and 11 are detailed analyses of perceptual processing at the levels of sensory registration and memory storage. Specific features are discussions of pattern and form perception as well as of attention and illusions.

Chapter 12 deals more specifically with the rich data on how learning influences perceptual identification.

Chapter 13 carries on the discussion of pattern perception by considering the determination of the perception of space and distance. Included is a discussion of recent data from space flights.

Chapter 14 extends space to motion and events.

Chapter 15 covers the broad scope of social perception, which includes the area of emotions, personality, and the perception of persons.

Chapter 16 is an exploration into extending knowledge of perception to throw light on the broader problems of cognition and motivation.

SUMMARY

This introductory chapter has attempted to define the nature of the information-extraction process in man. A discussion and an illustration of the importance of considering the two-way interaction between perception, learning, and thinking in an understanding of this process were presented.

We then looked at the problem of information extraction, ending with our conviction that modern psychology subscribes to an approach to psychophysical correspondence which believes that perceptual patterns or organizations begin with an intrinsic structure based on built-in programs and that these become modified through the specific effects of learning and practice. Following this experiential modification, the outflow of information from central cognitive structures dominates the act of perception.

Chapter 2

Hierarchical Organization of Perceptual Tasks

In Chapter 1 we discussed the four stages involved in producing the visual percept. These sequential stages were (1) sensory transduction of physical energy; (2) sensory registration; (3) perceptual selection and modification mediated by the cognitive structure of memory storage; and (4) the perceptual response.

Furthermore, the act of perception is not a unitary one, but can be broken down into levels. These levels can be ordered into a hierarchy from the simplest to the most complex, in which each successive progression up the hierarchy involves the extraction of progressively more information from the stimulus energy.

We shall first state this hierarchical order of perceptual levels and then go into an examination of the evidence which suggests its existence and complex organizational properties. The order listed, from the simplest to the most complex level, conforms to the following sequence:

I The *detection* of the stimulus *energy* (light) and a discrimination of change in stimulus energy.

II The *discrimination* of a *unified brightness, figural unity,* and *orientation* as separate from the background.

III The *resolution* of finer details which gives rise to a more *differentiated figure.*

IV The *identification* and *recognition* of a *form* or *pattern*.

V The *manipulation* of the identified form; this happens, for example, in *problem solving,* social *perception,* and where perception is related to values and motivation.

DIFFERENCE BETWEEN RECOGNITION AND IDENTIFICATION

Before continuing with the informational-levels approach, we should, for clarity, say more about level IV. While recognition and identification are often used as synonyms, a logical as well as experimental distinction exists between these two processes. Recognition means being able to say that something looks familiar, whereas identification means that we can say what it is or name it. Hochberg (1968) interprets some data of his as a reflection of the difference between these two processes. In his experiment he found no difference in the number of inspections (each for a fixed time period) required to match upright letters with upside-down letters when the stimuli were presented adjacent to one another. However, when the letters were separated by a distance big enough to require eye movements for both to be seen, fewer looks were required to match upright letters. Hochberg, reasoning that visual information was sufficient for matching adjacent letters whereas naming was probably used when they were further apart, concluded that memory was used only when naming was required. It takes more time to identify than it does to recognize.

Hochberg's experiment introduces us to the notion of hierarchical processing. What we are saying is that it takes time for information to be processed. Simpler information, requiring less time, is processed at lower levels, whereas more complex information, requiring progressively more time, is processed at progressively more complex levels.

One of the major reasons that different aspects of information are presented at different times is so that perceptual processing is manageable. Furthermore, the brain is presented with information that comes with time. As we saw in Chapter 1, this variation has significance.

Remembering that when we talk about energy we are referring to its informational aspects, it is not hard to see how the progression from level I to level V involves the extraction of progressively more information. Concurrently, it is to be expected that the brain as an active, selective agent also becomes increasingly involved as we ascend the hierarchy, and that perception becomes more constructive and creative. Having stated the order in this hierarchy, let us examine the additional evidence which suggests its existence.

DIFFERENCES IN THE AMOUNT OF STIMULUS ENERGY REQUIRED TO ACCOMPLISH PERCEPTUAL TASKS

One way of finding out whether a hierarchy exists is to ask whether more stimulus energy is required to accomplish the levels which are higher in the order. Stimulus-energy levels can be raised in three ways or in combinations of these ways. We can increase the intensity of the light, keeping its duration and spatial area constant; increase the spatial area of the light, keeping its intensity and duration constant; or increase the duration of the light exposure, keeping its intensity and spatial area constant. (The three laws relating intensity, time, and area in the production of energy levels are discussed in Chapter 4.) Finally, we shall conclude that it is the *time required to process information,* rather than stimulus energy per se, that is critical for the accomplishment of the more complex perceptual tasks. Since perception consists of higher-order tasks, processing time refers to the time required to effectively complete each level in the order.

Early Studies Which Suggest a Gross Hierarchy

One of the earliest experiments which investigated the relationship between stimulus energy and perceptual tasks was reported by Davies (1905). In this experiment the exposure duration necessary to detect a flash of light was compared with that necessary to identify a form. The subjects always reported that they could see the light before they could say what it was. We call the former, a low-information-processing task, *detection* and the latter, which requires more processing time, *identification.*

An experiment by Freeman (1929), which was also one of the earlier gross studies on the temporal effects of perception, demonstrated two additional dimensions of perceptual segregation. Inkblots and, in one case, eight silhouetted outlines of familiar forms were presented to subjects through a tachistoscope. (A *tachistoscope* is an instrument through which exposure time can be very accurately controlled.) The duration of exposure was increased from very short intervals to longer ones, and the subjects were permitted to give a phenomenological description and commentary on the course of the development of the percept. As the exposure time increased, three well-defined levels of development were obtained with the inkblots, beginning with a "preperceptive" vague awareness and ending with a verbal naming of the object. The first stage consisted of a vague apprehension of general extent, which developed into a primary qualification of extent as either far or near, right or left, up or down. The second stage involved the generation of "thingness," during which there emerged the awareness of clearer contours, and a figure was seen as having a "focus" and a "background." The development of this figure was from "something" to a "thing." Finally, there appeared a level of perceptive familiarity, during which recognition and then naming or identification of an object occurred. Although the first two stages were often apprehended, they were not clearly defined, and it is the third stage which corresponds closely to the perception of forms.

If we combine the results of these rather gross studies of Davies and Freeman, we get the suggestion of the first four levels in the above order. The first level uncovered by Davies was the *detection* of light, which was further differentiated into a second stage, *orientation,* by Freeman. The second stage of Freeman, namely, the development from "something" to a "thing," corresponds to levels II and III in our hierarchy. As the brightness patch, which is really what constitutes the gross figure, develops *sharper contours,* the differentiated figure emerges. "Something" represents the *figure,* level II, which becomes more differentiated in level III. Finally, we get the identification of form, which corresponds to our level IV, in the last stage of both studies. (We repeat that the identification of form probably requires even more information extraction than does recognition. However, we do not know whether there are two distinct levels.)

Elaborating Studies from Brightness or Figural Unity to Identified Form

Other, more precise, studies have, in general, obtained the same or a similar sequence of perceptual emergence. Thus, Dickinson (1926), who presented, tachistoscopically, nine letters to his subjects for 64 seconds, found that as the subjects continued to look at the letters, the perceptual process passed through three stages, which gradually evolved from one to the next. The first, or "visual-pattern," stage consisted of the mere awareness of thingness, a flat clearness which was clear in detail of illumination and contour but lacked logical meaning. During the second, or "generic-object," stage, parts began to stand out slightly in relief and took on the properties of an object without definite or specific meaning. These two stages represent the transition from the unified brightness or figure (level II) to the end of the differentiated-figure stage (level III). During the third, or specific-object, level, the forms rose out toward the observer, the ground receded, and the figure became stable (level IV).

A second study by Dickinson (1927) corroborated the above results. It also showed that, as perception varies from one level to another, the perception of *brightness* evolved through *contour* to *logical* meaning or identification.

A comparable study was performed by Wever (1927), who also presented stimuli tachistoscopically but who went into greater detail about the transition from level II to level III. He exposed 1,060 "nonsense figures" (irregularly formed fields) for durations of from less than 10 msec to more than 2 minutes, using the method of constant stimuli (a procedure to be described in Chapter 3). In general, as the exposure time was increased, there unfolded four levels which were elaborations of the ones previously reported. First there existed a given degree of heterogeneity of the visual field in which two regions were discriminated, representing the perception of a brightness difference between them. This stage of simplest "figure-ground" was followed by a transition (good figure-ground) in which the features were more pronounced and in which the figural field presented a primitive type of localization. Third, there emerged a contour which separated the two fields so that a primitive, poorly articulated form was perceived. Finally, the figure had a simple perceived shape. Throughout these stages depth localization or depth relief was least uniform and least subject to control, and *texture,* if present, *tended to appear at comparatively advanced stages.* We might add that texture, which presents a pattern, takes us toward level IV. Wever summarized his results as follows: "A given figure-ground experience, then, is but one of many possible stages of the complex perceptual phenomenon, and its precise nature is a function of the various components of the situation in their entirety" (1927, p. 226).

Wever reported the following temporal relationships between the perceptual structures and the temporal durations of exposure. There is no figural experience for durations of less than 10 msec; simplest figure-ground occurs at 10 to 13 msec; good figure-ground, at 15 to 10 msec; and "perfect" figural experience, at 25 or more msec. The increase of durations from a few seconds to 2 minutes was not followed by any increase in the experience of "goodness" of figure. So the essential range for the development of these four stages within the experimental conditions used by Wever was between 10 and 24 msec. It is particularly important to note that these values of time duration were obtained with one fixed, constant level of intensity and cannot necessarily be generalized.

An experiment by Bridgen (1933) extended the energy levels upward until the perception of a patterned form was experienced. Using a tachistoscope, he found that gross figure-ground differentiation ended at 10 msec (level II). This was followed by inaccurate discrimination of form between one-fifth and 2 seconds (level III). The final stage ended in the finest differentiation of patterns between 4 and 13 seconds (level IV). So it seems that the graduated segregation from a homogeneous field into unstable figure-ground, more differentiated figure, and finally pattern perception occurs at temporal durations of 10 msec to 13 seconds. At least this is true under the conditions utilized, which, in general, consisted of exposing dim lights or forms to constant intensity to dark-adapted subjects.

The trend of the quantitative values reported by Wever and Bridgen was generally supported by Helson and Fehrer (1932). They found that the recognition of form (level IV) required 25 times as much light as the just-perceptible discrimination of light (levels I to II) and that the perception of vague form (levels II to III) required a middle value of 15 times as much light.

The studies reported so far tell us that it takes time to go from one level to another. They do not tell us *what goes on* during these time periods. One clue as to what contributes to the accomplishment of the task during this time comes from a classic study on *contour* development by Werner (1935). He first presented a black patch in the shape of a square to the subject to inspect. Then, following an interval of 150 msec, he presented a spatially contiguous outline square with a double contour to mask the first one. The first square was not seen at all. If order of presentation of the two squares are reversed, both squares are seen.

Werner reasons that it takes time for the contour to establish itself and during this contour completion the form is also established. So that is one reason why more time is required for the processing of form to take place. (In the above experiment the outline square is not masked because the *double contour* is less easy to break up.)

It has further been noticed that the two squares do not have to be seen by the same eye for the masking of the first square to occur. (See, for example,

Kolers and Rosner, 1960.) Thus, even where memory is not involved, as it is not in this experiment, central (stage III) processing is still occurring.

Hake summarized an earlier review of similar work on stages as follows:

> The evidence shows a complexity of action including the ability to *detect the mere presence of light, to discriminate differences in brightness of large areas of the target, to resolve fine details of the target,* and *to appreciate the form* or general shape *of the whole target.* These several functions are not related to any useful degree. That is, the evidence does not permit the description of the visual system in terms of any simple sensing mechanism designed to sense or appreciate visual patterns. (Hake, 1957, pp. 6–7)

In order to clarify some of the work to be reviewed below, it is necessary briefly to define some concepts which are further explained in Chapter 5. They involve such concepts as threshold and cone and rod function. *Absolute threshold* refers to the minimum intensity of a stimulus that can just be detected 50 percent of the time. *Adaptation* refers to changes that take place after a particular level of stimulation has run its course. Thus *light* adaptation refers to the sensitivity level which is reached during daylight conditions. *Dark* adaptation refers to the fact that some retinal cells become more sensitive after we have been in the dark for a while. This process usually reaches its complete level after 30 minutes in the dark. The cells in and near the fovea, which take over in daylight-vision, are called the *cones.* The *rods,* which are on the periphery of the retina, take over in twilight conditions. Now for the evidence.

Clues to the kinds of organization involved at the different stage levels came first from Hebb (1949), who suggested three stages of perceptual organization:

I A primitive, sensorily determined unity, which refers to the unity and segregation of a figure from a background. The emergence of the figure seems to be a direct product of the pattern of sensory excitation and the inherited characteristics of the nervous system upon which it acts.

II The nonsensory, figure-ground organization, which is defined as one in which the boundaries of the figure are not fixed by gradients of luminosity in the visual field. This organization is affected by experience and other nonsensory factors, and is *not inevitable* in any perception.

III The identity of a perceived figure, which refers to the properties of association inherent in a perception. It is, of course affected by experience.

Question: Are these stages related to iconic, short-term, and long-term storage, respectively?

There certainly is evidence that levels I and II are related, but that these lower levels are not related to level IV. That is because the higher level depends more on LTM, while the first two are largely processed in the sensory register. In fact, Hebb has suggested that the perception of identity (our level IV) results after a fairly long, slow learning process during the first 4 months of life. (See also Fantz, 1961b.)

In a study by Craik and Vernon (1942) eighteen subjects were first completely light-adapted. The absolute thresholds (see Chapter 3) for various light stimuli were obtained continuously during 55 minutes of dark adaptation. Three results are relevant for the present issue: (1) The subjects exhibited characteristic individual differences between cone and rod function. Those who showed relatively high thresholds for cone adaptation showed relatively low thresholds for rod adaptation, and vice versa. (2) the low-cone-thresholds subjects were better at performing simple perceptual functions such as reading the position of a dial hand (level II). (3) Level IV function, the ability to perceive more complex patterns, such as silhouetted pictures, was, however, only partially related to the absolute thresholds for cone vision, and even less closely related to the threshold for rod vision.

Craik and Vernon state further that the perception of more complicated material was affected by a "variety of purely psychological" factors, such as intelligence, education, familiarity of the particular type of material or situation, and emotional attitudes.

The above fits in with the research of Hyman and Hake (1954) who found that the threshold for light (level I) is closely related to the threshold for the orientation of the gratings of a parallel bar (level II). Craik and Vernon found no such correlation between either of these, levels I and II.

In another significant study, Bitterman, Krauskopf, and Hochberg (1954) demonstrated that the kinds of mistakes subjects make in form identification are selective, and appear related to angles. Their subjects were dark-adapted for 10 minutes and then shown geometrical figures, each of which was illuminated for 0.5 second. Typical mistakes in identification of these figures were of the following kinds: a square was usually called a circle, a triangle a circle, a cross a diamond, an X a square, and so on. *A circle was usually identified correctly.* It is significant that, under these reduced conditions, complex forms (more angles— see Chapter 10) were simplified—that is, to a circle or form with fewer angles. This fact is related to findings by Hochberg, Gleitman, and MacBride (1948) and Krauskopf, Duryea, and Bitterman (1954) that there is a higher threshold for visual forms of shapes which have higher ratios of perimeter to area than those which have lower ratios.

Finally, we have the data from Piaget and Inhelder (1948), who found that there was an age progression in the development of form perception which involved increasing levels of abstraction. While children could differentiate, by drawing, curved from rectilinear figures at about four years of age, the discrimination between *triangles and squares* followed a gradual development and did not become accurate until a later age.

TIME FOR INFORMATION PROCESSING AT DIFFERENT LEVELS

So far in this chapter we have referred to pioneer studies which suggested that perception probably consists of relatively specific stages. Using the methods of the information-processing approach, later research has attempted to measure, more directly, the time taken to complete various levels of perceptual performance.

One such study was conducted by Posner and Mitchell (1967). In this study subjects were presented with pairs of stimuli, either letters or digits. Furthermore, the letters were all uppercase or uppercase and lowercase—for example, AA, Aa, AB, Ab. In one of two conditions subjects were required to signal as rapidly as possible whether two letters were the same or different in physical appearance ("physical identity" condition). The second letter would be the same for the first pair presented above but different for the other three pairs. In the second condition, they were to answer "same" or "different" with respect to name identity. In our example, both of the first two pairs would give rise to the answer "same." A and a are also identical with respect to naming.

The reasoning in Posner and Mitchell's study is that processing for physical identity would be at a lower level. Name identity would require LTM to retrieve the name and would thus require higher-level processing.

Here are the important results. Name matching always gave reaction times (RTs) that were significantly longer than physical matching. Moreover, when reaction times of same response with name identity instructions were compared, it was clear that those based on physical identity (e.g., AA) were much faster than those based on name identity (Aa, Bb, and Ee). However, the magnitude of the time difference depended on the task. Thus the time difference between CC and Cc was 71 msec under name instructions but only 20 msec under physical identity instructions.

In other experiments, Posner and Mitchell asked subjects to report whether the pairs of letters were both vowels or both consonants. The RTs for this task were even longer than those for name identity. The authors thus concluded that matches made on the basis of common names are processed faster than matches made on the basis of a common rule.

From the results obtained in the series of experiments, Posner and Mitchell proposed that there are at least three nodes at which different aspects of information are processed. A tree diagram illustrating the hierarchical arrangements of these nodes is presented in Figure 2-1. At node 1, physical similarity is processed, whereas name is processed at node 2, and rules at node 3. It is highly likely that these nodes are refinements within our level IV—node 1 being recognition, while node 2 concerns identification, and node 3 a more abstract form of identification.

Word and Letter Identification

Traditional research on form perception has generally used shapes as the stimuli. More recent work, especially since the dawn of information-processing models, has concerned itself more and more with letter and word recognition and identification. This kind of processing is, of course, central in reading skill. There is an obvious difference between the perception of a shape and a word (e.g., Δ

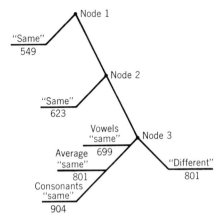

Figure 2-1 Tree diagram for experiment 4. (Numbers refer to mean RTs on last day for all subjects. For description of nodes, see text.) *(After Posner & Mitchell, 1967, p. 404.)*

versus triangle). Presumably, the information is given more directly in the shape, whereas it is more abstract in the word. An example of the relative ease of the former is that children can discriminate drawings at a much earlier age than they can words.

How does one, indeed, read a word? Do we process the letters separately, or do we form a new whole and process the letters as a group—a higher-order combination? Some clues came from pioneering research of Reicher (1969) and Wheeler (1970).

Consider the word WORD. We can present the stimulus tachistoscopically, mask it, then present two letters DK, ask the subject which of the two letters he had previously seen, and measure the identification time. We can further present the D in the nonword ORWD, or present it alone.

In the experiment by Reicher, it was found that the RT for choosing the correct letter was significantly shorter when it was first presented in a word than in a nonword. The finding was verified by Wheeler (1970). The finding that presenting the letter *alone* had an even shorter identification time has not been readily replicated.

Very systematic analysis in a series of experiments by Baron and Thurston (1973) throws light on this so-called "word-superiority" effect. They showed that the word-superiority effect holds just as strongly for pronounceable nonwords as for words, even when the critical letters are constant over all trials. For example, the subject does just as well (as regards time) recognizing the R in CORS (a pronounceable nonword) as in CARS, but takes significantly longer in CSRA.

In exploring this phenomenon further, the experimenters present additional data which suggest that the word-superiority effect might be positively affected by spelling rules or conventions. This suggestion comes from comparing the reaction times for chemical formuli spelled correctly with those when the spelling is reversed, using chemists as subjects. For example, the formula for salt is NaCl. Reversing the spelling would make it ClNa. In this experiment they used sixteen such formulas, half being reversed in spelling. By comparison with nonchemist controls, the chemist subjects had significantly lower RTs for the correctly spelled formuli than for the reversed ones.

The only conclusion one can reach after reviewing the many kinds of data like those reported in this section is that the human being has the potential for using a *multiple* information-processing system. Wickens (1972) indicates the extent to which this can be done. Subjects were presented with a word like GUN, which was masked before it could be clearly processed. Then two new words were presented and the subject was asked to choose the one which was the same as the one presented. (In fact neither was the same.) Subjects performed at a chance level. Finally, subjects were presented with two more words, one of which was KNIFE, and were asked which of the two words bore a similarity to the original stimulus. Significantly, KNIFE was chosen a greater percentage of the time. Even though the original word had not been clearly seen, a semantically similar word was seen as related to it.

It has also been shown that meaningful stimuli are not always processed more quickly. For example, Novik (1974) required his subjects to indicate whether each stimulus in a series of CCCs, CVCs, words (CVC type), and meaningful CCCs (e.g., JFK, LSD) was a word or a nonword. (C stands for consonants, and V for vowels.) RT was the dependent measure. While the typical word-superiority effect of Reicher and Wheeler was obtained, another important, and perhaps surprising, result was also found. Specifically, the RTs for distinguishing words from nonwords for meaningful CCCs were significantly longer than for meaningless CCCs. The conclusion is that these triads for word-nonword classification are processed in parallel. Thus, confusion or conflict occurs when meaningful CCCs evoke a word-like reaction but the subject has to say it is a nonword. The extra time taken to break the conflict or correct the confusion increases the RT.

Processing Time and Stimulus Information

The earlier studies reviewed in this chapter have shown that the duration of exposure influences the level reached in the perceptual act. The more recent studies show that the relative complexity of the perceptual task would affect the length of the RT. These relationships which are related to temporal duration could exist for a number of reasons. They could be determined by such factors as the energy level, size, and complexity of the stimulus. More systematic research will have to be done before we can catalog all these factors and their relationships.

One variable is, however, crucial for the position adopted in this chapter. That variable is processing time. Since we are postulating that more information is extracted at high levels, it is to be expected that more processing time will correspondingly be required. One study which measured processing time directly was performed by Haber and Nathanson (1969). They measured the effect of processing time on the number of sequentially presented letters the subject could report. The subjects were each shown 1,250 words, subdivided into five lengths (four, five, six, seven, and eight letters), five "on" times (10, 25, 50, 100, and 150 msec), and five "off" times (10, 25, 50, 100, and 150 msec). Thus, for each word length there were twenty-five cells representing different on-off combinations, each of which was tested with ten words per subject. Each letter acted as a visual noise field for the preceding letter. It should also be emphasized that the duration of each letter and the interval between each letter were varied independently. It was found that processing time, defined as time from the onset of one letter to the onset of the next letter, predicted the number of letters correctly reported, regardless of the partition between on time and off time. This relationship is presented in the graphs in Figure 2-2, which are self-explanatory. Michaels (1974) also verified that it was processing time and not exposure time that was the significant variable in identification.

It is evident that memory plays an important role in the above results as, indeed, it does in much of the work reported in this chapter. The studies cited show that it is not exposure time per se but time for processing which is needed. Presumably, the time must be long enough to transfer from STM to LTM if it is to affect the perceptual system in an enduring way. We shall argue in later chapters that what are remembered (or stored) are not "traces" of environmental stimulation but residuals of our own perceptual activities (Neisser, 1967; Posner, 1969).

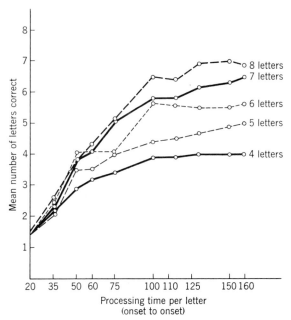

Figure 2-2 Mean number of letters correct as a function of total processing time, in milliseconds, for each of five word lengths. Data are combined over four subjects, and within each subject for different on-off combinations. The functions are terminated at a processing time of 160 msec, where they approach close to their asymptotic values. *(After Haber & Nathanson, 1969, p. 360.)*

To show the complexity and variety of these stored experiences, we now look at experience and learning.

LEARNING AND PERCEPTUAL EXPERIENCES

Levels in the perceptual hierarchy can also be distinguished on the basis of the extent to which experiences and memory play a role. A number of experiments using widely different methodologies all lead to the conclusion that, as we ascend the hierarchy of tasks, the role of experience becomes increasingly important.

Hebb (1937a, 1937b) compared the discrimination ability of rats who were reared in the dark with that of rats who were normally reared. He found that the two groups did not differ in brightness discrimination but that the dark-reared animals were inferior to normally reared animals in pattern discrimination. If we assume, for the moment, that the absence of light did not impair the optical mechanism (we shall have more to say about this later), then these results suggest that brightness discrimination is a more primitive phenomenon than pattern discrimination. Hebb's finding is further corroborated by Lashley (1938) who found that, after rats have learned to discriminate between two forms, the discrimination is completely lost if the brightness relationships are reversed. Thus, after a rat has learned to respond positively to a white triangle, no amount of training will produce a positive response to a black one alone. Brightness cues are dominant. In the rat, reaction to brightness appears to be largely innate, whereas form perception probably requires simple concept formation, and is thus highly subject to the influence of learning.

Similar results have been obtained with primates and human beings. Thus, Riesen (1947) compared the discrimination ability of four dark-reared chimpanzees with normally reared ones. He found that there were only little differences in brightness and color discrimination. When it came to pattern and form discrimination, however, the dark-reared animals were markedly inferior. In some cases the chimpanzees required weeks to learn. It might be argued that the visual nervous systems of the animals reared in the dark were probably damaged, but, more recently, Riesen (1958) reported similar trends when chimpanzees were reared under a dome which transmitted only unpatterned, diffuse light. The case of the learning of pattern perception appears to be well established.

Senden (1932) collected similar reports from clinical observations of human adults who were given vision for the first time in adulthood after congenital cataracts had been surgically removed. Again discrimination of brightness appeared fairly normal, whereas discrimination of forms required much learning, sometimes requiring 2 or more months. A more recent study (Gregory & Wallace, 1963), which we shall discuss in Chapter 12, analyzes in depth a case of recovery from blindness.

It does seem quite definite that brightness discrimination is a positive sensory phenomenon, and it is doubtful that anyone would want to argue for the significant importance of learning in brightness perception after considering the evidence. (In Chapter 7, in which systematic treatment of brightness constancy is covered, we shall examine additional evidence relevant to this point.) But the issues with respect to the role of learning in form perception are much more controversial.

Given the research cited above, it would be difficult to deny that experience plays *any* role in pattern recognition. What is at issue is the *nature* of the role of experience. One point of view which has been espoused by Haber and Hershenson (1965) is that experience directly influences the *clarity* of a percept. Thus, Haber and Hershenson, in their experiment cited above, interpreted their subjects' reports of more stimulus letters with repeated stimulus exposures as reflecting perceptual clarity. A second point of view (Köhler, 1929; Earhard & Fullerton, 1969) is that there is no effect of experience on *perceptual clarity*. Rather, the perceptual system is influenced in far more complex ways, as we analyze in Chapter 12.

An early experiment by Gottschaldt (1926) is relevant to this issue. This experiment was performed to determine the effects of repetitive experience in viewing a form on the ability to identify it when it was later imbedded in a more complex configuration. The subjects were asked to study simple figures for 1 second on each exposure. Some of the figures were presented three times only, while others were exposed 520 times. The observers were instructed to learn the figures. They were then presented with complex figures for each simple one. The subjects were asked to examine the complex figures for 2 seconds and told merely to describe them. In only 5 percent of the cases in which the simple figure had previously been presented 520 times did the subject notice, or even guess, that the simple figure was contained in the complex one. It does not appear from these data that the effect of repetition was one of enhancing *perceptual clarity*.

More recently, Earhard and Fullerton (1969) have reported a very elegant experimental test of the contrasting points of view as to the role of experience. They manipulated experience by varying the number of stimulus repetitions in the same manner as Haber and Hershenson (1965). Earhard and Fullerton reasoned that, if experience influenced perceptual clarity, then, with repeated exposures of the same stimulus, subjects should be able to resolve finer details of the stimulus (level III). Thus on each of twenty-four trials, the same four-letter consonant string was briefly (30 msec) exposed. However, on each trial, one of the letters was drawn *thinner* than the remaining letters. Which letter was thin was varied randomly over trials. The subjects' task was to indicate which letter was the thin one on a given trial. The results of this experiment were clear-cut. Subjects *did not* improve in this task over the twenty-four repetitions of the same stimulus. Subjects reported greater than chance accuracy at all repetitions. Thus, the result was not due to the task being too difficult to accomplish.

These data provide strong evidence that the role of experience is *not* to improve perceptual clarity. Apparently, experience influences memory processes which are more prominent in tasks involving stimulus recognition and identification (levels IV and V) than in tasks involving only detection (level I) or the resolution of the physiognomic details of a stimulus (levels II and III). This is not to argue that experience (memory) plays *no* role in these latter tasks. It is the *nature* and *complexity* of the role of memory which distinguishes the tasks in the hierarchy. Much of the remainder of the book will be directed toward elucidating this role. Specifically, Chapter 12 analyzes in detail the various ways that learning and sensory experience influence perception.

Finally, Michaels (1974) found that up to processing times of 40 msec there was no difference in the accuracy between reporting words and nonwords. After this time the percentage accuracy for words rose faster and reached an asymptote earlier. Thus length of processing time depends on the order of the perceptual task.

SUMMARY

In this chapter a hierarchical ordering of perceptual tasks is proposed. This hierarchical order consists of the following tasks: (1) detection of light and change in light energy, (2) the gross discrimination of a figural unity, (3) the resolution of a more clearly differentiated figure, (4) the identification of form, and (5) the manipulation or modification of form as in social perception and problem solving.

In general, more time is required to complete the more complex tasks. In addition, the further one proceeds in the hierarchy, the greater is the role of experience as represented in memory. Moreover, the time required to process this memorial information provides an explanation for the greater duration of stimulus exposure necessary to complete the more complex tasks. It is not exposure time but processing which is important. In addition, direct experiments indicate the importance of learning and perceptual experience in determining form perception but not processing at levels I and II of the hierarchy.

Sensory Psychophysics

When G. T. Fechner published his *Elemente der Psychophysik* in 1860, the first formal laboratory of experimental psychology, that of Wundt at Leipzig, was still nineteen years into the future. In this book, Fechner drew together scattered bits of methodology for measuring sensory experiences, systemitized these, and also presented a quantitative psychophysical law known today as Fechner's law. Fechner's psychophysics was only a part of a broad philosophical system he was developing over several decades. However, the impact of his methods on the young field of sensory psychology was immediate, and, in an only slightly modified form, these methods are still very much in use today. Fechner's law has been controversial from the start and still remains a consideration in present-day arguments on the "true" psychophysical relation.

Fechner regarded psychophysics as follows: "Psychophysics should be understood here as an exact theory of the functionally dependent relations of body and soul or, more generally, of the material and the mental, of the physical and the psychological worlds" (Fechner, 1966, p. 7). The point is that the relationship between our subjective experiences (e.g., loudness) and the physical properties of the stimulus to which we are responding (e.g., sound pressure) is not readily apparent. A pure tone does not appear twice as loud when we double the sound pressure. Loudness seems to double with every tenfold increase in sound energy. We generally cannot represent a change in our subjective sensory experience by directly applying the quantitative change occurring in the stimulus itself. Every psychophysical relationship has to be empirically determined.

Fechner's methods have traditionally been used to find one type of psychophysical relationship. This is a subject's discriminatory ability. This ability has been formalized as the concepts *absolute threshold* and *difference threshold*. Using the loudness example again, psychophysicists have asked the question: "What is the minimum sound pressure that a subject can hear?" This question implies an absolute threshold: i.e., stimuli weaker than some fixed value (below threshold) are undetectable, whereas those above this value (above threshold) are always detectable. Inconsistancies in our subject data would be due to shifts in attention, inexperience, judgment errors, and similar problems. The difference threshold concerns the subject's report of a change in sensory magnitude as an increase or decrease occurs in the physical values of the stimulus. A difference threshold for loudness would involve the question: "What is the minimum amount of change in sound pressure (from some specified level) that is necessary for the subject to hear the change?" The size of the difference threshold will depend on the level of the standard stimulus, the stimulus from which the difference threshold is being found.

Empirical findings about this relationship between the difference threshold and the standard stimulus led Fechner to formulate his psychophysical law giving a quantitative expression for the relationship between sensation and stimulus values. Such a law, if tenable, would certainly be the fulfillment of the psychophysicist's task. Obtaining data to test this type of law introduces a second type of measurement problem for the psychophysicist, namely, *psychophysical scaling*. If the subject is to report his sensory experiences for a wide range of stimulus values, not simply report the occurrence of changes in sensation such as in threshold determinations, he has to have some yardstick for measuring his subjective impressions. The problem of scaling is to determine the subject's yardstick or scale. Consider the importance of such a scale to the acoustical engineer who wants to measure the loudness of various kinds of sounds reproduced in an audio system.

In this chapter, the classical psychophysical methods for establishing absolute thresholds and difference thresholds will be presented first. This is followed by an introduction to signal-detection theory. This theory represents a current alternative to measuring a subject's discriminative abilities. The value of this approach is in recognition, evaluation, and inclusion of the nonsensory factors that influence discriminative performance. Next, there is a presentation of Fechner's law and some current reformulations of the psychophysical law that have been proposed to replace it. This section also includes a discussion of current psychophysical scaling techniques.

CLASSICAL PSYCHOPHYSICAL METHODS

Before discussing these methods, a word on nomenclature is necessary. The term *absolute threshold* will be abbreviated RL. This abbreviation is derived from the German phrase *Reiz Limen* and reflects the strong influence in psycho-

Table 3-1   Illustrative Data for Calculating the RL for a 1,000-Hertz Tone Using the Method of Limits

	Trials					
Stimuli, db	A_1	D_1	A_2	D_2	A_3	D_3
10.2						
9.8		Y				
9.4		Y				
9.0		Y		Y		Y
8.6		Y		Y		Y
8.2	Y	Y		Y	Y	Y
7.8	Y	Y	Y	Y	Y	Y
7.4	N	Y	Y	N	N	N
7.0	N	Y	N	N	N	Y
6.6	N	N	N		N	N
6.2	N	N	N		N	N
5.8	N		N		N	
5.4	N				N	
5.0	N					
RL	7.6	6.8	7.2	7.6	7.6	6.8
Mean RL = 7.27						

physics of the nineteen-century German investigators. Similarly, the traditional abbreviation for *difference threshold* is DL *(Differenz Limen)*.

Method of Limits

As an example of the application of the method of limits for calculating the RL, the data in Table 3-1 will be used. Let us presume that it was important in this experiment to evaluate, rather quickly, the subject's RL for the 1,000-Hz[1] tone used. Because of time constraint, fewer measurement trials were used than would ordinarily be the case. However, the criterion for number of trials used is the stability of the estimates of threshold obtained on successive trials. From this viewpoint, the six trials used here were probably sufficient.

A trial involves presenting a discrete series of stimuli in order of decreasing magnitude ("descending" trial) or increasing magnitude ("ascending" trial). The size of the steps used is a judgment of the experimenter. A large number of steps will be time-consuming and tedious, while too-few steps will impair the accuracy of the method. In the present example, 0.4-db[2] steps were used with alternating ascending and descending trials. The subject reports "yes" or "no" to indicate whether or not he hears the tone.

A measure of the RL is obtained for each trial. These are averaged to

---

[1]Hertz (Hz), after the physicist of the same name, is the unit of frequency, in cycles per second, of a pure tone stimulus. Subjectively, the physical parameter frequency is associated with the psychological dimension, pitch.

[2]Decibel (db) is the unit of sound intensity. Changes in sound intensity are detected, subjectively, as changes in loudness.

produce the final estimate of the RL. The RL is defined as the stimulus value midway between the transition from "no" to "yes" or "yes" to "no" responses for ascending and descending trials, respectively. Thus in trial A_1 (Table 3-1), the first ascending trial, the subject switches from a "no" response at 7.4 db to a "yes" for 7.8 db. The RL for this trial is thus 7.6 db. For D_1, the subject switches from "yes" at 7.0 to "no" at 6.6, giving an RL of 6.8 db. The mean of all estimates, 7.27, is taken as the RL.

It will be noted in the table that the experimenter chose to stop a trial after two successive new responses, e.g., a "yes" for 7.8 and 8.2 db in trial A_1 after the sequence of "no" responses. Traditionally, a trial is stopped after the first new response. A stricter criterion was used here because the subjects were untrained. Note the fluctuation of responses from trial D_3.

Two judgment errors are of particular importance with this method: the errors of *habituation* and *anticipation*. The habituation error occurs when the subject continues to give the same response in a sequence. It is akin to a response bias rather than an accurate sensory report. The error of anticipation occurs if a subject begins anticipating the location of the RL and switches his response before his subjective experience would necessitate it. The particular use of alternating ascending and descending trials is to balance out either error when it occurs.

The calculation of a DL using the method of limits involves very few changes from the RL procedure. The subject is presented a standard stimulus and a series of comparison stimuli covering a sufficient range about the standard. The latter stimuli are presented in discretely ordered steps. The manner of presenting the stimuli is again in alternating ascending and descending trials. The subject is then presented the standard followed by the comparison stimulus. His task is to judge the second stimulus as greater than, less than, or equal to the standard. A hypothetical DL problem is presented in Table 3-2. This problem concerns the DL for loudness for a standard of 2,500 Hz and 20 db. Looking in any column, for example, A_1, it is apparent that there are really two DLs measured on each trial. For A_1, the subject starts with "less than" responses, then crosses into a region of equal judgments, and then crosses again into a region of "greater than" responses. The lower threshold is termed DL_L here, and the upper threshold on each trial DL_u. Each is again calculated as the midpoint of the transition interval. Accordingly, DL_u is 22.25 db and DL_L is 18.75 db for trial A_1. The means for these two DLs over all trials are then calculated. The *interval of uncertainty* is defined as the distance between these two mean values. In this example, with reference to Table 3-2 again, this interval is 3.25 db. The DL is defined as one-half the interval of uncertainty, or 1.625 db, here.

Method of Constant Stimuli

This method (called the "method of right and wrong cases" by Fechner) is quite similar to the method of limits in terms of its demands on the subject; i.e., the subject's task is to report whether he detected the stimulus. However, in the constant-stimulus method, the stimuli are presented in a random order rather than sequentially. The errors of habituation and anticipation are thus avoided.

**Table 3-2 Illustrative Data for Calculating DL for a 2,500-Hertz 20-db
Standard Tone**

Comparison Stimuli dbs		A_1	D_1	A_2	D_2	A_3	D_3
					Trials		
	24.0				+		
	23.5		+		+	+	+
	23.0	+	+	+	+	+	+
	22.5	+	+	+	+	=	+
	22.0	=	+	=	+	=	=
	21.5	=	+	=	+	=	=
	21.0	=	=	=	=	=	=
	20.5	=	=	=	=	=	=
St	20.0	=	=	=	=	=	=
	19.5	=	=	=	=	=	=
	19.0	=	=	=	−	=	=
	18.5	−	=	−	−	−	−
	18.0	−	−	−		−	−
	17.5	−	−	−		−	
	17.0	−	−	−		−	
	16.5	−				−	
	16.0	−					

DL_u 22.25   21.25   22.25   21.25   22.75   22.25

Mean $DL_u = \overline{DL}_u = 22.00$

DL_L 18.75   18.25   18.75   19.25   18.75   18.75

Mean $DL_L = \overline{DL}_L = 18.75$

$IU = \overline{DL}_u - \overline{DL}_L = 22.00 - 18.75 = 3.25$

$DL = IU/2 = 3.25/2 = 1.625$

Key: − denotes judgment of "less than St"
+ denotes judgment of "greater than St"
= denotes judgment of "equal to St"

The computation of the RL and DL, however, are very different than in the method of limits.

In applying the method of constant stimuli to the calculation of the RL, the experimenter typically chooses from five to nine stimuli forming a range of values within which he believes the subject's RL exists. This may necessitate some pretesting with a more expedient method such as the method of limits. Each of these stimuli are presented a large number of times, in random order, and the percentage of "yes" responses is noted for each stimulus. Representative data are presented in Table 3-3. Again, an accurate measure of the weakest 1,000 Hz a subject can hear is needed. Six tones from Table 3-1 were used because they seemed to span the RL area for that subject. Let us presume that they were each presented to the subject 50 times in a random order and we obtained the percentage of "yes" responses given in the percentage column. The data are presented graphically in Figure 3-1, where the percentage values are represented on the ordinate and the corresponding stimulus values on the abscissa. The data are very typical in that they produce the figure of an elongated S curve. The RL is defined as the stimulus for which the proportion of "yes" responses is 0.50, i.e., the median or fiftieth percentile, of the distribution represented in Figure 3-1.

Table 3-3 Illustrative Data for Calculating RL for a 1,000-Hertz Tone Using the Method of Constant Stimuli

Stimuli, db S	Percentage "yes," p
7.8	98
7.6	90
7.4	70
7.2	38
7.0	18
6.8	3

The simplest way to get this RL value is by interpolating it from the graph, i.e., by drawing the intersecting line from 0.50 on the ordinate to the figure and then drawing the perpendicular to the abscissa and reading off the value.

There are several variants of the method of constant stimuli that are not presented here. Guilford (1954) lists seven ways to calculate the RL alone.

In calculating DLs with this method, an indirect statistical procedure is used. Typically, seven to nine above-threshold stimuli, centered about a standard, are used. Each comparison stimulus is presented with the standard, balancing the order in which the two are presented over all the judgments of the pair. The comparison stimuli are presented a large number of times in a randomized order. Usually, subjects are allowed only two response categories, e.g., greater or less than the standard. The proportion of greater judgments is calculated for each comparison stimulus. If, in plotting the data, with the proportions on the ordinate and the comparison stimulus values on the abscissa, the function is of the integrated normal form (S-shaped), a measure of the dispersion of the greater judgments, the semi-interquartile range, is used as the DL. It is half the difference between the 75th and 25th percentiles of the plotted function.

The method of constant stimuli is considered more accurate than the method

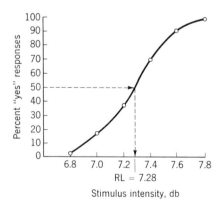

Figure 3-1 The graphical method of calculating the RL using the method of constant stimuli. The data are from Table 3-1. The method is described in the text.

of limits because of the greater number of judgments about the RL and its avoidance of the judgment errors typically produced by that method. A major drawback of this method is its tediousness and inefficiency. A very large number of judgments are required, and many judgment errors will occur because of the subject's shifting level of attention to the task. In some applications of this method, "catch trials" are used, in which no stimulus is presented, in order to gauge the subject's involvement in the task.

Method Of Adjustment

The method of adjustment, called the *method of average error* by Fechner, is probably the most natural for the subject. If an RL for loudness is to be calculated, the subject is supplied with an adjustable device for controlling the sound pressure to which he listens. His task is to adjust sound pressure to its least audible level. The mean of several adjustments is used as the RL. A DL is measured indirectly. In the loudness example, a particular DL would be obtained by presenting a standard to the subject, and having him adjust the intensity of the tone generator until it sounded equivalent in loudness to the standard. A large number of measures would be obtained. The standard deviation of the distribution of the subject's adjustments would be taken as the DL.

In summary, the method of adjustment can be used to calculate the RL and DL, although the latter only indirectly. The method demands a comparison stimulus that is continuously variable. It provides a natural task for the subject that is useful in sustaining his attention and interest. There is a problem of the subject's confidence in making adjustments. To be efficient, the method necessitates the subject's not taking inordinate amounts of time in making his adjustments. Some subjects insist, however, on quite long trials. Most of the studies on the constancies, reported in Chapters 8 and 9, use this method.

We have introduced three different methods for calculating RLs and DLs. In order to select a particular method, the experimenter must consider factors such as the availability of continuous or discrete values of the comparison stimuli, possible judgment errors, tediousness of the task, level of accuracy desired, and time available to collect data. All three methods are used extensively in the present research literature. An investigator must also consider whether to use naive or trained subjects. Naive subjects would be preferred if the final data are to be representative of the population to which they will be applied.

EVALUATING THE THRESHOLD CONCEPT

The concept of the sensory threshold itself is so pervasive in psychology that it is unlikely to be questioned. Traditionally conceived, the absolute threshold is a fixed point on the continuum of sensory experience. Stimuli that produce sensations below this point are not experienced, and subjects will make such statements as "The tone was too weak to be heard." One may question, however, what the concept actually means when three methods that are quite different in application can be used to measure it. In the method of limits the definition of the RL is straightforward: The point midway between the stimulus level at which the subject can report he detected the stimulus and the nearest level for which detection is not made. In the method of constant stimuli, however, the RL is an estimate of the stimulus value detected in 50 percent of the trials. One can ask: Why not 60 percent? Indeed, 60 percent is often used, as in the study by Hecht, Schlaer, and Pirenne (1942) on the minimum light energy for a visual RL. Finally, the method of adjustment has the subject attempting to find his own RL. He must keep adjusting the intensity level of the stimulus until he is as close as possible to that point at which the stimulus is barely detectable.

Can a concept so variable in operational definition be necessary and usable? With regard to necessity, there is no doubt. Rough estimates of the sensitivity of an individual's hearing or vision are often necessary since it is so variable across subjects, and such stimuli are common in psychological research. There is also the practical importance of hearing and vision tests. Consider, finally, with regard to how usable the concept of the threshold is that, most often, the various methods give comparable data.

One sticky problem, though, for the concept of the threshold is that of judgment errors. All the psychophysical methods for measuring thresholds that have been discussed have some procedure for balancing out "errors" in judgment that may interfere with the observer's ability to report accurately his sensory experiences. These errors may be, e.g., position, space, or time errors in the method of average error or errors of habituation and expectancy in the method of limits. Typically, an attempt is made to try to minimize these errors through experimental controls, such as the use of ascending and descending orders of judgment in the method of limits.

Consider the method of constant stimuli, however. One of the central issues in the early days of psychophysical methodology concerned the use of the "equal" response category in obtaining difference thresholds with this method. Subjects differed greatly in their usage of this response category and thus produced widely varying estimates of the DL. One had then either not to use this response category or preselect subjects who used it infrequently. Another disconcerting finding with this procedure was that catch trials, i.e., trials on which no stimulus was presented, often produced reports from the subject that he perceived the stimulus. The frequency of this latter error varied widely, of course, for the different subjects.

SIGNAL-DETECTION THEORY

The judgmental errors enumerated above are not necessarily antagonistic to the general concept of a threshold. However, the threshold cannot be easily defended as a stationary point along the sensory continuum. The occurrence of these errors, especially those on catch trials, would seem to argue that the level of the threshold is variable and influenced by motivational variables, judgmental considerations, and other personal factors. For proponents of the *theory of signal detection* (TSD), the threshold concept itself becomes superfluous (Green & Swets, 1966). These investigators have substituted in its place a model of

**Table 3-4   The Four Possible Outcomes of a
Signal-Detection Task and Their Associated
Probability of Occurrence**

Stimulus state	Response state	
	"Yes"	"No"
Noise alone	False alarm P(Y/N)	Correct rejection P (N/N)
Signal plus noise	Hit P(Y/SN)	Miss P(N/SN)

sensory processing that includes a separate evaluation of the *response biases and sensory factors* inherent in the responses produced in a psychophysical task. In the TSD model, it is not assumed that the subject merely reports his sensory experiences. Instead, he is making *a decision* as to whether the stimulus was presented. It is assumed that the "yes" or "no" response of the subject reflects his knowledge of the actual *probability* of the signal being presented to him on any one trial. Furthermore, he considers how his detection accuracy will be evaluated by the experimenter in consideration of any differential *rewards* (e.g., monetary) for correctness or costs for mistakes. Finally, the *sensitivity* of the subject to the actual strength of the signal must be considered.

Elements of TSD

Although it appears that the decision process of the subject cannot be a simple one, given all the considerations, the signal-detection model is able to refer the subject's decision to a solitary judgment scale or what is called a *decision axis*. In order to understand how the model accomplishes this, it is necessary to consider the design of a signal-detection experiment. One common signal-detection procedure for pure-tone signals has the following elements. The subject receives a warning signal that an observation interval is to begin. The observation interval contains either white noise[3] alone or white noise with a pure tone embedded in it. At the conclusion of this interval, a second warning light appears, indicating the start of a response interval. The subject's task is to respond "yes" (the signal was presented) or "no" (the signal was not presented) during the preceding observation interval.

A very large number of these trials are run, and the data are summarized in terms of the proportional occurrence of four possible outcomes (Table 3-4). It can be seen that there are two response possibilities, "yes" and "no," and two stimulus states, "signal and noise" and "noise alone," yielding four response-stimulus state combinations. A "hit" occurs when the subject replies "yes" and,

---

[3]A noise commonly used in psychoacoustic experiments to mask out extraneous noises. White noise contains all audible frequencies, each contributing equal energy.

in fact, a signal (tone) was presented. A ''false alarm'' occurs when the subject responds ''yes'' in the absence of a signal. Similarly, a ''miss'' occurs when the subject responds ''no'' when, in fact, a signal was presented during the observation interval, whereas a ''correct rejection'' indicates a ''no'' response coincident with the absence of the signal.

These outcomes will be referred to again later. The key to understanding the detection model of the observer's judgment behavior is to focus on the observation interval itself. When the subject makes his observation, it is with reference to some corresponding sensory representation or neural effect of the stimulus. One frequently applied model of the sensory consequences of the stimulus proposes that these effects are normally distributed, i.e., that the probabilistic distribution (the ''probability density function'') of possible sensory magnitudes related to any one particular stimulus is the familiar normal curve.

There are actually two normal distributions, one referring to the sensory effect of the noise alone and the other to the effect of the signal plus noise condition. In Figure 3-2, these two distributions are represented on a common axis. This axis represents the scale of magnitude of the sensory effect of the stimulus. It is also called the *observation axis* inasmuch as the subject's ''yes'' or ''no'' response depends on the size of the sensory effect he observes or feels for that stimulus. It should be noted that the noise distribution is to the left of the ''signal plus noise'' distribution. This results from the greater overall energy in the latter stimulus. On the other hand, the two distributions overlap. The overlap indicates that at times the probabilistic character of the neural effects will produce a sensory event for a noise trial larger than that with a signal trial. To the extent that the strength of the signal is increased, less overlap between the two distributions would be expected.

As an index of the subject's sensory response to the signal (his *sensitivity*), the measure d' has been introduced in TSD. This quantity is the distance between the mean of the noise distribution and the mean of the ''signal plus noise'' distribution using the standard deviation of the noise distribution as the unit of measurement. The manner in which d' is calculated will be presented later.

The observation axis is also called a *decision axis*. According to TSD, the subject establishes a *criterion* or point along this axis such that when the sensory effect is above this point he says ''yes'' and when it is below this criterion he says ''no.'' The decision comes in where this criterion or point is located along this axis. Once this decision is made, the probabilities of the four possible outcomes

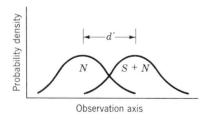

Observation axis

Figure 3-2 The two hypothetical normal distributions representing sensory observations to the presentation of noise alone *(N)* and to the addition of the signal to the noise *(S + N)*. The measure *d'* is the distance between the means of the two distributions.

are decided. In Figure 3-3, such a criterion is drawn over the same two distributions presented in Figure 3-2. It can be seen in this figure that "yes" responses to the right of the criterion will produce not only a region of hits, but also a region of false alarms. In the latter case, the "yes" response is being applied to a sensory effect arising from a noise trial. Similarly, the "no" responses given when the neural effect is below the criterion produce not only a region of correct rejections (saying "no" when in fact the signal was not presented) but also a proportion of misses occurring when the signal condition happened to produce a sensory effect below the criterion.

   Thus the criterion established by the subject guides his responses and controls the probability of the various outcomes. This criterion is directly under the control of the subject. According to the detection model, the subject attempts to establish an *optimum* criterion. In doing this, he must consider the actual (a priori) probabilities of the noise and signal events and any rewards or costs associated with the four possible outcomes of his judgments. Optimization, according to TSD, indicates that the observer is maximizing the expected value of his decision, i.e., he is *maximizing the rewards for his correct responses and minimizing the costs of his incorrect responses,* over a large, undefined number of trials. The use of certain elements of probability theory produces a mathematical solution to the optimization problem such that β, the optimum criterion, is found to be equal to

$$\beta = \frac{P(n)}{P(s)} \frac{Vn\,B + Kn\,A}{Vs\,A + Ks\,B} \tag{3-1}$$

$P(n)$ and $P(s)$ are the a priori probabilities of the noise alone or signal plus noise being presented, respectively. V and K stand for the rewards and costs, respectively, of the particular outcomes described by the subscripts (s = "signal plus noise," n = "noise," A = "yes," and B = "no"). Thus $Kn\,A$ is the cost to the observer of responding "yes" on a "noise-alone" trial, i.e., of giving a false-positive response.

   This value β can be referred to the observation axis (now called the *decision* axis) described previously. The value of β can also be viewed as the ratio of the value of the two probability density functions N and $S + N$ at a certain point along the observation axis. Consider the criterion line in Figure 3-3. The point at which

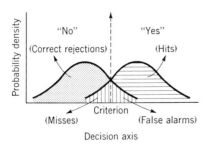

Figure 3-3 The probability distributions of the four outcomes to the signal-detection task as produced by the placement of the observer's criterion along the decision axis.

it crosses the N and $S + N$ distributions defines the probabilities that the "noise" or "noise plus signal" trials, respectively, produced that particular sensory observation. The ratio of these two probabilities defines a *likelihood ratio*, that is, a ratio of the probability, given a particular observation, that this observation was produced by the "signal plus noise" condition, divided by the probability that this observation was produced by the "noise-alone" condition. The observation axis can thus be considered a continuum of likelihood ratios going from small to large values, from left to right. β is then a point along this continuum.

At this point it would appear best to summarize the elements of the TSD model introduced so far. On any particular trial, the subject has a neural response which he observes. This observation is one of a distribution of neural responses that are possible, given the inherent probabilistic nature of the subject's response to both the "noise" and "signal plus noise" trials. The observer's sensitivity, denoted as d', and measured as the separation between the "noise" and "signal plus noise" distributions, is also considered at this point. Given knowledge of the a priori probabilities of the two signal conditions as well as the differential costs and rewards for the four possible judgment outcomes, a subject makes a decision that maximizes his payoff. He does this using a response criterion, β, that can be summarized as a point along his observation axis. *When this observation axis is considered as a continuum of likelihood ratios, β can be specified as a particular numerical value along this continuum.* The subject reports, "yes," he detects the signal when the observation exceeds his criterion and "no" when it is below the criterion. In this way the subject's behavior is explained by means of the tenets of statistical-decision theory.

The subject's responses are summarized in a signal-detection task through the use of a receiver-operating characteristic curve or *ROC* curve. Such a curve is represented in Figure 3-4. The ordinate of this graph represents the probability of a hit, whereas the abscissa gives the probability of a false alarm. The points of the curve, therefore, represent only the proportion of the subject's total responses that are "yes" when the signal did occur (hit) or did not occur (false alarm).

Each data point used to produce the ROC curve represents the proportion of hits and false alarms generated by a particular criterion. In a sense several experiments are run using the same signal and same signal intensity. In each, the subject uses a different criterion because of either a change in the a priori probabilities of n and s or because of a new "payoff matrix" for the four outcomes of his judgments.

By referring back to equation 3-1, that for β, the subject's optimum criterion, it can be seen that a change in signal and noise probabilities as well as changes in the payoff matrix will result in changes in β. The ROC function in Figure 3-4 was generated with the data presented in Table 3-5. Looking at the figure, it can be noted that the curve is produced from five data points, each representing a value for the hit rate, $P(S/s)$, and false-alarm rate, $P(S/n)$. These five points were generated by performing five subexperiments, each using a different value for $P(s)$, the probability that the signal would be presented. The strengths of the signal, and thus d', as well as the payoff matrix, were held

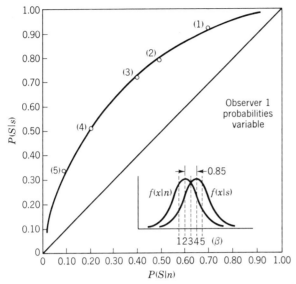

Figure 3-4 An ROC curve produced by shifts in the observer's criterion resulting from changes in the proportion of signal trials. The data are given in Table 3-5. *(From* Signal Detection Theory and Psychophysics *by John Swets and David Green. Copyright, 1966, John Wiley & Sons, Inc. Reprinted by permission of John Wiley & Sons, Inc.)*

constant throughout the experiment. In referring to equation (3-1), it can be seen that increasing the size of $P(s)$ produces a proportionally smaller value for β when the other factors in the equation are held constant; i.e., the ratio $P(n)/P(s)$ becomes smaller as $P(s)$ gets larger. The important point here is that these decreases in the value of β that occur as $P(s)$ increases are reflected in a movement of the response criterion to the left (toward the noise distribution) along the decision axis.

As the criterion shifts in this manner, the proportion of both hits and false alarms goes up (as we go from 5 to 1). This occurs because a greater portion of both the "signal plus noise" and "noise-alone" distributions are above the response criterion. In Table 3-5, these increases in hits and false alarms can be seen corresponding to increases in $P(s)$ from 0.10 to 0.90. The corresponding

Table 3-5   Data Used in Obtaining ROC Curve Represented in Figure 3-15

$P(s)$	Obtained β	Criterion position	$P(S/n)$ false alarms	$P(S/s)$ hits	Data point in figure
.10	2.20	5	.090	.335	(5)
.30	1.40	4	.205	.510	(4)
.50	.88	3	.400	.715	(3)
.70	.74	2	.490	.785	(2)
.90	.46	1	.690	.925	(1)

Source: Adapted from Green and Swets 1966.

data points, 5 to 1, can be seen in Figure 3-4. The shift of β to the left as $P(s)$ increases can be seen in the insert in the figure. Therefore, while data point 1 is produced by β position 1 which is the smallest β value, data point 5 corresponding to a $P(s)$ of 0.10, is produced by the largest β, at point 5 in the insert.

It is worth mentioning that β value 5 is often referred to as a strict or conservative response criterion, whereas value 1 would be considered lax. The terms have an obvious interpretation. The β value represented by 5 indicates that the subject will respond "yes" very infrequently as only a small proportion of the "signal plus noise" and "noise" distributions are above this value. On the other hand, if the subject uses a β value represented by 1, he will often be responding "yes." Of course, in the data being presented, this would appear to be sound strategy because this β corresponds to a $P(s)$ of 0.90; that is, the signal is nine times as likely to be presented as the noise.

As mentioned previously, shifts in β can occur because of changes in the payoff matrix used. Therefore, with reference to equation 3-1 again, to the extent that the total of the rewards for correct rejections and costs of false alarms ($VnB + KnA$) are less than the total of the rewards for hits and costs for misses ($VsA + KsB$), β will become more lax and farther away from the conservative end of the decision axis. Essentially, the subject is being reinforced for saying "yes," he detected the signal, under these circumstances, and this accounts for the shift in criterion. Reinforcing the subject for saying "no" is equivalent to producing a larger or more conservative β, i.e., a larger ratio of $(VnB + KnA)/(VsA + KsB)$.

It can be seen in Figure 3-4 that the d' for this particular ROC curve was 0.85. Figure 3-5 shows the general relationship between ROC functions and d'. As β changes, the various points along an ROC curve are mapped out. On the other hand, changes in d' indicate movement from one particular ROC curve to another. Specifically, d' increases as the curve gets more convex, i.e., moves to the upper left-hand portion of the figure. Thus with greater separation between the "signal plus noise" and "noise" distribution, regardless of the β chosen, the proportion of hits will be substantially larger than the proportion of false alarms, reflecting greater sensitivity of the subject.

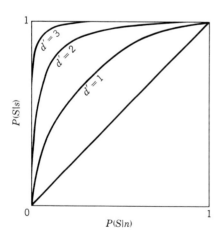

Figure 3-5 The relationship between d' and the ROC function. *(From* Signal Detection Theory and Psychophysics *by John Swets and David Green. Copyright, 1966, John Wiley & Sons, Inc. Reprinted by permission of John Wiley & Sons, Inc.)*

The "yes-no" signal-detection experiment is only one of several procedures that are commonly used to obtain the data necessary for producing ROC curves or obtaining estimates of d'. In the *forced-choice* procedure, the subject is given a number of observation intervals, e.g., two or four. His task, after attending to each observation period, is to report which interval contained the signal. The percentage of the total trials on which the subject is correct is then calculated. Reference is then made to tables that give d' equivalents for these percentages.

The *rating* method is somewhat more complex. Here the subject rates his certainty that the signal was presented during an observation interval. He may do this using a subjective scale, or he may assign a probability of being correct to his judgment. A number of ranges of certainty or categories of certainty are produced. Hit and false-alarm rates are established for each of these, and the resulting data are used to generate the points of an ROC function.

A very important adjunct of TSD that has not yet been mentioned is the *theory of the ideal observer*. The ideal observer is a mathematical model of the process or processes that may be used by the subject in detecting a particular type of signal. The performances of typical subjects are compared with that of the ideal observer to see how well the model predicts or matches actual detection behavior. Each type of detection problem can give rise to a unique ideal-observer model. The models may fit such complex stimulus situations as the subject attempting to detect any one of a number of pure tones differing in frequency. The manner in which the subject handles this uncertainty about the stimulus characteristics and how he then generates the necessary terms for the statistical-decision procedure underlying his detection performance are the elements of the model.

The ideal-observer concept has led to the application of TSD to many complex stimulus situations, such as the above, that represent, in their very complexity, more real-life perceptual tasks than would be represented by the simple yes-no detection procedure. The application of TSD methodology to areas other than psychophysics in psychology has been accelerating. A partial listing of these areas includes animal psychophysics, problems in sensory physiology, speech recognition, subliminal perception, and personality measurement. The common denominator in many of these studies is the need to distinguish response biases of many types from other behavioral measures. Another attraction is that the subject's responses can be viewed as the result of a decision process.

TSD is certainly one of the major theoretical and methodological innovations in psychophysics. *Its ability to directly distinguish the response criterion from sensory features in the subject's judgment solves one of the major and oldest problems in psychophysics*. Its conceptualization of sensory judgments as a decision process is a direct counterweight to the view of traditional psychophysics that the threshold denotes a discrete point below which there is no subjective experience of a stimulus. For TSD, sensory experience lies along a continuum. Variations in judgment reflect changes in the placement of the criterion for responding to given changes in stimulus probabilities or in motivational elements such as the payoff matrix. According to the TSD view, judgment variability is due not to the inherent variability of the stimuli or of the sensory apparatus but to the decision process used by the subject in making his judgments.

WEBER'S LAW AND THE PROBLEM OF A PSYCHOPHYSICAL SCALE

Calculating RLs and DLs can be viewed as a first step in quantifying our sensory capabilities. As an application of RL measurements, Figure 5-1 in Chapter 5 shows the relationship between a subject's brightness threshold and the particular wavelength of light energy he is responding to. A "visibility function" is obtained that indicates the nature of the differential sensitivity of our visual system to the component wavelengths of the visible spectrum, a very important finding.

The DL has been used as a unit of sensation, as a yardstick for measuring the magnitude of a subject's sensory response. This application follows directly from Fechner's theoretical elaboration of what he termed Weber's law, after his mentor E. H. Weber. In the 1830s Weber conducted a series of studies on the DLs, or as he termed them *just noticeable differences* (JNDs) for weight discrimination. He reported that no matter what weight he started with, the JND always turned out to be represented by the same proportional change in stimulus magnitude, about one-thirtieth of the standard (Boring, 1942). Thus a comparison weight would have to be 29 ounces (or less) or 31 ounces (or more) for a subject to distinguish it from a 30-ounce standard; in this example the JND or DL would be 1 ounce, and the ratio of JND to the value of the standard stimulus would therefore be 1:30. Similarly, if one starts with a 15-ounce standard, the JND would be 0.5 ounce, giving the same JND:standard ratio of 0.5:15 or 1:30. Weber generalized his finding into the statement that all the JNDs for any sense system would be a constant proportion of the standard, the constant being a function of the particular sense system. This is typically expressed today as $\Delta I/I = K$ where ΔI is the JND or DL, expressed in terms of the change in intensity necessary to achieve it, and I is the physical value or intensity of the standard.

Weber's Law has been tested innumerable times. The most common result is that the fraction $\Delta I/I$ is relatively constant over an intermediate range of stimulus values. For both relatively small and large stimulus magnitudes, the Weber fraction is larger than for the intermediate stimuli.

PSYCHOPHYSICAL LAWS

Fechner's Law

Since the JNDs for any one sensation (e.g., the loudness of a 1,000-Hz tone) are a constant fraction of the standard according to Weber's law, Fechner asserted that these JNDs all represented equal increments in sensation. On the basis of this logic a function can be derived that relates the subjective and physical values of these stimuli. Figure 3-6 is a graphical representation of this function. The

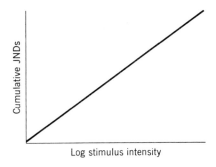

Figure 3-6 A representation of Fechner's law showing the linear relationship between cumulative JNDs and log stimulus intensity.

mathematical description of the figure (the "function") is as follows (Guilford, 1954):

$$\text{Cumulative JNDs (sensation)} = k \, \log \frac{S}{S_0} \tag{3-2}$$

where S is any above-threshold magnitude of the stimulus and S_0 is the RL value of the stimulus. Since $\log S/S_0 = \log S - \log S_0$, the formula may be rewritten as

$$\text{Sensation} = k \, \log S - k \, \log S_0$$

If we let $a = - k \, \log S_0$, the function becomes sensation $= k \, \log S + a$. This is, in reality, the equation of a straight line. In math texts, the linear equation is expressed as $Y = mx + b$, where m is the slope of the line and b is its intercept with the ordinate or y-axis. Here the ordinate is simply defined as sensation, and the abscissa, or x-axis, as $\log S$. Since Fechner considered the JNDs as units of sensation, all equal in magnitude for any sensory dimension, the sensation in Figure 3-6 is expressed as the number of accumulated JNDs above threshold (S_0). Fechner used R to describe the sensation, and his law is $R = k \, \log S + a$, or more typically $R = k \, \log S$, where S is understood to be measured as multiples of S_0.

The logical question at this point concerns the validity of Fechner's law, a consideration of which requires some background information on psychophysical scaling. It certainly would not be efficient to produce scales of cumulated JNDs related to stimulus magnitude. Furthermore, these scales would be based on a unit that can be measured only indirectly. Stevens (1960, p. 50) calls JND scales "confusion" scales "because the value of the JND is determined by the confusions an observer makes between stimuli spaced various distances apart on the sensory continuum." To appreciate this logic, note that if the constant-stimulus method is used to measure JNDs, the standard deviation of the distribution of "greater" judgments for the comparison stimuli is taken as the measure of the JND for that standard. What is needed is a *direct* scaling procedure (Corso, 1967) in which the subject directly reports the magnitude of his sensations.

At this point note that increasing a number by a constant ratio will, when logarithmic form is used, be equivalent to a constant arithmetic increment for example, $\log_{10} 1 = 0$, $\log_{10} 10 = 1$, $\log_{10} 100 = 2$. Fechner's law, $R = k \log S$, can therefore be viewed as stating that, as stimulus magnitude increases by equal ratios (above, from 1 to 10, etc.), sensation grows by equivalent incremental steps (above, from 0 to 1, etc.). The direct scaling methods of choice, used in conjunction with Fechner's law, are those in which the subject directly reports the incremental or interval changes in sensation that he experiences.[4]

The two most widely used of these methods are the *category judgment method* and the method of *equal-appearing intervals*. In the former, the subject is given a set of categories to be used, e.g., very loud, loud, medium, soft, and very soft if loudness is to be judged. It is assumed that subjects can make judgments of the *distance* between categories along their subjective scale for the particular stimulus dimensions. This assumption also implies that the subject can sense the *order* of magnitudes that he experiences, but it does not imply that he can locate a zero point on this scale, a point of no sensation. If the zero point were known, then *ratio* judgments could be obtained. Stating that a tone is twice as loud as another implies that it is twice as distant from zero sensation. Category scales are considered only interval scales because the subject's ability to sense the distance or intervals between stimuli is the most complex assumption made.

In the method of equal-appearing intervals, the subject is told to space stimuli so that they are equidistant steps from each other. In one variant of this procedure, he may be given two lights of different brightness and told to produce a brightness midway between the two by manipulating a voltage control to the lamp. He would then "bisect" these two new intervals. A scale would then be produced in which the stimuli would be subjectively spaced at equidistant intervals, each stimulus representing a unit along the scale.

Power Law

The power law (or Stevens' law, as it is often called, in honor of its chief proponent, S. S. Stevens) gets its name from the mathematical expression of the

---

[4]Stevens (1951) identifies four types of measurement scales. The scales are distinguished on the basis of the extent to which the properties of the numbers making up the scale are taken to reflect corresponding features about the magnitude of the psychological dimension being scaled. *Nominal* measurement occurs when numbers are used only to denote class of objects, e.g., numbers in a catalog. *Ordinal* measurement implies that the relative position, or rank indicated by the scale value, reflects the rank order of magnitude along the psychological dimension. IQ scores are probably ordinal measures where a greater score implies more of whatever IQ tests measure. For *interval* scales, not only are the ordinal properties of the numbers representing the scale meaningful, but so are the distances between these scale values. If a subject rates brightness on a 10-point equal-interval scale, the brightness difference between scale values of 5 and 7 would be the same as between 1 and 3, etc. A physical scale clearly interval in nature is that for temperature, either Celsius or Fahrenheit. There is only an arbitrary zero point, but distances between temperature values clearly represent the same movement of a column of mercury throughout the scale range. The highest order scale is the *ratio* scale. This is the type of scale that is produced when magnitude estimates are used. In addition to the properties of the interval scale, the ratio scale has the additional property of an absolute zero point. Consequently, the ratio of scale values is meaningful. Thus 10 units of brightness is taken to represent twice as much brightness as 5 units of brightness, etc.

law $R = kS_m$ (Stevens, 1957), where R, the sensory magnitude, is equal to a constant times the physical magnitude of the stimulus raised to a power, m. In logarithmic form, this equation becomes $\log R = m \log S + \log k$. This again is the equation of a straight line, where m, the exponent, is the slope of the line and $\log k$ is the intercept of the line with the ordinate. Thus if R and S are *both* plotted as log values, this law predicts the linear function shown in Figure 3-7. When expressed logarithmically, the essential difference between this law and Fechner's is in the $\log R$ term in the power law. Recall that Fechner's law can be interpreted as stating that equal ratio changes in stimulus magnitude produce equivalent arithmetic or incremental changes in sensation. Thus, the power law, when expressed logarithmically, states that equal ratio changes in stimulus magnitude produce equivalent *ratio* changes in sensation. These statements indicate that *the essential difference in the theoretical laws rests with the assumption concerning how sensory magnitude grows in proportion to changes in stimulus magnitude.* In other words, Fechner states that the subjective scale grows arithmetically for logarithmic changes in the physical scale, whereas Stevens asserts they both grow logarithmically.

This difference between Fechner's law and the power law, whether sensation grows incrementally or in ratio units as the stimulus intensity is increased by ratio units, is reflected in the scaling procedures used to obtain data for evaluating the theories. Whereas category and equal interval scaling are preferred for investigating Fechner's law, a ratio-scaling technique is typically used in evaluating the power law. The latter techniques are those that assume not only that the subject can report the subjective distances between his sensations for any two values of the stimulus, but that he can report the relative size or ratio of his two sensations, i.e., how much bigger or smaller one is than the other.

The ratio-scaling method typically used to provide data on the power law is the method of *magnitude estimation.* In the classic form of magnitude estimation (Stevens, 1957) the subject is given a standard stimulus and told that he should consider it as some value (e.g., 100) on his subjective scale. The subject is further instructed that all other stimuli should be evaluated as ratios of this standard. Thus, if a stimulus seems twice as large as the standard, it should be called 200; if it sounds one-half as loud, 50, etc. Magnitude estimation is, therefore, a direct ratio-scaling procedure where the subject is required to directly report the ratio of sensation between a comparison and standard stimulus. Magnitude estimation

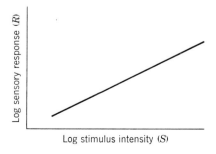

Figure 3-7 A hypothetical psychophysical function of the linear form predicted by the power law for responses and stimuli plotted in logarithmic values.

is the method of choice in power law studies. As applied currently, magnitude estimation does not always involve first giving the subject a number to apply to represent a certain standard on his subjective scale. Instead, many investigators instruct the subject to make only ratio judgments, i.e., to consider that a number twice as big as another implies twice as much sensation. The subject is then allowed to use any range of numbers with which he feels comfortable.

An impressive finding derived from experimentation on the power law concerns the data from *cross-modality matching*. In this experimental procedure, the subject reports his subjective estimate of one particular sense modality (e.g., loudness of pure tones) by adjusting a stimulus in another modality (e.g., force of handgrip) so that it appears subjectively equal to the first. When several values of the to-be-judged stimulus dimension have been "matched," *equal sensation functions* are produced which are linear when logarithmic units are used on the axes. In Figure 3-8 below (Stevens, 1962), force of handgrip in pounds was used to match the subjective intensity of stimuli from nine stimulus dimensions ranging from electric shock to white light.

Although the power law apparently does a good job in describing the relationship between direct ratio judgments (e.g., magnitude estimates) of sensation and the physical values of the stimuli, there is still much controversy over its validity as a psychophysical law. One of the major problems is the fact that there are sizable differences between individuals in the exponents obtained for virtually any stimulus dimension. In fact, even the correlations between exponents, when different response measures are used with the same stimulus dimension, have been found to be very small (Rule & Markley, 1971). Another important problem concerning the power law is that judgment data typically deviate from

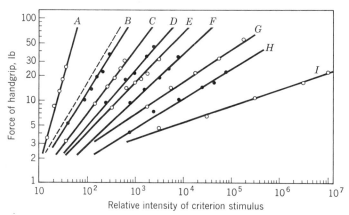

Figure 3-8 Equal sensation functions for nine stimulus dimensions produced by a cross-modality matching procedure using force of handgrip to represent the subjective intensity of the stimuli from the other modalities. All functions are linear when logarithmic coordinates are used, as predicted by the power law. The dashed line represents a line that would be produced by an exponent of 1 in the power function. Key: A, electric shock, 60 Hz; B, warmth; C, lifted weights; D, pressure on palm; E, cold; F, vibration, 60 Hz; G, white noise; H, 1,000-Hz tone; I, white light. *(From Stevens, 1962. Copyright 1962 by the American Psychological Association. Reproduced by permission.)*

the expected exponent when stimuli of small magnitudes, usually near absolute threshold, are presented.

As a final example of problems with the power law, there is the finding that ratio judgments are susceptible to contextual effects. This problem arises when the obtained power function is correlated to some feature of the stimulus distribution being judged, such as the range of magnitudes used. Category scaling procedures, the method of choice for Fechner's law, are also very susceptible to contextual effects. It is not at all clear, as for ratio-scaling procedures, whether these contextual effects are due to characteristics of our perceptual abilities or whether they reflect response biases or habits brought to the judgment task by the subject (Melamed & Thurlow, 1971).

EVALUATION OF THE PSYCHOPHYSICAL LAWS AND THEORETICAL INTERPRETATIONS

It would therefore seem that the power law is the preferred psychophysical relation if only for its reproducibility for many types of stimuli. An argument against this view is the common experimental finding demonstrated in Figure 3-9. These data are from a study by Gibson and Tomko (1972) comparing category and magnitude estimates of tactile intensity. The stimuli were trains of electrical pulses which were presented to the thumb and which felt like taps. Mean category judgments from an eight-point scale and the geometric means of magnitude estimates for the same stimuli are presented in Figure 3-9. The function relating the two sets of judgments is concave downward, whereas a linear function was expected. This linear function would be expected if, in fact, the category and magnitude estimation judgments are of the same underlying subjective intensity dimension. Category judgments have the subject employing an interval scale to reflect the apparent intensities, whereas magnitude estimates employ a ratio scale. The difference between these two procedures is in the implied origin or zero point for the ratio scale. The category scale should be linearly related to the magnitude estimate scale; i.e., using a constant to adjust for the origin should make this scale comparable to that of the magnitude

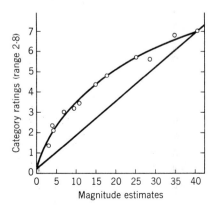

Figure 3-9 Data comparing the category and magnitude estimates of tactile intensity for the same series of electrical pulses. *(From Gibson & Tomko, 1972.)*

estimate scale. The data of Gibson and Tomko do not show this linear relationship.

The explanation offered for the concavity of the function relating the magnitude and category judgments is that there is a systematic bias built into category judgments (Stevens, 1961). Other approaches to the relationship between the psychophysical scales produced by category and magnitude judgments have been offered. Torgerson (1960) argues that the two types of judgment tasks merely represent the two standard ways we have of using numbers in measurement. He uses the amusing example of a rat and horse both gaining a pound during some time period. One can view the gains as equal, since each was a pound, or as unequal, considering that the weight gain was negligible for the horse but huge for the rat. A ratio scale of weight gain with a fixed zero point would allow us to say both gained the same amount. On the other hand, an interval (category) scale, when only unit size is fixed, would allow a statement about the inequality of the weight gains. In the latter case, a weight gain from 10 to 11 pounds for the rat is more nearly equal to a gain from 1,000 to 1,100 pounds for the horse, not from 1,000 to 1,001 pounds as for a ratio-measurement approach. Using numbers in these two ways, ratio and interval scaling, will produce the concave function in Figure 3-9, in which category and magnitude judgments are related. In other words, the obtained behavior reflects the number system the subject is forced to use by the instructions. The logic of this argument counters support for the power law that rests solely on the assumed superior validity of ratio-scaling techniques.

SUMMARY

Psychophysical methodology has a history as long as that of experimental psychology. The basic psychological methods for determining the absolute and differential threshold are still actively applied in much their original form. The concept of the JND as a unit of sensory experience has led to the development of a psychophysical law, Fechner's. Whether in fact equal interval changes in sensation are related to equal ratio changes in stimulus magnitude, as Fechner proposed, or whether equal ratio changes in sensation are produced by equivalent ratio changes in stimulus magnitude, as Stevens proposes, are still open questions. The data supporting either of these two laws seem to be tied to the type of scaling procedure, interval or ratio estimation, that was used in obtaining the data. One modern innovation in psychophysical methodology is signal-detection theory. By viewing psychophysical judgments as resulting from a decision process, this theory allows for a separate evaluation of the sensory and nonsensory factors that enter into these judgments. Signals no longer are viewed by this theory as above or below some absolute threshold value, determined by the characteristics of the sensory apparatus.

Chapter 4

Sensory Physiology
of Vision

This chapter is a survey of the physiological mechanisms of the eye and the major regions of the visual nervous system. The primary question in evaluating these mechanisms concerns the information within the stimulus they process and how this information may be related to our visual sensory experiences, the topic of Chapter 5.

VISUAL STIMULUS

While investigating the responses of the visual system to external stimulation, a clear statement must be made identifying the physical features of the stimuli that are being processed. The stimulus that initiates our visual experience is electromagnetic radiation of a very restricted range of wavelengths. "Light energy" has historically been conceptualized in two seemingly contradictory ways. As the use of the word *wavelength* indicates, energy is, on the one hand, considered to be transmitted in the form of an undulating wave. In other applications, such as in determining the minimal energy necessary for vision (Chapter 5), light energy is viewed as consisting of fundamental packets of energy, called *photons* or *quanta*.

Electromagnetic radiation, when considered as a waveform, consists of a wide spectrum of waves differing immensely in length. Cosmic rays are virtually infinitesimal, whereas radio waves may be miles long. From Figure 4-1, it can be seen that the range of wavelengths making up the visible spectrum is a very small fraction of the electromagnetic spectrum. Only stimuli of these wavelengths can be processed by our visual system, resulting in our subjective visual experiences. The range in wavelengths here is from approximately 400 nanometers (nm) or billionths of a meter to about 700 nm. The specification of the visual stimulus in terms of its wavelength is essential because the qualitative sensation of color is directly linked to this variable as indicated in the figure.

Specifying the intensive aspect of the visual stimulus is more involved than specifying wavelength. The amount of electromagnetic radiation that is being presented to our visual system can be specified in two ways. One is in watts, a power measure in the metrics of physics. The second type of scale, which emphasizes our subjective response to the visible spectrum, represents a scale of the *relative amount* of visible energy in the stimulus. Rather than measuring radiant energy, per se, this scale measures *luminous energy,* the latter term emphasizing the visibility of the stimulus.

The rate of flow of this luminous energy from some source to an intercepting surface is termed *luminous flux*. The *luminous intensity* of this source is measured in *candles*. Needless to say, there is some standard candle which serves as an international reference. These candles are no longer wax. Today, the term refers to incandescent lamps with certain electrical properties. The luminous flux emanating from this source is measured in *lumens*. When a point source of one candle of luminous intensity is placed in the center of a sphere, the amount of luminous flux within a unit solid angle of that sphere is one lumen. Since there are 4π such angles for the total sphere, the total luminous flux is 4π lumens, where $\pi = 3.1416$.

Luminance is the most widely used photometric concept, and it refers to the

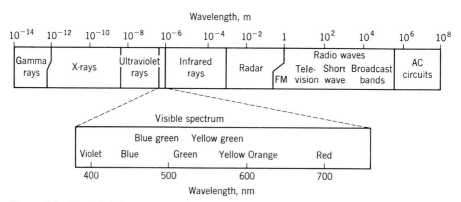

Figure 4-1 The total electromagnetic spectrum, ranging from the infinitesimal gamma rays to the circuits millions of meters in width. The portion of this spectrum that affects the visual receptors (the "visible spectrum") is the narrow region, from approximately 400 to 700 nanometers, shown in enlarged detail. (*From* The Human Senses, *2d ed., by Frank Geldard. Copyright, 1972, John Wiley & Sons, Inc. Reprinted by permission of John Wiley & Sons, Inc.)*

amount of luminous flux emanating from each unit of area of the source. The source is now considered extended and no longer a point. There are numerous measures of luminance. The most widely used measures are the *lambert*, defined as lumens per square centimeter, and the *millilambert* (ml), which is one thousandth of a lambert. Less used but considered the standard measure is the *stilb*, defined as one candle per square centimeter. Representative luminance values for common lighting situations range from 8,250 ml for direct sunlight to 0.00003 ml under night vision (Hurvich & Jameson, 1966). This is a ratio of intensities on the order of 100 million:1.

When the purpose of measurement is to determine the amount of light energy incident on a surface, *illuminance* is being measured. The units of measurement here refer to the density of luminous flux per unit of area. For a surface of one square meter, evenly distributed flux of one lumen produces a *meter-candle* of illuminance. a useful fact concerning illuminance is that it is inversely proportional to the square of the distance to the source.

VISUAL RECEPTORS

Figure 4-2 presents the anatomy of the eye. The analogy between the eye and a camera is often made (Wald, 1950). Some of the key aspects of this analogy are the *lens* of the eye and the *iris* of the eye, the latter serving to control the size of

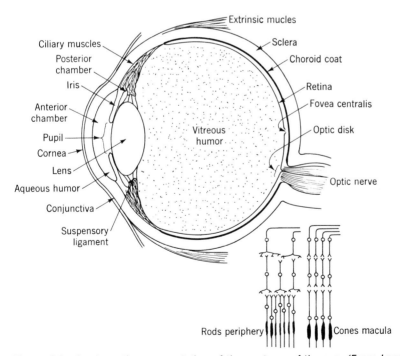

Figure 4-2 A schematic representation of the anatomy of the eye. *(From Langley, 1962.)*

the lens opening (pupil) as does the shutter on a camera. Further, the inside of the camera and the inner surface of the eyeball are coated black to increase light absorption and reduce light scatter. Analogous to film are the photochemical receptors on the retina, described below.

Three layers of cellular tissues form the eyeball. The outer layer is called the *sclera.* The *cornea,* ordinarily transparent, forms the front part of this layer. The central tissue layer is the *choroid coat* from which the *ciliary muscles* extend in front of the eyeball. These muscles control the shape of the lens and thus the focusing accommodation of the visual image on the innermost cellular layer, the *retina.* Within the retina are the actual visual receptors and their associated neural structures.

The light- or photosensitive receptors in the retina are of two kinds, the *rods* and *cones.* There are approximately 125 million rods and 7 million cones in the retina. These names derive from the general appearance of these receptors, as can be seen in Figure 4-2. The rods are most numerous in the periphery of the retina, whereas the *fovea centralis* represents a densely populated area in the central retina where cones alone are found. Cones are also found in the periphery of the retina, although not as profusely as the rods.

The density of cones steadily declines from the fovea centralis to the peripheral retinal areas, but the density of the rods increases at more peripheral areas, reaching a maximum at a point somewhere between 15 and 20° peripheral to the line of sight through the fovea.

The *optic disk* is a depressed area in the rear of the retina through which the fibers that form the optic nerve emerge from the eyeball. The "blindspot" is located at this position on the retina. One interesting thing to note in Figure 4-2 is the positioning of the rods and cones. They are oriented toward the back of the retina away from the source of light energy.

Light energy of the visual stimulus acts on various photochemicals in the rod and cone receptors. The structure of the molecules of these photochemicals changes as the light energy is absorbed, but this process of change is complex and only partially understood. Furthermore, there are a vast number of neural structures and other cells in the retina in the vicinity of these receptors that produce several types of electrical signals as the photochemicals are undergoing change in the receptors.

Photochemistry of Rods and Cones

The photopigment of the rods has been investigated since the midnineteenth century when many individuals reported the peculiar characteristics of a purplish substance found in many eyes. This substance, rhodopsin, becomes clear when exposed to light (i.e., "bleached"). The rhodopsin is found in the *sacs* that are piled up in the outer segment of the rod. These sacs consist of layers of rhodopsin molecules having a particular spatial orientation such that light energy is maximally absorbed when it is perpendicular to the long plane of the rod.

The rhodopsin molecule consists of a substance similar in structure to vitamin A (retinal) and a complex protein molecule, opsin. When a quantum of light energy is absorbed by a rhodopsin molecule, a complex sequence of stages is initiated in the transformation of this molecule into another vitamin A–related substance, retinaldehyde, plus the protein, opsin. Rhodopsin is continuously regenerated from the products of the specific conversion stage that may be reached given a particular stimulus. The regeneration of rhodopsin has been measured in the living human retina (Rushton, Campbell, Hagins, & Brindley, 1955), and appears to reach 50 percent regeneration in about seven minutes. There is some evidence that light may not only bleach rhodopsin but may act to regenerate it from out of the midconversion stages.

At this point it is clear that there is extensive and detailed knowledge about the structure and function of the photopigment that has been found in the rods. The expectation that a similar situation would be true for the cone receptor would be incorrect. In fact, no specific photopigment has clearly been identified in the mammalian cone. The search for photopigments in the cone system has been given direction, first by evidence that only the cone receptors are responsible for our color sense, and second, by certain psychophysical findings on color matching.

If a subject with normal color vision is presented with a patch of projected light of a particular color and is instructed to create a second patch of the same color by using projected lights of various hues, he will find it necessary to use three lights, each of a fixed wavelength composition in order to make a match. The subject is ordinarily establishing a second stimulus that he subjectively views as equivalent in color to the first, using a different mixture of component wavelengths than is found in the original stimulus. The two stimuli are then considered a *metameric pair,* or are *metamers.* These metamers would, of course, be different for different individuals, but color matching would still be trivalent, in all cases involving the mixing of three hues. The Young-Helmholtz theory of color vision is an elaboration of these metameric data. This theory proposes, in its modern version, three color receptors, each predominantly responsive to either short wavelengths (blue receptor), medium wavelengths (green receptor), or long wavelengths (red receptor). Our impressive color sense would be the result of neural events in which the primary color sensations resulting from the activities of the three cones would be "mixed." Since so much of the structure of the Young-Helmholtz theory of color vision as well as that of its rivals rests on psychophysical findings, particularly those having to do with color blindness, these theories will be discussed at length in Chapter 5, on visual psychophysics.

Given the existence of photopigments and the trivalent color theory, research on cone vision has been a search for three photopigments, each identified with a different cone and presumably all photolabile, i.e., breaking down when exposed to light. Although it is apparently straightforward to extract rhodopsin at present from a variety of species, the extraction of cone pigments has been almost universally unsuccessful. The only successful extraction has been that of *iodopsin* from chicken retinas (Wald, 1937). This substance maximally absorbed light energy of a longer wavelength than did rhodopsin. Surprisingly, there was only about a tenth of the amount of iodopsin that would be expected, given the proportion of rods and cones in the chicken retina.

The data used as support for the existence of the three photopigments come from studies on the differential absorption of light energy in the foveas of living retinas and in isolated foveal cones. Rushton (1957) detected two photopigments in the living human fovea that he termed *erythrolabe* and *chlorolabe*, red- and green-sensitive substances, respectively. Note that Rushton detected only the operation of two different absorption processes. He was not extracting or isolating photochemicals. Owing to defects in the method, he was not able to measure *cyanolabe*, the blue-sensitive material. In Rushton's procedure, the absorption of light energy for a series of wavelengths (the absorption spectra) of the retina is measured both before and after the retina has been exposed to a strong adapting light of blue, green, or red wavelength. The *difference spectrum* found by subtracting the postadaptation curve from the preadaptation curve represents the data of interest. This difference spectrum represents the particular response of the foveal photopigments to the adapting light stimulus. The two difference spectras found indicated that both red and green wavelengths (i.e., medium and long wavelengths) were being selectively absorbed by the photopigments of the retina.

Using the difference spectra technique with a refined apparatus, Marks, Dobelle, and MacNichol (1964) and Wald and Brown (1965) were able successfully to measure the absorption spectra for individual human and monkey cones. Evidence was found for the three predicted photopigments. Wald and Brown, using five human cones, found one which appeared to maximally absorb light energy of short (blue) wavelengths and two each of the red and green.

One other finding of particular note concerning types of cones is that of Tomita (1965) who was able to insert hyperfine micropipettes into individual carp cones and record their electrical activity in response to particular wavelengths of light. He did this by vibrating the retina against the pipette. Out of fifty recordings, 74 percent showed peak electrical activity for wavelengths in the red region, 16 percent in the blue region, and 10 percent in the green region. The averages of the wavelengths producing the maximum responses for these cones were 611, 529, and 462 nm.

Although the preponderance of physiological data seems to support the propostion that there are three cone receptors, distinguishable by the spectrum response of their pigments, an argument can be made supporting other interpretations of cone functions. Sheppard (1968) has listed a series of difficulties with the three-pigment theory and has proposed that more attention be paid to the physical structure of the outer membranes of the cones as a source of the differential wavelength responses of this receptor (Enoch, 1961). Sheppard's list includes the fact that only iodopsin, as a cone pigment, has been extracted; differential absorption by cones does not necessarily imply different photopigments, as physical features of the cones may be implicated; the "red cone" from human single-cone absorption data actually has an absorption maxima in the yellow region of the spectrum; the absorption data on individual cones is on peripheral rather than foveal cones where color discrimination is greatest. These two types of cones differ in physical features. Poisons that destroy rods do not destroy cones, implying that their chemical structure must be quite different.

NEURAL PROCESSES IN VISION

Retinal Processes

Once light energy has been processed by the visual receptors, electrical events occur both in the receptors themselves and in the neural tissues of the retina. In some manner, the evident fact of the bleaching of the photopigment leads to the transmission of electrical signals throughout the visual pathways. The manner in which this conversion of information from one form to another occurs is unknown at present. Many electrical phenomena within the retina have been recorded, however, and progress has been made in deciphering the information contained in these signals. The many types of cells in the retina, their density, and the complexity of their interconnections are the major difficulties faced by investigators in this area.

Figure 4-3 is a diagram of the types of nerve cells and their interconnections within a primate (e.g., human) retina. The rods (R) end in what are called *terminal spherules*. Each of these is associated with projecting fibers (dendrites) from several cells, mainly rod bipolar cells (RB) and horizontal cells (H). Each cone terminates in a type of pedestal to which sets of dendrites, three in number, are associated. These *triads* are thought to have as the middle dendrite a midget *bipolar* cell (MB), which is then flanked by the dendrites from two different horizontal cells.

The association between the rods and cones and nerve cells described so far involves evidence for the usual structures, at the point of juncture (synapse) between the cells, to promote the passing of the electrical signal from the receptor to the nerve cell. However, the cones also synapse with flat bipolar cells (FB), with the terminal parts of other cones, and with rod structures. It is unclear whether these points of contact involve the transmission of electrical signals.

The terminal fibers of the bipolar cells (axons) project to the next neural layer of the retina, that of the *ganglion cells,* of which there are two types. These axons also transmit to the *amacrine cells*. To make matters most complex, the amacrine cells, in turn, also project to the bipolar cells. The axons on terminal fibers of the ganglion cells form the *optic nerve fibers*.

In speaking of complexity, it should be made clear that several bipolar and horizontal cells are associated with each rod and that each of the bipolar cells connects to several rods. Similarly, several triads of connections exist for each cone cell. Furthermore, *several bipolar cells receive inputs from both the rods and the cones.*

It seems clear that *there is a complex signal-processing system throughout the retina.* The functions of the various interconnections will be apparent only when the information that they process about the structure and chromaticity of the stimulus can be clarified. It is usually stated that bipolar cells are connected

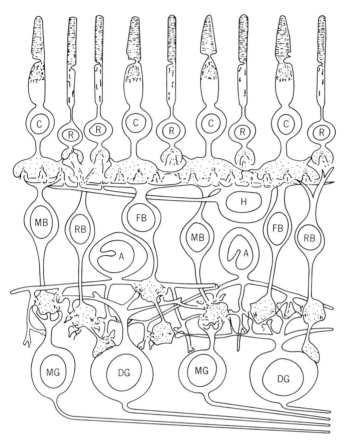

Figure 4-3 Types of nerve cells and their interconnections within a primate retina. Details are in the text. *(From Dowling & Boycott, 1966. Reprinted by permission of The Royal Society. Copyright, 1966, The Royal Society.)*

in a one-to-one relationship with cones and project in the same simple manner to the next, or ganglion, level of the visual pathway, this arrangement underlying the superb visual acuity or clarity found for this area of the retina. This type of statement is misleading in that there are at least four types of bipolar cells in the retina, one of which is the rod-associated type. In the fovea, the cones are still associated with the three other bipolar cells. The one-to-one relationship between receptor and nerve cell concerns only the midget bipolar cell (Sheppard, 1968).

The electrical activity of the cones has been discussed previously (Tomita, 1965). Similar data exist for rods (Penn & Hagins, 1969). The argument has been made that these responses result from the photopigment bleaching and do in fact represent the signals that rods and cones transmit to the neural layers of the retina (Brindley, 1970). The focus here will be on electrical activity of the retina that has provided much indirect information on the activity of the receptors and nerve cells found there. This phenomenon is the retinal slow or *s-potential*.

The s-potential   The s-potential is a graded electrical wave that arises in the retina in response to the light stimulus. It is graded in the sense that its maximum amplitude (the highest voltage of the response) is proportional to the intensity of the stimulus. This potential also lasts as long as the stimulus is present. Typically, fish have served as subjects in investigating these potentials, but so have mammals.

There are two types of s-potentials, both found when the recording microelectrode is inserted in what is termed the inner nuclear layer of the retina (MacNichol & Svaetichin, 1958). One response is achromatic, i.e., the response which is a rising negative potential is not dependent on the wavelength of the stimulus. The other s-potential is a chromatic response but of a complex sort.

The chromatic s-potential may be negative for one wavelength and then positive for another one. This is termed an *opponent process* by some because of its similarity to the opponent-process theory of color vision proposed by Hering as an alternative to that of Helmholtz. However, as opponent-type processes are commonly found at all levels of the visual system, it is important to clarify at this point what an opponent coding of hue information entails. The word *opponent* implies here a process by which the response of a visual cell or collection of cells codes wavelength information by exhibiting two antagonistic or "opponent" responses for two sets of wavelengths. Two such pairs of antagonistically coded wavelengths have been discovered to exist at all postreceptor levels of the visual system. One pair consists of the wavelengths from the yellow and blue regions of the spectrum, whereas the other pair contains wavelengths from the red and green regions. An example of an opponent or antagonistic process had already been indicated above for the s-potential. One linked pair of s-potentials recorded at one electrode (and therefore presumably produced by the same source) consists of a rising negative potential for "yellow" wavelengths and rising positive wave for "blue" wavelengths.

There has been much controversy in the literature as to whether s-potentials are being recorded from actual nerve cells in the retina or in intercellular spaces. Most likely, the achromatic responses come from horizontal cells and the chromatic type from the bipolar cells (Brindley, 1970).

Ganglion-Cell Responses

The final neural layer of the retina, that of the ganglion cells, has provided much support for the view that the retina is an active center for processing information about selected features of the visual stimulus. This information is coded in the form of action or spike potentials that are recorded via microelectrodes in contact with the ganglion cells. These potentials are very different from those producing the s-potential response. The action potentials are discrete electrical impulses that are produced by the ionic inversions that take place between the inside and outside of a nerve cell when stimulated. These pulses are always of uniform size and vary in number depending upon such features of the stimulus as its intensity.

A primary focus of the research on the information-processing aspect of the ganglion cell's response has been on the complexity of the spatial organization of its *receptive field*. The receptive field for a cell is simply that area on the surface of the retina which, when properly stimulated (usually by a small beam of light), produces changes in the number of action potentials in the nerve fiber. Presumably, that particular ganglion cell is connected via a complex organization of bipolar cells and receptors to that particular retinal area. The retina can be thought of as a mosaic of overlapping receptive fields or projection areas for each level of the visual nervous system.

Figure 4-4 represents a receptive field for a ganglion cell of a cat. In his studies on this receptive field, Kuffler (1953) showed that it has a three-part concentric organization. For an "on" fiber, there was a central circular region of its receptive field for which the presentation of a light produced a sharp increase in the number of action potentials (over the random spike activity that is always present) and then a decline as the stimulus persisted. The neuron was responding to the light being "turned on." In a concentric outer area of the receptive field, an "off" area was discovered. Presenting a light here only depressed the activity of the ganglion cell below its normal, unstimulated rate. However, turning the light stimulus off produced a surge of spike potentials similar to those obtained in the central "on" region. In between the "on" center and "off" surround was an area of the receptive field for which both the acts of turning the stimulus on and off produced surges of spike activity ("on-off" response).

A complementary pattern to that just described for "on" center, "off" surround ganglion cells was found for those cells having an "off" center, "on" surround receptive field organization. The size of the central region of a cat's receptive field is on the order of 0.5 to 2 ° of visual angle. The surround may be 10 times as large.

Another property of these receptive fields is the interaction between center and surround effects. When an "on" region is stimulated by the presentation of

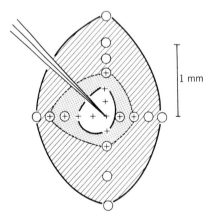

1 mm

Figure 4-4 The receptive field organization for a cat's ganglion cell. The central region, +, responded when the stimulus was turned on the large outer area, o, responded when the stimulus was turned off. Both responses were obtained in the intermediate region. *(From Kuffler, 1953.)*

the light, illuminating the "off" region at the same time cancels the "on" response produced by the first stimulus. Similarly, if a large stimulus which covers most of the receptive field is turned on or off, it will not produce a response in the ganglion cell because of the same inhibitory relationship between center and surround.

These interactive effects that can occur both within and across receptive fields, as well as the apparent coding of the temporal and intensive features of the stimulus, indicate *the complexity of information concerning the stimulus being screened and transmitted within the retina.* It should be emphasized, however, that the retina stage is only the initial stage in the processing of the informative aspects of the stimulus. Given the relatively smaller number of nerve fibers in the postretinal visual pathways than in the retina itself, it is not surprising that the processing of informative aspects of the stimulus is even more refined above the sensory receptor than in the retina.

Postretinal Processes

A schematic representation of the postretinal visual pathways is presented in Figure 4-5. The initial fibers are those of the *optic nerve* emanating from the retinal ganglion cells and departing from the retina at the optic disk. At the optic

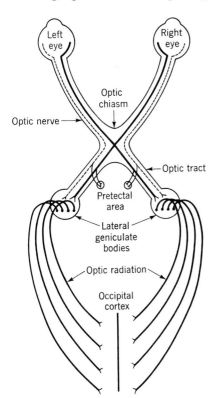

Figure 4-5 A schematic representation of the postretinal visual pathways. Details are in the text. *(From Langley, 1965.)*

chiasm, a sorting out of fibers from the nasal (inner) and temporal (outer) portions of the two retinas takes place. The temporal fibers (dotted lines) remain uncrossed, whereas the nasal fibers (solid line) cross over at this point. The result is that fibers from the left portion of the two retinas proceed to the left *lateral geniculate body* of the thalamus (at the base of the cortex), whereas fibers from the right side of the retinas arrive at the right body. Since the visual image is inverted and reversed on the retinas, the right and left retinal fields refer to the left and right side portions of the visual field, respectively.

From the optic chiasm to the lateral geniculate bodies of the thalamus, the nerve fibers are said to form the *optic tract*. It is only at this point, in the geniculate bodies, that the fibers, originally emanating from the retinal ganglion cells finally terminate. From this region, a second set of neurons form the *optic radiations* to area 17 of the occipital cortex.

Optic Nerve Fibers   Research concerning the types of visual information carried by the optic nerve fibers has revealed the highly interesting fact that in lower vertebrates, such as the frog, individual nerve fibers seem to be conducting very specific information about the spatial and luminosity characteristics of the stimulus. This is not surprising considering the comparative simplicity of the animal's nervous system. Furthermore, some of these cells seem to convey information that is necessary for the frog's survival in its ecology and suggest the importance of this consideration in evaluating any visual system in a comparative (cross species) manner.

Lettvin, Maturana, McCulloch, and Pitts (1959) discovered five types of optic nerve fibers while recording, with microelectrodes, at the point at which these fibers terminate in the animal's tectum (a noncortical area). Some fibers were processing information about the level of illumination. Others responded to complex characteristics of the stimulus, such as the degree of contrast between adjacent sections of the visual field (edge detectors). Most fascinating were the *complex edge detectors* or "bug perceivers." These cells responded maximally to small, dark, sharp edges moving into their receptive fields. They also responded to stationary objects as long as a background light was on. It is interesting to speculate that this type of cell is responsible for the frog's uncanny accuracy in catching bugs with its tongue.

It is important to emphasize again that a distinction should be made between the types of information conveyed in the frog's optic nerve fiber and in rabbits, pigeons, and ground squirrels (Michael, 1969). The information processed within the frog's optic nerve fiber is apparently more sophisticated than that in primates and certain other mammals. Responses to orientation and structure of the stimuli seem to be a property of cells in the visual cortex for these latter animals.

Lateral Geniculate Nucleus   In the human being, most optic nerve fibers proceed to an area of the thalamus called the *lateral geniculate nucleus* (LGN), a section of the lateral geniculate body. The thalamus is the important relay center for transporting sensory information to cortical areas. It is anatomically located between the midbrain of the brain stem and the cerebral hemispheres, and is part of the forebrain. Most retinal ganglion cells project to the LGN in primates. Some fibers avoid the optic tract and proceed to certain areas of the midbrain such as the superior colliculi. The function of these nerve cells seems related to registering the position of the stimulus as well as control of head and eye movements.

The type of visual information coded by the LGN cells has been extensively investigated in primates by DeValois (1965, 1971) and Wiesel and Hubel (1966). DeValois presented large patches (15 ° of visual angle) of light to the eyes of a variety of monkeys, usually the rhesus who appear, through both physiological and behavioral analysis, to have a very similar visual system to man. DeValois found that a minority of LGN cells, approximately 15 to 20 percent, were achromatic and responded to light of any wavelength presented to their receptive fields, with an increase in the number of spike potentials over some base line spontaneous rate. Some of these cells were termed *excitators* by DeValois and are similar to the cells found most frequently in the LGN of the cat. The firing rates of these cells were proportional to stimulus intensity, and were greatest for wavelengths in the middle portion of the visible spectrum. Cells that operate in an inverse manner were also found. These so-called *inhibitors* showed a decrease in firing rate, in response to the light stimulus. Their density, response to wavelength, and intensity parallel those of the excitators. Typical response patterns for these two types of cells are presented in Figure 4-6a and 4-6b.

The finding of De Valois that has caused the most interest has been that of the cell found most frequently, in 60 to 70 percent of the cases—the *spectrally opponent cells*. These cells give *both* excitatory responses to some wavelengths and inhibitory responses to others. The magnitude of either response depends upon the intensity of the appropriate stimulus. The operation of these cells is clearly that of an antagonistic or opponent process.

There are four types of these spectrally opponent cells: $+G-R$ (green-excitatory, red-inhibitory), $+R-G$ (red-excitatory, green-inhibitory), $+Y-B$ (yellow-excitatory, blue-inhibitory), and $+B-Y$ (blue-excitatory, yellow-inhibitory). Figure 4-7 shows a typical response pattern for each of these four cell types. Looking at the function for the $+R-G$ cell, one can see that for the shorter wavelengths, maximally so for the green region, there is an inhibition of the spike potential firing rate below the spontaneous level (dotted line). On the other hand, for the long wavelengths in the red region, presentation of the stimulus produces an increase in spike potentials over the spontaneous rate. Both the excitatory and inhibitory branches of the opponent process can be seen to be influenced by the intensity of the stimulus. These data are usually summarized as indicating either a long-wavelength excitatory (R or Y) and short-wavelength inhibitory (G or B, respectively) response pattern or the opposite.

One question that arises directly from DeValois' work concerns the number

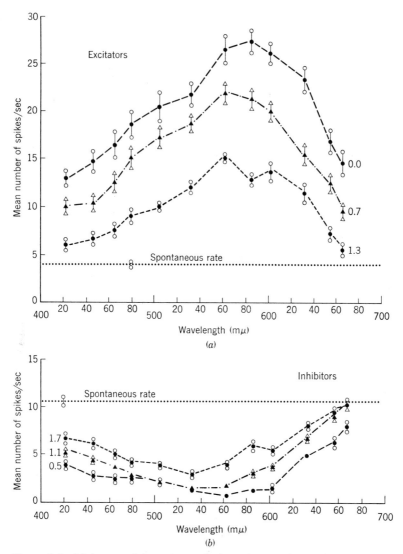

Figure 4-6 *(a)* Average firing rates to flashes of monochromatic light of a large sample of nonopponent *excitatory* cells. Top line: highest-intensity stimulus. *(b)* Average firing rates to monochromatic flashes of a sample of nonopponent *inhibitory* cells. Bottom line: highest-intensity stimulus. *(From DeValois, Abramov, & Jacobs, 1966.)*

of cone types in the retina. If there are, in fact, three different cones, why are there four hues involving the opponent cells: red, green, yellow, and blue? It is possible to eliminate one component of the opponent cell response, e.g., the excitatory response to red for a +R−G cell, and then measure the inhibitory response of the cell for the visible spectrum. This is done, in the present

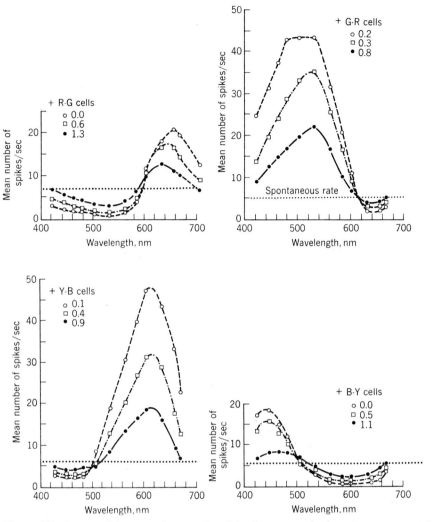

Figure 4-7 Average firing rates for samples of the four types of spectrally opponent cells for monochromatic stimuli of three intensity levels. Details are in the text. *(From DeValois et al., 1966.)*

example, by presenting a strong red light to the receptive field of the LGN cell and superimposing on this light another patch of light of various wavelengths. When this is done for all four types of LGN cells, at times inhibiting the excitatory response of the cell and at others, the inhibitory response, spectral sensitivity curves are obtained which show the degree of excitation or inhibition produced by the various superimposed wavelengths. These curves are remarkably similar to the absorption spectra of individual cones presented earlier (Wald

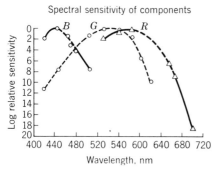

Figure 4-8 Spectral sensitivity curves of opponent cells after isolation of one component by the use of chromatic adaptation. *(From DeValois, 1965. Reprinted by permission of Academic Press, Inc. Copyright, 1965, Academic Press, Inc.)*

& Brown, 1965). It can be seen in Figure 4-8 that there are only three peaks of sensitivity for the spectrally opponent cells. This finding supports a model in which there are three types of cones, blue, green, and red, with both excitatory and inhibitory connections to the LGN cells.

Wiesel and Hubel (1966) used discrete, small, monochromatic lights to study the spatial organization of the receptive fields of the LGN cells. DeValois had used large, 15° patches of light. The most numerous of the small LGN cells had a concentric, center-surround organization. The spectral sensitivities of the center and surround were different, however. Examples of these cells were (1) red "on" center, green "off" surround and (2) green "off" center and red "on" surround. For the large cells, most had a center-surround organization but equivalent spectral sensitivities for both. Interestingly enough, about one-half of the LGN cells seem to be connected to rods as well as to cones. They show the spectral sensitivities of rhodopsin and have their center-surround organization after the eyes have been in darkness for a period of time.

At this point, a summary statement can be made concerning the physiological evidence for either a trichromatic theory of color vision similar to that of Helmholtz or one dependent on opponent neural processing of wavelength information. Most of the relevant sensory physiology has been reviewed up to this point in the chapter. There are very few cells in the visual cortex that respond differentially to stimuli on the basis of their wavelength (Hubel & Wiesel, 1968).

The physiological data appear to support both theoretical positions—but at different levels in the visual system. There is overwhelming evidence for the existence of three cones which respond primarily to wavelengths from either the blue, the green, or the red region of the spectrum. This evidence includes the work on the absorption spectra of human or monkey cones by Rushton (1957), Wald and Brown (1965), and Marks et al. (1964) as well as that on the electrical responses of individual carp cones to particular spectrum wavelengths by Tomita (1965).

On the other hand, there is equally overwhelming evidence for an opponent-process coding of hue information at the postreceptor levels of the visual system. In the retina, there are the s-potentials (MacNichol & Svaetichen, 1958) in which both yellow and blue, and red and green are paired opponent processes. The code has to do with the sign of the s-potential, being positive for a short wavelength and negative for the associated long wavelength or vice versa. For postretinal portions of the visual system, the work of DeValois (1965, 1967) and Wiesel and Hubel (1966), just reviewed, dramatically supports the opponent-process interpretations of the coding of hue information.

In physiology one cannot live with the dualism of, say, the wave and particle theories of light in physics. In physiology, both the trichromatic and opponent-process approaches to color vision must be correct. What is not known is the site and manner in which the trichromatically coded output of the cones is transformed into the opponent-process code of the postreceptor system. One model on how the three types of cones may be associated or linked to three neural opponent processes (red-green, blue-yellow, and white-black) is described in the next chapter (Hurvich & Jameson, 1974).

Cortical Cells of the Visual Pathways   The LGN fibers in man project mainly if not entirely to an area at the central rear of the cerebral cortex, called the *striate* or striped cortex. This is commonly called area 17 of the cortex. Adjacent to the striate area are two other visual areas, 18 and 19, which compose the *nonstriate cortex*.

Hubel and Wiesel (1962, 1965, 1968) have explored the responses of cells in these three visual areas through the use of microelectrode single-cell recording using cats and rhesus monkeys as the experimental animals. They have discovered essentially five types of cells. The simplest cells are those that seem to respond in a manner similar to LGN cells, having a circular-concentric receptive field (so far found only in monkeys). The remaining cortical cells have receptive fields that are elongated and rectangular in shape. These fields are particularly unresponsive to diffuse light and have a very well-defined and restrictive spatial structure.

Typical receptive fields can be seen in Figure 4-9. One common organization has a central strip that is narrow to varying degrees and is flanked on both sides by areas of contrasting activity (e.g., an excitatory central region with inhibitory flanks). Other fields have only two adjacent rectangular areas of contrasting function. Stimuli presented to these receptive fields are most effective when they are linear, of high contrast with their background, and when presented directly along the dividing line between the two portions of the field.

The most effective stimulus has a very specific locus and orientation on the retina for any particular receptive field. *Simple* cells have a very narrow region within their receptive field for which the particular stimulus of correct orientation can be maximally effective. *Complex* cells, on the other hand, have a larger region within their receptive field for which properly oriented stimuli can produce the maximum discharge of spike potentials. This suggests that complex

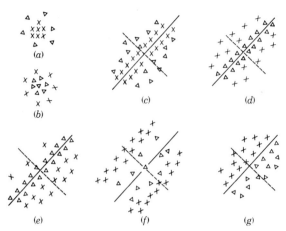

Figure 4-9 Geniculate (a and b) and cortical receptive fields (c to g). Crosses indicate "on" responses and triangles "off" responses. *(From Hubel & Wiesel, 1962.)*

cells may be associated with a number of simple cells of the same orientation.

There are two types of *hypercomplex* cells—lower-order and higher-order. These cells have been found in both cats and monkeys, primarily in areas 18 and 19 for the cat. These cells respond to various features or transformations of the stimuli appropriate for the simple and complex cells. Thus, *lower-order hypercomplex cells* respond only when the linear stimulus is properly oriented. However, the line must terminate within the receptive field or the response of the cell diminishes or stops altogether. For some cells, the stimulus may be bent so that it is properly oriented over only part of the receptive field. For some cells, the stimulus must be terminated at one end within the receptive field, but the other end may extend outside the field or terminate within. Finally, some cells of this type seem to be responding to a specific angle that may be formed by intersecting two linear stimuli. *Higher-order hypercomplex cells* seem to be associated with several lower-order hypercomplex cells in that they respond to similar stimuli but over a wider region of the retina.

Another interesting facet of Hubel and Wiesel's work is the finding (Hubel & Wiesel, 1963) that cells of all types with similar receptive-field orientations are arranged in columns perpendicular to the cortical surface. A similar columnar arrangement can be found for cells that have similar ocular dominance; i.e., their response may be limited to stimulation of one eye, of both eyes with equal sensitivity, or of both eyes but unequal sensitivity.

The data provided by Hubel and Wiesel have obvious implications for human perception. Consider the area of form perception which includes such ordinary yet complicated abilities of human beings as the discrimination and recognition of the different letters of the alphabet or of different faces. Hubel and Wiesel's data can be used to argue for a type of feature abstraction process underlying form perception and recognition in which "features" are the kinds of simple spatial elements of a pattern that seem to be processed by complex and hypercomplex cells. The problem still remains as to how the processing of features is controlled and how these features are resynthesized or put together again for the completion of the form experience. A further discussion of these problems is given in Chapter 10 which covers the information-processing approach to perception.

SUMMARY

This chapter serves as an outline of current knowledge about the sensory physiology of vision. It is clear that any analogy of the eye to a camera is a superficial analogy for a very complex system. Light energy is absorbed via the molecular structure of specialized photochemicals. The activity of these photo-chemicals initiates a series of neural events that encode very selective features of the total stimulus event. The receptive fields of neurons at the various levels of the visual system process information about not only the illumination levels of the stimuli, but also their spatial orientation, contour, and wavelength. It is as if the nervous system for vision is processing certain "perceptual elements" that are recombined as our perceptual experiences. Before such a position can be maintained, however, techniques must be developed for exploring the relation-ship between these neural units and the manner in which supraordinate integration of the processed perceptual elements occur—much in the manner of Hubel and Wiesel's hypercomplex cells. What can be explored at present is the extent to which psychophysical relationships in vision can be understood, given our present knowledge of the sensory receptors for vision and their associated neural networks. What these phychophysical findings are and how they may be related to certain physiological processes in vision is the business of the next chapter.

Visual Psychophysics

This chapter focuses on the experiential correlates of the physiological processes described in the last chapter. The data are psychophysical in that estimates of such sensory quantities (psychological) as the RL and DL are related to levels or the amount of the particular stimulus dimension (physical) in question. It is interesting to note that the early history of visual psychophysics concerns the same individuals (e.g., Helmholtz) who were the pioneers in sensory physiology.

Many of these early investigations of the late nineteenth century and the early part of this century were concerned with what has been termed the *duplicity theory* of vision. It was as if there were two processes in vision, one that could be measured under low illumination and one under high illumination. Today, this duality is generally ascribed to characteristic differences in the functions of the two retinal receptors, the rods and cones.

VISUAL SENSITIVITY FUNCTIONS

The absolute sensitivity of the human visual system varies with the wavelength of the stimulus and the retinal locus of its application. For reasons that will be discussed subsequently, the usual experimental procedures for measuring sensitivity involve controlling the preexposure dark interval, size of the stimulus, and its length of exposure. When absolute thresholds are measured (with one of the procedures of Chapter 3), using a small light source (for example, 4' of arc) presented to the fovea centralis, and a series of wavelengths covering the visible spectrum, the *photopic visibility function* of Figure 5-1 is obtained. The *scotopic visibility function* is obtained when the stimulus is presented in a peripheral retinal area (for example, 10° off-center).

It is apparent from both functions that sensitivity is greatest for midrange wavelengths and decreases at both the blue and the red ends of the spectrum. For the scotopic function, the decrease in sensitivity is much greater for the long wavelengths than for the short ones. The point of maximum sensitivity (lowest threshold) is at a different point in the two functions. It is at approximately 505 nm (green) for the scotopic function and at approximately 555 (yellow-green) for the photopic curve.

Since the fovea centralis contains only cones, whereas the peripheral area contains primarily rods, the photopic curve is considered to reflect the activity of the cones, whereas the scotopic curve reflects the activity of the rods. It is apparent from Figure 5-1 that the rods are considerably more sensitive than the cones for all but the longest wavelengths. It should be noted, finally, that the scotopic stimuli all appear as a dim gray while the photopic stimuli do have apparent hue.

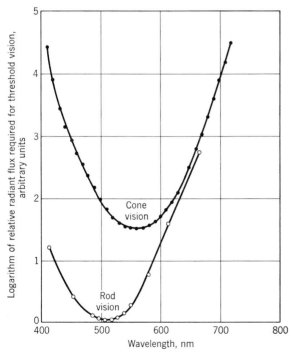

Figure 5-1 The photopic (cone) and scotopic (rod) sensitivity functions. The functions show the relative amounts of energy needed for the RL as a function of wavelength for foveal (cone) and peripheral (rod) stimuli. *(From Chapanis, 1949.)*

Since the scotopic function indicates that the rods are more sensitive in weak illumination than the cones, it is common to speak of *night vision* when referring to the scotopic function and *daylight vision* when referring to the photopic function. When our environment goes from daylight to twilight to darkness, there is a corresponding switch from photopic or daylight vision to scotopic vision corresponding to the decrease in general illumination.

This duplicity of function in the visual system is identified with a common sensory experience first noted by Purkinje in the early part of the nineteenth century, and therefore called the *Purkinje shift*. When one goes from daylight to twilight, i.e., from photopic to scotopic vision, colored objects at the red end of the spectrum lose their brightness more quickly than objects at the blue end of the spectrum. The explanation for this phenomenon is the fact that the point of maximum sensitivity for the scotopic function is 50 nm or so more toward the blue end of the spectrum than that for the photopic curve (cf. Figure 5-1). Thus the shift to the scotopic function in twilight produces a precipitous drop in relative brightness for the longer wavelengths (red).

Spatiotemporal Factors in Vision

Since the rods and cones vary in both their distribution in the retina and in their underlying associations in the first level of the visual nervous system, one would expect that the threshold measurements would reflect spatial factors. There is both temporal and spatial summation of stimulus energy in the visual system. For temporal summation, *Bloch's law* states that there is a simple reciprocal relationship between stimulus intensity (I) and duration (T) for the critical amount of stimulus energy E_c necessary for detecting the stimulus at threshold: $E_c = I \times T$. This equation implies that threshold energy can be maintained by, for example, increasing stimulus intensity proportionally by the factor that its duration is shortened. The product of I and T only has to remain a constant value. Thus, if a subject can detect a stimulus of 10 ml at 0.005-second duration, he should also be able to detect one of 5 ml where duration is now doubled to 0.01 second. $E_c = 0.05$ in both cases. The temporal limitation on this relationship is that the stimulus duration should not exceed 0.01 second for perfect summation.

Two laws, those of *Ricco* and *Piper,* are used to describe the relationship between size or area of the stimulus (A) and intensity (I) in producing the critical threshold energy, E_c. Ricco's law, $E_c = I \times A$, has intensity and area reciprocally related in producing the E_c value. Theoretically, therefore, one could, for example, double the stimulus area and halve its intensity and still produce a stimulus of threshold detectability for the subject. This law, when pertaining to extrafoveal (peripheral) stimuli, has a limitation on the size of the stimulus for which it holds. The size varies in an increasing manner with the distance of the stimulus from the subject's fovea. The range of areas has been reported as between 30' and 2° for a maximum fit of the law (Hallet, Marriott & Rodger, 1962). For foveal stimuli, the area of the stimulus should be less than 10'.

Piper's law holds that intensity and the square root of the area ($\sqrt{A}$) are reciprocally related in producing the appropriate threshold detection energy: E_c

$= I \times \sqrt{A}$. Although this law apparently contradicts that of Ricco, in actual application it does not since the range of stimulus size and location in the retina for which it is said to hold are different than for Ricco's law. It has been proposed that Ricco's law holds best in the fovea (photopic vision), whereas Piper's is appropriate for peripheral (scotopic) viewing. On the other hand, many studies show what might be termed a transition point for stimulus area for extrafoveal stimuli such that for stimuli from about 2° and up, Piper's law is more consistent with the data than Ricco's.

Brightness Discrimination   A further type of visual-sensitivity function concerns the measurement of the DL or JND (ΔI) at various stimulus intensities. If Weber's law was entirely correct, $\Delta I/I$ would produce a constant fraction for the entire range of stimulus intensities. However, the typical findings (Hecht, 1934) are that $\Delta I/I$ varies inversely with I for low stimulus intensities and approaches 1 for the weakest stimuli. In the latter case, ΔI for these stimuli is almost as large as the stimulus intensity itself. However, for a broad range of moderate stimulus values, the value $\Delta I/I$ is relatively constant but very small, on the order of 0.01, or less in some cases.

ADAPTATION

Sensitivity depends not only on certain physiological properties of the receptors, which we have already discussed, but also on the effects of prior stimulation—thus, on temporal factors. Some indication of how extensive this change in sensitivity can be is given by the common experience of trying to find a seat in a dark movie theater after entering from a bright lobby. To avoid an accident, we need someone with a flashlight to guide us. Yet, after the movie, the lobby appears so bright that we have to shut our eyes to avoid the glare. Or take the example of a darkened bedroom. If we awaken in the middle of the night, we have no trouble seeing clearly about the room. In both examples, our eyes have undergone tremendous *dark adaptation*. In fact, the human visual threshold is more sensitive by a factor of nearly 100,000:1 after a period of about 45 minutes in a totally darkened room. The fact that our eyes quickly adapt to the increased illumination upon leaving the movie theater attests to the process of *light adaptation,* obviously a much quicker process than dark adaptation.

Figure 5-2 presents what might be considered the "base-line data" for an investigation of dark adaptation. In this study, the subject's threshold was measured after varying periods of darkness. The stimulus was a white light, large enough to cover both foveal and peripheral regions of the retina. The ordinate represents the *decreases* in intensity of the threshold stimulus (increases in sensitivity) in common log units. Thus -1 represents a tenfold drop in threshold, -2, a hundredfold drop, etc. After approximately 30 minutes, the threshold is about $\frac{1}{100,000}$ of its initial value.

The function clearly has two branches and reflects the duplicity of the visual system. The initial increase in sensitivity is rapid and levels off in less than 10

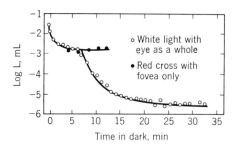

Figure 5-2 The classic dark-adaptation data of Hecht (1934). The ordinate gives the RL values for the test target; the abscissa gives the time in the dark subsequent to a preadaptation exposure to high-intensity white light. *(From Hecht, 1934.)*

minutes. A second process of increasing sensitivity, more gradual and sustained than the first, begins where the first terminates. The increase in sensitivity due to the latter process is 1,000 times or more as great as that produced by the first.

That the first process is associated with cone vision and the second with rod vision is quite easy to demonstrate. If a very small stimulus is used and restricted to the fovea, only the first portion of the dark adaptation function is obtained. Restricting this stimulus to a point about 10° toward the periphery of the visual field produces the rod function of Figure 5-2. The scotopic origin of the second function can also be demonstrated by using a small peripheral stimulus that is of a long red wavelength. Recalling that the rods are relatively insensitive to these long wavelengths, we are not surprised that the second portion of the dark-adaptation function does not materialize under these circumstances.

The increasing sensitivity of the rods as time in darkness increases could be explained by postulating a series of equilibrium levels within the rhodopsin regeneration cycle. With increasing time in darkness, increasing amounts of rhodopsin would be present in relationship to the products of rhodopsin's breakdown. However, the weight of evidence clearly rules out such a model. Certainly incompatible are the data of Campbell and Rushton (1955), who showed that 50 percent of the rhodopsin in the human eye is regenerated within 7 minutes. However, the threshold at this point has been lowered by a factor of 500 (for large stimuli), not 2.

The current theories of scotopic adaptation relate the state of adaptation to the amount of rhodopsin bleached by the adapting stimulus in a complex manner. These theories involve neural messages from the receptors to some neural "regulatory" center that controls sensitivity. Two prominent theories are those of Barlow (1964) and Rushton (1963, 1965). Both theories propose that the bleaching of rhodopsin by the light-adapting stimulus produces signals to the regulatory center indicating that a certain level of bleaching has been reached in the receptors. These signals continue after the stimulus has been turned off, and act to inhibit the visual system's ability to respond to subsequent stimuli. The retina is responding to a "dark light" (Barlow, 1964).

The theories differ with regard to the uniqueness of the signal conveying the bleaching information. Barlow proposes that this signal is indistinguishable from those in response to light energy, whereas Rushton sees the two kinds of signals as distinct. The data to which both theories are addressed concern such findings as those showing that the time course of dark adaptation is positively correlated, at least for moderate intensities and above, with the intensity of the light-adapting or background stimulus presented at the beginning of the experiment (Dowling, 1967). It is as if each level of sensitivity reached in dark adaptation is equivalent to, or synonymous with, the effect of a light-adapting stimulus of a certain intensity. After a sufficient amount of time in the dark, depending on the preadaptation intensity level, the now-decreased neural messages allow for greater sensitivity.

Minimal Stimulus in the Dark-adapted Eye   One of the most acknowledged studies in sensory psychology is that of Hecht, Shlaer, and Pirenne (1942). These investigators attempted to determine the minimal amount of light energy necessary to produce a threshold experience for a fully dark-adapted subject. The specific set of conditions for this measurement consisted of a 510-nm stimulus source of 10' visual angle, placed 20° from the center of the fovea, an area that contains 350 to 500 rod receptors. The stimulus was presented for only a millisecond. Following an analysis of the amount of light energy that would be reflected or absorbed by such structures as the lens and fluids of the eye, and the efficiency of the rhodopsin in absorbing the energy, it was determined that between 5 and 14 quanta of energy were necessary for this particular group of subjects to detect the stimulus on 60 percent of the trials (60 percent was their criterion for threshold).

Since the probability that any rod receives more than 1 quantum is quite small, these data are generally interpreted as indicating that five to fourteen rods must be stimulated for the perception of the light source. Stimulation then must be the absorption of only 1 quantum of light energy in one molecule of rhodopsin for each of five to fourteen rods.

TEMPORAL RESOLUTION: FLICKER

The visual system has a limited capacity for processing discrete stimuli in a manner consonant with the temporal occurrence of the stimuli. As the reader might guess from what he has repeatedly met so far in this chapter, the magnitude and form of this limit are different for the photopic and scotopic systems. This has been demonstrated in literally thousands of studies from the nineteenth century to the present involving the *critical fusion frequency* (or critical flicker frequency), abbreviated as CFF. In one common procedure, the subject looks monocularly down a long tube at a circular patch of light produced by a bulb positioned behind a rear filter. A flicker is produced in the stimulus by interrupting the light (blocking it) periodically. This is accomplished by means of a circular disk, one portion black and one clear. The speed at which the disk revolves determines the number of flickers or interruptions of the stimulus. This variable is usually expressed in cycles per second and can be thought of as the number of times the stimulus is turned on and off per second. The case being considered here is that in which the interrupting disk is half black and half clear.

For any given stimulus intensity and interruption rate, the CFF is found such that the flickering in the light source is no longer perceptible. The light now appears steady, uninterrupted, and somewhat dimmer than the actual uninterrupted light source.

A host of subject and stimulus variables can be considered in a CFF experiment (as can a series of methodologies for measuring the CFF point itself). An excellent review of this area can be found in Brown (1965). Important variables include intensity, wavelength, and size of the stimulus, area of the retina stimulated, state of adaptation, and nonvisual organismic variables such as the arousal or activation level of the subject. The latter set of variables refers to the fact that the processing of sensory stimuli can apparently be enhanced or depressed by the activity of certain midbrain structures such as the reticular formation, that mediate our arousal level.

For the effect of stimulus wavelength and intensity on the CFF, reference can be made to the classic study of Hecht and Shlaer (1936). Their data, presented in Figure 5-3, show the relationship between CFF and intensity for seven stimulus wavelengths. There are several things to consider about these functions. The stimulus used was large enough to cover both the foveal and peripheral retinal areas. It is apparent from Figure 5-3 that there are again two distinct parts to the CFF figure. If stimuli of varying size and location are used on the retina, it can be shown that the multibranched lower portion of the function, where intensity and CFF are similarly low, is due to the activity of the rods. The remainder of the function can be shown as a photopic or cone function.

From Figure 5-3, it can be seen that the CFF function is asymptotic at about 60 Hz, the apparent limit for the influence of intensity on CFF. This point can be considered as a second inflection point or point of change in the CFF function

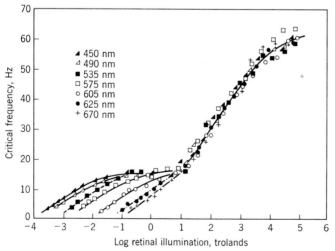

Figure 5-3   Relation between critical fusion frequency (in hertz) and the intensity of the light for seven stimulus wavelengths. *(From Hecht & Schlaer, 1936.)*

(the point at which the function changes from a rod to cone type when *I* reaches sufficient intensity being the first) and is interpreted as indicating the point at which the physiological system underlying CFF can no longer follow the temporal characteristics of the stimulus. Jung and Kornhuber (1961) present evidence for this physiological interpretation from their work on the cortical visual cells of cats.

It is clear from Figure 5-3 that wavelength effects on CFF are negligible for the cone portion of the function. At low stimulus intensities, the greater sensitivity of the rods for the short wavelengths is reflected in the quickly asymptoting functions for these wavelengths compared with the steep, cone-like functions for the red stimuli, where the rods are quite insensitive. The function for 670 nm is virtually coterminous with the cone function.

SPATIAL INHIBITION: MACH BANDS

It was pointed out earlier that both within and between receptive fields, inhibition commonly occurs when multiple stimuli are presented. The phenomenon of *lateral inhibition* between optic nerve fibers has been extensively investigated in *Limulus,* the common horseshoe crab.

Limulus has a compound eye with several large receptor units, called ommatidia, which can be stimulated individually. The neural plexus associated with the ommatidia contain the axons of eccentric cells derived from the receptors. These axons come together, along with another group of cells, to form the optic nerve of *Limulus*. Recordings of action potentials are made from the eccentric cells in the optic nerve. The kind of inhibition that occurs between these optic nerve fibers is called *recurrent* (Ratliff, Hartline, & Miller, 1963). The amount of inhibition produced by one receptor unit (unit A) influencing another (unit B) is the result of the activity level of unit A, which in turn is the sum of negative inputs (the amount of inhibition coming from unit B) and positive ones (from the excitatory stimulus).

The *Mach bands* are a special case of brightness or border contrast for which the data on the *Limulus* eye have led to some interesting physiological explanations (Ratliff & Hartline, 1959; Ratliff, 1965). A brightness contrast occurs when two regions of homogeneous but different intensity are juxtaposed. At their common border, an enhancement of apparent brightness occurs. This enhancement occurs precisely where an *abrupt* change or discontinuity in stimulus intensity lies. In Figure 5-4, a disk is presented (a) which produces the apparent brightness pattern (b) when spun on a color wheel. In *b*, there are two Mach bands. The first is the bright band which, in terms of the test stimulus, is located at the point where the star tips emerge. The second band is an area darker than its background, and can be found at the ends of the star tips in the test stimulus.

The actual distribution of luminance for the rotated test figure is indicated at the bottom of Figure 5-4. There is a gradual increase in luminance from the end of the star points to the white inner area of the figure. The distribution of apparent

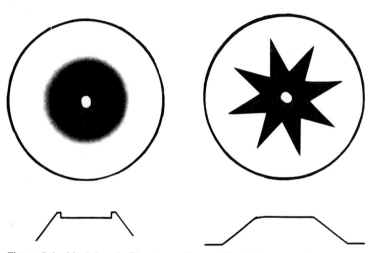

Figure 5-4 Mach bands. The star pattern on the right was used to generate a gradient pattern of luminance that resulted in the appearance of the light and dark mach bands appearing in the rotated figure on the left. The graph at the bottom of the star pattern shows the actual physical gradient of luminance produced by both the stationary *and* the rotated patterns. The graph at the bottom of the rotated pattern shows the apparent brightness distribution over this figure. The notches indicate areas of increased and decreased apparent brightness corresponding to the perceived bands. *(Courtesy of Richard Goldman.)*

brightness, as evidenced by the appearance of the Mach bands, does not follow the distribution of stimulus energy. There is a decrease in brightness at the point where the luminance begins its increase and an increase precisely at that point where the luminance gradient levels out.

By analogy to the spatial interaction found in the visual system of *Limulus*, Ratliff and his co-workers view the dark band as resulting from the abrupt transition from a region of minimal inhibition to one of active inhibition. The bright band, on the other hand, occurs when there is an abrupt change from a region of maximum inhibition to one of decreased inhibition. Although explaining human psychophysical data by way of analogy to data on *Limulus* can only be tenuous, there is no doubt that sensory inhibition is also crucial in the human nervous system. Békésy (1967) describes the importance of inhibition for many sense systems. His application of inhibitory processes to pitch perception is discussed in Chapter 6.

COLOR VISION

The one sensory response to the visual stimulus that is perhaps most fascinating is the experience of the hue or chromaticity—"color"—of the stimulus. The starting point in an analysis of color vision is the visible spectrum, that range of wavelengths from approximately 400 to 700 nm to which our visual receptors respond. The range of "spectral" colors produced by the visible spectrum has been shown in Figure 4-1. The most familiar light sources such as the sun and incandescent lamps provide a mixture of wavelengths from throughout the visible spectrum—white light.

Dimensions of Color

The color of an object is in actuality a multidimensional attribute. We experience color as having not only a characteristic *hue* but also a degree of *saturation* or color purity. A rose may be a deep red or have only a touch of pink. We apparently discriminate the degree of the color experience. A third attribute of color as a stimulus dimension is its *brightness*. The stimulus may be a deep red but have so little energy that it appears black. On the other hand, the stimulus may have so much energy, and thus appear so bright, that it is virtually white with only a tint of color, whether or not that color is a saturated one.

The usual way of depicting the three subjective attributes of color in one figure is to represent them as the three dimensions of a solid figure. The color solid shown in Figure 5-5 is a double cone. The center slice of this solid represents the *color circle* whose circumference is composed of the spectral hues with the addition of a range of nonspectral purples that lies between the short wavelength blues and the long wavelength reds from which they are formed. The

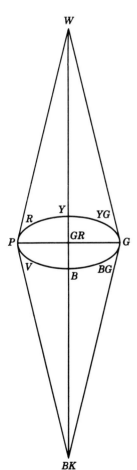

Figure 5-5   The color solid with a central slice revealing the color circle.

colors on the circumference have the greatest saturation. Along any radius of this circle, saturation decreases, with the center of the circle being a neutral gray. The brightness dimension is represented along the longitudinal axis of the solid. The end points of this axis, being black and white, represent a neutral gray of low and high intensity, respectively.

Color Mixing

The color circle can serve as a guide in predicting the hue and saturation that will result from the mixing of two or three of the saturated colors from its periphery. It should be pointed out that *additive* color mixing is being described in this section as in mixing lights of different hues. There is also *subtractive* color mixing that occurs when pigments are mixed. In the latter case, the resultant hue would depend upon what wavelengths are absorbed by one or the other of the pigments and which are reflected by both.

Any diagonal of the circle runs through the neutral gray and terminates at two saturated colors. These hues are complementary. When mixed in the appropriate proportions, a neutral gray will be produced. If the component hues are intense enough, a white will be produced. Interestingly, complementary colors do not produce any other unique hues. The resulting hue will be determined by whichever of the two contribute more to the mixture. Its saturation will depend upon the relative amounts of the two components. Consider yellow and blue. No mixture of yellow and blue will produce a yellowish-blue or bluish-yellow. Either a gray or one of the components will be produced. If considerably more blue is added than yellow, a blue of somewhat less saturation than that on the circumference of the circle is produced. If only a slight edge of blue over yellow is included in the mixture, the result will be a very unsaturated blue located near the center gray of the blue radius line. Any color can be desaturated by mixing it with its complement.

Any color along the circumference of the circle can be matched by mixing, in equal proportions, two wavelengths, selected so that one is as far below the target color as the other is above it. Thus orange can be produced by mixing equal amounts of the red and yellow of the color circle. Spectral green can be obtained by mixing blue-green and yellow-green, etc. All these color mixtures have less saturation than the colors on the circumference of the circle. If the two noncomplementary colors are mixed in less than equal proportions, the resultant color will be biased toward the predominant wavelength. Using more red than yellow will produce a more reddish-orange than that centered between red and yellow on the color circle.

Color Systems

There are two approaches to designating or specifying colors. One is the color atlas approach in which a select group of distinguishable color samples are presented. Some schema for organizing them is used that reflects a number of subjective attributes of color. Such attributes may include color brilliance, saturation, lightness or darkness, and hue—as well as others that are not as directly comprehensible. It is this focus on the attributes of color *sensations* that makes this approach phenomenological in orientation. The Munsell color system is the most widely applied of these systems.

The second approach is directly concerned with specifying color in terms of the physical composition of a color mixture that subjectively matches it. Colors are not organized by a system of subjective attributes but with reference to the composition of their matching color mixture. This approach reflects the fact that any hue can be matched by the proper additive mixture of three "primary" wavelengths. Therefore, a specific color is designated by a series of numbers indicating the relative amounts of each of the primary hues necessary for a successful match. A hue of any saturation can be represented in this manner. The practical value of such a system is immense. One need only consider the need for rigorous color specification in photography, television, and chemical-test indicators in medicine and industry. One such system, the CIE method, is described below.

CIE System   The Commission Internationale de l'Eclairage (CIE) system of color measurement, unlike the Munsell, allows one to specify a color in an exact, reproducible manner. In order to do this, the spectrum or wavelength composition of the stimulus must be measured and the trichromatic color matching characteristics of the "standard observer" for these wavelengths known. The latter requirement refers to *trichromatic colorimetry* whose validity depends on two observations (Wright, 1964): (1) That a color can be matched by a mixture of three wavelengths (with some restrictions as to complements, etc.), and (2) that an additive mixture of two colors will be matched by the sum of the trichromatic mixtures for matching each individually.

A trichromatic color match can be given by the following equation (Wright, 1964):

$$C(C) = R(R) + G(G) + B(B) \tag{5-1}$$

In this equation, (C) is the color that the subject is to match by mixing together certain amounts of three primary colors, (R), (G), and (B). The equation reads, "C amount of color (C) is matched by mixing R amount of (R), G amount of (G), and B amount of (B)." Although this relationship is written as an equation, the equals sign should be interpreted as "is matched by." R, G, and B are called *tristimulus values* and are not expressed in either radiance or luminance units. A unit of each of the tristimulus values is defined as the amount of the stimulus necessary to include in a mixture of the three wavelengths to match some standard white. It is argued that white is the one mixture where the three wavelengths make equal contributions.

Figure 5-6 is the standard CIE chromaticity chart. This chart allows one to represent graphically the amount of each of the color primaries that must be mixed to produce a match with some standard. The chart is actually based on the

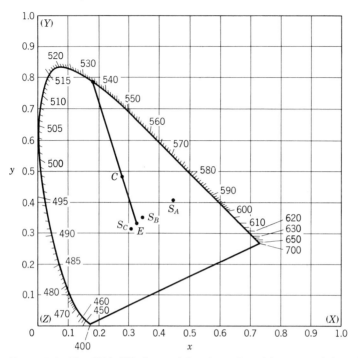

Figure 5-6 The 1931 CIE chromaticity chart plotted in terms of the reference stimuli X, Y, and Z with units based on an equal-energy white, E. The locations of the illuminants S_a, S_b, and S_c are shown. The first illuminant is an incandescent source; the other two are phases of sunlight. *(From Wright, 1964.)*

CIE reference stimuli, X, Y, Z, rather than the R, G, B primaries discussed. Although they do not represent real stimuli, these new standards can be defined via the R, G, B matching system. The reason for the selection of these standards was primarily technical. One definite purpose was to make all coordinate values positive, eliminating the problem of the negative (R) values needed for matching blue-green stimuli.

In Figure 5-6 the amounts of color primaries, X and Y, that are necessary to match a spectral color are given as the coordinates of the figure. The amount of Z does not have to be shown on this figure because the CIE system has been devised so that the amount of X, Y, and Z (mixed) always adds up to 1. Therefore, $Z = 1 - (X + Y)$.

To demonstrate the use of the chart, consider a spectral "blue" of 495 nm. This hue is equivalent to a proportional mixture of approximately 0.42 or 42 percent from the Y primary (obtained from the diagonal from 495 on the chart to the y-axis), 0.03 from the X primary, and 0.55 of the Z primary, derived from the equation $1 - (0.03 + 0.42)$.

Deficiencies in Color Vision

The topic of deficient color vision is inextricably caught up in the development of the theories of color vision. Historically, all these theories have been evaluated primarily on how well they accounted for the clinical findings in color vision. It is therefore necessary to summarize the major types of color blindness before critically evaluating these theories.

Trichromatic Color Blindness   Individuals who have deficient color vision are classified as *dichromats* or *trichromats,* depending upon the number of hues necessary for making color matches, using the usual colorimetry methods. Like individuals with normal color vision, trichromats can match any hue by using a mixture of three others. This mixture, however, would be different from that obtained from normal persons. Their color deficiency is considered a "weakness," an anomaly. It primarily amounts to a need for greater stimulus intensity than would be required by normal persons in matching stimuli from certain portions of the spectrum.

The *anomalous trichromats* are divided into the classifications *protanomalous* and *deuteranomalous.* The former refers to persons with a weakness in the red region of the spectrum, the latter, to those with a weakness in the shorter wavelengths, in the green region. The decreased sensitivity of the anomalous trichromats is usually accompanied by an increase in the size of the JND or DL for color discrimination in their weakness region. This is not always true, however. Some of these individuals show quite normal color discriminations. In fact, the degree of color weakness can vary from almost indiscernible to quite large. These individuals may reflect only the extremes of the distribution of color sensitivity in the general population.

The incidence of trichomacy is quite high, approximately 6 percent for males and ½ percent for females (Wyszecki & Stiles, 1967).

Dichromatic Color Blindness   Dichromats are those individuals who need only two hues, one from a long and one from a short wavelength, to match any other hue. These individuals apparently perceive only two hues and would therefore seem to lack one of the three cone systems. This type of deficiency is clearly more than a color weakness. A dichromat may be a *protanope, deuteranope, tritanope,* or a *tetratanope.* The first two types of persons have forms of red-green blindness and the latter two have yellow-blue blindness. Red-green blindness is quite common in males (2 percent), while rare in females, whereas yellow-blue blindness is very rare for both sexes (Wyszecki & Stiles). Red-green blindness is a sex-linked genetic trait that is handed down from maternal grandfathers to their grandsons. The female intervening here would most likely not present the symptoms of color blindness and only act to transmit the trait.

Protanopes and deuteranopes both divide the spectrum into a blue and a yellow region—that is all. There are several differences between protanopes and deuteranopes. The yellow region begins at about 530 nm for the deuteranopes and at about 520 nm for the protanopes so that the former group does have a more extensive blue region. The protanopes also show a decrease in sensitivity for long wavelengths (red) compared with normal individuals. Comparable brightness matches necessitate much greater stimulus energy for the former group. On the other hand, deuteranopes show a decreased sensitivity in the blue-green region and normal sensitivity in the red (Graham & Hsia, 1958). Both protanopes and deuteranopes perceive a gray or bluish-gray for a narrow band of wavelengths within the transitional region between the two perceived hues. The center of this gray band is shifted slightly toward the longer wavelengths for the deuteranopes. Finally, the wavelength of lowest absolute threshold (highest luminous efficiency) is at 540 nm for the protanopes and at 560 for the deuteranopes.

It is not uncommon to explain red-green blindness on the basis of a loss of red cones (protanopes) or green cones (deuteranopes). The loss of these cones would not explain the regions of yellow sensation for these individuals. There is an interesting hypothesis on the origin of the yellow sensation for the red-green blind, which is discussed in the next section. Geldard (1972) points out that the visual acuity of the dichromats is normal, a finding inconsistent with the notion of missing visual receptors. Regardless of the origin of red-green blindness, there is very direct evidence on the color sensations of those who experience it. What is necessary is to have a subject with one normal eye and one eye red-green blind. Then color sensations in the deficient eye can be matched by hues presented to the normal eye. This would certainly lead to more reliable data than those obtained by asking a color-blind subject what color he or she sees. There is no guarantee that the color names used by dichromats refer to the same color sensations experienced by normal viewers. Dichromats have simply learned to apply a name, e.g., green, to the hue aspect of a familiar object, e.g., grass.

The characteristics of yellow-blue blindness, which is a rare condition, resemble those of the red-green type. The tritanope has a neutral band in the yellow-green area of the spectrum. Hues of greater wavelength appear red, whereas shorter ones appear green, even into the violet range. The tetratanopes have two neutral points, one where the normal eye sees a pure yellow (580 nm) and another where the eye sees a pure blue (470 nm). The visible spectrum is split into three segments by the neutral bands. The central segment has a characteristic hue of green, whereas the spectral bands on either side appear red for all wavelengths (Geldard; Hurvich & Jameson, 1957).

Monochromatic Color Blindness   The final type of color blindness is that of the *monochromat*. In the pure form, these are individuals who do not have any color vision. The entire spectrum is seen as a series of grays differing in brightness. Apparently the monochromats do not have any cone receptors, only rods. These individuals are rarely encountered, and many do have a weak color sensation, especially in the blue region. The latter finding would indicate a remnant of cones.

Theories of Color Vision

Young's Theory   Thomas Young, at the beginning of the nineteenth century, offered some changes to a model of color vision originally proposed by Newton in the seventeenth century. This revised theory has remained to the present day as one of the most influential conceptualizations of color vision. Young's contributions were twofold. He did not feel that Newton's idea of the retina consisting of an infinite number of particles vibrating in unison with the impinging light waves was tenable. Instead he felt there were only three types of particles (sense receptors?) responding (by vibrating) to three fundamental wavelengths or colors. These were originally red, yellow, and blue but subsequently became red, green, and violet. The importance of this schema lies in the notion of three independent sensory processes for three fundamental color sensations.

Young's other contribution was in extending his analysis beyond the physics of the problem and interpreting problems of color mixing and our experiencing of nonfundamental spectral hues in terms of sensory processes; the solution to the problem of color vision would be found in the characteristics of the observer and not in the physical makeup of the stimulus. "Thus the sensation of yellow is produced by a mixture of red and green sensations while blue is also a compound sensation, being produced by the mixture of green and violet sensations. White light (light we experience as white) is produced by mixing red, green, and violet light in proportions of two parts red, four green, and one violet, with respect to the quantity or intensity of the sensations produced" (Young, 1845).

Young-Helmholtz Theory Helmholtz, acknowledging Young's primacy, elaborated on his theory and produced what is commonly called the Young-Helmholtz theory of color vision. Helmholtz argued that there were three fundamental color sensations. His physiology, as expected, was different from Young's. The eye contains three types of nerve fibers. Stimulation of each produces a unique color sensation; red for the first, green for the second, and violet for the third. Helmholtz' set of primary color sensations is clearly the same as Young's. However, the nerve fibers that give these discrete sensations are stimulated by *all* wavelengths. Only their maximum response is to stimuli from the red, green, or blue-violet region of the spectrum.

Consider Helmholtz' diagram, given in Figure 5-7. The three types of fibers are represented vertically while the spectral wavelength regions are presented along the horizontal axis. Focusing on the "red"-sensitive fiber, one can see that it is most stimulated by long wavelengths in the red-orange region. Its sensitivity then decreases progressively from the yellow region to that of the shortest, or violet, wavelengths. The sensory experience is "red" though, whenever this

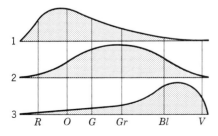

Figure 5-7 Helmholtz's schematic representation of his color theory. Fiber 1 is red-sensitive; 2 is green-sensitive; 3 is violet-sensitive. *(From Helmholtz, 1896.)*

fiber is excited, irrespective of the wavelength of the stimulus. Similar descriptions hold for the other fibers.

For a further clarification of this model, consider the effect on the three receptors of a green wavelength stimulus (G). It produces a large effect in the green fiber, a small effect in the red fiber, and a very weak response in the violet fiber. The sensation of a spectral "green" is then, in reality, a mixture of a large green sensation, a small red sensation, and a weak violet sensation, all three proceeding from the activity of their respective color fibers. The reason for the latter complexity in the model is that spectral hues are in actuality considered mixed colors or sensations. The purest color sensations are only those that involve large responses in one fiber and extremely weak ones in the other two. The only "pure" color sensations, in this sense, are a certain red, green, and violet. "Pure" yellow is produced by an equal moderate stimulation of both the red and green fibers, as can be seen in Figure 5-7.

How acceptable is the Young-Helmholtz theory? Certainly, it explains the facts of trichromatic color mixing well, as would be expected. There are two principal areas of data where difficulties do exist. The first concerns color sensations themselves. Many theorists are antagonistic to the Young-Helmholtz theory because of its physicalistic approach to the explanation of color mixing. The Young-Helmholtz theory has yellow and white as derived colors resulting from mixed sensations. Yet to its antagonists, these colors are as primary in *experience* as blue (or violet), green, and red. Yellow and white are not experienced as color mixtures in the same way as purple, brown, or blue-green. They seem indivisible as sensations. In fact, if blue, green, red, and yellow are for the moment all considered unique color sensations, it is interesting that certain color mixtures are never experienced as such, e.g., yellowish-blue and greenish-red.

Following this same approach, how can one account for such phenomena as complementary afterimages, or simultaneous color contrast, without yellow's being designated a primary or unique color sensation? Complementary afterimages occur when one views, e.g., a blue stimulus for a fairly long duration and then looks at a neutral gray area. This neutral area then takes on a yellowish appearance. Similar findings occur for red and green stimuli. As an example of *simultaneous color contrast,* a gray patch viewed on a blue background will appear yellowish. Helmholtz attempted to explain such phenomena as being due to the "self-light" of the retina after fatiguing certain receptors. Such an explanation ignores the possible brilliance of the complementary afterimages (Ladd-Franklin, 1932).

Color blindness and the Young-Helmholtz theory   The original interpretation of color blindness according to the Young-Helmholtz theory was that specific receptors or fibers were missing. As more information accrued about color deficits, especially for unilateral color blindness, the inadequacy of this interpretation became clear. Not only does the dichromat see yellow throughout most of the green and red range, there are also one or two gray bands visible in the spectrum. If white (or gray) is a derived sensation, in which all three primary sensations play a role, how does the dichromat experience white in the absence of one of the receptors? Why is yellow perceived in the absence of a green receptor by deuteranopes and also in the absence of a red receptor in the protanope?

Hering's Theory and Hurvich and Jameson   Although there are several theories of color vision besides the Young-Helmholtz formulation, the one initially proposed by Hering has had the greatest support. Hering sought to alleviate the major problems of Helmholtz' theory as viewed by those theorists who saw the primary data of color vision in the sensations of the observer rather than in the rules of color mixing. Hering proposed that yellow, white, and black, as well as red, green, and blue, were basic, nonderived color sensations. He proposed a model of *retinal physiology* which never found much favor nor support but schematically has been of great importance in interpreting the activity of the visual nervous system.

Hering (1874) spoke of an "optic substance" composed of a mixture of three chemically different and independent substances each of which could undergo processes of dissimilation (breaking down) and assimilation (building up). These two processes produced a pair of color sensations for each of the three substances. The three primary color pairs were yellow-blue, green-red, and black-white. Hering proposed that white was produced by dissimilation and black by assimilation for their substance but did not take a stand on which process produced a particular color sensation for the other pairs. This is truly an *opponent process* because the production of both chemical processes in any optic substance, e.g., by the application of the appropriate stimuli from the spectrum, would cause both of the paired sensations to be canceled out. White appears when mixing complementary lights because of this antagonistic process.

It should be apparent that Hering's model has decided advantages in explaining certain features of color vision such as the purity of yellow and white sensations, dichromatic color blindness, simultaneous and successive color contrast, the absence of yellowish-blue and reddish-green sensations, and some more subtle effects such as the predominance of red and green hues at low illumination levels and yellow and blue at high levels (Hurvich & Jameson, 1957). Nevertheless, previous information in Chapter 4 on the spectral absorption properties of the cones indicates rather clearly that there is no support for this model as a description of retinal receptor processes.

Hurvich and Jameson (1974) have shown, however, how a Hering opponent-process model can be used to represent the activity of the color-vision system at a neural level in a manner consistent with the existence of three color receptors. Figure 5-8 is a schematic representation of the Hurvich-Jameson (1974) neural opponent-process model. There are three receptors or cones having absorption maxima at 440 nm (α), 530 nm (β), and 570 nm (γ). At the neutral level we have three opponent-process pairs: blue-yellow, green-red, and white-black. For indicating the opponent nature of the neural processes, the blue, green, and black systems are arbitrarily considered negative processes, whereas yellow, red, and white are considered positive. The arousal inputs from the receptors to the op-

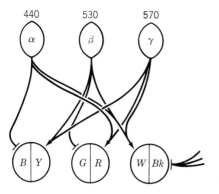

Figure 5-8 The relationship between three-cone absorption processes and the neural opponent process in color vision as proposed by Hurvich and Jameson (1974). *(Copyright, 1974, by the American Psychological Association. Reproduced by permission.)*

ponent system are *signed,* i.e., those indicated by arrowheads in the figure are positive inputs and those ending in a flat line are negative.

With regard to these arousal inputs, it should be noted that the neural response within any of the three systems is determined by the sum of the signed inputs from the three receptors. Again consider the signs as arbitrary. If the stimulus is predominantly composed of short wavelengths (blue) of high energy content, it will be absorbed to a greater extent by the alpha than by the beta and gamma receptors. The result of a strong alpha signal of negative sign and two weak receptor signals of opposite sign from the beta and gamma receptors will result in the blue state of the blue-yellow opponent process. The sensory-experience blue now arises in response to this neural process. It is not linked directly to the receptor process as in the Young-Helmholtz model. One other feature of the Hering-Hurvich-Jameson model to be emphasized is that black is *not* directly produced as a result of the sum of inputs from the receptors. Further, it is not produced by an absence of input, either. In the latter case, a gray sensation would be experienced. Black results as a contrast phenomenon following or preceding the presentation of a stimulus.

In deciding between the Young-Helmholtz model and a Hering-type opponent-process model for color vision, the current explosion of information in sensory physiology, as summarized previously in Chapter 4, supports the former theory at the receptor level but an opponent process at all neural levels of the visual system. At present, the most workable approach seems to be of the sort proposed by Hurvich and Jameson (1974) and investigated by DeValois (1965) where a three-receptor system is associated through neural outputs to an opponent neural system for coding information.

SUMMARY

The fact that the visual system includes two distinguishable classes of visual receptors with different photochemical properties is clearly evident in the photopic (cone) and scotopic (rod) portions of several psychophysical functions. These include the enhanced sensitivity of the rods as shown in the visibility functions, the two portions of the dark-adaptation function for large stimuli, and the relationship of CFF to stimulus intensity and wavelength. That the whole story of these sensory phenomena is not at the receptor level is revealed by the incompleteness of the explanations for dark adaptation and CFF that refer to photochemical events alone. Neural events, specifically the integration of information from several receptors, underly the temporal integration findings summarized by Bloch's law, and those on the spatial integration of brightness indicated by Ricco's and Piper's laws. The Mach bands indicate a further important feature of neural processing, that of mutual or reciprocal inhibition in the various neural networks underlying some of the more complex visual phenomena.

Because of the enormous breadth of research, color vision encompasses a large portion of this chapter. The relevance of the various nineteenth century theories of color vision to present sensory physiology is evidenced by the support at the receptor level for the Young-Helmholtz theory and at the neural level for the theory of Hering.

Chapter 6

Audition

Human beings are often characterized as visually oriented. Our reliance on vision is said to dominate whatever inputs we receive from our other senses. The scope of problems investigated in audition, however, is as broad as that in vision. Furthermore, the history of psychophysics, including its methodology and laws, is quite closely associated with auditory investigations. Helmholtz published an elaborate treatise on the auditory sense at the same time he was investigating problems in optics. Applied work in audition has spawned such extensive fields as audiology and acoustical engineering.

The purpose of this chapter is to explore the same issues and findings that were covered in Chapters 4 and 5 for vision. The first part of this chapter parallels Chapter 4 and describes the auditory stimulus and the anatomy and sensory physiology of hearing. The latter part of this chapter is concerned with auditory psychophysics.

AUDITORY STIMULUS

Physical Parameters

While responding to sound stimuli, the auditory receptors encode the features or dimensions of a pressure wave that is displacing the eardrums. Sound waves are generated by vibrating bodies in an elastic medium. The density of this medium can be changed continuously by the movements of the sound source within it. Sound waves do not have a consistent, constant speed as was true of the visible spectrum. The speed of sound waves depends upon the medium through which they are traveling. In air at 0°C these waves travel at about 340 meters per second (m/sec) or about 760 miles per hour (mi/h), commonly called mach 1 (after Ernst Mach who also discovered the Mach bands discussed in Chapter 5). The speed of sound is greater in denser mediums such as water.

In Figure 6-1 the pressure wave induced in air particles by the movement of a vibrating body, such as a tuning fork, is schematized. This wave moves laterally by the transfer of the energy of this motion of air particles to their neighbors. The resulting motion is similar to that of an ocean wave as it proceeds to shore. The pressure wave in this figure represents the instantaneous pressure changes occurring at one point in space as the wave moves through it over a finite time period.

The pressure changes depicted in Figure 6-1 are described as sinusoidal. These simple harmonic or oscillatory changes of the waveform over time are those of a particular waveform, the *sine wave*. As for any waveform, the sine wave has a characteristic wavelength (λ) which is the distance traveled by the wave as it completes one harmonic *cycle*. In Figure 6-1, various *phase angles* are given along the abscissa. A complete cycle of harmonic or sine motion is 360°. The first 180° of phase is the period of compression in Figure 6-1, whereas the cycle is completed at 360° of phase when the period of rarefaction ends. During rarefaction the pressure goes below atmospheric level, and the particles travel in the opposite direction. Two equivalent sound waves are considered "in phase" when they begin together and thus are always at the same phase position. When they do not originate at the same instant, they are considered "out of phase" by an amount specified by the phase position of the first wave at the same

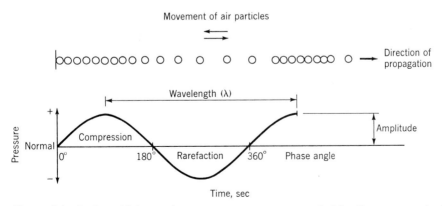

Figure 6-1 A sinusoidal sound pressure wave as represented by the movement of air particles and schematically. (*From* The Experimental Psychology of Sensory Behavior *by John F. Corso. Copyright 1967 by Holt, Rinehart, and Winston, Publishers. Reprinted by permission of Holt, Rinehart, and Winston, Publishers.)*

time the second one begins. These two sound waves are thus 90° out of phase when the second sound begins just as the first reaches its peak of compression. *Phase* is an important parameter in the stimulus which provides auditory information (about space, for example).

Another important parameter of the sound wave is its *frequency,* or the number of cycles occurring in a specified time period. Frequency is measured in cycles per second, and this measurement is abbreviated *Hz* (after the physicist, Hertz).

The amount of "pressure" in the sound pressure wave is, of course, related to the force with which the vibrating body was set into motion. This force translates into amplitude (or extent of peak movement of this body) during its oscillations. The amplitude of the sine wave is indicated in Figure 6-1. The pressure (force per unit area) imparted to the medium is measured in dynes per square centimeter. The weakest sound pressure that can be detected (the "softest" sound) by the "average" listener is 0.0002 dyne/cm² for a 1,000-Hz tone. The distance that the eardrum moves in response to this pressure is incredibly small. In extent, it is about one-tenth the diameter of a hydrogen molecule. As Davis and Silverman (1960) point out, nature has apparently gone the limit in establishing our sensitivity to the sounds our auditory receptors can process. Any greater sensitivity would lead to a constant disturbing noise from molecular interactions.

On the other hand, we also respond to sound pressures that are of the order of 2,000 dynes/cm². This enormous range of sound pressures encoded by human beings would make the use of absolute pressure measurements very cumbersome. Instead, sound intensity is measured in units derived by taking the logarithm of the ratio of two pressures, the one being measured and some standard reference pressure. This unit is the *decibel* (abbreviated db). The number of decibels for any sound pressure is given by the following formula:

$$N \text{ (db)} = 20 \log_{10} \frac{P_1}{P_0} \tag{6-1}$$

where P_1 is the pressure being measured and P_0 is the standard reference pressure, usually taken as 0.0002 dyne/cm², the threshold pressure of the average listener for a 1,000-Hz tone.

The transformation from an absolute pressure scale to a logarithmic one drastically reduces the range of the actual numbers used to measure intensity. With reference to equation 6-1, it can be seen that every time the sound pressure is multiplied by a factor of 10, the number of decibels increases by 20. Recall that a common logarithm for any number is the power to which 10 must be raised to produce that number. If P_1 is the strongest intensity to which one can respond and still have an intact eardrum (about 2,000 dynes/cm²), and P_0 is 0.0002 dyne/cm², the ratio of P_1/P_0 is 10,000,000:1 or 10^7:1. Applying equation 6-1, we have

$$N \text{ (db)} = 20 \log 10^7 = 20 \, (7) = 140 \text{ db}$$

Table 6-1 Sound-Pressure Levels of Some Familiar Sounds Expressed in db - SPL

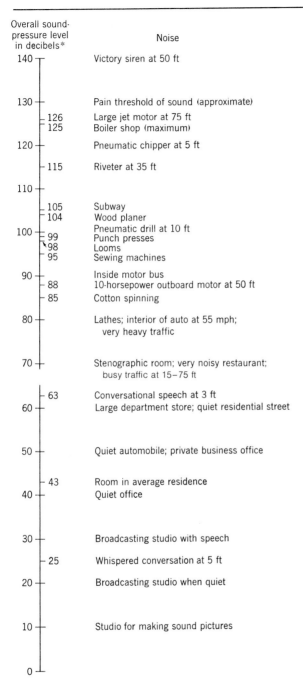

Overall sound-pressure level in decibels*	Noise
140	Victory siren at 50 ft
130	Pain threshold of sound (approximate)
126	Large jet motor at 75 ft
125	Boiler shop (maximum)
120	Pneumatic chipper at 5 ft
115	Riveter at 35 ft
110	
105	Subway
104	Wood planer
	Pneumatic drill at 10 ft
99	Punch presses
98	Looms
95	Sewing machines
90	Inside motor bus
88	10-horsepower outboard motor at 50 ft
85	Cotton spinning
80	Lathes; interior of auto at 55 mph; very heavy traffic
70	Stenographic room; very noisy restaurant; busy traffic at 15–75 ft
63	Conversational speech at 3 ft
60	Large department store; quiet residential street
50	Quiet automobile; private business office
43	Room in average residence
40	Quiet office
30	Broadcasting studio with speech
25	Whispered conversation at 5 ft
20	Broadcasting studio when quiet
10	Studio for making sound pictures
0	

*0 db = 0.0002 dyne/sq cm

Source: From Corso, 1967, as adapted from McCormack, 1957.

It can be seen that converting from an absolute pressure scale to the decibel scale has reduced the range of the scale by a factor of about 1 million ($10^7/140$).

Table 6-1 shows the decibel equivalents for many common noise situations. It is perhaps surprising that most of our daily noise experiences are in the 60- to 90-db range.

One often sees the term SPL or SL after a decibel statement, for example, 20 db SPL. SPL stands for *sound pressure level* and indicates the number of decibels above the reference or threshold pressure of 0.0002 dyne/cm². The later figure may not, in fact, be the actual threshold pressure for a particular subject and, after all, was originally determined only from a 1,000-Hz tone. Thresholds actually vary with the frequency of the stimuli. SL refers to the *sensation level* of the stimuli. When decibels are reported as SL values, this indicates that these are with reference to the subject's measured threshold for that stimulus rather than to 0.0002 dyne/cm².

The sound pressure wave depicted in Figure 6-1 is that of a simple sine wave. As such it produces the sensation of a *pure tone* (cf. Figure 6-2a). Subjectively, the pitch of a pure tone increases with its periodicity or frequency. This topic will be explored at length in a later section of this chapter. At this time it is necessary to point out that almost all the sound stimuli we encounter in our daily routines are not of this simple physical structure. Complex stimuli that

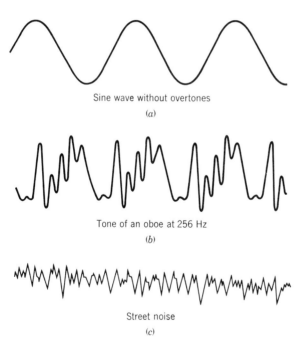

Sine wave without overtones

(a)

Tone of an oboe at 256 Hz

(b)

Street noise

(c)

Figure 6-2 A comparison between the straightforward periodicity of (a) a pure tone, (b) a complex tone with stable phase relationships between its component frequencies, and (c) a nonperiodic noise stimulus. (*From* Speech and Hearing, 2d ed., by H. Fletcher. Copyright 1953, D. Van Nostrand Co. Reprinted by permission of D. Van Nostrand Co.)

appear tonal to us are ordinarily composed of some *fundamental frequency* and a series of *harmonics* or overtones. The complex vibratory patterns are produced by the simultaneous vibration of the sound source as a whole and in parts. Imagine a guitar string vibrating as a whole at some fundamental frequency f. If it also vibrates simultaneously along each one-half of its length, a second frequency component of the complex tone of $2f$ is produced. This is the second harmonic. The harmonics of a complex tonal stimulus always stand in this simple integer relationship to each other: f, $2 \times f$, $3 \times f$, $4 \times f$, etc.

Given that various harmonics will sum to produce the complex tonal wave-form, the exact shape of this waveform will reflect the manner in which the various periods of compression and rarefaction of the harmonics add together given their phase relationships. The complex waveform of an oboe with a fundamental frequency of 256 HZ is given in Figure 6-2b.

The most complex sounds are what we intuitively would call "noise." Subjectively, noise is clearly distinguishable from tonal stimuli, whether complex or simple. The defining characteristic of noise is its lack of periodicity. This is clearly seen in Figure 6-2c. Although the waveform for the oboe is also quite complex (Figure 6-2b), its periodicity or cyclical nature is evident. The lack of periodicity in noise is due to the random nature of the characteristics of the constituent sound waves at any one moment. When all audible frequencies are represented with equal intensity in the noise and when phase relationships are sufficiently random, the noise has a characteristic "sh" sound. This is *white noise* and is commonly used as background noise to mask out stray sounds in many psychological experiments.

ANATOMY OF THE EAR

It is common practice to distinguish between the outer, middle, and inner ear. Reference should be made to Figure 6-3. The *outer ear* consists of the pinna or auricle, the external auditory canal, and the tympanic membrane or eardrum.

The *middle ear* is an air-filled cavity lying between the tympanic membrane and the inner ear, or cochlea. It is quite small in volume, about 2 cc. The major elements of the middle ear are the three tiny bones or ossicles that transmit the pressure wave from the tympanic membrane to the oval window of the inner ear. In sequence, these bones are the malleus, incus, and stapes (hammer, anvil, and stirrup). The three middle-ear bones are held rather tautly in place by two muscles, the tensor tympanic and the stapedius.

The point of contact between the middle ear and the fluid-filled inner ear is at the *oval window* of the latter where the footplate of the stirrup is attached. Another elastic membrane can be seen in Figure 6-3 immediately below the oval window. This is the *round window* and serves to dissipate the energy imparted to the fluids of the inner ear by the movement of the stapes. The inner ear itself is a series of very complicated channels cut into the temporal bone. This is the *labyrinth* which includes the three semicircular canals, the vestibule, and the *cochlea* (cf. Figure 6-3). The cochlea contains the auditory receptive apparatus,

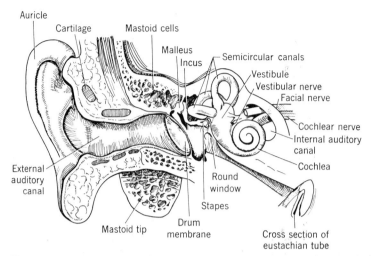

Figure 6-3 The major components of the outer, middle, and inner ear. In this view, the temporal bone has been cut away to reveal the semicircular canals, the vestibule, and the cochlea. A detailed discussion of the anatomy of the ear is given in the text. (*From* Hearing and Deafness, *3d ed., by Hallowell Davis and S. Richard Silverman. Copyright 1947, 1960, 1970 by Holt, Rinehart, and Winston, Publishers. Reprinted by permission of Holt, Rinehart, and Winston, Publishers.*)

whereas the other portions of the labyrinth contain the receptors for responding to linear and rotary acceleration which underline our sense of balance.

The cochlea has three internal channels formed by membranes, ligaments, etc. The three divisions of the cochlea are the *scala vestibuli* which extends into the vestibule itself, the *scala media,* and the *scala tympani.* The end of the cochlea nearest the stapes is the basal end. The apex, at the tip of the innermost coil, is the opposite end. At the apex, the scala vestibuli and scala tympani connect via an opening between the two channels called the *helicotrema.* This produces a direct path for the pressure wave to travel from the oval window to the helicotrema and back for dissipation at the round window.

An expanded cross section of the scala media is given in Figure 6-4. The conglomeration of cells resting upon the *basilar membrane* and bounded on the upper surface by the *tectorial membrane* is the organ of Corti. The key elements of the organ of Corti are the *inner* and *outer hair cells* that lie on internal and external sides of the arch of Corti, respectively. These hair cells are the auditory receptors that are stimulated via the passage of the pressure wave through the fluids of the cochlea. They are the "rods" and the "cones" of the ear although, of course, their mode of operation is quite different. The auditory nerve, a branch of the VIII cranial nerve, innervates the hair cells of the cochlea. The complexity of the neural connections between the auditory nerve and the hair cells is reminiscent of that between the rods and cones and the bipolar cells in vision. Auditory-nerve fibers receive inputs from a number of different hair cells of a particular type, and each hair cell innervates a number of neurons.

Our major concern is sensory *transduction.* How are the hair cells able to

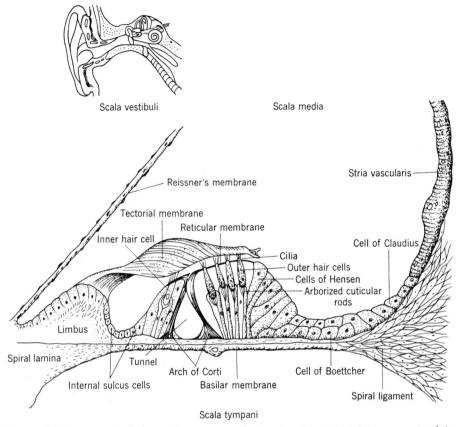

Scala vestibuli   Scala media

Reissner's membrane

Stria vascularis

Tectorial membrane

Reticular membrane

Inner hair cell

Cell of Claudius

Cilia

Outer hair cells

Cells of Hensen

Arborized cuticular rods

Limbus

Spiral lamina

Tunnel

Internal sulcus cells   Arch of Corti   Basilar membrane   Cell of Boettcher

Spiral ligament

Scala tympani

Figure 6-4   An expanded view of the scala media showing the essential components of the organ of Corti. (*From* Hearing: Physiology and Psychophysics *by W. L. Gulick. Copyright 1971 by Oxford University Press. Reproduced by permission of Oxford University Press.*)

transmit information about the auditory stimulus to the auditory nerve? How is the mechanical movement of the hair cells produced by the pressures in the inner ear fluids converted into the neural signal? For vision, there was a "bleaching" process in the photochemicals of the rods and cones in response to the light energy. For audition, there are mechanical stresses applied to the taut hair cells. Clearly, the sensory processing of sound energy must be very different from that for light energy.

The common name for the electrical response originating in the hair cells is the *cochlear microphonic* (Wever & Bray, 1930). Interestingly, this response was first recorded from the auditory nerve and was thought to reflect its neural signal. The very nature of the cochlear microphonic made this hypothesis untenable. This potential reproduces very accurately and also amplifies the vibration patterns of the sound stimulus. One can even detect speech from the microphonic. Since many sound stimuli have components of over 1,000 Hz and since no nerve can fire at a greater rate than this, the source of the microphonic was sought elsewhere. It is clear that this response is produced by the hair cells for a number of reasons (Somjen, 1972), the most obvious one being that destroying the hair cells, e.g., by poison, immediately stops the microphonic.

At this point, what must be clarified is the role of the cochlear microphonic in producing the activity of the auditory nerve. Davis' (1965) theory proposes two possibilities. The first is that the generator potential in this nerve (the electrical event that causes a "spike" to be generated) is directly produced by some direct transfer of current from the hair cell to the dendrites of the nerve. The second is that the generator potential is produced by some release of a chemical "transmitter substance" caused by the microphonic that then migrates across the junction to the auditory nerve where the generator potential is produced.

AUDITORY NERVOUS SYSTEM

Central Auditory Pathways

By comparison with the visual nervous system, the outstanding characteristic of the auditory pathways is their great complexity. Figure 6-5 is a schematic diagram of the ascending auditory pathways (pathways toward the cortex). In this drawing, the hair cells of the organ of Corti are considered the first-order neurons of the auditory system. The auditory nerve (2) leaves the cochlea and proceeds to the medulla of the lower brainstem. The nerve splits and sends fibers to two portions of the cochlear nucleus. There are then many lateral connections within the medulla with other centers of the auditory system such as the superior olivary nucleus. Some of these third-order neurons proceed directly from the cochlear nucleus to the inferior colliculus, the second major brainstem area for audition. Others connect to fourth-order neurons in projecting to this area. The next major auditory center is in the medial geniculate nuclei of the thalamus from which fibers radiate to the widespread auditory centers in the cortex, primarily in the temporal region.

Although stimuli as diverse as clicks and speech have been used to produce electrical responses at various levels of the auditory system, the majority of studies have employed stimuli which varied simply in frequency, intensity, or both. The survey of findings presented here will concentrate on such studies. Physiological processes underlying sound localization will be presented within the section of this chapter dealing with the psychophysics of that area.

Responses of the Auditory Nerve

Recordings can be made of the auditory nerve activity as a whole, or else microelectrodes can be used to obtain a single record from one of the 31,000 individual neurons of the cochlea. Recording from the whole nerve produces what is called a *compound* or *summated action potential*. The actual complexity of the compound potential will depend upon the intensity and complexity of the acoustic stimulus.

Rose, Brugge, Anderson, and Hind (1967) recorded an interesting phenome-

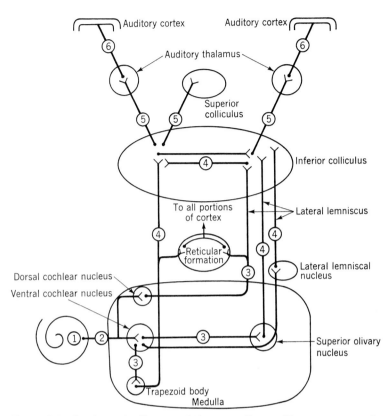

Figure 6-5 A schematic diagram of the ascending auditory nervous system. The numbers indicate the successive order of the neurons in the ascending chain to the cortex (6). The hair cells of the organ of Corti are considered the first level of these pathways (1); the auditory nerve (2) defines the second level of this system. *(From Uttal, 1973.)*

non from individual cells of the auditory nerve. They found that a nerve cell can follow the frequency wave of the stimulus when it is fired. It does this not by firing on every cycle, which would be beyond its capacity for high-frequency tones, but instead it fires in synchrony with the wave on a certain proportion of the cycles, e.g., every fourth or fifth one. This is called *phase locking.*

Somewhat analogous to the receptive fields of visual neurons are the response areas of auditory neurons. The threshold intensities (for spike discharges) for a wide range of frequencies are determined for an individual cell of the auditory nerve. Typical response areas for several cells of the auditory nerve of the cat are presented in Figure 6-6*a*. Each of the response areas has a "best" frequency, the frequency at which the threshold intensity is lowest. These areas show that "frequency tuning" takes place within the auditory nervous system. The response area is quite narrow at the lowest threshold intensities. None of the response areas in Figure 6-6*a* are of the symmetrical variety but of the more common asymmetrical variety, i.e., the cutoff of the cell's responsiveness to high-frequency stimuli is very sharp, whereas the responsiveness to ones below

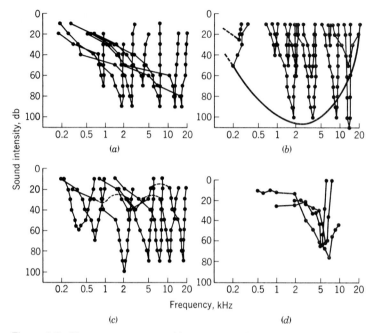

Figure 6-6 The response areas of four neurons from various levels of the ascending auditory nervous system: *(a)* cochlear nerve, *(b)* inferior colliculus, *(c)* trapezoid body, and *(d)* medial geniculate body. Frequency tuning for these neurons is evident in the narrowing of the response area in the region of the minimum threshold. (*Reprinted from* Sensory Communication *by W. A. Rosenblith by permission of the M. I. T. Press, Cambridge, Massachusetts. Copyright, 1961, by the Massachusetts Institute of Technology.*)

the best frequency only gradually declines. It should be pointed out that even at this lower level of the auditory system, neurons can be found that are not affected by auditory stimuli or are affected by only complex stimuli such as clicks or noise bands.

The relationship between stimulus intensity and the amount of spike activity in individual auditory nerve fibers is unclear at present. The most elaborate study is that of Kiang (1965). Instead of showing more spike potentials per unit time as stimulus intensity increased, most fibers studied increased firing up to a certain intensity level, then either decreased or leveled off their firing rates as intensity was further increased. Some of the cells did not respond until a stimulus level of 40 to 60 db SL was used.

Subcortical Auditory Centers

Katsuki's findings (1961) about the response areas for auditory nerve fibers (Figure 6-6*a*) have already been described. The remaining portions of Figure 6-6 show the response areas for the neurons in progressively higher centers in the auditory system. These data, along with those of similar studies, indicate a narrowing of the response areas as the various levels of the auditory nervous system are ascended. This progression does not continue into the auditory cortex. Cortical neurons have both wide and narrow response areas. Oonishi and Katsuki (1965) found cortical neurons with several "best" frequencies which were not harmonically related. At some lower levels the response areas for excitation of the neuron are surrounded by zones of inhibition. Certain ranges of frequency inhibit the activity of the neuron. This kind of border contrast between frequency regions for a particular neuron may serve to allow the detection of the unique elements in a complex stimulus (Whitfield, 1967).

An area of particular interest in the processing of frequency information is that of the *tonotopic* distribution of neurons, i.e., the extent to which the location of neurons in terms of their best frequency is ordered in some manner. A tonotopic distribution of neurons has been found for several levels of the auditory nervous system, although not in the medial geniculate (a subcortical structure).

The response of subcortical auditory neurons to the intensity of the stimuli has not been found to be a simple one. As an illustration of these findings, Rose et al. (1963) found cells in the inferior colliculus that reponded to increases in intensity of the stimulus with increases in their discharge rate only up to a certain intensity. At this point and for subsequent increases in intensity, they stopped responding.

Auditory Cortex

There are many auditory areas in the temporal region of the cortex. Evidence from animal research strongly argues that the cortical areas are not necessary for "simpler" auditory processing such as for frequency or intensity discrimination. For complex auditory-pattern discriminations, such as would be involved in discriminating a melody, the cortex is very much involved. Removal of tissue from several auditory areas, at least for the cat (Goldberg, Diamond, & Neff, 1957; Kaas, Axelrod & Diamond, 1970) destroys the ability to make auditory pattern discriminations.

THEORIES OF HEARING

The concern of this section is with the various theoretical treatments of the manner in which the frequency of the stimulus is encoded or processed within the auditory nervous system. The frequency of a pure tone is related to the sensation of pitch that it produces in much the same manner that the wavelength of a light stimulus is associated with the sensation of color or hue. Pitch and hue are qualitative sensory dimensions unlike those of loudness and brightness. The subjective experience of the observer is not directed toward how much pitch or hue but toward what type: high or low pitch, red or green hue.

Frequency Theories

The significant feature of the frequency theories is that they all propose that the frequency or periodicity of the stimulus is reproduced in the activity of the neurons of the auditory system. Any analysis of frequency would have to occur, presumably, at some cortical center. The best known of the early frequency theories, that of Rutherford (1886), assumed that neurons could follow the frequency of the signal up to a rate of 14,000 Hz. A major and unsurmountable problem for this version of the frequency theory is that it is now known that neurons cannot produce action potentials at a rate greater than 1,000 times per second, far below the upper limit of 20,000 Hz for human pitch perception.

Wever (1949) had the creative insight that it would not be necessary for each member of a neuronal system, such as the auditory nerve, to fire in synchrony with the frequency of the stimulus. On each cycle of the stimulus, it is only necessary that some subset of neurons fire. A collection of subsets of the nerve could then cover the frequency of the stimulus without any neuron exceeding the limit of firing of 1,000 Hz. As an example, consider a 10,000-Hz tone. One subset of fibers could fire on the first, eleventh, twenty-first, etc., cycles. Ten subsets firing in staggered volleys such as these would be sufficient to encode the frequency information in this 10,000-Hz tone. This *volley theory* of Wever's accordingly extends the theoretical limits of the frequency theory beyond the limits imposed by the maximum discharge rate of individual auditory neurons. The intensity of a stimulus could be encoded by the number of fibers composing each subset. An increase in intensity would increase the number of neurons firing at each cycle by recruiting more and by causing some to fire at a faster cycle rate than they ordinarily would.

Place Theory

Although the place theory of pitch perception has a long history going back to at least the seventeenth century (Wever, 1949), it is associated today with the name of Georg von Békésy, who received the Nobel prize for medicine in 1961 for his work on the dynamics of cochlear activity. For historical perspective on his theory, it is necessary to first describe the *resonance-place theory* of that nineteenth-century intellectual giant, Helmholtz. This theory proposed that the transverse fibers of the basilar membrane could resonate independently of each other. Furthermore, each of these fibers (a different "place") was thought to be tuned to resonate at a different frequency. Helmholtz used the fact that the basilar membrane increases in width from its base (the stapes end) to the apex (helicotrema end) to associate the former region with high-frequency stimuli and the latter with low-frequency stimuli. It may help in conceptualizing this theory to think of the basilar membrane as sort of a tuned harp where plucking the long strings produces the low tones and plucking the short ones produces the high tones. It is not necessary to actually pluck these strings, because they can be induced to vibrate by a sound pressure wave of sufficient intensity, traveling through the fluids of the cochlea.

Modern studies in sensory physiology do not support Helmholtz's model. The place theory proposed by von Békésy resembles that of Helmholtz only in terms of the spatial or place encoding of stimulus frequency. In von Békésy's theory, the basal end of the basilar membrane is again the location for resolving high-frequency sound stimuli with a decrease in the frequency being resolved as the location on the basilar membrane moves toward the apex.

The manner in which a place along the basilar membrane becomes the site of activity for any particular frequency is explained by von Békésy via some of his findings on the mechanical properties of the inner ear. Much of this work is summarized in von Békésy (1960). Essentially, von Békésy used two techniques to elucidate the mechanical properties of the cochlea: (1) direct observation of human and animal cochleas with openings produced by surgical techniques which he developed, and (2) mechanical models of cochleas.

In order to understand von Békésy's *traveling-wave* version of the place theory, it is necessary to note that the basilar membrane, in man as well as in other animals, is a complicated *elastic* membrane. It not only becomes continuously wider from the stapes to the helicotrema end, this membrane also becomes less stiff, by a factor of about 100:1 in human beings. Von Békésy (1956) observed that pressure waves emanate from the oval window into the fluids of the inner ear surrounding the basilar membrane and that these traveling waves of pressure distend the basilar membrane, i.e., push it in and out in a continuous series of locations as they move from the stapes end to the helicotrema where the pressure is finally dissipated.

The major point of von Békésy's findings is that the *location of the maximum displacement* on the basilar membrane produced by the traveling wave varies with the frequency of the stimulus applied to the stapes. In an important study, von Békésy (1949) measured the place of maximum vibration in a human cochlea in which the basal end of the basilar membrane was exposed. To stop the action of this membrane, a stroboscopic light was used and silver crystals were placed on Reissner's membrane to make it visible. The latter membrane vibrated coincidentally with the basilar membrane. The data are presented in Figure 6-7. Clearly, the location of the maximum vibration or displacement moves away from the helicotrema and toward the stapes as the frequency of the tone

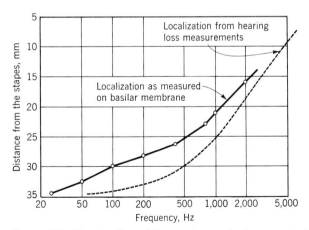

Figure 6-7 The location of the maximum displacements along the basilar membrane produced by pure tones from 25 to 2,000 hertz. Note that as the tonal frequency increases, the location of the maxima produced by the traveling wave moves towards the stapes. This figure also shows the great similarity between these actual observations on a human cochlea and predicted loci based on hearing deficiencies. *(From Békésy, 1960.)*

increases. Frequencies as low as 20 Hz had identifiable maxima at the basal end of the membrane.

An important consideration in evaluating the place theory is the finding that the maxima are quite broad, in terms of distance along the basilar membrane. The "broadness" increases, in fact, as the frequency of the stimulus decreases. At low-frequency levels, for example, 50 Hz or less, most of the basilar membrane vibrates. The finding that the maxima of vibration are rather broad, as is the whole effect of the traveling wave, has served as an argument against the adequacy of this place theory as a general explanation for pitch perception. More will be said on this later.

Von Békésy (1956) has used data collected from a mechanical model of the cochlea, upon which an arm is positioned, to demonstrate how these broad response areas may not be a handicap to the place theory. These models are long, fluid-filled tubes with rubber ("basilar") membranes that have pistons in one end which serve as stapes. Vibration of these "stapes" are felt along the arm, whose nerve supply to the hairs is similar to that found in the basilar membrane. Apparently, the trained observer detects very precise areas of localization even though vibratory stimuli cause widespread effects in the model just as tones do in the inner ear. Von Békésy has introduced the concept of *funneling* to explain these precise localization effects. According to this concept, there are neural and mechanical processes that sharpen and localize the response area for the stimulus. They are apparently demonstrable, at least for tactile vibration using the model of the cochlea. Similar processes may be involved for the cochlea to the extent that the physiology of the inner ear resembles that of the tactile sense of the arm.

An Evaluation of the Place and Volley Theories

There is a great deal of neurophysiological evidence that is consonant with von Békésy's place theory. This evidence, as well as other findings supportive of the volley theory, can be found in the excellent evaluation of the two theories provided by Uttal (1973). Some highlights of this material will be presented here. Strong support for the place theory comes from the work of Stebbins, Miller, Johnsson, and Hawkins (1969) who used antibiotics to destroy hair cells within the basilar membrane of rhesus monkeys. It was found that the region of destruction was as sharply defined as were regions of hearing loss measured by audiograms. An important feature of these findings was their agreement with von Békésy's observation that high-frequency stimuli are resolved at the basal end and low frequencies toward the apex of the cochlea.

Another area of agreement with the place theory concerns the organization of activity in the subcortical auditory nervous system. The response areas of auditory neurons at various subcortical levels have been described previously in this chapter. Although these response areas are relatively broad, the point that Uttal makes is that most response areas indicate that there is a restricted range of frequencies, even for high-intensity stimuli, to which the neuron will fire. This indicates, furthermore, that a restricted region of the basilar membrane is involved, supporting the place theory.

Evidence is not lacking to support the volley theory proposed by Wever (1949). The data concern the findings of "phase locking" for various subcortical auditory neurons that were described earlier. It is hard to interpret the phase-locking data because the stimulus-frequency range for which phase locking occurs decreases as the various levels of the auditory nervous system are ascended. There is no phase locking in the cortex (Brugge, Dubrovsky, Aitkin, & Anderson, 1969). What happens to phase-locked signals, that apparently exist at the lower levels of the auditory system, is unclear, as is their purpose. Nevertheless, their existence does indicate that a frequency code of the volley type may exist for coding the low-frequency stimuli for which a place of resolution on the basilar membrane does not exist. The most common evaluation of the pitch theories at present has both Wever's volley theory and von Békésy's place theory involved in pitch coding.

This combination, *volley-place theory,* has the volley principle accounting for the coding of low-frequency stimuli and the place theory operating at higher-frequency levels. The transition point at which one goes from the frequency code to the place code is unclear. Since phase locking can occur up to 5,000 Hz, a model could have all frequencies lower than this encoded by the volley principle and all higher ones by the place mechanism. More commonly, the transition point is assumed to be in the vicinity of 50 to 100 Hz.

AUDITORY PSYCHOPHYSICS

Sensitivity Functions

Absolute Thresholds The most elementary psychophysical function in audition is that for relating the absolute threshold to the frequency of the sound stimulus. The parallel to the visual-sensitivity function is obvious.

One major problem in obtaining this function is in specifying the point at which the sound pressure at threshold is measured. In minimum audible field (MAF) tests, the sound source is placed in front of the listener and presented via speakers. This is an "open ear" procedure. The threshold intensity is measured by means of a recording device situated at the same relative position as the subject's head.

In the minimum audible pressure (MAP) procedure, the subject is wearing earphones. The sound pressure of the stimulus is determined at the eardrum, e.g., by means of some probe microphone that can be inserted into the ear canal. The MAP procedure may be less naturalistic than the MAF, but neither adequately reflects the ordinary listening conditions that contain all kinds of stray, complicated sounds which mask the sound upon which attention is focused.

An additional procedural problem concerns the number of ears used. Monaural thresholds are always higher by at least a few decibels than binaural (two-ear) ones. Further problems concern the experience level of the subjects, their age, the psychological method used, and the duration of the stimulus.

In Figure 6-8, several MAF and MAP measurements of the auditory sensitivity functions are shown. For most frequencies, the MAP threshold is 6 to 10 db SPL greater then the MAF thresholds. The lowest thresholds for both

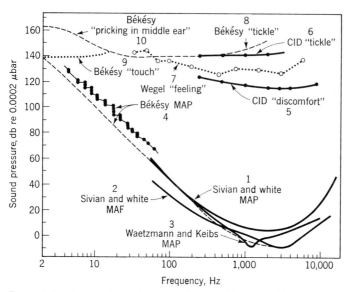

Figure 6-8 Several determinations of the auditory sensitivity functions and the thresholds of "feeling" for acoustical stimuli. MAF = minimum audible pressure in a free sound field, measured by microphones placed where the listener's head had been; MAP = minimum audible pressure at the eardrum, measured by a probe microphone. (*From* Handbook of Experimental Psychology *by S. S. Stevens. Copyright, 1961, by John Wiley & Sons, Inc. Reprinted by permission of John Wiley & Sons, Inc.*)

functions are the stimuli in the 1,000- to 4,000-Hz range, a range important in perceiving speech. The highest thresholds are for the lowest frequencies. Also in this figure, the "pain" functions from several studies are summarized. These show the sound pressure levels at which noticeable discomforting sensations such as tickling and prickling occur for the various stimulus frequencies. The stimulus intensities range from 120 to 140 db SPL for these functions. It is interesting to note that the thresholds for pure tones as low as 2 Hz (using MAP) and 23,000 HZ (using MAF) have been obtained (Corso, 1967).

Difference Thresholds: Intensity It will be recalled from Chapter 3 that the unit of differential sensitivity is the JND or difference threshold defined as the minimum change in a stimulus dimension that the subject can detect. The size of this JND depends very much on the psychological procedure used and the experience level of the subject. Classic data for the JNDs of intensity for pure tones (which the subject actually perceives as a change in loudness) are those of Riesz (1928), presented in Figure 6-9. Several features of this graph should be noted. The intensity values are given in sensation levels, decibels above threshold. The statistic $\Delta I/I$ is presented on the left ordinate, whereas the actual values of the DL are given on the right ordinate. Recall that Weber's law states that $\Delta I/I = K$, that the DL is a *constant* proportion of the stimulus intensity, I.

Riesz' data clearly indicate that the DL for intensity depends very much on

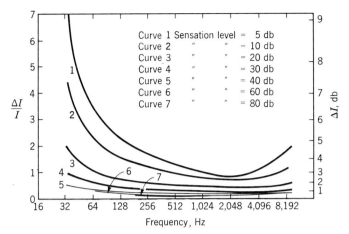

Figure 6-9 The classic data of Riesz (1928) on the DLs for intensity for pure tones. The Weber fractions (*I/I*) are presented for ten frequencies at several SLs. (*From* The Human Senses, *2d ed., by Frank Geldard. Copyright, 1972, by John Wiley & Sons, Inc. Reprinted by permission of John Wiley & Sons, Inc.*)

both the values of I and of f. The ratio $\Delta I/I$ is not constant for any of the stimulus frequencies used. The largest spread occurs for the 35-Hz tone, whereas the smallest range of $\Delta I/I$ occurs at approximately 2,500 Hz in the figure. The latter stimulus frequency can be considered as the one for which the auditory mechanism has greatest differential intensity sensitivity; i.e., the value of $\Delta I/I$, averaged over I values, is lowest here. Note also that the Weber constant gets progressively smaller as stimulus intensity increases.

Harris (1963) has shown that if trained observers, using the method of constant stimuli, are employed in measuring the DL for intensity, the size of the DL is considerably smaller than those proposed by Riesz. They were also fairly constant at all but the smallest levels of I. For a 1,000-Hz tone, one DL varied between approximately 0.75 and 1.25 db for values of I ranging from 5 to 80 db SL.

Difference Thresholds: Frequency When we investigate the ability of subjects to discriminate a change in frequency of a pure tone of constant intensity, the subjective attribute of the stimulus we measure is its *pitch,* or tonality. Pitch generally increases or gets "higher" as the frequency of a pure tone increases. Our sensitivity to slight changes in pitch is incredibly acute. In fact, changes in frequency of 1 Hz can be detected as changes in pitch for some stimuli.

The Weber ratio, $\Delta f/f$, comparing the DL frequency, Δf, to the frequency level of the standard, f, is of considerable interest. For loudness ranges from 30 to 40 db SL, Harris (1952) found that the ear is most sensitive in the 1,000- to 2,000-Hz region; i.e., the lowest Weber ratios are obtained in this region. The overall functions obtained showed constant Weber ratios for middle-range stimuli and tended to show increasing values for both ends of the stimulus range used. This finding is consistent with the limitation noted in Chapter 3, namely, that Weber's law holds for middle-range-stimulus values.

Binaural Difference Thresholds   The absolute binaural threshold for a pure tone is about 3 db SL lower than the monaural threshold. SLs are used because the sensitivities of the two ears must be equated in these procedures. There is no systematic relationship between frequency of the tone and the binaural-monaural threshold shift (Hirsh, 1952). The DLs for both intensity and frequency are lower for binaural listening. The binaural advantage is very small, however, in both cases. Only at very low frequencies is the Weber ratio for frequency appreciably lower in the binaural condition.

Masking

Unless an individual spends all his time in a soundproofed environment, the discriminability of any sound being attended to (signal) is affected by the presence of other sources of sound (masker). In a typical office environment, there may be 50 to 60 db of background masking noise, a jumble of complex sounds produced by the lighting, machinery, voices, etc. How the loudness of a target sound source, a signal, is reduced by the presence of some masker is a problem with a fairly long history in psychoacoustics. In the laboratory the signal and masker are well defined and isolated, unlike the situation in the naturalistic setting. Nevertheless, a large variety of experimental situations are possible. The first consideration concerns whether the signal and the masker are both presented to the same ear, different ears, or both ears.

A second consideration concerns the structure of the signal and the masker. Either or both may be pure tones, combination tones, broad-band noise containing a wide spectrum of frequencies such as white noise, or narrow bands of noise covering a smaller frequency range. Finally, some note must be taken of the time interval between the presentation of the masker and of the signal. In this section, the data reviewed are for simultaneous presentations of signal and masker. If a masker precedes a signal, *forward masking* is being investigated. When the signal precedes, *backward masking* is occurring.

Monaural Masking: Tone Signal and Tone Masker   Perhaps the most quoted study in the masking literature is that of Wegel and Lane (1942) in which a pure tone signal and pure tone masker are presented to the same ear. The data presented in Figure 6-10 are representative of their findings. In this particular experimental condition, a 1,200-Hz masker was presented at three SLs. Various signal frequencies, from 400 to 4,000 Hz, were presented coincidentally. The data points represent the amount of masking of the signal produced by the 1,200-Hz masker at the various intensities, i.e., the increase in intensity above its masked threshold that is necessary to make the signal just barely audible. The greatest amount of masking takes place for signals close to the masker in frequency. This holds for all intensity levels of the masker. The dips in the

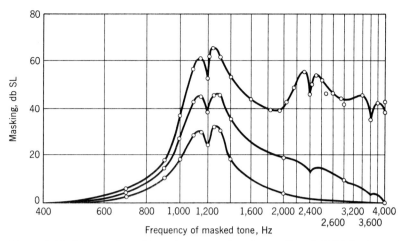

Figure 6-10 Monaural masking of one pure tone by another. A 1,200-hertz masker was presented at three SLs. The signal frequencies ranged from 400 to 3,200 hertz. Although the greatest amount of masking takes place in the vicinity of the masker's frequency, there is considerable asynchrony in the overall masking functions. Frequencies higher than the masker are more successfully masked than lower frequencies. *(From Wegel & Lane, 1924.)*

functions represent areas where beats occur because of the similarity in frequency between the signal and masker. The beats apparently make the signal more discriminable at these values. The most quoted aspect of Wegel and Lane's study deals with asymmetry in the 80-db plot (top). Pure-tone maskers of a high intensity level produce a greater degree and range of masking at frequencies higher than the masker than at lower frequencies.

Monaural Making: Tone Signal and Wide-band Noise Masker Hawkins and Stevens (1950) did an extensive study on the relationship between the masked threshold of pure tones and eight intensity levels of a white noise masker. Recall that white noise includes all frequencies in the audible spectrum at an equal intensity level. The data presented in Figure 6-11 represent the masked thresholds for a series of signals from 100 to 9,000 Hz at eight masking levels. The lowest curve in the figure is the typical sensitivity function for pure tones. The most striking feature of these data is the parallel nature of the masking functions. At low intensity levels of the masker, the thresholds of the midrange frequencies are most affected, i.e., elevated. However, by the 20-db noise level the masked thresholds show relatively little difference over the range of signals from 100 to 9,000 Hz. As the masking level is increased beyond this point, the thresholds of the signals are increased by a factor equivalent to the rise in the masking level.

Binaural Masking: MLD Binaural masking reflects the influence of the central nervous system in the processing of auditory information. There are now two independent channels of sensory input that must be integrated. The

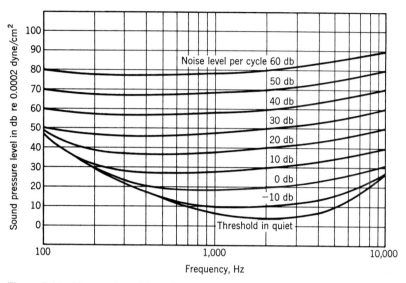

Figure 6-11 Monaural masking of pure tones by white noise at different energy levels. These idealized masked threshold contours show that the masked thresholds are relatively constant for all signal frequencies when the masker level exceeds 20 db. *(From Hawkins & Stevens, 1950.)*

masking level difference (MLD) is a measure representing the difference between the masked threshold obtained for a particular signal in binaural masking and that obtained from monaural masking. Binaural thresholds, for most listening procedures, will be lower than the corresponding monaural ones.

A large MLD can be obtained in the following situation. The monaural threshold involves presenting the pure-tone signal and the white noise masker to the same ear. The binaural situation involves presenting the white noise and signal to both ears. Further, the noise and signal are presented in such a manner that their interaural phase conditions are opposite. A signal or noise would have an interaural (between the two ears) phase difference of 0°, if the phase of the stimulus at each ear is the same at each moment. Thus, the eardrum is being pushed in by the sound pressure wave at both ears at the same instant, etc. In the 180° interaural-phase situation, one eardrum would be responding to the peak of condensation in the sound stimulus while the other would be responding to the peak of rarefaction; i.e., one eardrum is moving in to exactly the same extent that the other is moving out. The stimulus is perfectly "out of phase" at the two ears. When the noise and signal have different interaural phases, for example, 0° of interaural phase for the signal and 180° for the masking noise, the MLD is greatest.

This "unmasking" or lowering of the masked threshold by the use of binaural rather than monaural masking procedures may be of the order of 10 to 15 db for high masker levels and certain frequencies of the signal. Interestingly, the advantage for binaural listening holds only for the condition where the phase relationships are opposite for the signal and noise. When the interaural phase relationships are the same, for example, 180° out of phase for both signal and masker, the monaural threshold is lower than the binaural.

Critical Bands and Masking   If a pure tone is masked by white noise, it is being presented in the midst of every audible frequency, each presented at the same amplitude. White noise is the broadest of the broad-band noise maskers. High and low cutoff filters can be used in conjunction with the white noise to reduce the "bandwidth" of the masker. Perhaps only the frequencies from 500 (low cutoff) to 2,500 Hz (high cutoff) will be used in the noise band. A noise band can be made of any width beyond that producing only complex tones. Consider a pure tone embedded at the center of a relatively wide noise band. The amplitude of the noise can be raised until the tone is masked. As the band is made narrower, the tone is not automatically unmasked, i.e., does not go above threshold. *No change* in the masked threshold occurs until a certain minimal bandwidth is produced symmetrically about the tone. Once the masker's band of noise is reduced beyond this point, the tone is unmasked, and its loudness quickly grows as the bandwidth is narrowed. The latter phenomenon is referred to as *loudness recruitment. The minimum bandwidth that maintains the masking level is the critical band.*

The existence of critical bands indicates that only those frequencies in the noise band of sufficient proximity to the tone are involved in masking it. It makes one cognizant of the place theory of pitch perception and leads to speculations about some kind of local interference along a region of the basilar membrane as the source of masking. Scharf (1970) reviews the evidence that the critical band represents a spatial neural unit of lateral inhibition along the cochlea.

Classification of Auditory Sensations

Pitch   Pitch is that auditory sensation most directly associated with the frequency characteristics of the stimulus. For pure tones, one speaks of low to high pitch as the frequency of the tone increases. This kind of correspondence is really only a crude approximation of the actual relationship.

Although pitch changes are directly tied to the frequency of the stimulus, there is also a complex relationship between pitch and two other aspects of the stimulus, its duration and intensity. With respect to duration, any pure tone is heard as a "click" when its exposure is sufficiently short, on the order of 100 msec or less. Doughty and Garner (1947) found subjects able to discriminate a "click pitch" for clicks that last somewhere in the 100- to 200-msec range. Longer stimuli produce stable "tone pitches" that do not gain in tonality as the duration of the stimulus increases.

The nature of the relationship between the intensity of a pure tone and its pitch is a subject of controversy at present. The study by Stevens (1935) is, perhaps, the most widely quoted one on this topic. He found that pure tones of fairly low frequency (for example, 500 Hz and below) undergo a *decrease* in pitch proportional to any *increase* in their intensity. On the other hand, for fairly high frequencies (for example, 4,000 Hz and above), pitch *increases* are directly related to *increases* in the intensity of the tone. For 8,000 and 12,000 Hz, the increases in pitch were tremendous at high intensity levels. Stevens only used one subject. His procedure involved presenting, successively, two tones of different pitch. The subject adjusted the *intensity* of the comparison stimulus so that its pitch was equated to the standard. Ward (1970), in reviewing several studies on this same problem, concludes that Stevens' data are those of an "atypical observer." The typical result, as reviewed by Ward, shows very little effect of intensity on pitch.

One other "mystery" surrounding these intensity influences on pitch is that these effects, when measurable, are restricted to pure tones. Complex tones, such as those produced by musical instruments, do not show apparent pitch changes as intensity is increased. Any speculation on the source of this pitch stability would seem to have to wait on a resolution of the conflict over the existence of the intensity effect for pure tones themselves.

Loudness   The apparent loudness of an acoustical signal of whatever form is directly related to its power or intensity. Although the loudness of a signal does depend upon its frequency and duration, as will be discussed subsequently, much of the research interest in loudness has focused on developing a psychophysical scale relating loudness and intensity. The great impetus to this research has been the practical importance of such a scale in all the varied areas of applied acoustics.

The most widely accepted scale of loudness, in fact it is used as an international standard, is the *sone* scale. This scale in its original form was devised by Stevens and Davis (1938), using a ratio-scaling procedure. One sone is defined as the loudness of a 1,000-Hz pure tone at 40 db SL. Recall from Chapter 3 that the data summarized by Stevens plus subsequent research indicated that the loudness of pure tones of 1,000 Hz and similar intermediate frequencies doubled every 10 db. This led to the power law formulation of subjective loudness in which loudness (e.g., in sones) is an exponential function of the stimulus intensity. Stevens (1956) found the n, or exponent, in the equation R (sones) $= kI_n$ to be 0.6 for binaural judgments.

As frequency and intensity interact in producing the pitch of a pure tone, it is not surprising that a similar interaction occurs for loudness. The functions relating loudness to the frequency of the tone are the *equal-loudness contours*. As this name implies, these are functions showing the intensity necessary for tones of various frequencies to appear equal in loudness. The original set of equal-loudness contours was provided by Fletcher and Munson (1933). An extended revision of these functions was undertaken by Robinson and Dadson (1956). This finding is presented in Figure 6-12.

A major problem in treating these loudness contours was to find an appropriate referent to represent the loudness of an entire contour. In an examination of Figure 6-12 it can be seen that each contour has a number associated with it, except for the bottom one which is actually the MAF threshold function for these subjects. These numbers represent the "loudness level" in *phons* of each

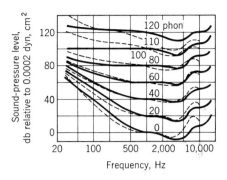

Figure 6-12 Equal loudness contours at two age levels. Solid line = age 20; dashed line = age 60. *(From Robinson & Dadson, 1956.)*

contour. Although each frequency is at a different intensity level in each equal-loudness contour, the loudness level is the same. The phon level of any tone whose loudness is being evaluated is defined as the SPL of a 1,000-Hz tone that appears equal in loudness. Thus, all tones on the 20-phon contour line were judged equal in loudness to a 1,000-Hz tone of 20 db SPL. Figure 6-12 actually shows the equal-loudness functions for two age groups, 20- and 60-year-olds. The major difference is in the elevated intensities for high frequencies in the older group. As would be expected, all the functions are flattest in the 500- to 2,000-Hz region where acuity is greatest.

Volume, Density, and Tonality The *volume* of a sound refers to its spaciousness, how well it fills an area. Low-frequency tones are judged reliably by subjects to have greater volume than high-frequency stimuli. Subjects are also able to judge the *density* of a sound, how compact it appears. High-frequency pure tones are judged as denser than low-frequency tones. There is evidence that density is not simply the subjective inverse of volume, as might appear. The final subjective attribute to tonal stimuli that has been experimentally investigated to any degree is *tonality*. This term refers to the unique character of certain tones that stand in some frequency relationship to each other, such as the similarity of pure tones that are an octave apart. A C of 256 Hz (middle C) sounds more similar to a C of 512 Hz (high C) than it does to stimuli, closer in frequency, within the octave. As Gulick (1971) puts it, there is something of "C-ness" about the note, a kind of identity that most listeners perceive.

A controversy exists concerning the independent existence of these three auditory experiences as valid dimensions. Gulick does not accept volume and density as bonafide dimensions, particularly because of the lack of evidence for any related physiological process. On the other hand, Geldard (1972) accepts these two dimensions primarily on the basis of psychophysical evidence. Gulick accepts tonality as a dimension because, in addition to the sensory data supporting its existence, there are good models, such as in the tuning curves for auditory neurons, which suggest associated physiological operation. Geldard, on the other hand, sees tonality as a very weak bet for a legitimate dimension because of the lack of sufficient psychophysical data to support it. Future work will more likely resolve these differences between sensory, psychophysical, and physiological data.

AUDITORY SPACE PERCEPTION: SOUND LOCALIZATION

There is no doubt that sounds have a spatial aspect in much the same way that visual stimuli are localized in extended space. Sounds, however, can not only be localized in space; they can also produce a "sound image" along a lateral line running between the two ears. This image occurs when stimuli are presented binaurally via earphones. Furthermore, sounds can be localized,although errors are common, behind as well as in front of the listener. Auditory space curves 360°, forming a sphere around the individual. Visual space is, of course, more limited.

The distance at which sound can be localized, on the other hand, is much more limited than visual distance. Although the speed of sound does not change for a constant medium, the energy level of the sound stimulus, like that of the visual stimulus, will depend on its distance from the listener. Finally, the geography of the body, especially the size and shape of the head and the features of the cartilage of the pinna, must be considered in evaluating the acoustical information that the subject has in localizing a sound source.

Acoustical Cues for Sound Localization

Consider the orientation of the subject in Figure 6-13. Assume that a circular plane of indefinite extent exists that is parallel to the floor and coincident with a line connecting the subject's two ears. This plane is the subject's *lateral plane* because of its coincidence with the lateral line between his two ears. When a stimulus is presented at some point along the circumference of this plane, its

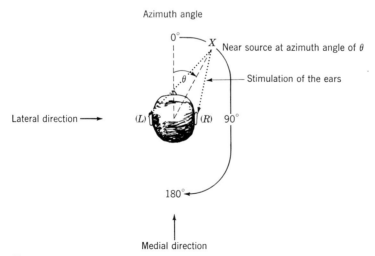

Figure 6-13 Spatial direction and the azimuth angle in sound localization.

position is defined with respect to a medial line running from front to back, bisecting the subject's head at right angles to the lateral line. This *medial line* defines a stimulus of 0° azimuth. The location of the source on the lateral plane is specified by the angle formed by its projection to the medial line (0°) at the center of the head. In Figure 6-13, the azimuth angle is indicated as Θ. A source at 90° azimuth is perpendicular to the right ear in this figure. A source at 180° is directly behind the listener on the lateral plane.

Of course, a sound source may be located above or below the lateral plane. Its direction may still be specified with respect to the lateral plane that has been defined. If the stimulus is located directly above the center of the subject's head, it is at a point on the circumference of a *medial plane* bisecting the head and located perpendicular to the floor. Actually, an infinite series of planes could be specified because the head is really at the center of a spherical auditory space.

If one takes the head to be a perfect sphere and the ears to be holes (no external cartilage), approximate values for the distance of the external sound source from each ear can be calculated for any stimulus azimuth. These *binaural distance differences* are directly associated with *binaural differences* in the acoustic cues used for sound localization.

Intensity as a Cue: the Interaural Intensity Difference

The interaural intensity difference (IID) is the difference between the ears in the sound pressure received from an external sound source. This difference in intensity will vary with the binaural distance difference which, in turn, will be dependent upon the actual distance and azimuth of the sound. Intensity differences based directly on these distance differences would be very slight. The major source of intensity differences at the two ears is the *sound shadow* produced by the head. This shadow can be thought of as a filter which passes low frequencies but hinders, via reflection, the movement of high frequencies about the head.

Figure 6-14 shows the relationship between azimuth angle and the IID for pure tones from 200 to 6,000 Hz. These measurements were taken with actual observers in position. For low frequencies, for example, 200 and 500 Hz, the IID is quite small, even at 90° azimuth where it might be expected to be quite large as the sound source is opposite the right ear. The complex interaction of azimuth and frequency is seen in the 10 to 20 db IIDs for the stimuli of 1,800 Hz and above. As will be discussed later, these findings indicate that IIDs are effective cues only for relatively high-frequency tones or complex stimuli with high-frequency components, where the sound shadow is particularly effective.

Temporal Cues

There are really two temporal cues available in the binaural stimulus. For clicks, short tone bursts, white noise bursts, and, initially, pure tones, there are differences in the time of arrival of the sound pressure fronts to the two ears that depend on a binaural distance difference and thus on the azimuth and distance of the source. The interaural time difference (ITD) is greatest for the 90° azimuth

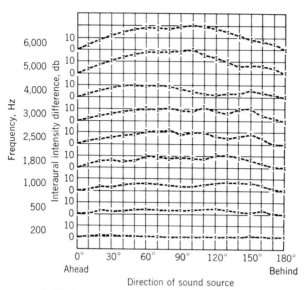

Figure 6-14 Interaural intensity differences as a function of the direction of the source and its frequency. *(From Fedderson et al., 1957.)*

position. Values decrease symmetrically to zero (for 0° and 180° azimuth) from the maximum.

The second time cue is the *phase* relationship between the sound waves at the two ears. For tonal stimuli, not only will a difference in binaural distance produce an ITD, but, depending upon the frequency of the stimulus, a certain degree of phase difference will exist between the two ears. The exact amount will depend on the azimuth and frequency of the stimulus. This can be grasped intuitively when one thinks of the binaural distance difference in terms of the increased number of cycles or parts of a cycle of the tone that the sound wave has to travel in order to get to the far ear. Phase can be an ambiguous cue, and it certainly is for stimuli above approximately 1,500 Hz (Mills, 1972). When the ITD is such that more than a half-cycle of phase lead is produced, it becomes uncertain as to whether an ear is leading in phase or is actually lagging behind in phase.

Lateralization Studies Stimuli presented in the field provide both temporal and intensity cues to the listener. In order to study these cues separately, and their interaction, under controlled conditions, lateralization procedures are used. Several variants of the procedure have been developed, but the essential element remains the localization of a sound image along the lateral line of the head which runs between the two ears. Binaural stimuli are presented via earphones, and a unitary sound image can be lateralized, e.g., in the center of the head or toward one or the other ear, as long as the temporal and intensity discrepancies of the binaural stimuli resemble those of actual external sources.

A traditional lateralization approach involves the determination of a trading ratio, defined as "that ITD/IID where the two interaural differences will just balance each other in determining the subjective location of the sound image" (Molino, 1974, p. 139). To clarify matters, consider that a sound image will shift laterally toward one ear with the more intense stimulus when ITD is zero, and will shift toward the ear receiving the earlier stimulus when the IID is zero. Trading ratios show the amount of ITD necessary to balance out 1 db of IID.

The study by Harris (1960) is an example of a centering procedure in lateralization studies using trading ratios. The subjects were required to adjust the ITD of the stimulus to compensate for (i.e., to bring the sound image back to the center of the head) a lateral displacement of the signal brought about by some IID imposed by the experimenter. The data of this study are important because they show the influence of the frequency components of complex stimuli on the trading ratio. Stimuli (clicks) with components over 1,500 Hz were found to need considerably larger changes in ITDs to compensate for each 1-db shift in the IID than stimuli with frequencies restricted to components of 1,400 Hz or below. Thus the ITD is a much more powerful cue in lateralization at low frequencies than at high ones.

Molino (1974) has criticized the relevance of lateralization studies to the localization of sounds in real space. In a study that bridges lateralization and localization procedures, he presented, *by earphones,* the appropriate IIDs and ITDs that stimuli at various frontal azimuth angles in real space would produce. However, as in localization studies, he had the subjects indicate these azimuth positions rather than the location of the sound image along the lateral plane of the head. The response procedure was novel. The subject had his hand positioned at some azimuth angle to give strong proprioceptive cues for that azimuth. He then indicated, by button presses, the apparent position (right or left of the hand) of the source presented via the earphones. Subjects were very accurate. Some gave data that were very similar to the localizations actually produced by real sources presented in an open-field control condition using the same azimuth positions and response measures.

Role of Head Movements in Localization

In the natural environment we do not localize sounds with our heads in a fixed position. In locating the source of a sound we particularly use those alterations in the signals received by our ears that are specifically produced by head movements. Head movements produce dynamic cues for determining the relative elevation of the sources.

The classic studies on the role of head movements are those of Wallach (1939, 1940). One finding by Wallach was that sounds that remain in the median plane of the listener as he rotates his head are localized in the vertical plane of the head, usually above the head. The reason for this judgment is apparent in that only stimuli from the vertical plane would be immune to transformations in IID and ITD as the head rotates. On the other hand, stimuli of nonzero elevation (out of the horizontal plane) should show changes in these two interaural parameters when the head is pivoted, i.e., moved between a shoulder and its natural upright position. Thurlow and Runge (1967) did not find that such pivot movements were much help in judging the elevation of a source.

Pinnae and Sound Localization

In the real world the processor of auditory information has ears, really appendages of cartilage, over the openings in his or her nonspherical head. Furthermore, these ears are not symmetrically placed about the lateral plane of the head nor even directly on it. What are commonly called ears are technically pinnae (singular, pinna). The shape of the pinnae includes several irregular hollows and rises. A number of studies, e.g., Batteau (1967), have shown that the pinnae alone are sufficient for distinguishing signal locations directly behind or in the front of the listener as long as the stimuli have sufficient high-frequency components, that is, 8,000 Hz or greater. Batteau has shown this with microphones fitted with artificial pinnae. Subjects listening to the output of the microphones, via earphones, did a good job in localizing both the azimuth and elevation of high-frequency stimuli. Localization was poor when the microphones were used alone.

Two hypotheses have been proposed concerning the cues for sound localization provided by the pinnae. The *shadow theory* asserts that the pinnae produce a transformation in an acoustic wave front containing high frequencies that serves to distinguish anterior from posterior stimuli. The transformation for the posterior azimuth would be much greater than for stimuli in front of the listener. We have already discussed the head itself as a sound shadow for high-frequency stimuli such that IIDs are the most effective cue for high-frequency stimuli. The ITD is very ineffective for these stimuli because they do not bend around the head as readily as low-frequency stimuli; they are reflected.

This notion of reflected wave fronts relates to a second theory of the *pinna reflections*. These reflections are actually echoes off the various surfaces of the pinna. The echoes would have various delay periods depending upon the angle of incidence of the wave fronts of sound pressure. These temporal delays would be very fine cues for resolving the azimuth of high-frequency stimuli.

Gardner (Gardner & Gardner, 1973; Gardner, 1973) has done some very precise and ingenious experiments on the role of the pinna in localizing sounds presented along the median plane. This plane is the one that bisects the head in the front-to-back direction. Gardner has developed plugs to occlude (block out) various portions of the pinnae or the whole pinna, leaving a small hole for the sound pressure wave to enter the ear canal. In investigating the localization of a series of speakers about the anterior portion of the median plane, Gardner found that localization is very poor when both pinnae are occluded. The amount of error is quite low when only one ear is occluded. One active pinna does quite a good job in aiding sound localization for these wide-band noise signals.

Neurophysiological Correlates of Sound Localization

Two centers in the ascending auditory pathways as well as portions of the auditory cortex itself have provided evidence that binaural information is being processed. The superior olivary nucleus of the medulla, located in the lower portion of the brainstem, seems to be the initial area of the ascending auditory system at which cells can be found that respond to binaural inputs. Stotler (1953) had shown the convergence of fibers from the two cochlear nuclei onto the cells of the medial superior olivary nuclei. Galambos, Schwartzkopff, and Rupert (1959) found cells that responded to both interaural temporal and intensity differences in dichotic-click stimuli. Goldberg and Brown (1969) found similar cells that responded to tonal stimuli. Their data are particularly congruent with the psychophysical evidence concerning the cues for localization. Goldberg and Brown found that cells with a high-frequency response area were most sensitive to intensity differences between the dichotic stimuli. On the other hand, cells with response areas predominantly in the low-frequency region showed greater responsiveness to phase than to intensity differences.

The second noncortical region of binaural interaction is in the inferior colliculi. These nuclei are located in the midbrain, and send fibers to the thalamus and cortex. There is some speculation that any response to temporal cues at this level reflects earlier processing at the superior olivary. Rose, Gross, Giesler, and Hind (1966) have examined all types of cells in the inferior colliculus that may play a part in sound localization. Using binaural tonal stimuli, these investigators found two collections of cells, those mainly sensitive to phase cues and a second type primarily responsive to intensity differences. Individual cells had a characteristic phase or intensity value that would produce the greatest amount of spike activity.

Although the neural processing necessary for sound localization takes place in subcortical regions of the auditory system, the auditory cortex is intimately involved at some level in the production of localization *responses*. Neff and Diamond (1958) had originally shown that larger, extensive, lesions through all the auditory areas of the cortex produced very large localization errors in cats. Masterton and Diamond (1964) did find that localization based on intensity differences was somewhat less impaired. Since the auditory cortex seems most involved in processing the higher-order patterns of acoustical stimuli rather than their structural features, it may be that their ablations and lesions are disrupting the animal's ability to incorporate stimuli within a representation of acoustical space.

SUMMARY

The sensory physiology of the auditory nervous system can be distinguished from that of vision most readily at the level of the receptive system. The audiology and physiology of the cochlea indicate that an initial mechanical transduction of the acoustic signal is transformed into electrical activity that is associated with particular spatial locations along the basilar membrane dependent upon the physical characteristics of these signals. The organization and complexity of the postreceptor levels of the auditory system show the same type of receptive field and excitatory-inhibitory coding patterns evident in the visual system.

The range of psychophysical investigations in audition also parallels that for vision. The principal issues discussed in this chapter were the absolute and differential sensitivities of the auditory sensory system and masking. Scaling and delimiting of the various acoustic sensations such as pitch, loudness, and volume were discussed. The various binaural and monaural cues contributing to the auditory space sense, discussed in the last section of this chapter, indicate a dependence of this ability on a precise encoding of stimulus features at lower portions of the auditory nervous system.

Context for Brightness and Color Constancy

The analysis presented in the first six chapters indicates that it is rare indeed that a focal stimulus is perceived independently of the context of stimulation within which it is presented. These contextual effects can be produced in four ways: (1) simultaneous presentation of two stimuli; (2) successive presentation of two stimuli; (3) contextual effects produced by short-term experience such as in sensory adaptation; and (4) contextual effects produced by long-term storage, learning, and memory.

A major thesis of this chapter and Chapter 8 is that certain categories of stable perception—later designated as brightness and hue constancy—are organized in the first three ways listed above and are not subject to the effects of past learning or memory. Other kinds of stable perceptual phenomena, later designated as size and shape constancy, are organized in the fourth way described above—that is, are influenced by interpretation in a learned context which is stored in memory. Our aim is to study the organizational and relational determination of these constancies and deviations therefrom.

In this chapter we shall specifically emphasize the contextual determination of brightness context. Besides any interest that it might have in its own right, studying brightness constancy leads to understanding all classes of contextual effects—thus, whether the perception contains constant properties of an object depends on a variety of *stimulus relationships.* Learning and experience are negligible as necessary determiners.

FUNCTIONAL OR ADAPTIVE SIGNIFICANCE OF PERCEPTUAL CONSTANCIES

A little reflection on how we adjust to our daily environment will reveal that, if we responded to all the changes in the dimensions of stimulation, living in our world would be virtually impossible. More specifically, it would not be very adaptive to see colors changing simply because their incident illumination changed or to see sizes and shapes undergoing transformation because their distance or spatial orientations were altered. Rather, we must be able to respond to certain *constant properties* of objects—such as color, size, shape, space, and volume—in order for the world to be sufficiently reliable and predictable; otherwise there would be too much uncertainty to make adaptive behavior possible.

Designating Perceptual Constancies

The first constant property of perception is organized at the *second level* of the perceptual hierarchy—that is, below the levels requiring memory or the contextual involvement of long-term storage. This property, called *color constancy,*[1] includes both achromatic and chromatic light. The former constancy is variously called brightness, lightness, or whiteness, while the latter is called hue, or simply color. Strictly speaking, though, color constancy equals brightness plus hue constancy, since color equals brightness plus hue.

The brightness of an object is not determined solely by the intensity of the light illuminating it. Intensity by itself produces the sensory effect called *luminosity.* Brightness is also determined in part by the proportion of the incident light which is reflected from the surface of the receiving object. The other factors, such as contrast, size, and reflectance of surround, are considered later in this chapter.

Of major importance, though, is a constant property of objects which give us a constant relative reflection surface. We all know that the whites, grays, or blacks (on the achromatic scale) of objects remain relatively constant under ordinary everyday conditions, irrespective of whether they are seen in shadows, cloudy conditions, twilight, or bright sunlight. This invariant property, object brightness, is called *brightness constancy,* and exists because of the index of reflection or the albedo of the object. The term *albedo* refers to the proportion of light received by an object that it reflects back. An albedo of 0.80 means that the object reflects back 80 percent of the received incident illumination; it looks white. Similarly, *hue constancy* (the invariance of the colors in the spectrum) exists because the object reflects a specific wavelength (blue, green, red, etc.).

---

[1]We define more fully the nature of brightness, size, and shape constancy as we go along in this chapter and Chapter 8.

The other constancies, size and shape, are organized at levels III and IV of the hierarchy. The comparison and analysis of the three experiments in the next section show that this is so.

Size constancy refers to the fact that the perception of objective size does not decrease with distance from the object (as retinal size does) but remains constant.

Shape constancy refers to the phenomenon that perceived shape of an object remains relatively invariant with respect to the changes in spatial orientation. Thus, a rectangular book tilted away from the observer still looks like a rectangle even though its image on the retina becomes trapezoidal.

It is not hard to understand why all the constants have traditionally been explained by a unitary principle since they describe situations in which perceived or psychological dimensions remain relatively invariant with respect to changes in the physical dimensions. But we shall also see that the organization of brightness and color constancy is determined at the level of stimulus factors, while determination of size and shape constancy requires experience, learning, memory, and attitude. Our task will therefore be to ascertain why level II is sufficient for the organization of brightness constancy while levels III and, perhaps, even IV are invoked in the appropriate operation of the other two constancies.

TWO EXPERIMENTS: ORGANIZATION OF SIZE CONSTANCY AT A HIGHER LEVEL THAN BRIGHTNESS CONSTANCY

The purpose of the first experiment to be considered (Gilinsky, 1955) was to determine the effect of attitudes on the reported sizes of objects. Four triangles of different lengths were, one at a time, located at various distances directly in front of the subject; a variable triangle, i.e., a triangle whose size could be altered, was located at a distance of 100 feet from the subject and at an angle of 36°26' to the right of the line of sight. The triangles, which were made of white-colored sheet aluminum, were seen against a background of grassy terrain, remote trees, and buildings at the far end of a field. The heights of the four standard triangles varied in 1-foot steps from 3½ to 6½ feet.

The subject judged the height of one standard triangle at a time, the height of the variable being altered until he considered it equal to the height of the standard. This was done by instructing the experimenter to lower or raise the variable in a pit in the ground; that is, the two sides of the variable triangle would be lowered or raised to adjust its height to apparent equivalence with the distant standard. Such judgments were made of the four standards, located at distances up to about 4,000 feet. This is called the *method of adjustment*.

Judgments of height at each distance were made under two sets of instructions. Under one set, the subject was asked to alter the variable until it equaled the size of the standard, if we were to measure it, despite appearances to the contrary. These judgments were called *objective* matches since they were estimates of the actual size of the object. Under the second set of instructions, the subject was told to alter the size of the variable until it equaled the size of the standard as it appeared at the moment, even though he knew it was bigger. These judgments were called *retinal* matches because the subject was instructed to follow as closely as he could the reduction in retinal-image size with distance. The average results of Gilinsky's experiment are shown in Figure 7-1.

It is quite clear from an inspection of Figure 7-1 that the two sets of instructions led to different-sized matches. We know that the size of the retinal image of an object decreases as its distance from the eye increases. This is shown in the retinal size curve in the figure. We see that the retinal matches follow this curve very closely. It would be safe to say that the retinal matches resulted from the discrimination of immediate sensory stimulation on the retina, with little intervention from central processes. But what about the objective matches? Here we see that size constancy closely followed the object size level; in fact, there was overconstancy—i.e., the subject overestimated the size of the distant standard.

It is indeed remarkable that the human organism is able to give two widely differing reports of size under the same condition of retinal stimulation. In fact, Jenkin and Hyman (1959) in another study concluded from a factor analysis of their data that perceptual judgments under retinal and objective attitudes were independent of each other. Further verification comes from V. R. Carlson (1960) who found no relationship between judgments of apparent and objective size.

We turn now to a brightness experiment, performed by Gelb (1929), which reveals that the observer *cannot* give two such different judgments under the same pattern of stimulation. In a room where several objects are faintly lit by a ceiling light, a rotating *black* disk, illuminated by an intense but concealed

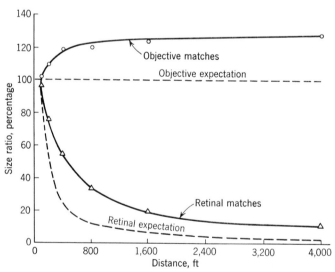

Figure 7-1 Objective and retinal matches plotted as ratios of the size of the variable to the size of the standard. *(After Gilinsky, 1955, p. 183.)*

lantern, is placed in the foreground. The beam of the lantern falls exactly on the area of the disk, no additional light being cast on the background. Observers report seeing a *white* disk standing in a dim light, and this impression is very compelling. A small piece of white paper is then brought into the rotating disk. Instantly the disk is reported as "turning into" its objective black color, and the beam "becomes" very intense. When the white paper is removed, the disk dramatically changes back to white. These sudden reversals of perceived brightness can be induced with perfect consistency merely by moving the white paper in and out of the beam. *Knowledge makes no difference* in the perception.

In comparing these two experiments, we should note that in the first one the subject could ignore the relationship between size and distance if he wished, whereas in the second he could not ignore the relationship between the light reflected by the black disk and the light reflected by the white paper. That is, in the first experiment the subject could report an objective or reduced size when distance cues were present, whereas in the second experiment he could give only one class of response constancy, when cues to illumination conditions were present.

We use these two experiments to introduce a discussion of the perceptual constancies. The first example is an illustration of size constancy, and it shows that perceived size does not regularly follow changes in the retinal size of the object, providing there are adequate cues to distance. But it is very important to keep in mind that the observer can give *either constancy or retinal matches under these conditions of adequate cues to distance perception.* When cues to distance have been removed, he naturally can give only a retinal match. In the case of brightness constancy, however, as shown in the second experiment, the subject can give *only one discrimination* in each of the conditions: a sensing of illumination intensity when he is not able to compare the brightness of the objects and a perception of objective brightness when he can compare the brightness of an object with that of at least one other object.

Vernon (1970, pp. 170–171) uses data from Landauer and Rodger (1964) to back up her claim that brightness is not organized at a lower level than size, clearly taking issue with the view expressed in the last paragraph above. In order to address ourselves to her argument, it is necessary to present the essence of the experiment, although we shall go into this kind of research in greater detail later in this chapter.

Briefly stated, Landauer and Rodger used a modification of the standard experiment of Katz (1935), shown in Figure 7-2. In one chamber the standard disk on the color wheel had a white sector of 89°. The subject had to adjust the white sector on the variable so that the two disks appeared to be equally white in his judgment. The reflectances of the white and black sections of the standard and the variable were identical, and each chamber had *identical sources of illumination* produced by a 200-watt incandescent lamp.

The variable of particular interest was the *instructions* given to the subjects. Each of three groups received a different instruction: (1) *reflectance,* which instructed subjects to pay attention to illumination differences and albedo, (2)

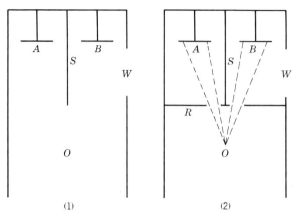

Figure 7-2 Plan of an experiment in brightness constancy, viewed from above. *(After D. Katz, 1911, p. 181.)*

*luminance,*which instructed subjects to ignore albedo differences and concentrate on illumination differences; (3) *apparent brightness,* which instructed subjects to pay attention to how bright the standard disk appeared without further amplifications.

Vernon used the fact that the average white sector for the reflectance instructions was 93.2°, for the luminance instructions, 126.7°, and for the "apparent brightness" instructions, an intermediate 111.2° as evidence to support her claim that brightness constancy determination, too, consists of a compromise between stimulus factors and attitudes.

A number of considerations make this conclusion questionable. Consider the following:

1   The reported results of Landauer and Rodger might very well be an artifact of their experimental conditons. Since *both* the albedos of the disks and the illumination intensities in the two chambers were identical, the usual question of brightness constancy does not even arise. The only time we really have a problem is when the albedos are *constant* but the reflected illumination intensities are *variable*. The usual question concerns how the individual extracts the former as a constant if the latter, which is what reaches his eye, is variable. Gelb's experiment, and the others described in the next section, show that under reduced conditions complete destruction of constancy takes place, whereas under nonreduced conditions constancy prevails. Under the latter condition one cannot obtain complete separation between reflectance and luminance, whereas Gilinsky's experiment clearly shows that one *can* attain complete separation of objective size and retinal size under nonreduced conditions. It is obviously more legitimate to consider memory and nonsensory factors in the case of size constancy.

2   When the basic condition for constancy is already maximized in both chambers, it is not at all surprising that experiential sets can produce modifications in one direction or the other. After all, attitudes can even influence simple detection as we saw in Chapter 3. So the demonstration of attitudinal modification in no way proves memory determination of the basic phenomenon on the basis of memory.

3   Finally, an unstable range of constancy findings with color wheels is consistent with Burzlaff's (1931) results reported in the last section of this chapter. Burzlaff found much higher and more stable constancy when an ordered scale of brightnesses was used to measure the constancy responses. It is evident to us that the case has been made that brightness constancy results from immediate sensory judgment; memory, if any, plays a very minor role. Let us see how this sensory judgment is made.

BRIGHTNESS AND COLOR CONSTANCY

David Katz (1935), in his famous work on the phenomenal appearance of color, noted that there was a tremendous dissimilarity between the scale of perceptible illumination changes and the scale of detectable whiteness differences. In fact, the ratio of the highest illumination in which objects are detectable to the lowest illumination in which they are noticeable is of the order of several thousand to one. The corresponding ratio of the whitest white to the blackest black is only 60:1. In the latter case we are looking at light reflected from an object. Although Katz pointed out the important fact that there was a difference between the illumination scale and the whiteness-constancy scale, he actually referred to the latter phenomenon as *brightness constancy*.[2]

It is now customary to talk about *brightness* and *whiteness* as synonyms, and to use the terms *luminance* (physical) and *luminosity* (psychological effect) to refer to changes caused by variations in illumination. The rest of this chapter analyzes the nature of brightness constancy.

Early Phenomenological Description

Katz was one of the first psychologists to give a good phenomenological description of the modes of appearances of color under a variety of physical conditions. The first important distinction he made was between surface and *film* color. The latter refers to color or light which seems to be amorphous and "unattached" to any object. Surface color, on the other hand, is seen as "belonging" to the surface of an object (Katz, 1911). In surface color, for example, the brightness is seen as an integral part of a *segregated unit* or *figure* (level II in our hierarchy). Thus *brightness constancy will hold only for surface colors*, and a surface color must have a constant physical property to correspond to its psychological counterpart. In the case of brightness constancy, this constant physical property is termed *albedo*.

Albedo   Every object which has any reflecting surface has a property, an index of reflection, which is called *albedo*, defined earlier in this chapter. A

---

[2]Koffka (1935) has stated it would be more accurate to speak of whiteness constancy.

good white has an albedo of 0.85 or 85 percent, which means that it reflects about 85 percent of the light it receives. Similarly, the darkest gray or a black has an albedo of 0.14 or 14 percent, and intermediate grays have albedos which range between these limits. (Theoretically, a pure black does not exist since it would have an albedo of zero, and we would not see it at all.) We can express albedo by the formula $A = R/I$, where A is albedo, R the intensity of reflected light, and I the intensity of incident light. Thus, if an object receives light with an intensity of, say, 200 cd/m² and reflects 160 cd/m², it has an albedo of 0.80 or 80 percent. If it receives 150 cd/m², it will reflect 120 cd/m². (The abbreviation cd/m² refers to candles per square meter and is a measure of luminance.)

In everyday life the objects around us are numerous and have varying albedos, ranging from very low to very high. Even though incident illumination varies from bright daylight to the shadows of twilight, the objects will, under ordinary conditions, maintain their relative brightness because a constant proportion of the light they receive will always be reflected, that is, *the ratio of the light they reflect must be constant because their albedos are constant.*

Maintenance of Brightness Constancy when Illumination Conditions Provide Information about Relative Albedos

The three techniques described in this section show the general conditions which must be met if brightness-constancy perception is to prevail.

Standard Experiment: Shadow Method and Its Implications   The experimental situation is illustrated in Figure 7-2. The observer sits in the experimental room as shown. Color wheel A contains a white disk. Color wheel B, which is in good daylight illumination, contains a white disk and a black disk which overlap so that the proportion of white in relation to black can be varied before the wheel is spun. In situation 1, there is fair constancy—that is, a high proportion of white on color wheel B, whereas in situation 2, constancy is almost zero—that is, the color wheel B has almost all black in it.

Method of Illumination Perspective   Katz used this method while distinguishing the second of his phenomenological categories, which he referred to as psychological qualities of *pronouncedness* and *insistence* of brightness. The observer sits in a dark room under a high-powered lamp. An ordered series of eighteen achromatic colors, from white to black, is presented in front of him at a distance of 1 meter. Farther away, at approximately 5 meters from the observer, various grays, whites, and blacks are presented to him, one at a time in random order. His task is to equate one of the colors in the near series with the one presented farther away. When the far color was white, the subject chose a white from the near series which reflected approximately 20 times as much light (absolute intensity) as the distant white. In other words, despite the fact that the far color received one-twentieth as much illumination as the near color, the subject perceived the two whites as being almost equal; i.e., there was a high degree of *whiteness constancy.*

There were, however, two differences in appearance. The nearer white seemed "lighter" or "livelier." Katz called this a difference in *insistence*. Some observers also reported that the nearer white appeared more genuine, whereas the distant one appeared "darker" or "veiled in darkness." Katz referred to this as a difference in *pronouncedness*. The white in the better illumination is therefore both more pronounced and more insistent. This distinction between pronouncedness and insistence is even more vividly demonstrated when the distant color is black. Again the observer chooses a black from the near series which is close in albedo to the distant black, but now the distant black looks more pronounced; i.e., it is a better black. The near black reflecting absolutely more light is still more insistent. Thus a constant brightness, with a fixed albedo, always looks most insistent in strongest illumination. But there is an interaction between albedo and illumination with respect to pronouncedness. In general, the whites and light grays look more pronounced in *better* illumination, whereas the blacks and dark grays look more pronounced in *poorer* illumination.

In this regard we recall Wallach's (1948) experimental work which shows that under high ratios of reflectance, subjects are more capable of detecting luminosity from "albedo." Yet it would seem that high-contrast conditions do not provide the basic explanation for constancy but rather specify conditions of phenomenological elaboration.

Separately Illuminated Subfields   The technique of using separately illuminated subfields was introduced by Hsia (1943). The observer is seated in front of two separately illuminated, open-ended chambers, at his right and at his left. At the back of the chambers, some 5½ feet distant, a heavy black drapery is drawn across to provide a common background and eliminate any direct contrast effects. This is a variation of the shadow method, in which the two chambers receive different incident illuminations.

A number of "standard" grays were used in this experiment. The standard gray disk was located in one chamber, and the intensity of the illumination reflected from it was varied by lowering or raising a ceiling light which illuminated this chamber only. The comparison gray disk was always presented in a constant "reference" illumination which was provided by another ceiling lamp. The observer, who could not see the sources of either light, had to make a brightness match of the comparison gray with the standard gray. This was done by adjusting the brightness of the variable disk with the aid of a spotlight. Four experiments were presented under varying illumination intensities, and twelve individuals served as subjects.

A typical result obtained with a standard black of 0.12 albedo is presented in Figure 7-3. It is clear that the actual match fell between the expected whiteness match and the expected illumination match. Although there were wide individual differences, with some observers closer to an illumination match and others showing greater brightness constancy, the average was about midway between the two. If the perception of the standard followed changes in illumination directly, then the actual match should have been close to the illumination match.

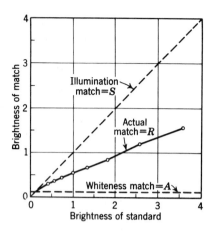

Figure 7-3 Condensation of Hsia's experiment. Whiteness constancy as a function of difference in illumination. *(Modified from Hsia, 1943.)*

If constancy were perfect, then the actual match should have followed the whiteness-match curve. Neither of these results occurred. Instead, we again find partial constancy.

The shadow method, separately illuminated subfields, and the method of illumination perspective all show that moderate brightness constancy can be obtained if the observer has a constant frame of reference which indicates that incident illumination on the two objects is different. In such cases the observer does not compare the two objects directly but judges each one relative to its background. Since the ratio of the object's albedo to its background albedo is constant, the whiteness ratios also are constant. But if the backgrounds are hidden, the subject lacks a constant frame of reference. He then has to compare the absolute reflected light of two objects directly. These luminosities change with changes in incident illumination, and there is no basis for a constancy response. We now turn to the conditions producing such effects.

Destruction of Brightness Constancy under Obscured Illumination Conditions

Katz had argued that constancy is destroyed when surface (object) color and film color are not distinguishable. Another way of stating this proposition would be to say that constancy is destroyed or greatly reduced when the stimulus conditions preclude a perceived separation between the illumination reflected from the total field and that reflected from a specific object—that is, when there is a fusion between luminosity and reflectance. One technique by which this unification of general illumination and object (or surface) color can be achieved is described in this section.

Hering's Fleckschattenversuch (Shadow-spot Experiment) This research on shadow spots was first reported by Ewald Hering. When a small shadow is cast upon a piece of white paper, it looks like a fuzzy gray-shadowed spot, and the part of the paper under it retains its white color. The gray shadow is clearly seen as superimposed on the white paper. But if we now draw a heavy black line around the shadow so that the contour coincides with the shadow's usual penumbra, the white paper in the shadow instantly "turns" gray. Removing the penumbra apparently makes it difficult to detect the shadow as special low-incident illumination. Thus the shadowed part is actually seen as having a darker color; luminosity dominates the perception. Another way of producing the same effect is to create unrecognizable shadows (MacLeod, 1940) or remove the penumbra of a shadow (MacLeod, 1932). Both techniques reduce or destroy brightness constancy. That is to say, we see the *whole* visual space and its subsidiary elements, with their various shades and brightness. "When the reduction screen is used . . . it is to be noted that only unification not a reduction to a more retinal seeing has occurred" (Gelb, 1929, p. 676).

Apropos of Gelb's assertion about field articulation, it is interesting to note that Stewart (1959) found a similar effect by using a somewhat different technique. A very large black disk was presented with a smaller white disk in front of it. On successive trials the size of the white disk as well as its distance from the center of the black disk to the outside of its margin were varied. As might be expected, the black disk looked darker the larger the white disk was, and the closer it was to the center of the black disk.

Stewart's experiment is rather interesting because it suggests that the relationship between unification *(fusion or assimilation)* and articulation *(differentiation or contrast)* is not simple at all but very complex. *Fusion* is facilitated by spatial proximity and extensity, but so, up to a point, is *contrast*. Differentiation is facilitated by heterogeneity as well as by spatial extensity and distance, but again, only to some limit. If the spatial separation between two surfaces is too much, there will not be any interaction or influence at all.

The extent of this complexity is further demonstrated in the experiment of Newson (1958). A gray square suspended by an invisible thread was illuminated by an intense beam of light, and thus appeared white. When another lighter surface was introduced into the beam, the square turned gray. The depressing effect of the inducing surface was greater the closer in contact it was, and the higher its albedo. However, when its reflectance was higher than any other surface in view, it controlled the brightness of the test square, even if it was not in contact with it.

Contributing Field Factors

We have seen how Gelb accounted for brightness constancy in terms of the articulation of the perceptual field. One way of affecting articulation is through contrast, which is illustrated in Figure 7-4, an example of brightness contrast.

Relation of Contrast Effects to Constancy   Some significant studies deal with this complex interaction. First of all, Wallach (1948) and Wallach and Galloway (1946) have attempted to explain brightness and color constancy as aspects of contrast phenomena. A schematic representation of Wallach's experiment is shown in Figure 7-5.

In general, the experiment proceeds in the following manner. By using

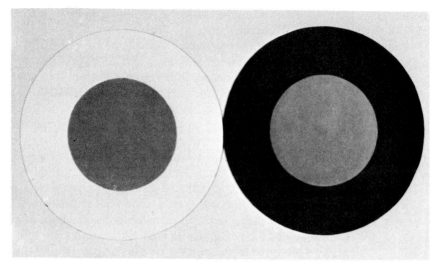

Figure 7-4 Which inner circle looks brighter?

sensitive episcotisters (an episcotister is a device which regulates proportion of whatever is reflected) and projection lanterns, the standard, which consists of a light disk surrounded by a light ring, is presented to the observer. The brightness ratio of the disk and the ring can be set at a fixed value by varying the intensity of light and the episcotister setting. The comparison stimulus is projected on the same background, using the same technique. The comparison ring has a different brightness from that of the ring of the standard, and the observer has to vary the comparison's episcotister setting until the disk appears as bright as the standard. The rest of the room is dark.

In the example shown in Figure 7-5, the ratio of ring to disk was 360:180, or 2:1, for the standard. Wallach predicted that the same ratio should hold for the comparison. Hence, since $2:1 = 180°: x$, $x = 90°$. Four observers actually gave a mean of 85°, which is fairly close to the expected 90°. A number of variations

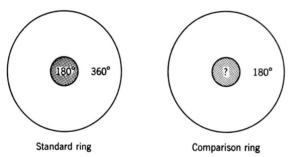

Standard ring   Comparison ring

Figure 7-5 Example of Wallach's experiment (1948). The ratio of surround to standard disk is 2:1. Therefore, expected reflectance for the comparison disk is 90°.

were performed, but the results were basically similar. Thus, our example is fairly typical of Wallach's general findings.

Wallach concludes that brightness constancy and the formation of surface colors are strictly a function of the *intensity ratios* because he found that he could change perceived brightness merely by changing the ratios between two spots of light. If the ring was darkened, the disk appeared to be brightened, and vice versa. Wallach appears to be explaining brightness constancy in terms of contrast factors, as do he and Galloway in their experiment on hue contrast (Wallach & Galloway, 1946).

In another study Wallach (1936) investigated the effects of relative proximity of contrast on constancy and contrast. Alternate light and gray vertical bars were exposed. The subject reported the outer as luminances while the inner ones were not seen as such. However, when the bars were in close contact, only degrees of surface whiteness and grayness were seen. Here is an example where close contact enhances constancy differentiation, while lack of contact enhances luminous contrast.

Finally, Wallach also showed that intensifying the brightness contrast between a chromatic color and its surround also affects the appearance of a hue. For example, an orange disk looks brownish when a ring of light around it is increased in intensity. Similarly, on a very bright day, the blue sky looks "washed out" or quite desaturated. If one now concentrates on a small part of the sky, by, for example, looking at it through a small tunnel made with one's fingers, one will see a bright and rich blue.

Very early in this chapter we saw, in A. A. Landauer's work, that experimental instructions can affect brightness judgments. And we have just seen that viewing attitudes can affect the appearance of hue. A further experimental demonstration that instructional attitudes can affect assimilation and contrast was provided by Mackavey (1969), using Koffka's ring as the target.

First, consider Koffka's ring in the insert in Figure 7-6. We can have a black-white divided ground. Both Koffka (1935) and Helson (1943) had reported that the gray ring will maintain a uniform brightness throughout. It is only when the ring is divided by a line or some other marker that the expected contrast phenomena will be observed—namely, that the part of the ring against the black ground will look white, and vice versa.

Now, Mackavey trained individuals to look at *parts* (ten segments in all) of the ring and make separate brightness judgments for each segment, using a rotating Polaroid filter to make the brightness match. The results are shown in Figure 7-6.

It is interesting to note two important facts: (1) There is a gradient of contrast effects. The gray ring looks *brighter* as we go from the center to the end along the black-ground side. Similarly, it gets *darker* as we go from the center to the end along the white-ground side. (2) The only significant effect of the divider was to eliminate the depression of brightness of the ring as we moved toward the end of the white ground.

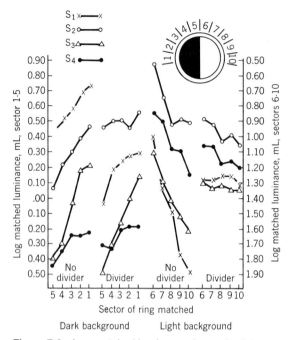

Figure 7-6 Log matched luminance for each of the ten sectors of Koffka's ring shown in the insert. (Matched luminance values for sectors 1 to 5 are to be read from the left-hand scale. Matched luminance values for sectors 6 to 10 are to be read from the right-hand scale. For all sectors 6 to 10 all data for S2 have been displaced downward by 1 log unit, as have the divider data for S4 for sectors 6 to 10. The no-divider data for sectors 6 to 10 for S4 have been displaced downward by 7 log units.) *(After W. R. Mackavey, 1969, p. 407.)*

Ratios Attenuated by Interacting Process The experiments described above, with particular reference to the constant ratios reported by Wallach, presented one object at a time against a background. In everyday life we usually encounter a number of objects of different albedos against a variety of backgrounds. What kind of *approximation* to constancy do we obtain under such conditions? A suggestion of an answer to this question comes from an experiment of Jameson and Hurvich (1961).

In the Jameson and Hurvich experiment a number of adjacent rectangular gray patches of different reflectances were presented simultaneously. While the illumination of the array was varied over one log unit, thus presenting variable luminance of the surround and the patches, the ratios between them remained constant. The subjects were required to match a comparison patch presented in each level of illumination to each of the five test patches. If constancy were to prevail, these matches should be constant, despite variation in the luminance of the surround. This indeed was found to be true for a *middle range of luminance*. When the illumination was larger than this level, there was an increase in the matches of the patches—that is, the surface seemed to get lighter. Of even more significance and surprise was the observation that when the luminance was lower than this level, the patches seemed to *grow darker*.

Hochberg (1971), referring to earlier work of Hering, reasons that a low level of luminance may not be clearly visible, hence the darkening effect. However, Jameson and Hurvich (1964) and Hurvich and Jameson (1966) argue that complex interactions take place between the test field and its surround. The surround induces, through interaction, some kind of opponent process in the test figure. While this theory is supported with corroborating data, it has also met opposition (Flock & Freedberg, 1970; Flock & Noguchi, 1970; Jameson & Hurvich, 1970). Since the controversy is young, we shall not pursue it here. Rather, we go into other research pointing to the complex field factors and stimulus interacting effects influencing brightness constancy and contrast phenomena (see Freeman, 1967, and Hochberg, 1971, for additional discussion of these factors).

CONTEXTUAL FRAMEWORK FOR EVALUATING CONTRAST EXPLANATIONS

It must be clear by now that a variety of factors all interact to determine the main effect of color constancy and its secondary elaborations in the various contrast phenomena. Examples of these interacting cues are relative albedos, cues to the conditions of the illumination, ratio between contiguous light intensities (contrast), spatial proximity, and extensity, and viewing set.

Of all the factors listed above, *viewing set* is probably the most central, under everyday conditions. However, this directional set in color perceptions is primarily organized at level II of the hierarchy—i.e., by the sensory pattern of stimulation. We have seen that this sensory unit or differentiation can be modified by instructional set. This was true in detection and will again be seen to be true in Chapter 12 when we discuss stabilizing of figural differentiation.

To say, however, that attitudinal set can modify sensitivity is a far step from saying that it is a necessary condition for sensory discrimination. In fact, the evidence reviewed so far leaves little doubt that level II organization is all that is necessary for brightness constancy to function. There are, however, a number of complex stimulus factors, such as luminance, size, and spatial distribution which interact with albedo ratios.

One of these complex issues concerns the nature of contact between the surfaces. Some studies have shown that close contact enhances constancy (e.g., Wallach, 1948). Other studies (Henneman, 1935; Hsia, 1943; Katona, 1929; MacLeod, 1940; and Mackavey, 1969, just reported at the end of the previous section) have found, however, that the surround affects constancy even if the figure and ground are not in direct contact, but close enough for the effect to spread. Furthermore, the magnitude of the effect of the surround also depends on its energy level in relation to that of the figure, the sharpness or gradualness of the brightness gradients between the figure and ground, and other related factors as seen in the following experiments.

MacLeod investigated the effect of the magnitude of the brightness gradients between the object and its surround on perceived whiteness constancy (MacLeod, 1947). In his experiment, two overlapping color wheels, the inner one smaller than the outer, were rotated behind a neutral gray disk. They appear as two concentric rings around the disk. The physical brightness of the first wheel was periodically varied, while that of wheel 2 was held constant. When variations of wheel 1 were gradual so that there was a gradual increase in brightness from the disk through ring 1 to ring 2, whiteness constancy was fairly high. When, however, there was a sharp increase in wheel 1, so that it was much brighter than either the disk or wheel 2, whiteness constancy was significantly lowered. Ring 1 was then seen as a sharply demarcated contour around the disk, which appeared to be darkened.

This experiment shows that when changes of brightness in the area between object and general background are gradual, constancy is fair, but when a sharp brightness gradient intervenes between object and background, this gradient creates contrast effects which depress constancy.

The problem of the enhancement or depression of brightness due to the inducing effects of the surrounding field has been more fully investigated. In one report, Diamond (1953) reasoned that previous studies on contrast were hard to assess since the stimulus was presented to both eyes; hence any interaction between the eyes would complicate the data. If in one study the object and its surrounding field were presented to one eye and the comparison object and its surrounding field were presented to a noncorresponding part of the other eye, the interactions between the two retinas could be controlled. Heinemann (1955) used this method in a study diagramed in Figure 7-7. The luminances of the central parts and inducing fields (surrounds) were produced by techniques similar to those employed by Wallach. Monocular presentation was used. The test field T and the inducing field I_1 were presented only to the right eye, and the comparison field C with its inducing field I_2 only to the left eye. The observer had to match the apparent brightness of C and T as I_2 and I_1 were varied.

In the earlier study, which was similar, Diamond found little inducing effect if the inducing-field luminance was *less* than the test-field luminance. For example, if C and I_1 were held constant and I_2 was varied, the expected variation in the equality brightness match on T did not occur if I_2 remained below the luminance of C. In other words, the constancy of the brightness ratio $T/I_1 = C/I_2$ breaks down if the luminances of the inducing fields are below those of the center

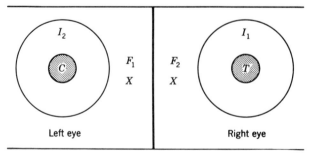

Figure 7-7 The comparison field C, the inducing field I_2, and the fixation point F_2 are presented to subject's left eye only; the test field T, the inducing field I_1, and the fixation point F_1 are presented to the right eye only. *(After Heinemann, 1955.)*

fields. Conversely, the depression of test-field brightness by the inducing field occurs when the luminance of the inducing field is greater than that of the test field.

This result was verified in Heinemann's extended study, which also pointed to new complexities. When the luminance of the inducing field is below that of the test field, the brightness of the test field is increased very slightly. With equality of luminance, the brightness of the test field starts to decrease progressively as the luminance of the inducing field continues to rise. What is most puzzling is that, if we start with a lower inducing-field luminance and gradually increase it, the test field begins to show a depressed brightness even before the inducing-field luminance reaches the level of the test field.

In a second study, Heinemann found other complicating factors, such as how much higher the luminance of the test field was than its surround and whether the comparison field had an inducing field at all. He concluded that the function relating the inducing-field luminance and test brightness is not linear but curvilinear. That is to say, a unit effect is not obtained on the brightness of the test field for every unit change in the luminance of the inducing field. Rather, sometimes there is a very slight change, sometimes no perceptible change, and sometimes a corresponding change. Heinemann concluded that an explanation of these effects should probably be sought at a level above the retina.

Other findings corroborate the complex relationship between perceived brightness of the test field and the luminance differences between the inducing and the test field. Keep in mind that in Heinemann's conditions the induction effect is greatest if the inducing-field luminance is greater than the test-field luminance.

Beck (1966a), using line figures against gray paper backgrounds, found that the figure tended to be assimilated by the background when the latter was lighter, whereas contrast in the figure was enhanced when the background was darker (than the figure). Moreover, repeated judgments (practice effects) have little effect on contrast per se, but reduce assimilation—that is, as darkness and width of line increase, assimilation gives rise to contrast following repeated judgments.

In the next section we see, moreover, that, under the same conditions of stimulation, whether contrast assimilation occurs can be affected by attention. The spatial dimensions seem a little more clearly understood at present. Following the work of MacLeod, Heinemann, Wallach, and others already reviewed, some more recent articles throw further light on the mechanism underlying the influence of proximity.

One interesting study was conducted by Oyama and Hsia (1966) using chromatic colors. In a rather complicated design, the subjects, which consisted of the two experimenters, were required to set a chronometer to the "best" blue, green, yellow, and red. Each of these primary hues constituted the test field, which was exposed with a surrounding inducing field of blue, green, yellow, and red, and with six separations between inducing and test fields (0°, 0.5°, 1°, 2°, 4°, and 8° visual angles). That is, all combinations of four test-field hues, four inducing-field hues, and six separation conditions were completed by each of the two subjects in eight sessions. The separation between the two fields consisted of a black paper ring. During the rest periods a white card was used to maintain light adaptation.

For each test field, a chromatic setting was made before and after exposure in the inducing field. The mean of these settings constituted a reference value for wavelength (λ_0). For each condition or inducing color and separation, the shift of the mean wavelength setting (λ_t) from the reference value (λ_o) was considered as a compensation for the contrast produced by the inducing field on the test field.

Statistical analysis supported two hypotheses in a reliable way: (1) Compensatory shift occurs in the direction of the spectral position of the inducing color. For example, a yellow in a yellow inducing field gives rise to a green test setting. Probably the yellow became bluish because of the contrast of the inducing field. To compensate, the setting had to move from the contrast to the required test-field hue. (2) Color contrast decreases as separation between inducing field and test field increases.

Another study is singled out because it used depth separation rather than the usual two-dimensional separation (see Chapter 13 for discussion of space and depth). The apparatus was so constructed that a circle of lights could be seen in *front* of a darker surround. It was possible to move the figural light to or away from (approaching the subjects) the surrounding ring.

Typical contrast effects were obtained. The dark surround enhanced the lightness of the figural circle of light. Furthermore, this enhancement decreased with increase in depth separation. However, when the stereoscopic depth effect was removed by going from binocular to monocular regard, the decrease did not take place. That is, enhancement was present and uniform, irrespective of the magnitude of physical depth separation. Hence it is perceived or *subjective,* rather than actual, distance which is the effective variable.

The complexity of the spatial proximity variable is also shown in an experiment by Cole and Diamond (1971). A technique somewhat similar to Heinemann's was used. The area of the surround was held constant, but its spatial distribution was varied—that is, it was either a large quadrant spread out to one side of the test field or else it was a concentric circle around the test field. It was found that as long as the distance from the center of the test field to the center of the surround was held constant, the test-field apparent brightness was *not* affected by the amount of inducing field surround. However, the apparent brightness of the test field *increased* significantly as the separation between the centers of the test field and inducing fields was increased. That is, if an inducing field of constant area always borders upon a test field, it will change in *effective separation* from a test field as it changes from an adjacent to a surrounding field. This is because the average distance of the receptor elements in the inducing (retinal) field changes with respect to the elements in the test field (Cole & Diamond, 1971, p. 127). This explanation might be related to the lateral inhibition which is described at the end of this chapter.

To summarize: Constancy results from an interaction between albedo and cues to viewing conditions. Modifying influences are produced by contrast and assimilation. These modifications, in turn, depend on the differences in intensity ratios and spatial factors. *These factors operate through creation of a directional or perceptual set.*

There are a number of other articles which deal with theoretical analysis of contrast, or with investigating the sensory scale of lightness judgments. These references are beyond the scope of this book, but we list them for the interested reader: Diamond (1960, 1962) for theory; Freeman (1967), summarizing and evaluating contrast interpretations of lightness constancy; Tanaka, Uemura, and Torif (1967), testing, in part, the theoretical issues raised by Diamond.

Reflectance Ratios in the Context of the Albedo

The above studies concern reflectance ratios and contrast, but do not relate them to albedo. Hambacher (1956), in a partial replication of Wallach's study (1948), varied the albedos of the disks. An illumination of 100 footcandles was cast on a standard disk with an albedo of 21, and the surround was an albedo of 83. The comparison surround, with an albedo of 42, and its disk were illuminated by 50 footcandles. The rest of the room was dark. The distance between the centers of the two wheels was only 18.25 inches. The observer instructed the experimenter to vary the percentage of white of the variable wheel until it appeared to be as white as that of the standard. If the constancy were perfect, X would be 21. If Wallach's brightness ratio holds, we should have $X/21 = 21/83$ (not $X/42$, since the variable receives only half as much incident light as the standard does). Hence, $X = 5.25$ footcandles (approximately).

In Hambacher's experiment, the albedos of both the standard and the variable stimulus were obtained by overlapping white and black disks. Using an illuminometer, Hambacher stated that a brightness of 5.25 footcandles from the variable disk would require a white sector of 10.56 percent. The mean obtained by eight subjects was actually 15.01 percent. The difference between Wallach's prediction and the obtained value is highly significant and much larger than any reported in his own study. Hambacher thought that the results could be handled better in terms of *whiteness* ratios than *brightness* ratios.

It is an established fact that the function relating perceived whiteness and reflectance (albedo) is not linear. The Munsell achromatic series of equal-whiteness steps takes this relationship into account. The approximate relationship expressed in Table 7-1 contains eleven equal steps of apparent whiteness. If we transform the albedo values in the table into whiteness steps, we have the following:

Standard disk = 21 = 5.13
Standard background = 83 = 9.20
Variable background = 42 = 6.95

The ratio is

$$\frac{X}{6.95} = \frac{5.13}{9.20}$$

**Table 7-1   Relationship between Reflectance (Albedo) and
Whiteness**

Whiteness	Reflectance	Whiteness	Reflectance
0.0	0.00	6.0	0.29
1.0	0.01	7.0	0.42
2.0	0.03	8.0	0.58
3.0	0.06	9.0	0.77
4.0	0.12	9.5	0.88
5.0	0.19	10.0	1.00

Source: After Newhall et al., 1943.

Thus X is 3.88 whiteness, which, when converted back, is 0.1123 reflectance (albedo). Now, the obtained mean white sector on the variable wheel was 15.01 percent, the black disk taking up the remaining 84.99 percent. The fused albedo of this variable wheel was 0.1224, which is not significantly different from the calculated 0.1123.

It is not surprising that albedo plays the vital role in whiteness constancy, since without it we would not have whiteness constancy at all. It is the albedo which is the constant property of the object.

ORGANISMIC FACTORS AND SUBJECTIVE SET

We have already seen from the views and work of such people as A. A. Landauer and R. S. Rodger, Magda Vernon, and W. R. MacKavey that instructional set can influence the perception of brightness. Moreover, we reviewed studies which pointed to the conclusion that whether assimilation or contrast took place depended very heavily on what kind of directional set was created by the stimulating conditions. This raises the more general question of subjective or "experiential" direction of brightness judgments. A brief summary of some pertinent findings follows.

A relevant study was performed by Hochberg and Beck (1954), who found that a *fixed* intensity looks brighter if it comes from a surface *parallel* to the line of sight than if from a surface *perpendicular* to the line of sight. Evidently the brain codes retinal brightnesses within a field context on the basis of experiences in the natural world; but in this coding it cannot break up the sensory pattern as it can in certain conditions of size and shape. How high a level of organization is represented in this coding of the sensory pattern in brightness?

A further study by Beck (1965) showed that whether a surface was divided vertically into two halves or horizontally into two halves makes a difference in contrast phenomena—the fact that there is more contrast between two halves in the vertical orientation could relate to an experiential expectancy that light usually comes "from above." Furthermore, a photograph like that shown in Figure 13-11 will exhibit different light-shade distribution and, therefore, different lightnesses depending on whether the photograph is viewed upright or upside down. A similar explanation concerning assumptions about where the source (or sources) of incident light is was also presented by Beck (1969).

Beck (1971) also presented two objects of individual luminance to subjects. One of the objects acted as a shadow caster. Its brightness appeared to be less bright than the other object—as if the former were in special illumination.

Mershon and Gogel (1970) have shown that even the spatial proximity effect is subject to these experientially related cues. They duplicated the Gelb experiment reported at the beginning of this chapter. However, there were three conditions: the Gelb condition, another condition in which the comparison paper was spatially removed from the black disk and viewed binocularly, and a repeat of condition 2 but viewed monocularly. Conditon 3 gave the same result visually as the Gelb condition. However, the effect of the white paper on lowering the brightness of the disk to its objective black was *less* in the binocular-depth condition. It is as if the fact that the white reference paper was nearer to the subject had the effect of making it "have to be white." Actually in this effect, the black disk looked less black.

Finally, in studying the contrast-assimilation phenomenon with a disk surrounded by an inducing field, Festinger, Conen, and Reven (1970) found that contrast will only be effected when the disk is focused upon. Otherwise, assimilation takes place—that is, the surround will "absent" the figure. The theory is that the visual system transmits information about *changes* that are on the retina, not about steady states. Absolute brightness levels are arrived at by averaging over the entire visual field. Moreover, those areas to which the observer pays attention are overweighted in arriving at the average, absolute, brightness level.

A more technical theoretical analysis and critique of spatial location influence on brightness judgment is presented in a sophisticated experiment by Flock and Freedberg (1970).

To go to developmental experience, most of the phylogenetic and ontogenetic data indicate that whiteness constancy is organized at a fairly primitive level (Brunswik, 1929); for example, it is present in fish and very young children. As shown by Brunswik, however, some developmental modification does take place. What the organism possibly learns can be inferred from a comparison of two studies performed by Burzlaff (1931).

In the first study Burzlaff used the method of illumination perspective, just as Brunswik had done. Forty-eight grays, ordered in equal brightness steps, were placed far from the window. Each of the better-illuminated grays was designated as the standard at different times. Using the method of constant stimuli, the observer considered all the grays of the near series, comparing their whiteness with that of the distant series. Despite the fact that the distant grays received only one-twentieth as much illumination, the matches showed near equality. About 90 percent constancy was obtained for all subjects, and there was no difference between 4-, 5-, 6-, and 7-year olds and adults. The curve relating age to percentage of constancy was practically a straight line, parallel to the age scale. Two features of this experiment should be noted: (1) The observers had an immediate scale on which to base their discrimination, which is probably why the percentage of constancy was unusually high. Recall the use of color wheels by Landauer and Rodger which, by contrast, did little to constancy. (2) The gray paper had good microstructure.

In a second study Burzlaff used a similar method but this time employed color wheels for the standard and the variable; i.e., he used the method of adjustment. In this case he found two important results. When the standard was more than 6 percent white, constancy was low for both children and adults: about 22 percent for the 6-year-olds and younger children and about 32 percent for the 7-year-olds and adults. But when the standard was 51 percent white, there was a sharp increase, ranging from 30 to 85 percent, in whiteness constancy for the 5- to 7-year-olds and adults. Whatever development took place in whiteness constancy was completed by the time the child was *7 years old.*

Beck (1966) compared children between 5 and 6½ years of age with adults in lightness discrimination. The study, performed in a dark room, showed that adults were more stable about the judgments they made. Note again that a dark room is more ambiguous and, therefore, leaves more scope for experiential intervention.

Physiological Explanation

Cornsweet (1970, pp. 371–373), in addition to other theorists, has attempted to explain brightness constancy in terms of lateral inhibition and logarithmic transformations. His first assertion is that, early in the process of brightness excitation, there is a logarithmic transformation of excitation. This transformation is given by the equation

$$e = K \log (LR)$$

where e is the excitation input to the lateral inhibitory system, K is a constant of proportionality, L is the intensity of incident illumination, and R is the albedo (reflectance) of the object.

Suppose we apply this formula to the case of two objects whose albedos are 0.80 and 0.10 in an illumination of 1,000 units. Then,

$$e_1 = K \log (1,000 \times 0.80) = 2.9 \, K$$
$$e_2 = K \log (1,000 \times 0.10) = 2.0 \, K$$

Now let us double the illumination:

$$e_1 = K \log (2,000 \times 0.80) = 3.2 \, K$$
$$e_2 = K \log (2,000 \times 0.10) = 2.3 \, K$$

Therefore, we have increased each e by the same amount, in this case, 0.3 K.

Since the excitation input is the same, the lateral inhibition (always directly proportional to excitation) will also be the same—they cancel one another. Hence, constancy prevails.

As ingenious as Cornsweet's explanation is, it can tell us about only the basic cellular process. Such factors as "cues to conditions of illumination," which fit more into the realm of cognitive expectancy, must still be taken into account.

SUMMARY

The studies reviewed, which used primarily the psychophysical methods of adjustment and constant stimuli, suggest that brightness constancy operates because the organism responds innately to differences between the intensity of reflected light relative to the intensity of pooled reflected light coming from a common background or frame of reference.

If the common background is missing, or illumination conditions are such as to preclude this relative perception, then illumination matches based on absolute differences between the intensities are made.

The theory offered to explain these facts is based on the ratios of reflected light, taking into account albedo and absolute intensity. It also subsumes color-contrast phenomena.

Brightness constancy is a sensory fact, not appreciably affected by learning; that is, the organism does not have to learn to respond to *relative differences* between the reflectance of each object and its background (instead of absolute differences between the two objects). Although the observer responds innately to this relation between the object and background reflectance, the accuracy with which the ratio is matched is affected by field experiences in the natural world and by attitudinal set. We can, however, account for the basic process of brightness constancy in terms of lateral inhibition.

How Size and Shape Constancy
Are Mediated

In order for adaptive behavior to exist, the perceived world must be predictable. Yet space-time relationships vary as a function of distance and orientation. The problem of size and shape constancy is to explain how perceived size and shape remain constant despite variations in retinal size and shape with distance and orientation, respectively.

Now in order for the perceived size and shape to approximate constancy, it follows, from the last paragraph, that *the perceiver must have mechanisms for accommodating these spatial variations*. As has so beautifully been stated by one of the most original thinkers among perceptual researchers, "The brain must function in such a way that these environmental vicissitudes are allowed for, or in some way enter into the process of underlying perception" (Rock, 1970, p. 254). Understanding how these accommodations are effected constitutes the study of size and shape constancy.

NATURE OF SIZE CONSTANCY

The objective match in size constancy, as we could see from the first experiment in Chapter 7, appears to be an estimation in which judgment plays an important role. In this judgment or estimation, the subject must be relating visual angle to some other variable which he ignores in the retinal match. This "something" which he takes into account appears to be the fact that the retinal size decreases as a function of distance (this view has caused debate with which we deal later). If this statement is correct, we can predict that objective-size constancy should *decrease* as we decrease cues to the estimation of distance. That is, the size of the retinal image alone provides ambiguous information about the objective size of an object. This uncertainty is reduced as more cues to distance are provided, and the objective size becomes more available to the perceiver.

Determination of Size Constancy

Perhaps a concrete example will help us to understand the situation in size constancy. Let us suppose that a stake whose objective size, *AC*, is 20 feet is moved from a spot just in front of the subject so that it is four times as far away. Since its distance has increased by four times, its relative retinal size *(AR)* will have been reduced to one-fourth of its original size, that is, from *AC* to *AR*, or, in our example, from 20 to 5 feet.

Clearly, if the person judges the new size to be only 5 feet, then constancy would be 0. If he judged it to be 20 feet, then constancy would be perfect. Let *AP* represent the perceived or judged size. As *AP* approaches *AR*, constancy approaches 0; as *AP* approaches *AC*, constancy approaches 1.

It is not necessary to think that the perceiver first senses the retinal size and then converts it to the objective size by taking distance into account. In fact, this probably does not happen, since Brunswik (1944) has found that there is more variability in retinal than in objective judgments. We simply mean that the subject can separate retinal-size information from distance information even though the ordinary viewer is not usually aware of doing this. Certain individuals, such as artists, who adopt a more analytical attitude, do frequently separate retinal size and retinal distance. We shall return to this point later.

Measurement of Size Constancy and the Brunswik Ratio

In Figure 8-1, we have schematically diagramed the typical size-constancy experiment. The subject, who is located at *A*, observes an upright standard stake, 50 centimeters high, situated at *C*, 500 centimeters away. A series of stakes of variable heights is located at *B*, 100 centimeters away. The subject has to judge which variable stake has the same height as the standard stake. Suppose that he chooses a stake of 46 centimeters. This is an application of the method of constant stimuli. How much constancy exists?

One measure is the Brunswik (1929) ratio. BR= $(P - R)/(C - R)$, where $R=$ relative retinal size, C = objective size, and P = perceived size. Brunswik

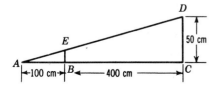

Figure 8-1 The components for measuring size constancy. Although the relative retinal image size is *EB*, size constancy requires a perception of objective size, *CD*.

reflects the extent to which perceived size approximates objective size. Thouless (1931a, 1931b) uses logarithmic transformations. In the above example, the relative retinal size $R = 10$, since at 500 centimeters the size will be $\frac{1}{5}$ that of 100 centimeters, or $\frac{1}{5}$ of 50, which is 10. Therefore (the Brunswik ratio):

$$\frac{P - R}{C - R} = \frac{46 - 10}{50 \quad 10} = \frac{36}{40} = 0.9 \text{ or } 90 \text{ percent}$$

We pointed out that the individual can make an adequate judgment of object size only if he has cues to the relative distance of the object from him. We must now examine this important aspect of size constancy.

Relationship between Perceived Size and Physical Distance

As we have noted, it is an established law that the retinal size of an object is inversely proportional to its distance from the eyes. Hence, if R equals the retinal size, C the object size, and D the distance, then $R = C/D$, or $C = RD$.

If the subject has no way of judging D, then C will be judged in terms of R, the retinal size, and constancy will be poor. The better his judgment of distance, the better should he be able to perceive the true, objective size C. The important condition exists when the subject judges the size of an unfamiliar object. (Familiar objects are perceived from memory.) In this case he must use D if he hopes to judge C fairly accurately. This is neatly shown in a very ingenious experiment performed by Holway and Boring (1941) which supports the *size-distance invariance hypothesis*. This hypothesis states that, for the perception of objective size to remain constant, the product of perceived retinal size and perceived distance must be constant ($OS = RS \times D = K$). The experimental arrangement of Holway and Boring is shown in Figure 8-2.

The experiment was conducted as follows. The subject sat at the intersection of two corridors. Down one corridor he could see a spot of light, Ss, which was projected by the projector P. This spot always subtended a visual angle of 1°, even though its distance from the subject was moved between 10 and 120 feet.

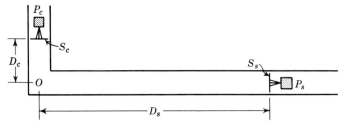

Figure 8-2 Plan view of the corridors. S_c indicates the position of the comparison stimulus located at a constant distance ($D_c = 10$ feet) from O. S_s a distance D_s from O indicates one of the positions occupied by the standard stimulus. The standard stimulus always subtended a visual angle of 1°. Distance from O to the standard was varied from 10 to 120 feet. P_c and P_s indicate the position of the projectors. *(After Holway and Boring, 1941.)*

This could easily be done, of course, merely by altering the opening of the projector. The spot of light on the variable, Sc, was adjusted to match the apparent size of the standard, Ss, at each distance of the latter. Functions relating apparent size to distance were obtained from five subjects, using the method of repeated adjustments, under four sets of conditions. The conditions were created to produce successive decreases in distance or depth cues, as follows: (1) binocular viewing, in which the subject viewed with two eyes; (2) monocular viewing which reduced depth cues by eliminating binocular disparity; (3) monocular viewing through an artificial pupil (the latter, cutting down the surround, reduced the depth cues further); and (4) monocular viewing through an artificial pupil and a long, black reduction tunnel, stretching from the subject to the standard stimulus, and eliminating most of the visual spatial frame of reference. The results of this experiment are presented in Figure 8-3.

The following factors are relevant when interpreting the results. Since the visual angle was held constant, one would expect the function relating size to distance to be a line parallel to the abscissa, as shown in the lower dotted line in the graphs of Figure 8-3. This would hold if the apparent size were based only on the visual angle or the size of the retinal image. In size constancy, however, the function relating size to distance would be represented by the upper dotted line in the graphs of Figure 8-3. This line is derived from trigonometric or geometric functions, from which it can be shown that a 1° angle will be projected from a size 8½ inches at 40 feet, 17 inches at 80 feet, and 25½ inches at 120 feet.

With binocular viewing, in the presence of good depth cues, size constancy was very good—a slight overconstancy existed. As depth cues were progres-

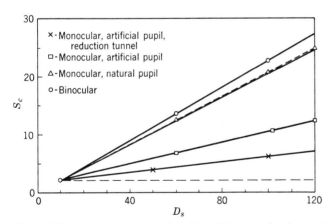

Figure 8-3 Apparent size as a function of distance for four sets of conditions. The figure is based on the averages of all the data obtained in the present experiment. The slope of the functions relating apparent size to distance diminishes continuously as the mode of regarding the stimuli is altered from direct binocular observation to monocular observation through the artificial pupil and a long black reductional tunnel. As the number of extraneous cues is diminished, the slope of the function approaches zero as a limit; i.e., it approaches the law of visual angle. The top broken line represents prediction from the law of size constancy; the bottom one represents prediction from the law of visual angle. (*After Holway and Boring, 1941.*)

sively reduced, size constancy progressively diminished toward the size of the retinal image. We can thus conclude that the unobscured judgment of distance is a necessary condition for adequate size estimation.

Hastorf and Way (1952) were concerned that Holway and Boring obtained any constancy at all in condition 4 described above. The actual computed constancy ratios were 1.09, 0.98, 0.44, and 0.22 for conditions 1, 2, 3, and 4, respectively. They noted that the reflected light present in the Holway and Boring experiment might have produced some cue to distance. Consequently, they conducted the experiment under monocular regard in a black-painted, unilluminated room. In their first experiment they presented circular light areas at four different distances but with the same visual angle as in Holway and Boring's experiment. The match followed the law of visual angle. In experiment 2 the light at four different distances had the same objective size. Again the matches followed the law of visual angle. In both experiments the authors were successful in reducing the constancy ratio to zero. Thus size constancy is determined by complex factors.

The size-distance invariance hypothesis has generated much research and controversy. Many studies have produced supportive data. For example, Gogel and Koslow's (1971) experiment has generated data showing that estimates of size are more accurate when distance cues give good perception of distance. As cues to distance are reduced, so is the perception of size. This supports the size-distance invariance hypothesis. The data of Teghtsoonian and Teghtsoonian (1970), in which magnitude estimates of both size and distance were the dependent measures, also support the size-distance invariance hypothesis in a general way.

However, Weintraub and Gardner (1970) have warned that the size-distance invariance hypothesis, also called Emmert's law, operates quite differently under two conditions. The law of retinal size ($RS = OS/D$) holds with great accuracy. However, the law of the size constancy is subject to a variety of factors. In their experiment they demonstrated that falsifying cues to space will alter phenomenal distance, and thus phenomenal size. The research discussed in the next section indicates that *two mechanisms*—one inborn and the other affected by experience—can be used to categorize the factors which affect the perception of objective size.

How the Distance Variable Is Involved

The ability to abstract the stable qualities of environmental objects is necessary for adequate orientation to the environment. Whether this ability is innate or learned has been debated since the arguments of Hering and Helmholtz, the former favoring a nativistic position, the latter an empiricist interpretation. Gestalt psychology favored the former.

Rock (1970, pp. 241–282), after commenting on the lack of specificity in the gestalt explanation, discusses, in very involved ways, how complex and multidetermined the operation of constancy probably is.

In the course of developing a cognitive theory of perceptual constancy,

Rock points out that any knowledge which might be used to stabilize perception does not have to be learned. Furthermore, the individual might have the ability to perceive both objective size and visual angle directly, in which case the requirement of transforming visual angle into objective size, by taking distance into account, would not be needed.

Rock and McDermott (1964) report that subjects will give ambiguous estimates of both retinal size and distance under reduced conditions. Moreover, they were also capable of giving different matches between an object viewed under reduced conditions and another object located at two different positions and viewed binocularly. They thus conclude that subjects are capable of estimating retinal size directly and can also ignore knowledge of objective size if that is the attitude they are adopting. Subjects, like artists, can be trained to judge retinal size quite accurately.

It is important to notice that there is controversy about whether subjects can judge distance under reduced conditions. Gogel (1970) has concluded that when objects are located close to each other under reduced conditions, subjects will perceive size as if the distance were equal. This was not so in the Rock and McDermott experiment because subjects had to turn their heads through 90° to make their matches. Thus the distance judgments were ambiguous.

It seems evident from the preceding findings that the relationship between objective size, retinal-image size (visual angle), and distance in perception is probably more differentiated than any competing traditional theories postulated.

In a very careful and creative analysis, Oyama (1974) varied visual angle and convergence while keeping the stimulus at the same distance and controlling for other relevant variables. There were five conditions for visual angle (size) which varied from 1° to 3°. There were also six conditions of convergence angle, from 1° to 4°. The dependent measures were judged size and judged distance.

Judged size was proportional to visual angle—that is, perceived size increased as a linear function of increased visual angle. Conversely, perceived size decreased linearly as convergence increased. This is understandable. If the stimulus size remained the same and the object was seen as coming nearer (because of increased convergence), it would have to appear to be getting smaller.

Judged distance decreased as a function of both increased convergence and visual angle. That is as it should be, since objects get bigger and convergence increases as objects approach the perceiver.

The question about the relationship between size and distance was more complex. The ratio of perceived size to perceived distance was constant—a finding consistent with the size-distance invariance hypothesis. However, the correlation between perceived size and distance when visual angle and convergence varied was zero. It was only when *one* of these variables was held constant that a significant correlation between size and distance was obtained. These findings plus more sophisticated analysis to determine the order of relationship led Oyama to conclude that size and distance are not directly correlated.

Rather, the size-distance effect exists because both are related to other variables such as convergence and visual angle. This is in keeping with the view of Gruber presented later in this chapter.

The relation between distance and size perception was further investigated by Broota and Epstein (1973). They found that, under reduced conditions, it always took longer to make a size judgment as the distance increased. However, there was no corresponding increase in the judgment of distance, but the distance judgment always took a shorter time.

The complexities of the way distance might mediate size perception is further complicated by the existence of innate and learned cues. Bower (1964, 1965, 1966a, 1966b) reports the existence of size constancy in 2-month-old infants. In the earlier Bower studies, motion parallax, an innate cue (see Chapter 13), was probably an important factor which enabled distance perception and, thus, size constancy. In more recent work, Bower et al. (1970) have also shown that even in 9-day-old infants cues to depth, such as optical expansion of approaching objects, already function effectively.

Leibowitz (1971) has couched pertinent research on innate and learned determiners of size constancy in the theoretical formulation of von Holst and Mittelstaedt (1950). These investigators have claimed that the individual can distinguish between changing stimulation which results from movement of the stimulus and that which results from movement of the individual or parts of his body (e.g., eye movements). The principle governing the former is called *exafference*, while that governing the latter is *reafference*.

Leibowitz creatively applies the reafference principle to cues to distance variation, which are effective at rather short distances. These cues, listed in order of distances (short to longer) at which they are effective, are accommodation, convergence, and binocular disparity (we shall call them *organismic* cues).

In a specific experiment, Harvey and Leibowitz (1967)—in a usual kind of size-constancy measurement, using the method of adjustment—had adult subjects set a variable rod to equivalence with a standard rod under unrestricted and reduction screen vision. Under the latter condition, only the short-distance cues can function—i.e., the other cues such as texture, density, and pattern gradients cannot function (see Chapter 13). The results of the experiment are shown in both parts of Figure 8-4. Notice that there is no difference between the two conditions up to 120 centimeters, both giving perfect constancy. After that there is very good constancy for the unrestricted condition, with a much lower degree of constancy under the restricted condition.

Suggestion that these organismic cues are more nativistic, while the pattern cues are developed through experience (and therefore founded in learning), can be seen when we compare the graphs in Figure 8-4 with the age-distance curves of Zeigler and Leibowitz (1957) presented in Figure 8-7 toward the end of this chapter. Note that there is no difference between children and adults at the short distance. It is only with longer distances that the adults became increasingly superior to the children. A logical deduction from these two sets of data would be that children and adults, being equally good at short distances, are equally

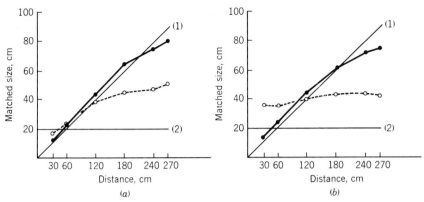

Figure 8-4 (a) Matched size as a function of distance with unrestricted vision (solid lines) and with a reduction screen (dashed lines), under continuous (top graph) and short-duration (bottom graph) illumination. (1) Prediction based on the law of size constancy. (2) Prediction based on the law of retinal image. (b) Matched size as a function of distance with unrestricted vision (solid lines), and with a reduction screen (dashed lines), under continuous (top graph) and short-duration (bottom graph) illumination. (1) Prediction based on the law of size constancy. (2) Prediction based on the law of the retinal image. *(After Harvey & Leibowitz, 1967, p. 252.)*

effective in utilizing reafference organismic cues to generate the objective size. More experience or learning would be needed to utilize pattern cues to distance to generate objective size at longer distance.

Methods and Attitudes Affect Size-Distance Relationships

The variations reported in the last section depend, in part, on methods used and what the subject is focusing upon. Thus, in his *ecological research* Brunswik (1944) found that average errors were much greater for estimates of retinal size than for estimates of distance and object size. Different ways of measuring the three parameters were used. Also Gruber (1954), in a laboratory setting, found that the different constant error for distance and size estimates were not in accordance with the size-distance hypothesis. The controversy and equivocal findings stem from three sources: Different ways of obtaining the subject's response are used, different investigators interpret these various meanings of size and its relation to distance in different ways, and instructions given to the subject are not always clear enough. The subject might have doubt about what is expected from him, or the procedure used under one condition might give rise to greater error than that used under another analysis.

As an example of the above, we recall that Gilinsky (1955) found that subjects could give separate and quite reliable judgments of objective and retinal sizes under nonreduced conditions. Furthermore, Jenkin and Hyman (1959), after correlating and factor-analyzing judgments given under retinal and objective instructions, established that there was no significant relationship between these two (and, therefore, independent) responses.

When we add the third variable, distance, the picture becomes even more complex. We have already reported Brunswik's finding that objective-size judgments were more accurate than retinal-size judgments. In addition, objective-size judgments were reliably correlated with real, not judged distance. Furthermore, V. R. Carlson (1960) finds that both objective-size judgments and projective-size judgments correlate reliably with distance judgments, but that apparent-size judgments do not. (*Apparent size* refers to the way the size appears; i.e., it is usually a compromise between projected size, which is visual angle, and objective size.) The following issues suggest themselves. Firstly, Carlson's study was closer to laboratory conditions and used shorter distances than Brunswik's ecological research. Secondly, subjects might have a hard time knowing the meaning of apparent size. Thirdly, since distance judgments of nearer positions are more reliable than those of points farther away, one is more likely to get accurate perceptions of the relationship between distance and various aspects of size for the shorter ranges.

In a related study, Carlson and Tassore (1967) verified that apparent-size instructions do not produce as stable results as either objective- or projective-size instructions. All three instructions were effective in producing very different size judgments, consistent with previous findings. The distances, however, were much shorter, being 10, 20, 30, and 40 feet. During the first four trials, separated by about a week, the subject was presented with the standard at only one distance. On the fifth day, he was presented with standards at all the distances. What is interesting is that there was more relationship (consistent with size-distance invariancy) between size and distance on the fifth day than during the first four days. (As might be expected, apparent size still showed no stable relationship.) This suggests either the positive influence of practice or the contextual effect of a distance series, when the latter is presented in a close span of time.

The fact that instructions make such a powerful difference and that training improves the expected relationship between distance and size (projected and objective) led Carlson to conclude that there is little basis for assuming that individuals vary in the degree of size constancy they possess. Rather, they differ in the extent to which they judge a verbal concept. These differences are more related to cognition, attitude, and motivation.

If, indeed, we are dealing with assumptive and conceptual processes, there is no reason to expect automatic relationships between size and distance. Sometimes they will be consistent with one another, sometimes they will not, depending on the subject's set, on the methods of measurement or analysis employed by the experimenter, or on both.

Relevant to the last factor mentioned, we can point to a dispute between two research teams as typical of the kind of controversy which is grounded in attitude rather than irrefutable objective fact.

Following a demonstration by Epstein and Landauer (1969) that estimates of size and distance could be obtained in the absence of distance cues, Landauer and Epstein (1969) presented, under reduced conditions, a disk at four distances so that visual angles of 8, 4, 2, and 1° were projected. They asked subjects to estimate size and distance by choosing a match from a variety of familiar objects as outlined in Table 8-1. The results were that estimated size went up proportionally with increase in visual angle, whereas the estimated distance decreased proportionally.

These results are different in one respect from those of Gogel (1969). He presented, also under reduced conditions, three different-size objects at the same distance. He found that the estimated visual angle varied systematically with the three different-size objects, but that estimated distance did not. It is the last finding that Landauer and Epstein see as contradictory to their own; they also regard these results as inconsistent with the size-distance invariance hypothesis, while they see Gogel's as consistent with it. But is that really the case? Let us see.

Objective size equals visual angle times distance. Therefore, as visual angle goes up, distance goes down, and vice versa. That is exactly what Landauer and Epstein found. Since there were no cues to either objective size or distance, the left side of the equation is nonexistent. The subject was operating with the right side—that is, using visual angle as a cue to distance and doing it reliably. Gogel (1971) also analyzes the theory and data to conclude that the results are consistent with the size-distance invariance hypothesis, in a way consistent with our explanation which follows.

As far as Gogel's (1969) experiment is concerned, it is important to note that the three different-size objects were actually located at the same distance. The

Table 8-1   Items on the Equal Step Size and Distance Scales on which Subjects Located Their Judgments.
The Scale Values in Parentheses (Millimeters for Size, Centimeters for Distance) Did Not Appear on the Scale Shown to Subject

Size judgments	Distance judgments
Pinhead (1)	Length of finger (8)
Nail head (4)	Span of hand (18)
Small shirt or blouse button (8)	Length of a 12-inch ruler (31)
Dime (17)	Length of extended arm (65)
Quarter (22)	Span of both arms extended (140)
Half dollar (31)	Length of a bed (200)
Ping-pong ball or golf ball (43)	Length of standard Chevrolet car (350)
Tennis ball (64)	Length of large station wagon (500)
Baseball (73)	Length of a bus (1,100)
Large grapefruit (130)	Width of State Street (1,600)
Bowling or volleyball (220)	Width of a football field (4,900)
Large L.P. record (305)	Length of a football field (9,200)
Car wheel (450)	
Bus wheel (900)	

Source: Landauer and Epstein, 1969.

finding, therefore, that visual angle in this case did not give the illusion of varying distance would be connected with the fact that the subject was always focusing at the same point—distance did not vary. Only such a convergence could have provided information about this condition. Recall that the principle of reafference by Leibowitz holds that these innate mechanisms work at short distances.

If we want the total size-distance relationship to be provided, one is best off with *providing a number of cues* and then varying the distances or the way the cues are presented. Such variation is reported by Blessing, Landauer, and Coltheart (1967).

In Blessing's experiment, it was decided to vary apparent distance in two conditions by creating false-perspective cues. This was done by having the subject look at the standard (a rectangle) through two tunnels, each of which had the same length of 450 centimeters. Tunnel A was falsely made to appear shortened by making the viewing end 25 by 25 centimeters, while tunnel B appeared longer with a viewing end of 75 by 75 centimeters; the far end of each tunnel was 50 centimeters. Moreover, the inside of each tunnel had eleven lines of uneven width, unevenly spaced to augment the illusion that tunnel A was shorter and tunnel B longer.

Using the method of adjustment for both size and distance, each subject made four adjustments of the variable for the size and distance of the standard rectangle located at the far end of each tunnel. The results for the thirty subjects indicated that both the judged distance and judged size were lower in tunnel A than tunnel B. The differences were statistically significant.

These findings are consistent with the size-distance invariance hypothesis. Since the visual angle was constant, the perception of greater distance would obviously lead to the perception that the objective size was bigger, and vice versa.

The correlation between judged size and judged distance for the thirty subjects was close to the line of best fit for a linear relationship. The correlation is positive and significant.

Naturalistic Research Further Considered: Attitude and Information

The research discussed so far makes it clear that there is a relationship between objective size and distance. Perception of these two variables at short distances is accurate. When distances get larger or when we use reduced conditions, we might confuse the subject; *the subject's assumptions are always crucial.* This is clearly seen when we vary distance and the richness or reliability of distance cues. Some additional findings comparing naturalistic and experimental research, and showing the effect of instructions, are relevant to this point.

In a very insightful analysis Leibowitz and Harvey (1967) pinpoint a seeming paradox in the study of size constancy and distance perception. What is the ostensible paradox? It is that size constancy demands *invariant size* over distance and yet *decrease in size* is used as a cue to distance. Both the ability to perceive objective size and the ability to respond to changes in distance are, significantly enough, important aspects of adaptive behavior.

When we look at the problem from the perspective of *what the person is trying to do,* the paradox resolves itself. We have already seen from a number of studies (Gilinsky, Carlson & Gogel) that, when so instructed, subjects are able to show (in their size judgments) that they can see the retinal size decrease with distance. Since this has to be a reversible function, it therefore is quite clear that the subject can use relative (retinal) size as a cue to distance, if the latter is the task upon which he is focused. Leibowitz and Harvey (1967) present additional evidence that in a natural surround "apparent-size instructions" do produce matches much closer to retinal than object size (Brunswik ratios in the order of 0.36 and below), and that apparent-size judgments do decrease as a function of distance. (They used distances of 400 to 1,100 feet in a natural terrain on a college campus.)

In the experimental situation, when we give "objective size instructions," we are essentially asking the subject to ignore retinal, apparent, or phenomenal size. In such cases, depending on viewing distance and presenting conditions, subjects will use the cumulative effect of distance cues—oculomotor adjustment, binocular disparity, contextual effects, familiarity, and pattern gradients—to make a judgment of objective size. Leibowitz and Harvey (1969) have found that the judgments of a familiar object (a human being) will be closer to the predicted outcomes for all three types of instructions than the judgments of a less familiar object (a board). Moreover, using the method of limits, Leibowitz and Harvey showed, in a dramatic demonstration, that a natural terrain, "rich" in distance cues, produces judgments closer to objective size, under all three conditions of instructions, than a natural environment "poor" in distance cues. The results of this experimental demonstration are presented in Figure 8-5.

In discussing the work of Leibowitz and Harvey, we saw, in one set of experiments, that familiarity does aid in the accuracy with which objective size is

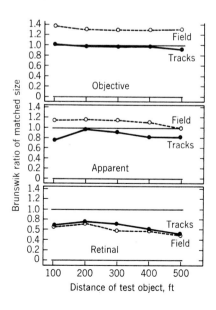

Figure 8-5 *Leibowitz and Harvey (1969).*

judged. Corroborating evidence is reported by Bolles and Bailey (1956). An experiment by Schiffman (1967) throws additional light on this variable because it indicates that the *effect of familiarity is influenced by other information—giving cues in the stimulating environment.*

In Schiffman's experiment, the sizes of six familiar objects—a cigarette package, playing card, toilet roll, examination booklet, manila folder, and magazine cover—were compared with those of six identical off-size objects (three larger and three smaller) and six unfamiliar objects whose sizes were equated with the off-size objects. Comparisons between these three sets of objects were obtained under three viewing conditions—near, far, and far-reduced.

The results are highly informative. *Under the near-viewing condition,* two-thirds of the differences between familiar and off-size objects were statistically significant, whereas none of the estimates between off-size and unfamiliar (equated in size) were. In this case, therefore, information provided by the stimulus conditions and distance cues played the decisive role.

In the far-viewing condition, only two of the comparisons between familiar and off-size objects were significantly different, whereas two-thirds of the differences between off-size and unfamiliar were statistically significant. Similarly, under far-reduced conditions, two-thirds of the latter comparisons were, i.e., between off-size and unfamiliar, statistically different, whereas more of the differences between familiar and off-size were significant. Clearly, as we move from near to far to far-reduced, the information in the stimulus field becomes less dependable, and thus the subjects rely more on familiarity and memory.

It must be clear by now that a variety of stimulus-presenting (situational) conditions and organismic factors can influence the perception of size and distance. Some other situational factors should be noted. Leibowitz, Bussey, and McGuire (1957) and Weber and Bicknall (1935) report that constancy is better with real objects than photographic reproductions. Moreover, the latter study found that this three-dimensional stereoscopic presentation improves constancy—even helps size constancy. Also, the transactionalists, e.g., Kilpatrick and Ittelson (1953), emphasized that subjective or afferent distance rather than real distance can influence perceived size. For example, if accommodation is paralyzed by atropine injection, perceived size is reduced.

The transactionalists have, indeed, demonstrated the complex aspects of cues even as primitive as accommodation and convergence. Other investigators have reported that the effects of convergence are neither uniform nor universal. For example, Richards (1971) has found that about 67 percent of the subjects exhibited a strong effect of convergence on perceived size and distance. The relative reduction or increases in convergence, over the entire range, was never greater than a factor of 1 in 4, so it cannot account for all size constancy.

Moreover, Leibowitz, Shiina, and Hennessy (1972) showed that oculomotor cues are effective only at very short distances. Accommodation was accurate up to 1 meter; beyond that distance underaccommodation occurred.

Cognitive and Physiological Mechanisms   At longer distances (more than 1 meter) a variety of perspective, pattern, and other cognitive factors are influential. Vogel and Teghtsoonian (1972) studied the effect of three viewing conditions on size and distance judgments: converging walls, parallel walls, and diverging walls. By comparison with the parallel-wall condition, distance was 1.4 as big for the converging condition, but only 0.95 as big for the diverging condition. However, the relationship for size was not as uniform. There was no significant effect for the first condition, but the apparent size decreased with apparent distance in the diverging condition. The authors note that, for each condition, the ratio of apparent size to apparent distance (S/D) was a monotonic increasing function of visual angle, but the rate of growth varied among the three conditions. Thus the size-distance invariance hypothesis is not a sufficient explanation of their data.

From the above it is evident that perspective cues are complex and important (see also Chapter 13). Carlson and Tassore (1971) have also found that differences between perceived height and distance of two objects (a human being and a board) were consistent with the perspective attitude but not the size-distance invariance hypothesis.

Moreover, Coltheart (1970), increasing our knowledge of cognitive influence, has shown that *verbal* information about size enables subjects to estimate distance, when viewing a blank triangle under completely reduced conditions.

Finally, Humphrey and Weiskrantz (1969) found that partial lesions in the posterior (back) part of a monkey's cortex produced no deficit in size constancy. However, lesions in the inferotemporal (bottom) lobe caused severe breakdown in size constancy, with almost no recovery. These researchers reasoned that the inferotemporal lesions interfere with the organism's ability to relate distance and size perception—that is, they process each area separately. This is an intriguing and plausible notion given the complex research findings we have reported earlier in this chapter.

Conclusions on Size Constancy

Unlike the situation of brightness constancy, in the judgment of size we can get either a constancy (objective) or retinal (visual angle) match, depending on instructions or the attitude of the viewer.

At short distances the estimation of visual angle, objective size, and distance are accurate and regulated by *innate, reafferent* principles such as accommodation, convergence, and binocular disparity. At further distances these oculomotor factors are not very effective, and learned, exafferent patterned cues are necessary. Whereas for distances, the correlation between objective size and real (measured) distance is positive, all other correlations are low. This is probably because the error in visual angle, perceived size, and distance becomes greater. In this case attitude and familiarity become more important, and providing "rich" distance cues aids accuracy.

Apparent distance is dependent on a number of interacting factors. Experiments have shown that apparent distance is influenced by actual distance, the assumed horizon, distance cues, and attitudinal and organismic factors, plus the frame of reference which is provided. Under natural viewing conditions there is a close relationship between judged size and physical distance. When the subjective scale of distance is distorted from the physical distance, this distortion usually shows up in the perceived size. Mechanisms underlying the relationship between size and distance are suggested.

SHAPE CONSTANCY: METHODS, DATA, AND THEORY

Shape constancy defines the phenomenon whereby a shape is perceived as constant even when it is tilted away from the frontal-parallel plane. Shape constancy is observed when the object is rotated either vertically or horizontally in space. We have all observed that a desk top looks rectangular even though the retinal image is not. Also, if a square is tilted away from the observer, it still looks square even though the retinal image becomes trapezoidal.

Application of the Brunswik Ratio in Determining the Index of Phenomenal Regression

The index of phenomenal regression in shape constancy can be experimentally determined as follows, applying either the Brunswik or Thouless ratio. The standard consists of an equilateral triangle outlined in a white or a black panel, which can be clamped to a ring stand in such a way that the triangle is viewed at an angle to the subject's line of sight. The variable triangle is outlined by white metal strips against the black background of a second panel. These strips can be adjusted to produce a continuous series of triangles with a constant base (equal to that of the standard) and two equal angles.

The subject sits with the standard triangle and the variable triangle 5 feet from his eyes. The experimenter tilts the standard triangle through a predetermined arc by tipping the top edge of its board away from the subject. The subject then directs the experimenter to raise or lower the adjustable screen until the variable triangle appears to have the same shape as the standard.

The procedure for computing the index of phenomenal regression can be followed with the help of Figure 8-6. *A* represents the location of the subject's eyes. *BC* is the altitude of the standard triangle when it is perpendicular to the line of sight, and *BD* is the altitude of the triangle when it is tilted through θ degrees. The relative change in the retinal-image shape is represented by the relative change in the altitude; we compute the projected altitude at the vertical plane, i.e., *EB* in our diagram. Since the base and bottom angles of the standard triangle remain the same, the change in its shape, as it is tilted, is represented by

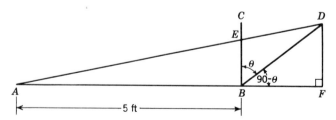

Figure 8-6 Diagrammatic representation of shape-constancy demonstration.

a change in its altitude; i.e., the triangle becomes "flatter." The relative projected altitude is EB. Applying the principle of trigonometry, we have

$$\frac{DF}{BD} = \sin (90-\theta)$$

Therefore

$$DF = BD \sin (90-\theta)$$

And

$$\frac{BF}{BD} = \cos (90-\theta)$$

Therefore

$$BF = BD \cos (90-\theta)$$

Now we have BF, and we are then able to calculate EB as follows. Let ABE and
ADF be two similar triangles. Then

$$\frac{EB}{DF} = \frac{AB}{AF}$$

Therefore

$$EB = \frac{DF \cdot AB}{AF} = \frac{DF \cdot AB}{AB+BF}$$

Therefore in our example

$$EB = \frac{BD \sin (90-\theta) \; 5 \text{ ft}}{5 \text{ ft} + BD \cos (90-\theta)}$$

Since BD, the true physical altitude of the standard triangle, and θ, the arc of tilt,
are both known, the equation is easily solved. The index of phenomenal regression can now be determined by applying the Brunswik ratio,

$$\frac{P - R}{C - R}$$

where P = the average of the equated altitudes of the variable triangle
$\quad\quad C = BD$, the object or physical altitude of the standard triangle
$\quad\quad R = BE$ as calculated above (the relative retinal stimulus)

In experiments similar to the ones just described, it is found that with normal viewing conditions the index of phenomenal regression lies between 0.60 and 0.80.

Dependency of Shape Constancy on Spatial Cues

Since the retinal shape changes as the object's spatial orientation is changed, it follows that shape constancy should be reduced as cues to spatial orientation are reduced or distorted. Many experiments have dealt with this problem. Some of the earliest and most extensive work in this area was performed by Thouless (1931a, 1931b, 1932). In his first experiment he used as a standard a circle which was placed obliquely to the subject's line of sight. Under these conditions the retinal shape would be elliptical. The variable consisted of a series of ellipses between a "flat" ellipse and a circle, which was placed at a right angle to the line of sight. The subject had to choose one of these variables which he thought had the same shape as the standard circle. In general, it was found that the subject chose an ellipse which was less elliptical than the calculated retinal shape; i.e., he chose a shape which approximated that of the circle. Indices of phenomenal regression ranged between 0.60 and 0.80. Under these conditions, where the subject could clearly observe the differences in spatial orientation, shape constancy or phenomenal regression averaged about 70 percent. Similar results were later obtained with squares and other shapes.

In subsequent experiments, Thouless found that if spatial cues are eliminated, the index of phenomenal regression can be reduced to zero. Thus, if the standard shape was viewed monocularly against a black-velvet background, the perceived shape approximated the retinal shape; there was no shape constancy. Monocular perception reduces the depth cues of retinal disparity and convergence, and the black-velvet background reduces texture cues to space. A similar demonstration was provided by Ames (1946), who rotated a window in its frame until it appeared almost end-on to the observer; i.e., its retinal shape had almost no width. Nevertheless, it still looked like a rectilinear window. But when the image of the same rotating window was cast on a photographic plate so that most depth cues were eliminated, its shape changed continuously, always approximating the retinal shape. Koffka (1935) postulated that there exists a tendency to perceive the shape the way it is at a "neutral level," i.e., the way it appears in the frontal-parallel plane. In other words, he is asserting that shape remains invariant with respect to its shape in the frontal-parallel plane. The reference points should be the vertical and horizontal planes. If Koffka was on the right track, we might deduce that shape constancy would be higher if the opportunity for judging the relative tilt or rotation of the object were increased. Conversely, shape constancy should decrease if the subject had difficulty in perceiving the relative tilt or rotation in space.

Relationship between Perceived Shape and Spatial Orientation A direct test of Koffka's hypothesis was conducted by Eissler (1933). In the vertical plane he tilted the standard object at varying degrees, and the subject had to judge both its shape and the relative amount of tilt. Eissler obtained three results of relevance. First, he found that phenomenal regression increased as tilt increased, i.e., the subject continued to correct for tilt as the latter increased. Second, regression was not complete because the discrepancy between perceived shape and real shape increased as the angle of tilt became more extreme. Third, he did find some degree of relationship between per- ceived shape and judged tilt; i.e., shape constancy did sometimes increase as the amount of judged tilt increased. This relationship, however, was by no means linear. In other words, increase in shape constancy was not always accompanied by an increase in the amount of judged tilt.

Koffka has criticized Eissler's somewhat inconclusive data by pointing out that some of his subjects were one-eyed and could not therefore perceive space very well. Subsequently, Stavrianos (1945) repeated a modification of Eissler's experiment. Her experimental design was superior, and her controls were better. She also found little relationship between the perception of shape and the judgment of tilt. Whereas shape constancy was generally good, judgment of tilt showed more fluctuation and error.

With a few subjects, however, there was some relationship between the perception of shape and that of tilt *under monocular vision,* although this relationship was not present for normal vision. In another experiment binocular vision was employed, and the subject selected appropriate shapes from a number of rectangular forms varying in height and width (rather than using the method of average error). The results seemed to indicate that under some conditions the correspondence between the perceived shape of an object and its perceived tilt was marked but not perfect. The subjects appeared to be accepting a relationship between shape and tilt and to see the objects as *three-dimensional* identities which remained the same even though the spatial coordinates changed. Work by Langdon (1955a) tends to corroborate the latter statement. He found that forms which can be modified so as to change their shape are perceived as three- dimensional objects of fixed shape which are changing their position. Apparently the natural preference in perception is to maintain the integrity of the object's shape and to change its perceived orientation if necessary. Orientation, as we shall see in the next chapter (e.g., Beck, 1971), is a primitive determiner of organization.

How the Orientation Factor Might Be Engaged: Innate and Experiential Determiners

The principles of *exafference* and *reafference*—introduced during our analysis of size constancy—can be applied in trying to make sense of the complex results coming from studies of shape constancy.

A possible demonstration of the reafference principle exists in the experiments of Bower (1965), who apparently found the existence of shape constancy in 2-month-old infants. These infants were shown a 50 by 25 by 2.5 centimeter board rotated through 45° and located in front and to the left of them. The board acted as a conditioned stimulus (CS); that is, *upon presentation,* if the infant turned his head to the left and looked at the stimulus, the experimenter would "peek-a-boo" him by raising his head from beneath a counter in front of the infant. "Peek-a-booing" provided a reward or reinforcement.

In a generalization test, four different stimuli were presented, each for 30 seconds and repeated four times. The four generalization conditions were: (I) the original CS; (II) the CS in the frontal-parallel plane; (III) the projected shape of the CS in the frontal-parallel plane; (IV) number III presented at a 45° rotation. Having been conditioned to the board tilted through 45°, the experimental question asks: To what extent will the infant generalize his responding to stimuli that have some degree of similarity to the board?

The results are very interesting, indeed. The mean number of responses for the four presentations were: (I) 51; (II) 45.13; (III) 28.50, and (IV) 26.00. The difference between (I) and (III) was highly significant, while the statistical equivalence of (I) and (II) suggests the presence of shape constancy. Comparisons of either I or II with either of the other groups were not significantly different.

From the two subsequent experiments in the same sequence, where systematic controls were set up, it was concluded that these infants do *not* do well at responding either to orientation or projected shape.

While these research findings will require much replication and while the "peek-a-boo" game might complicate the interpretation of the infant's response, Bower's research does raise a very important question. If shape constancy does exist in infants, what mechanism organizes it?

Bower (1971) has adopted an extreme nativistic position with respect to the perception of the shapes, sizes, and spatial orientation of objects. He asserts that infants not only possess wired-in programs for organizing spatiomotor abilities, but can also anticipate the tactile consequences of motoric behavior. However, this extreme position must be viewed with caution since data reported by other researchers question that infants have such abilities (see White, 1971; Kravitz & Boehm, 1971).

What spatial ability, then, does exist at birth? Bower's (1965) study supports our earlier suggestion that size constancy is present in infants because of the distance cue of motion parallax. This is so since binocular and monocular viewing of the objects give rise to size constancy—it is inferred that head movements could produce relative displacements of objects and spaces in the visual field sufficient for depth discrimination and, thus, constancy. This displacement could not occur when the stimulus was only a projection of a scene because the objects in the picture are flat—hence no constancy in infants. Moreover, Bower, Braughton, and Moore (1971) themselves reply that subjects respond differently to moving and stationary objects. Responses made to objects in motion did not generalize to a condition when the object was presented in stationary position.

A direct test of what cues function without learning comes from the work of Gibson and Walk (1960), which shows clearly that the depth cue of motion parallax is present at birth. (See Chapter 13 for a complete analysis.) Moreover, the principle of reafference (applied to size constancy) states that oculomotor feedback (and probably binocular disparity) gives an innate foundation to size constancy. Reasoning analogously, we would postulate that these innate cues make the principle of reafference applicable in the case of shape constancy as well.

Other research findings show that, in the more experienced adult, there is a strong tendency for conditions to be perceived in such a way as to maximize the constancy of shape. Some experiments by Langdon (1951, 1953, 1955b, 1955c) indicate ways to enhance shape constancy.

In one experiment (1955b) performed in the dark, Langdon used a fluorescent circular outline of wire rotating on a vertical axis from the direct line of vision through various angles to 90° and then back to direct vision again. The subject compared the shape of the rotating circle with fifteen different outline ellipses representing various rotations of the circle to his line of regard. These matches were compared with the condition in which the circle did not rotate spontaneously. In this case the subject could rotate the circle so as to equate the circle with the ellipses. There was practically no constancy present when the circle was stationary, but constancy was found with the moving-circle condition; the constancy increased with increasing speed of sweeps of the circle, up to ten sweeps per second. The deformation of the stimulus as the circle moved enabled the observer to perceive the outline as a three-dimensional form having spatial orientation.

In another experiment Langdon (1955c) located two sets of standard outline circles and comparison ellipses in a distorted room. One set of circle and ellipse was undistorted, but the other was distorted so as to appear undistorted in the distorted room. He reported that estimates of the perceived shape of the distorted forms corresponded to the space occupied by the shape. The overall results of the Langdon experiments show that the degree of constancy can be reduced by the removal of such perceptual depth cues as movement, texture, and shadows.

Further verification that the shape of an object is determined by the spatial framework is provided by the experiment of Beck and Gibson (1955). These investigators found that the phenomenal (perceived) slant and, therefore, the shape were determined primarily by spatial frame of reference provided by a textured background surface. This conclusion held irrespective of the physical slant of the object.

Finally we have the work of both Thouless (1932) and Klimpfinger (1933), who showed that artists, who possess a more analytical attitude, have poorer shape constancy than average individuals. Moreover, both Klimpfinger and Brunswik (1933) found that *shape constancy can be improved by instructing subjects in the synthetic or objective attitude* and lowered by instructing them in the analytical attitude.

A Possible Mechanism   At the end of the section on size constancy we stated that size constancy requires responding to size and distance in some related way, although the relationship may work indirectly through perspective cues. The organism is born with wired-in programs for coding some of these cues (reafference) and learns to code others through modified programs (exafference). An analogous mechanism likely operates in shape constancy. The reafferent programs code movement parallax, whereas exafferent programs code perspective cues to orientation.

One experiment which suggests how this shape constancy develops was performed by Shinar and Owen (1973). Their subjects were given eight irregular shapes to memorize. Then they had to choose a match to each memorized shape from a set of shapes which were *rotated*. The mean RT to make the match varied from 1,020 msec for 0° rotation to 1,150 msec for rotations of 60 and 90°. However, following practice in a number of trials, the RT decreased to 780 msec, and there was no variation of the degree of rotation. The author reasons that shape constancy operates when the subject attends to aspects of the stimulus complex which are invariant with respect to rotation—that is, the perception consists of shape and rotation in some related way. Future research will work out the function of these relations, and their *underlying* physiological mechanism.

COMPARISON OF THE PERCEPTUAL CONSTANCIES

We have stressed throughout this chapter that it is incorrect to consider brightness, shape, and size constancies as parts of a unitary process. This view is strongly supported by the extensive study of M. R. Sheehan (1938), based on the universally low correlation he and Thouless (1932) obtained when comparing the three constancies. They asserted that it is logically and experimentally indefensible to use the term *constancy* if it implies the existence of a unitary trait.

Furthermore, Leibowitz, Mitchell, and Angrist (1954) and Leibowitz, Chinetti, and Sidowski (1956) found that under reduced exposure time brightness constancy is improved, size constancy unaffected, and shape constancy destroyed.

Influence of Age, Development, and Learning on the Constancies

Other generalizations reveal differences between the three constancies. Brunswik (1956) compared his work on brightness constancy with Klimpfinger's work on shape constancy and Beyrl's work on size constancy. Size constancy was found to be 90 percent complete in the 2-year-old, and to improve with age until it is 100 percent complete in the 7-year-old. Shape constancy, on the other hand, is less than 15 percent in the 3-year-old and improves to almost 60 percent in the 14-year-old. Finally, brightness constancy is almost 30 percent in the 3-year-old and improves only slightly, to about 44 percent in the 16-year-old. Note that brightness constancy remains relatively low and that size constancy is much higher (in fact 100 percent) than shape constancy in adults.

Relative to the last point, Ghent (1960) presented monooriented forms (forms usually seen in a particular orientation) in various orientations. She found that 3- to 7-year-old children were more accurate in judging objective shape when the forms were presented in their characteristic position. The older subjects did equally well for all orientations of the shapes. In a second study (Ghent & Bernstein, 1961) it was observed that preschool children express strong preferences for orientation in the perception of geometric forms.

Other studies describe development trends. Cruikshank (1941) worked with 73 infants whose ages ranged from 10 to 50 weeks. The standard stimulus consisted of a large rattle, which was always located at a distance of 75 centimeters from the infant (condition C). The variable consisted of a smaller rattle (one-third as big as the standard), which was sometimes located at a distance of 25 centimeters (condition A) and sometimes at a distance of 75 centimeters (condition B). The three rattles were presented one at a time, and the reaction of the infant was noted.

Now, it would be expected that if conditions B and C elicit the same reaction, then size constancy (distance relationship) is operating. If conditions A and C exhibit the same reaction, then the visual angle rather than size constancy is determining the responses. Some of the results follow. Up to 22 weeks of age A was responded to more frequently, followed by C. Thus, size constancy is poor during the early age period. Between the ages of 4 and 5 months A and B began to confuse the infants. Finally, at the age of 6 months a differentiation between A and C developed, with a more similar response between B and C. Thus, much learning of size constancy takes place very early, and Cruikshank concluded that size constancy occurs as early as in the 6-month-old infant. Learning of size begins at 6 months, shows very rapid increase up to 2 years, and then shows slower increase until it is nearly complete in the 6-year-old.

Liebowitz, Bussey, and McGuire's (1957) study indicated, however, that learning continued to a later age. Children, consisting of eight boys between the ages of 7 and 9 years, and five male adults matched a comparison with one of a series of standard objects located at various distances up to 100 feet. The sizes of the standard objects were so adjusted as always to subtend a constant visual angle. The results are contained in Figure 8-7. It is clear from inspection of this figure that the adults exhibited almost perfect size constancy, whereas the children showed much poorer constancy, and that learning of size constancy continues beyond 9 years of age when longer distances than those employed by Cruikshank are used.

Additional data of Leibowitz and Judisch (1967) show that aged individuals (mean, 73.6 years) have even better constancy than college students, but only at a distance beyond 25 feet. (See Figure 8-8). These authors also report that shape constancy drops sharply after about age 45.

We shall have to await future definitive research to really know why shape

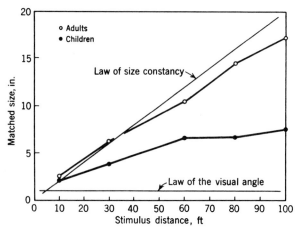

Figure 8-7 Mean matched size as a function of stimulus distance for a group of adults and a group of children. The size of the test object was adjusted so as always to subtend a constant visual angle. *(Ziegler and Leibowitz, 1957.)*

constancy decreases with age, but it may have to do, in part, with the fact that separating shape from its background (which is what breaking down constancy entails) requires more analytical ability and this is more likely to occur in older persons. Relevant to this issue, Leibowitz, Waskow, Loeffler, and Glaser (1959) have found that rhesus monkeys exhibit high degrees of shape constancy. The following order in terms of decreasing constancy was found: mental defectives, slow learners, college students in elementary psychology courses, and Ford Foundation scholars. And, of course, artists have highly trained abilities to break down shape constancy. These data are further verified by Leibowitz and Sacca (1971) who found that, when shape judgment is measured by use of matching and drawing responses, the highly intelligent individuals exhibit a lower tendency toward shape constancy.

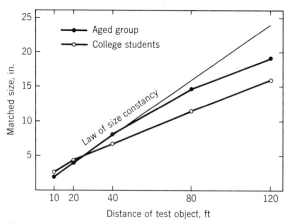

Figure 8-8 Older people have higher size constancy than college students. *(After Leibowitz and Judisch, 1967.)*

SUMMARY

Unlike brightness constancy, which is uniformly determined by innate factors, two principles affect size and shape constancy. At short distances and in young individuals, size and shape constancy are determined by reafference mechanisms which are innate and regulated by oculomotor factors. With experience, size constancy improves because exafferent cues, such as the pattern gradients, are processed. On the other hand, shape constancy first increases, then decreases with age because more analytical instructions and attitudes play a major role in affecting size and shape judgments. We further suggested that possible mechanisms underlie the processing of brightness, size, and shape constancies.

Emergence
and Organization
of Figure

In many ways the organization of perception concerns itself with the balance between *assimilation* and *differentiation*—that is, between fusion into a unit and segregation into separate entities. Our discussion of brightness induction and contrast in Chapter 7 included these two complementary processes. Level I of the hierarchy represents relative homogeneity, that is, the mere detection of a signal, nothing else. Brightness constancy involves the discrimination of one brightness as characteristic and different from another. This is representative of level II of the hierarchy. In this chapter we shall deal with transition from level II to level IV—that is, with how we go from a brightness unity which might be quite unstable, involving the fluctuation of a figure and its background, to a figure which is more stable. Remember that level III of the hierarchy involves the finer differentiation of the unity, and that is precisely how figures become stabilized.

Our discussion will be organized around three topics: first, what happens when there is not heterogeneity in the stimulus; second, the nature of the unstable or ambiguous figure and its ground, leading into a discussion of the conditions which make the figure more stable and definite; third, the gestalt laws of perceptual organization and the innovations and theory to which this approach gave rise.

HOMOGENEOUS FIELD OR GANZFELD

If the entire field which stimulated the receptors consisted of a homogeneous distribution of energy, it is obvious that no segregations could be perceived. Some differentiation in stimulus energy is necessary for a figure to be seen as separate from a background.

A field which gives a homogeneous distribution of energy is called a *Ganzfeld*. While it is technically difficult to achieve a completely homogeneous field, some investigators have succeeded in producing adequate *Ganzfelden* (W. Cohen, 1957, 1958b; Hochberg, Triebel & Seaman, 1951). Hochberg et al. did it by having each subject wear half of a table-tennis ball over the eye. In this way they could study, for example, certain color phenomena in such a monocular *Ganzfeld*.

Cohen constructed a *Ganzfeld* which consisted of two intersecting translucent spheres. Each sphere had the following characteristics: (1) it was painted white on the inside, and (2) it was so constructed that any light entering it was evenly diffused over the entire inside surface through multiple reflections. If the illumination in the two spheres is identical, the subject sees a uniformly illuminated field if he looks with one eye into the *Ganzfeld* through a small opening in the first sphere.

Using this apparatus, Cohen reports some interesting findings. For example, if the *Ganzfeld* is uniformly illuminated with a highly saturated hue, the color gradually fades. First the subject reports seeing a poorly saturated, diffused hue which, within about 3 minutes, becomes gray. Very often the gray is seen as denser and nearer than the hue. Thus, we note that the *Ganzfeld* not only gives a perception of uniform light energy but also makes the *ground unstable*—that is, changes some of its characteristics, such as distance and hue. In order to perceive a stable ground, it is necessary to perceive a stable figure as well.

For color to be maintained, some heterogeneity had to be introduced. One way to do this was to introduce an achromatic stimulus into a chromatic field; e.g., a gray disk introduced into a red *Ganzfeld* would be seen as a blue-green circle in a red background. It is interesting to note that the figure (disk or circle) took on the complementary color of the *Ganzfeld* and was seen as more saturated than the ground.

Another way of producing heterogeneity was to introduce *intensity differences*. Thus, if the second sphere had a lower luminance than the first sphere, a dark circular area was seen where the spheres intersected. In the phenomenon reported in the last paragraph, an intensity difference produced both a spatial separation of the circle from its background and a sharpening of its contour. Thus a figure was produced.

To show further that *Ganzfeld* stimulation produced the same effect as if there were no stimulation at all, we turn now to a brief description of the autokinetic effect. The reason for introducing that phenomenon at this point is to demonstrate that while the autokinetic effect is usually produced in a dark room, a similar condition can be created in a *Ganzfeld*.

Autokinetic Effect

The subject is located in a completely dark room, into which we introduce a spot of light. This can usually be done by placing a light source in a completely black box that has a pinhole through which the spot of light is seen. The subject is told to fixate the light, and after a short while he reports that he sees the light moving. The perceived motion of a light under such conditions, where there is no background, is called the *autokinetic effect*.

While no fading of the stimulus occurs, as was true in the *Ganzfeld*, the two phenomena appear to be related. First of all, the autokinetic effect also represents a case in which the percept is unstable; the light wanders in many directions which are not systematically predictable. Furthermore, Cohen (1958a) reports that a similar phenomenon occurs in a bright *Ganzfeld*. A stationary target was located in the Cohen *Ganzfeld,* which was homogeneously illuminated. The subjects saw the target as moving. Finally, Luchins (1954) found that the standard autokinetic effect could be reduced by making the background more heterogeneous. He did this by gradually increasing the background intensity in a modification of the typical autokinetic demonstration. As the brightness of the background increased, thus bringing more differentiation of the background into sight, the amount of autokinesis decreased until finally very little or no movement of the spot figure was seen. There are other ways of ensuring change in the stimulation, such as the optic tremor which continuously changes the stimulation of the retina (see Chapter 12).

The findings from these experiments on the *Ganzfeld,* and the autokinetic effect, suggest that the perception of *stability of both the figure and its background* requires heterogeneity in stimulus energy. This heterogeneity can be produced by differentiation in intensity (or, more fully, energy level), wave composition, spatial extensity, or temporal sequence. We shall return to this subject later. First, we go on to see what happens when a figure is shaped only by contour, with little else to differentiate it.

FIGURE-GROUND PHENOMENA: PRIMITIVENESS AND INSTABILITY OF FIGURAL UNITY

The discrimination of a figure from an amorphous background occurs at a higher threshold than that required for the discrimination of a formless brightness difference. This is probably so because a greater amount of information must be extracted in figure-ground differentiation. The many studies reviewed in Chapter 2 on energy levels and time for processing are relevant here.

The development of the figure goes through stages from instability to greater stability. These stages are illustrated in the experiment of Wever (1927), who exposed nonsense forms tachistoscopically from short to longer time intervals. When the figure-ground stage was reached, it appeared to have two steps. First, the figure was simple and not very stable, and then it developed into a better figure which could be grossly located in space.

The fact that figure-ground perception can be stable as well as unstable may be shown in other ways. If one looks at a Necker cube, which is produced by an outline perspective drawing, the perception is very unstable. The cube fluctuates in the third dimension, now coming toward the observer, then receding from him. Similar demonstrations were made by Rubin (1921), using the ambiguous figure, an example of which is presented in Figure 9-1. Looking at this picture leads to fluctuation in perception. Sometimes the middle vase is seen as a figure with the rest the background; at other times the two profiles emerge as figures with the middle receding to the background. Such reversals in figure-ground are spontaneous and very difficult to control. We note in these stimuli that the brightness is fairly homogeneous, with *the only differentiation existing at the contours.* Such figures are quite unstable with much fluctuation between figure and ground.

One clue as to how fluctuation might be reduced comes from the study of Dugger and Courson (1968), who reported that, within the limits of the sizes used by them, a larger visual angle was more stable than smaller visual angles. In their experiment the target figure was a Necker cube (see Figure 11-9e). Subjects fixated a dot in the center of each cube, which was situated left-face-forward down for 2 minutes, and counted aloud the number of reversals, i.e., spontaneous changes in orientation of the cube. Three black India ink outline drawings of a Necker cube were used. The dimensions of the three drawings were 13½, 8¼, and 3 inches, corresponding to visual angles of 13, 8, and 3°, respectively, at a viewing distance of 5 feet.

At the end of each 2-minute trial, the experimenter recorded the number of reversals reported by the subject, who was also asked to report any unusual phenomena. If fading and disappearance of lines were mentioned, the subject was asked to indicate which lines were involved. If fading was not reported spontaneously, he was asked whether it did occur.

The 3, 8, and 13° visual angles gave mean number of reversals of approximately 35, 33, and 28, respectively. The differences between 28 and the other two are statistically significant ($P < 0.01$). More fading was also reported for the bigger figures: thirty-seven subjects reported fading with a 13° visual angle, twenty-seven with the 8°, and only twelve with the 3° figure.

We conclude that there is more stable eye fixation on the larger figures. The clue? Direction of *eye fixation contributes to the stabilizing* of fluctuating, reversible, or ambiguous *figures.* Actually, directed eye fixation (or relative movement) is part of a larger context, namely, focused attention, as can be seen from Rock and Kremen's reformulation of Rubin's research which is analyzed in the next section.

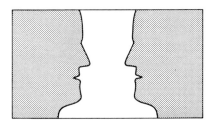

Figure 9-1 Ambiguous figure to illustrate fluctuations in figure-ground.

Attempts To Make the Figure More Stable

Rubin (1921) tried to show that the figure-ground relationship would be more stable if the brightness gradients between two areas were sharper and the observer attended to one of these as the figure. By using a projection lantern, he was able to project on a screen a green irregular shape surrounded by a black area or a black shape surrounded by a green area. These stimuli were exposed for 4 seconds. In one experiment the observer was first given nine of these fields and told to see the enclosed figure; then he was given nine more and asked to see the enclosing figure. In the critical test these eighteen fields, now with reversed figure-ground relationships with respect to color, were randomly presented with nine more fields, and one observer was asked to look at the *enclosed* field only, while another was asked to see the *enclosing* figure only. The results indicated, in general, that the observer had difficulty in recognizing the figure when the color relationships were reversed. Apparently the organism had been responding to specific color patterns, so that reversing the color relationship impaired recognition. This statement is verified in another experiment in which Rubin found that figure-ground relationships were moderately persistent even at these lower exposure times. On successive exposures, the observer reported seeing the same part of the figure about 64 percent of the time.

A modified replication of Rubin's research throws some light on the probable cause of his results (Rock & Kremen, 1957). A comparison between the two experiments and an understanding of the significance of the results will be aided by reference to Figure 9-2. In Rubin's experiment the entire figure was exposed during the training period, and the subject was instructed to look at one part, either the figure or the surround. In Rock and Kremen's experiment only one-half of the test figure was presented during the training period. If it was the left half, it belonged to set A; if the right half, to set B.

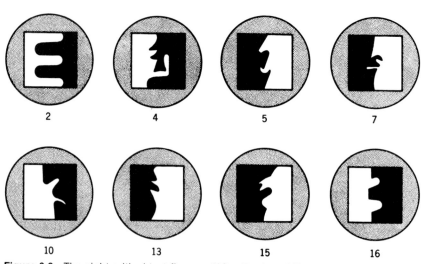

Figure 9-2 The eight critical test figures. *(After Rock and Kremen, 1957, p. 25.)*

Since only eight of eighteen figures gave a 50:50 split in choice between A and B in a control group, only data from these eight figures were used to analyze the results obtained from the experimental groups. The figures are shown in Figure 9-2. In looking at the results, we should keep the following points in mind. For the eight critical figures there were seventy-six responses to set A halves and seventy-one to set B halves. Counterbalancing for black on the left and black on the right, and vice versa, was followed. In the test figures four had black on the right, and four had black on the left. The number of subjects (out of fifteen in each experimental group) who showed a preference for either the training half or the nontraining half, together with the control data, were summed over the eight figures.

The differences between the distribution of results for group A (56:51) and the distribution of the control group (76:71) and that between the distribution of results for group B (63:84) and the distribution of the control group (71:76) are not statistically significant. Comparisons of the total number of responses to the figures exposed during the training period with the responses to those not seen during the training period (119:99) for the combined experimental groups were also not statistically significant.

The importance of the difference between Rubin's results and Rock and Kremen's lies in the following fact: Rubin tried to "influence" his subjects in the training period by exposing the entire ambiguous figure and instructing them to attend to one part. Rock and Kremen gave no instructions and used only half of the ambiguous figure for several exposures during the training. Rubin's method significantly increased the probability that a response would be made to the training part rather than the nontraining part, while Rock and Kremen's method did not. The effect of presenting the entire ambiguous figure with instructions to attend to one part is to provide a *context* within which the figure is perceived. When the subject views the figure subsequently, he does not merely present a "blank" slate waiting for the stimulus to register sensorily. Instead he sends out *testing stimuli* or *sets* from the brain which select the part to be received and reacted to. This interpretation is consistent with the general outflow model presented in Chapter 1.

Our interpretation is supported further by the following facts. The kind of results obtained by Rock and Kremen are believed to be determined by the crucial characteristics of the stimulus that the subject *first saw*. These authors also raise the question of how rewards and punishment can influence the probability of a perceptual response when repetitive exposure does not. Certainly verbal intent or some other motivational effect like reward or shock is demonstrably more effective in accentuating certain sets or classes of responses to stimuli. That these directional sets can result from short-term as well as long-term experience is demonstrated in the two research findings reported next.

Instructions Affect Stabilization   An experiment conducted by Pelton and Solley (1968) assessed the effect of induced subjective attitudes on relative figural stability while subjects viewed the Necker cube. Fifteen subjects were assigned to the "switch" condition and were instructed to switch perspectives as frequently as possible. The fifteen subjects in the "hold" condition were instructed to hold any perspective being perceived at the moment for as long as possible.

During the experimental procedure the reversal phenomenon was briefly described to each subject with the help of a Necker cube, one of whose frontal faces was drawn in red while the other was in blue. The subject was asked whether he alternately saw a cube with a blue front and a cube with a red front. Then the instructions were read, and the reading was followed by the presentation of a black test cube which was exposed for a single 3-minute interval. The subject made his response by pressing a left key when he saw the left-perspective square (red) and a right key when he saw the right perspective. In addition, the specific instructions, "switch" or "hold," were inserted at this point. Fifteen-second intervals were marked off on the recording paper, and the number of reversals that occurred during each of the twelve 15-second intervals was counted. The mean reversal per interval for the thirty subjects was very different for the two conditions—the "switch" condition producing three times as many reversals (six versus two, which is significant).

Prior Learning Affects Reversal Rate The previous section told us that short-term set—for example, experimental instructions—can affect the relative stability of figural perspective. The next experiment shows that longer-term set, in this case practice, can influence the rate of reversal. Smith, Impater, and Exner (1968) showed that, in order of presentation, practice in reversing on 15, 25, 50, 100, and 15 percent outlines of a Necker cube yielded a reversal rate on the last 15 percent cube nearly equal to that of the 100 percent cube (the smaller the percentage, the less line segments there are).

In this experiment 107 sophomores were tested in four groups, approximately equal in number. Each subject was given a test booklet which had a Schroeder staircase on page 1 and a 15, 25, 50, 100, and 15 percent Necker cube on pages 3, 5, 7, 9, and 11, respectively. The even-numbered pages were blank. It was explained to the subject that the Schroeder staircase was a reversible figure and that he should observe it until the figure started to reverse. Thereafter, the subject had to make a tally on the bottom of the page each time any of the figures reversed themselves during a 3-minute exposure period for each of the five cubes.

The mean numbers of reversals for all subjects on the 15, 25, 50, 100, and 15 percent cubes were 23.12, 39.36, 51.76, 60.60, and 57.78, respectively. Inspection of the means shows a monotonic increase for the first four cubes which is associated with joint effects of practice and degree of completeness. The difference between the first two cubes is statistically significant, and each of them is significantly different from the last three cubes ($P < 0.05$ in all significant comparisons). Since the differences between the 50, 100, and second 15 percent cubes were not significant while the difference between the first and second 15 percent cubes was significant, practice or perceptual learning may be more important in this situation than the degree of figural completeness. Note that the second 15 percent cube gave rise to more than twice as many fluctuations as the first 15 percent cube.

Research from Rubin through Rock to the last two studies described gives ample evidence that organismic set created by method of presentation, instructions, and practice significantly affects the perception and relative stability of unstable figures.

Set or Attentional Directors   Rock and Kremen also thought eye movements create directional sets. Related to this fact are some interesting observations. Hochberg (1964), for example, notes that a contour can delineate only one of the two areas which it shapes. This is also true of edges in three-dimensional objects, but there is a crucial difference between a contour and an edge. A contour can shape only one area *at a time,* but it can shift the direction of which side it shapes as the individual looks down on it. This cannot happen when an individual looks at an edge. Thus the fluctuation in figure stability when there is only a contour to separate the figures can be caused by the ease with which the direction of shaping can change. One way of altering this condition is to make one side dominant; an edge does this. Another way is to make one figure more articulated than the other. In an experiment on binocular rivalry, Breese (1899) showed this to be true. In an experiment of this type two different targets are presented, one to each eye. The targets may merge or alternate, or one may "win out over the other" in the perception. In Breese's experiment the more articulate side won out. The gestalt laws also describe articulation.

GESTALT LAWS OF PERCEPTUAL ORGANIZATION: GROUPING AND FIGURAL UNITY

The question raised by Max Wertheimer in his classic article (1923) can be introduced by considering Figure 9-3. For perceptual discrimination to take place, the physical world of stimulation must contain some degree of heterogeneity. At the other extreme, we encounter the fact that the number of segregations

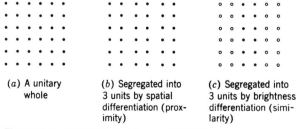

(*a*) A unitary whole

(*b*) Segregated into 3 units by spatial differentiation (proximity)

(*c*) Segregated into 3 units by brightness differentiation (similarity)

Figure 9-3   Illustration of the gestalt laws.

that the observer can perceive is limited by his capacity to process separate units. In *a* of the figure the individual cannot process the thirty-six dots at one glance. Consequently he is just as likely to say, "I see a collection of dots" or "I see dots making up a square." In *b* and *c* spatial proximity and similarity decrease the uncertainty or variability in perceptual reports. Most people are likely to report seeing three columns of dots in *b*, and in *c* something like two columns of white dots bordering a column of black dots.

The perceptual field tends to be organized into a limited number of wholes or units. It is to the question of determining the principles which govern the grouping of the elements into these units or figures that Wertheimer addressed himself. The fruits of his insight were contained in gestalt laws of perceptual organization, the essence of which we shall attempt to describe in the following sections.

Law of Prägnanz

This is the basic or master law which governs the segregation of the perceptual field into separate units. The elements of the field tend to segregate into units which are most stable or which create a minimum of stress. To quote Koffka, the law of *Prägnanz* states that "psychological organization will always be as 'good' as the prevailing conditions allow. In this definition the term 'good' is undefined" (1935, p. 110). Nevertheless, when we study Koffka's examples and those of Wertheimer, it becomes clear that a good or *Prägnanz* form is one which constitutes the simplest stable structure. The criteria for Prägnanz form is one which constitutes the simplest stable structure. The criteria for Prägnanz embrace such properties as regularity, symmetry, simplicity, inclusiveness, continuity, and unification. Examples of the way the master principle of *Prägnanz* works are illustrated in Figure 9-4. The rest of the gestalt laws, similarity, proximity, closure, and good continuation, which are shown in Figures 9-3 and 9-4, are ways of attaining *Prägnanz*. Inclusiveness is diagramed in Figure 9-9, and perception of causality, as studied by Michotte, described in Chapter 15.

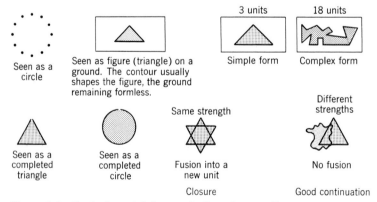

Figure 9-4 Illustration of *Prägnanz* in figural perception.

Generalization of the Gestalt Laws

Although the illustrations presented by Wertheimer and by Koffka are very striking, we might still wonder how general these principles of grouping are. That these laws operate to some extent has been demonstrated by the gestalt psychologists. But other studies (e.g., Hochberg & Silverstein, 1956; Rush, 1937) have been performed to determine in a more experimental manner under which conditions they operate, and these indicate that the laws interact in complex fashions, sometimes supporting each other and sometimes acting in opposition. Furthermore, the laws are more prominent with older than with younger subjects, indicating a possible experiential or maturational effect.

Hochberg and his associates have attempted to study the operation and strength of these laws quantitatively. In one experiment Hochberg and Silverstein tried to determine how much closer elements had to be (proximity) to overcome a stronger influence of brightness (similarity) which was pulling them in another direction. The stimulus materials are shown in Figure 9-5.

The brightness of the squares in the rows was alternatively dark gray and light gray. The apparatus was so constructed that columns could be moved, bringing the second column closer to the first, the fourth closer to the third, and the sixth closer to the fifth. Correspondingly, the distance between the second and the third and between the fourth and the fifth columns would increase. That is to say, as the distance b decreased, the distance c increased. What these experimenters essentially did was to determine how much smaller the distance b (relative to c) had to be so that there would be vertical organization (seeing columns) which would overcome the force toward horizontal organization caused by differences in brightness between the rows, that is, so that proximity would win significantly.

Hochberg and Silverstein found that when they increased the difference

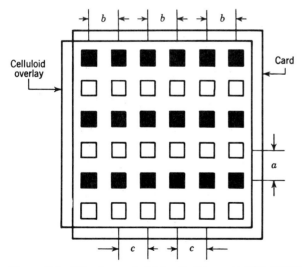

Figure 9-5 Stimulus material for Hochberg and Silverstein's experiment.

between the brightness of the rows, the difference between the columns had to be increased correspondingly to go from horizontal to vertical organization. A second result of perhaps greater interest is the fact that the amount of closeness depends on whether we begin with the presence of horizontal or vertical organization. Thus, if we begin with horizontal organization, we must move the columns to distance X to produce vertical organization. When we move the columns from the other direction back, we have to go beyond X to produce horizontal organization again. This is called the *factor of direction;* it influences the relative strengths of similarity and proximity.

In a further experiment Hochberg and Hardy (1960) found that as distance between rows decreased (proximity), there had to be a corresponding within-row increase in brightness differences (producing alternating columns which were dark and light) to reorganize perception from apparent rows into columns.

In the final study to be considered here, Hochberg and McAlister asserted that the utility of translating the organizational laws depends on the empirical determination of dimensions of abstraction along which information can be scored (such as number of angles, number of line segments, or some weighted combination of the two) and upon the "demonstration of a quantitative dependence of response frequency on the 'information scores'" (1953, p. 362). In one experiment they presented tachistoscopically each of the Kopferman cubes a number of times and observed the frequency with which subjects gave bidimensional (as opposed to three-dimensional or depth) responses to each. The Kopferman cubes are presented in Figure 9-6. The results indicate that the two cubes (Y and Z) which require fewer lines, segments, and angles (the lowest "informational" scores of these two dimensions of the four cubes) to be seen as bidimensional give rise to bidimensional responses more frequently than the other two cubes. This is an example of the operation of redundancy in the determination of figural goodness.

The above-mentioned spatial factors in figural organization lead us to consider the more recent work of Beck which shows how *spatial orientation* directs the effectiveness of similarity in giving rise to grouping or segregation.

In the first experiment, Beck (1966c) demonstrated that similarity is not necessarily a good predictor of how grouping will take place; spatial orientation is more predictive. In this project fifteen subjects were shown twelve target patterns, three of which are illustrated in Figure 9-6. The pattern is made up of three sections; the subject is asked to divide the pattern into two regions, at the boundary where the most natural break occurs. The results are presented in

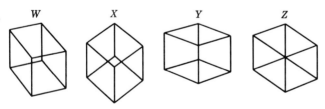

Figure 9-6   The Kopferman cubes. *(After Kopferman, 1930.)*

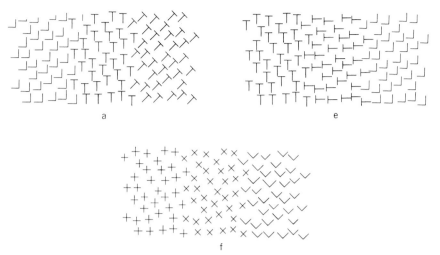

Figure 9-7 Targets a, e, and f—three of the twelve targets used in the experiment. The targets are shown in their upright position. *(After Beck, 1966b, p. 300.)*

Figure 9-7. The number under the figures represents the quantity of subjects (out of sixteen) who divided the pattern at that point. It is evident that figures which had the same *orientation*, rather than the same shape, were seen together.

In another study Beck (1966b) verifies the above results using a different measuring technique. A pattern of illuminated figures (e.g., upright T's) was exposed to the subjects. Then a pattern of another set of figures was superimposed on the first set. The luminance of the standard figure was reduced until two separate patterns were seen. It was assumed that the less the luminance had to be lowered, the greater was the tendency to segregation.

Statistical analysis of the luminance values showed that rotating some of the figures in a field from a vertical position to a slant of 45° facilitates segregating the field into separate perceptual groups. In contrast, changes in the shape or orientation of the figures, which have their component lines *vertical* and *horizontal*, do not reliably aid grouping.

In the third experiment, Beck (1967) apparently demonstrated that shape as an organizing principle could be subsumed under orientation—that is, in order to be effective, shape must change orientation from the vertical-horizontal plane to the 45–135° plane. In this figure, the standard pattern of upright T's was exposed at three different lower luminance values with a pattern of other figures superimposed. The subject had to rate the extent that the two sets of figures segregated from one another. The rating was done on a six-point scale, with 0 meaning no segregation, and 6 meaning very clear-cut segregation. Using both two-line and three-line figures for the comparison, Beck found that patterns which maintained a horizontal or vertical orientation were not segregated out (even if dissimilar), whereas *figures which were in transverse planes segregated from figures in the vertical-horizontal plane even when they were similar in shape to the figures in the other plane.*

Underlying Mechanism and Organizing Principles   Beck's work is important. It suggests that the gestalt laws of perceptual organization can be reduced basically to organizing principles of brightness and spatial extensity. Thus, other grouping principles, such as similarity and closure, are probably phenomenological categories involving brightness and spatial aspects. Beck suggests that processes involving grouping are most sensitive to those properties that are selectively respondent at an early stage in the visual system. In that context, the processes in grouping are based on spontaneous direct response to relatively simple properties such as *brightness, size,* and *line direction.* The basic importance of line orientation is consistent with J. J. Gibson (1950), who has suggested that it is a basic element in the perception of figure, and Hubel and Wiesel (1962), who found specific detectors for line orientation when studying neurons in the visual cortex of the cat.

The importance of the mechanism of line detection as a figural organizing principle is also suggested in the experimental results of Gillam (1972), who used the rotary-motion illusion discussed at the beginning of Chapter 14. The stimulus that oscillated consisted of two lines. The two parameters which varied were (1) whether the two lines were parallel or converged (up to 50°), and (2) the amount of spatial separation between the lines.

If the lines were seen to move together in the same direction, including reversal, they were seen as forming a figural unit. The data indicated that converging lines moved independently, and separation up to 2.5 centimeters produced asynchrony. Parallel lines tended to move together, and separation made only a slight difference. The results are tentatively attributed to the distribution of line detection in the cortex reported by Hubel and Wiesel (1968).

In tasks similar to those of Beck reported in the last section, Olsen and Attneave (1970) presented displays similar to the one depicted in Figure 9-8 to their subjects. The subject's task was to state which quadrant was different, and RTs were taken. It was found that the slope of the stimulus elements made no difference, with horizontal-versus-vertical orientation giving the fastest RT. This is congruent with Beck's data. The author concluded that segregation depends on identities and difference between descriptions which, in turn, represent relationships between the stimulus array and an *internal cartesian reference system.* Could this internal system be caused, in part, by the line detection reported by Hubel and Wiesel?

Finally, Bear (1973), taking off from Garner's work in uncertainty and "goodness of pattern," presented dot patterns to subjects. Usually four dots were presented, and the subject was asked to predict where the fifth one would be. It was found that redundant patterns (see Chapter 10) gave the highest percentage of correct predictions (95 percent or higher). Bear concluded that a stimulus pattern which is perceived to belong to a surround, redundant subset, will be a good figure. Redundant implications are provided by the following conditions or tendencies:

Complexity and straight line
Inferring that dots are symmetrical
Connecting dots in a subpattern containing an isolated element

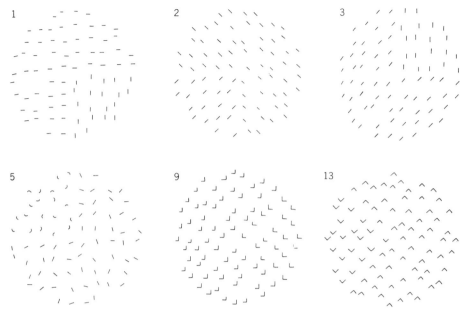

Figure 9-8 Sample displays from experiment 1. Other categories are illustrated in a 45° rotation of the figure; note especially that category 9 rotates into category 13. *(After Olson and Attneave, 1970, p. 5.)*

Contributions from Information Theory

Another empirical demonstration that the gestalt laws are probably derived from reponse to the simple properties of the stimulus and form redundancy was presented by Attneave (1954a) who utilized an ingenious application of information theory in an attempt to explain why the gestalt laws operate the way they do. Information theory was developed within communication engineering and was a systematic attempt to handle the transmission of messages through communication channels. Psychologists, however, became aware of its application to the living organism as the communication channel (Quastler, 1955).

Messages of stimuli containing a certain amount of information are encoded (perceived) and transmitted through the channel. The decoding of the message or stimulus material is indicated by the response of the organism. The communication channel for orthodox information theory is a static one, a "black box"; but when the living organism is the channel, the system must be treated as dynamic. Thus the encoding of the message is effected by the internal characteristics of the organism, namely, its physical characteristics and life experiences. Attneave suggests the way information theory might be used to quantify the gestalt laws of organization. The laws of organization operate essentially to give us information on the basis of which we make discriminations. Presumably a certain amount of information is required before we are able to make visual discriminations. The articulation of the visual field is so constituted as to transmit a certain amount of redundant information. This ensures discrimination and the perception of certain patterns or configurations.

Attneave presents some ingenious illustrations of how this information-transmission concept might be used to quantify the gestalt laws which govern the segregation of the stimuli in the visual field into certain good configurations. He begins by asserting that much of the visual information received by any higher organism is highly redundant; i.e., it contains unnecessary repetitive information. He gives examples of how this hypothesis might be tested by employing Shannon's "guessing-game" technique, which consists of presenting a series of elements to the subject at one time. The subject has to guess when the color, duration, or some other dimension of the stimulus will change. (This is a more complicated version of Bear's technique.) For example, if we were to present the subject with the diagram of a black ink bottle on the corner of a brown table against a uniform white background, he would be able to see this with little effort. The guessing-game technique, however, demonstrates that much of the information transmitted by such a field of stimuli is highly redundant. The redundant visual stimulation results from either (1) an area of homogeneous color or brightness, or (2) a contour of homogeneous direction or shape. It can, therefore, be concluded that essential information is concentrated along contours (i.e., regions where color or brightness changes abruptly) and at those points on a contour at which its direction changes most rapidly, i.e., at angles or peaks of curvatures.

Symmetry constitutes another form of redundancy, since the information received from one side of a symmetrical figure is predictable from that received from the other side. Symmetry, it will be recalled, is one of the criteria of *Prägnanz.* In the same way the other gestalt laws of organization like similarity, good continuation, and proximity reduce uncertainty of perception by giving certain redundant information. The value of symmetry and redundancy is more complex than can be indicated here, however, and we shall return to the subject later in this chapter.

Furthermore, it would seem that the visual machinery is so constituted as to maintain redundancy at a certain level and not to overload the communication channel. Thus, the organism is required to encode little information. The gestalt laws of organization play a necessary role in this process, in which they operate to transmit economical information by providing a maximum amount of redundancy.

This work which Attneave has started seems very promising for the task of quantifying the gestalt laws of organization. The construct "economy of information transmission" seems to be a very useful tool to apply not only to principles of discrimination, but also to concept formation and efficient problem solving.

We end this section by emphasizing that information can be quantified, with *maximum information being transmitted where the greatest change occurs in contour direction and brightness.* Furthermore, transmission of this essential information is *ensured by redundancy.* Therefore, the various gestalt factors, including symmetry, good continuation, and other forms of regularity, may all be considered to constitute redundancy in visual stimulation (Attneave, 1954a, p. 209).

Mackworth and Morandi (1967) have combined an information analysis of complex pictures (e.g., an aerial photograph of Baja California) with a study of the directed eye movements of the subject in viewing the picture over a 10-second period. The picture was divided into sixty-four sections, and the informativeness of each section was determined by a panel of subject raters. The subject's eye fixations were primarily directed toward those sections of the pictures rated high in informativeness. Particularly, fixations were directed toward the nonredundant contours on the map. These points occur where there are abrupt changes in the contour of the coastline viewed in the relief map. There is evidence that the subject skims the outline of the figure peripherally, then uses foveal vision to fixate on the informative, nonredundant aspects of the figure.

Postulated Mechanism for Organizing Form   In the section on gestalt grouping we referred to a theory based on line orientation and the distribution of line detectors in the cortex. In Chapter 12 we also present evidence that indicates that these cortical detectors are subject to significant modification from experience. At this point we want to describe some evidence which suggests that eye movements are related to the way the cortical patterns, which we propose underlie the organization of form, might change with learning. Such a hypothesis is germane to a wide range of theories about form perception which we take up in the next chapter.

The evidence comes from the innovating research of Noton and Stark (1971). Their work was guided by their belief that pattern recognition is a serial operation in which the brain processes the pattern, feature by feature. (This view is similar to that of Hebb and the Gibsons described in the next chapter.) Their research was aimed at investigating the order in which these features are processed.

They presented patterns (e.g., faces) under conditions of poor visibility. A special technique was used to measure (monocularly) the saccadic eye movements from feature to feature to reveal the order of processing. Subjects, three females and one male, first viewed five patterns for 20 seconds each. These patterns were then intermingled with five others during a recognition task.

They discovered fixed patterns, which they called *scanpaths*. These scanpaths consistently follow a fixed path. Also, during the recognition phase, the first few positions from the learning phase show up repeatedly. In the case of the human face and upper body, 65 percent of the eye movements focus on the nose, chin, hands, eyes, and back of head (see also Yarbus, 1967, chap. 7).

Noton and Stark believe that these eye patterns suggest how patterns are remembered and recognized by subjects. In a way similar to Hebb's theory, they consider the directed pattern to be an integral part of the *memories* on which recognition is based. These memories are an integrating sequence of sensory and motor memory tasks, recording alternately a feature of the pattern and eye movements required to reveal the next feature. Under normal viewing conditions the eye movements are believed to be replaced by an interval attention mechanism which processes successive features of the pattern. (This view is consistent with the theory of the Gibsons.) Lastly, since the scanpaths are markedly different (yet characteristic) for different subjects, it is postulated that this mechanism must be central, rather than solely peripheral. If we relate the theories of Attneave and Noton and Stark, it would be consistent to expect that the memory mechanism also works so as to make the "storage" of remembered forms more economical. G. A. Miller (1956a, 1956b) has considered how organisms tend to encode information in "chunks" so as to minimize strain. If encoding for economical memory functioning actually occurs, we would expect the brain to perform a certain amount of encoding in agreement with the gestalt laws. The effect of this hypothetical brain process should be evident in reproductions from memory of previously perceived forms. Some evidence relevant to such a process comes from the work of Wulf (1922).

Wulf presented various outline forms, one at a time, to observers and asked them to inspect these figures. The observers were then required to reproduce the forms at various intervals after the original exposure. The delay between inspection and reproduction consisted of such intervals as 30 minutes, one day, one week, a few months, and so on. Each observer made several reproductions of a specific form. Of interest is the fact that sucessive reproductions reportedly showed changes in the direction of the greater *Prägnanz*. The most important change appeared to be the accentuation of certain structural features. This accentuation, or emphasis, is illustrated in the principles of sharpening and of leveling. In sharpening, differences are accentuated, while in leveling, they are assimilated (see Chapter 16).

We may apply informational concepts to these principles. Thus it can be hypothesized that sharpening results from both redundancy and economical encoding, i.e., extracting the essential information into suitable chunks. Since the information is concentrated at the angles where the direction changes abruptly, encoding operates to accentuate the angles and make them sharp. This also results in a certain amount of redundancy since the angles become more or less equal. The redundance which results from leveling is obvious. Through leveling the distance between the two lines becomes uniformly equal, and the essential information (curvature) carried by one line is repeated by the other. This is supported by the "unity" in movement of parallel lines described earlier.

Wulf's studies raise an important question, which has to do with whether these changes operate independently of experience. He had theorized that changes in the reproductions resulted from autonomous changes in the "memory trace" existing in the brain. These autonomous changes occurred in the direction of greater *Prägnanz* and operated independently of experience.

Wulf's conclusions have been evaluated experimentally by E. M. Hanawalt (1937) and by Hebb and Foord (1945). If the forms are reproduced only once by a subject and if each subject reproduces the form at different times after exposure, there is no evidence of slow, spontaneous changes in the trace. That there is a change is apparent, but the subject who reproduces a form after one month, for example, does not necessarily show more change than one who makes a reproduction after one day. Thus what Wulf apparently showed was that the progres-

sive changes were a result of the subject's trying to *remem'*
easier to draw things more symmetrically or parallel to each
remember them this way. Again, we have maximization of reᴗ
tion to produce economical decoding of information. The memory
tion is consistent with contemporary theories of perception.

The importance of making this distinction between what is seen ᵥ
attempts to reproduce what is seen can further be appreciated by looking at the
data from experiments of Rock and Engelstein (1958). Three separate experiments, each using different figures and different subjects, were performed. When
a specified period elapsed since original exposure to the figure, each subject had
either to reproduce or to recognize the original. Recognition response was made
by choosing the match from ten figures, which ranged in similarity from 1 to 10,
10 being identical and 1 being least similar to the original. This scale of similarity
was obtained by pooling the determinations of many judges, and a different set of
judges scored the reproductions. While there might be some question about the
compatibility of the data, since the judges were different, the results are still
informative. The two recognition curves were very close to the original figure,
even after four weeks, as opposed to the three reproduction curves, which
deviated very markedly from the original. Rock concludes that the changes
which occurred in the reproduction were probably response phenomena, dic-
tated by a tendency to draw things more or less regularly when there is no
adequate memory in consciousness to the contrary. That these changes do not
represent changes in the memory trace per se is attested to by the excellence of
recognition memory.

To continue with the effect of experience, earlier in this chapter we referred
to an experiment by Gottschaldt (1926) which demonstrated that mere repetitive
experience in inspecting a figure does not increase its discriminability if it is a part
of a more inclusive whole (see Figure 9-9). The experiment was conducted in the
following manner. The experience consists of inspecting a number of A figures
(which is the left figure), each of which is presented for 1 second. Some of the
figures were shown three times, whereas others were shown 520 times. During
the test situation B figures, each containing an A figure embedded in it, also were
shown. The observer was merely told to describe the B figure. Only rarely did
the observer mention that it contained an A figure. The results show that the A
figure was mentioned in 6.6 percent of the cases in which it had been exposed
three times, and in 5 percent of the cases in which it had been shown 520 times.
Gottschaldt concluded that the quality of the perceived form depends most
strongly on the structural features of the stimulus; there is a very strong tendency

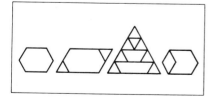

Figure 9-9 Illustration of inclusiveness.
(After Gottschaldt, 1926.)

perceive the form which represents the "best" gestalt. Repetitive experience with a figure does not increase the probability of its detectability if it is embedded in a larger, more complex whole. It should be noted, however, that the directions given to the subjects were of a general nature. More than 6.6 percent of the subjects might have noticed *A* in *B* but did not indicate this fact because of the generality of the instructions. *Inclusiveness* is at work since *B* includes *A*.

The limitation of this principle of inclusiveness is indicated in the experiments by Djang (1937) and N. G. Hanawalt (1942), previously cited. These experiments indicated that experience does play an important role in the hidden-figures task.

Djang's experiment is very instructive. It not only shows the kind of forms in which experience does play a role but also deals with the complex nature of the various possible interactions between stimulus structure and learning. He showed that if the *A* figure in the first place does not represent a good gestalt, experience will facilitate its separation from a larger whole.

Further Exploration of Redundancy and Memory for Form   Now that we have seen the importance of structural organization and the way learning interacts with it, we might ask whether forms which are more definitively structured will be remembered more easily than forms which are more equivocally structured. A study designed to answer this question was performed by Attneave (1955). In this study, as in the earlier one, he attempted to quantify the gestalt laws by using the approach of information theory; but here he was interested in the memory of perceived forms. A total of 149 subjects was randomly assigned to one of five groups, each of which was shown sixty patterns of dot cells. Each pattern was shown one at a time, and the subject was required to reproduce the pattern afterward. There were five classes of patterns, as shown in Figure 9-10.

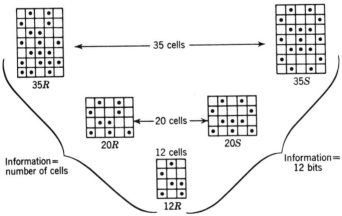

Figure 9-10   Examples of the five classes of patterns. The symmetrical patterns 20S and 35S are matched with the random patterns 20R and 35R. With respect to informational content, they are matched with each other and with 12R; i.e., 12R contains all the information necessary for the construction of either 20S or 35S. *(After Attneave, 1955, p. 210.)*

The figure contains one of the 60 patterns in each class. In the pattern 12 *R* dots were inserted into cells at random. There were twelve "bits" of information. The other two random conditions, 20 *R* and 35 *R,* contained twenty and thirty-five bits of information, respectively; but 20 *S* contained only 12 bits since the pattern is symmetrical about the vertical axis. Likewise, 35 *S* also contained twelve bits of information since the pattern is symmetrical about both the vertical and the horizontal axes. Each group was presented with only one class of patterns.

Example of Bits   The reader may wonder why there are twelve bits (units of information) in the twelve cells. If we apply the formula $\log_2 A$, each cell will have one bit of information, since there are two alternatives (a dot or no dot) for each cell, and $\log_2 2$ is 1. Therefore for twelve cells there are twelve bits of information, which seems to be true intuitively in any case.

As far as the 20 *S* condition is concerned, the pattern simply contains two examples of the 12 *R* condition in a symmetrical relationship. Hence Attneave feels no additional information is put in. The same is true of 35 *S* which contains 12 *R* repeated in horizontal and vertical symmetry. Attneave therefore concludes that the 12 *R*, 20 *S*, and 35 *S* conditions each contain twelve bits of information. We shall question whether this is strictly correct after we have examined his results.

Three measures of memory were employed: (1) immediate reproduction, which consisted of reproduction of the pattern into blank cells immediately after exposure; (2) delayed reproduction, which consisted of reproduction 15 seconds after exposure; and (3) identification, which consisted of learning the names of the patterns and then identifying them by their names. The results of the three measures gave similar trends. The patterns 12 *R*, 20 *S*, and 35 *S* each contain only twelve bits of information, but 20 *R* and 35 *R* each contain more than do 20 *S* and 35 *S*. In all cases the errors were counted only from the twelve cells in each pattern which were identical. This was obviously done so that we could compare equal probabilities for making errors. The maximum number of errors which could be made is twelve, with a chance probability of six. First we compare 12 *R*, 20 *S*, and 35 *S*. Here we note that these patterns differ only in the number of elements but not in the amount of information concerned. It is clear from the data that symmetry is not the whole answer since more numerous errors are made for 35 *S* than for 20 *S*. Similarly, we compare 20 *R* with 20 *S* and 35 *R* with 35 *S*. In this comparison we truly see the benefit of symmetry in the reduction of the amount of information from 35 *R* to 35 *S* and from 20 *R* to 20 *S*. In this case, symmetry (redundancy) does indeed make it easier to discriminate the patterns.

We should add that the effect of symmetry was greater in the delayed reproduction than it was in the immediate reproduction. Evidently the effect of redundancy in facilitating encoding has more chance to operate after delay.

A study by Adams, Fitts, Rappaport, and Weinstein (1954) found that subjects learn to identify symmetrical shapes more easily than asymmetrical shapes when the two are matched with respect to number of lines and angles.

Fitts et al. (1956), however, have indicated that symmetry of figures may either hinder or facilitate form recognition, depending upon the manner in which they are presented. Likewise, Rappaport (1957) has shown that redundancy (provided by figures with repetitious outlines) is effective only when "noise" is present. More will be said in Chapter 10 about the structural factors influencing form identification.

Relative to the Attneave study, however, we might add that the assumption that no further information is generated when the symmetrical portion of a pattern is added may be questionable. Intuitively we see that the information content should not double, but it appears reasonable to assume that some small amount of information is added. If this were not so, the two patterns would be identical, which is definitely not the case. If we allow for an addition of a minimal amount of information (beyond that of 12 R) for the symmetrical figures 20 S and 35 S, the results are more understandable. We can then say that the number of errors tends to increase with increasing amount of information contained within the stimulus pattern and conclude that symmetry does improve information encoding and memory. Studies are needed to determine how the mechanisms operate and interact. The studies reported here serve to clarify the gestalt principle that figural goodness may be favorable to memory.

In brief, it appears that responses which are primitive or initially more dominant are not necessarily the ones which remain dominant in the repertoire of the adults' behavior. Experiential factors can compensate for a lack of structural factors and can in certain cases become more dominant than responses to unlearned forms, possibly through an encoding process involving chunks of information rather than bits or pieces of information. "Doing what comes naturally" may be true for the naive child, but after the experienced organism has learned the functional utility of responding to certain forms, the latter become important cues to behavior. As a matter of fact, the whole question of how experience influences form discrimination is a very complex one which cannot be answered by one overall principle, as Köhler has tried to do. In the next three chapters we shall present recent views and research on the effect of controlled practice on perceptual discrimination.

SUMMARY

This chapter was divided into three main sections. The first described results which show that a certain amount of heterogeneity in stimulation is needed for the perception of figure. Demonstrations within the homogeneous field or *Ganzfeld,* known as the autokinetic effect, show that a differentiated ground is necessary for the emergence of a figure. The second section dealt with conditions determining the relative stability and instability of figure-ground phenomena including set and eye fixation. A description of the gestalt laws of visual perception, especially as initiated by Wertheimer, was presented in the third section. Attempts to reduce the gestalt laws to simple response reaction were also described.

Recent attempts using information theory to clarify why gestalt laws work the way they do, especially the pioneering work of Attneave, were introduced to throw light on the organization of elements into figures, patterns, groupings, or configurations. The thesis is that gestalt laws operate to establish a certain amount of redundancy which in turn ensures us against maladaptive error in perception. The channel capacity of the human organism as a processor or receiver of information is limited. While the amount of information we receive is relatively low, we can rely on that information for effective behavior.

The relative importance of stimulus factors and experience in the determination of figural detection and recognition was assessed. Figures which are relatively simple (have *Prägnanz,* according to gestalt principles, or are *redundant,* according to Attneave) are more readily perceived and recognized. It is in the case of more complex stimulus patterns that the role of experience becomes more important in the establishment of a stable, more permanent figure.

Information Processing Part One: Form Perception and Pattern Recognition

At the beginning of this book, and also in the description of the perceptual hierarchy, we stated a fundamental difference between detection and recognition, the two fundamental tasks in the problem of the perceptual extraction of information. We also distinguished recognition, noticing familiarity, from identification, knowing what it is. The preceding chapters have dealt with the tasks of detection and the higher stages of the hierarchy which precede the task of form perception. We have now arrived at the point where it is necessary to analyze the nature of the perception or recognition of a form or a pattern. In doing this, it is first necessary to consider in general terms how we shall define form or pattern. Most of the material that follows deals with recognition, although identification is sometimes involved.

In Chapter 9 we described a variety of principles, commonly called *perceptual laws of organization,* which the gestalt psychologists had proposed to describe the way elements in the perceptual field congregate. It is important to repeat here that these principles were merely subclasses of a master principle, the *principle of Prägnanz. Prägnanz* is a kind of esthetic principle since it deals with the distribution of elements into a condition which the gestalt psychologists described as the best, or a good fit. Although the gestalt psychologists did not really define good figure in operational terms to the satisfaction of subsequent psychologists, the work of Attneave (also previously reviewed) indicated that the principle of *prägnanz* really concerned itself with the economy and accuracy of information transmission. That is, since the human channel capacity is limited, the individual cannot see everything in the field without his perception becoming very unreliable or error-prone. Consequently, we tend to see little, but what we do see we can rely on: this is called *maximization of redundancy*. In actual terms, as we showed in the preceding chapter, this means that the perception will tend to consist of a configuration which is simplest—that is, one which has the smallest amount of elements or, in the case of a single figure, the smallest number of directional changes in the contour.

It must have become evident to the reader that the gestalt laws of organization describe how elements are grouped, but do not tell us how elements come together to form a particular meaning or a particular identity which we can recognize. For example, the gestalt laws of organization probably cannot account for what constitutes or defines a particular face that we can recognize. To repeat, we do not think that one can use any of the gestalt laws of organization to describe what it is about a particular woman's face that a particular infant can *identify* as being his mother's face as distinguished from the face of some other human being. It is this kind of problem—namely, of identity as distinct from unity or grouping—that Hebb has defined as constituting the central problem in the perception of form.

There are at least two ways (or aspects) of considering what constitutes a particular form pattern or what defines form. Consider the figure diagramed in Figure 10–1. One may raise the question, "What is it?" Perhaps many readers will say that it looks like a triangle; but it has four interior angles rather than three. Now, when we consider this problem, it becomes clear that *one aspect of a form,* namely, *its complexity,* probably depends on the number of angles or directional changes in contour or the number of separate features or elements that one can identify. Thus, we would probably say that an octagon is a more complex form than a square, which, in turn, is a more complex form than a triangle. Or, putting it another way, we could say that a human face, because we can identify at least five features—namely, hairline, eyes, nose, mouth, and curvature of head—is a more complex form than a bull's-eye, which simply has one feature that repeats itself, a set of more or less concentric circles, and is

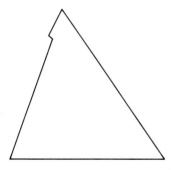

Figure 10-1 A five-sided figure that resembles a three-sided one, the triangle.

therefore relatively redundant. But consider further a square and a rectangle. Both consist of four angles. That is not going to tell us that a square looks different from a rectangle. Furthermore, two human beings will have the five features which we described before, but, again, that does not tell us what makes them different. Finally, in the example presented in Figure 10-1, the figure has four angles but, in fact, looks like a triangle. Clearly, in addition to the number of elements or, for example, the number of angles, there also exists the problem of the *relationship* between the angles, or the relationship of one part to another. That needs to be understood in order for us to have a clear definition of form.

Let us look into this relational aspect, considering the examples of the square and the rectangle. It is apparent that the characteristic distinguishing a square from a rectangle is the ratio of one side to the other. It is true that these sides must be joined by the four angles, but what makes the two forms different is the fact that in the case of the square the ratio of one side to another is equal to 1, whereas in the case of the rectangle the ratio of one side to another is different from 1. It is conceivable that similar kinds of distinguishing patterns or relationships operate in the way we tell one face from another—such things, for example, as not only the acuteness of the curvature of the jaw, but also the slant of the face and eyes, and the space between the eyebrows and the hairline. Somehow the human being develops amazing capacities to tell these very, very fine relationships apart and also to put them together to create the final product for defining the particular form or identity.

METRICS OF FORM

A number of psychologists (e.g., Attneave, 1955, 1957b, 1962; Attneave & Arnoult, 1956; Michaels & Zusne, 1965; Zusne, 1970; Brown & Owens, 1967; Hochberg, 1962; Garner, 1970b, pp. 350-358) have focused primarily on the first problem that we mentioned above, namely, the determination of the complexity of form.

The work of Attneave is probably the most appropriate place to start since he represents a transition from the classical work of gestalt psychology on figural organization to the more modern work of the information processors, which we shall analyze in the second part of this chapter.

Before specifically describing and considering Attneave's statement of form perception, we should provide the theoretical context for this work. Attneave started his investigation by applying the *concept* of information theory which was developed by Shannon and Weaver (1949). Let us consider the pattern in Figure 10-2, which consists of thirty-two cells. Suppose we play a game in which the subject is required to discover which one of these cells we have previously decided to be the "correct" one. If the subject *extracts* information most efficiently, he will be able to discover this cell with the minimum number of questions. He could proceed by eliminating one cell at a time, but intuition tells us that this would obviously not be the economical way of selecting a strategy. A more efficient way of extracting information would be to elicit answers which

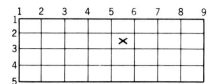

Figure 10-2 A pattern of thirty-two cells for illustrating the strategy in information extraction.

would eliminate the greatest number of alternatives for each question asked. The strategy might proceed somewhat as follows:

Question 1   Is it to the left of column line 5? Answer: No.
             Hence it must be to the right of this line.
Question 2   Is it above row line 3? Answer: Yes.
Question 3   Is it to the left of column line 7? Answer: Yes.
Question 4   It is to the right of column line 6? Answer: No.
             Therefore it must be in one of the two cells bounded by column lines 5 and 6 and row lines 1 and 3.
Question 5   Is it above row line 2? Answer: No.
             Therefore it must be the cell marked by X in the figure.

By using the procedure outlined above, the subject was able to eliminate *half* of the number of alternatives by asking each question in such a way as to elicit the most informative answer. Measurement in information theory is based on some operation of a binary choice (such as using the yes-no questions above). The unit of measurement is called the *bit,* which is a contraction of *binary digit.*

How do we go about measuring the bits of information? Let us look at the example above. We started with thirty-two alternatives, and by five questions reduced the alternatives to one. Since each question involves the choice between two alternatives, we can measure the bits by determining to what power 2 has to be raised to arrive at the number of alternatives. In the example above, $2^5 = 32$. Therefore five bits of information are contained in the pattern of cells. If all the information is transmitted, the individual will solve the game by asking only five questions. The general equation of measuring the amount of information in bits is:

$$A = 2^H$$
$$H = \log_2 A$$

where A represents the number of alternatives, and H is the symbol for expressing the amount of information in bits. (In our example above, $32 = 2^5$, or $H = \log_2 32 = 5$.) This equation holds only when all A's are equally probable. A somewhat more complicated but equivalent expression is necessary when all A's are not equally likely.

How can this way of measuring the amount of information be applied to the analysis of form or pattern discrimination? Let us consider the situation schematized in Figure 10-3. This schematization by Miller (1953) of the communication channel can be concretized in the situation of form perception in the following

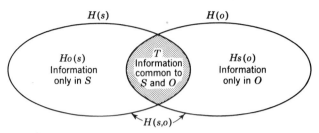

Figure 10-3 Schematic representation of the several quantities of information that are involved when messages are received from two related sources. *(Modified from Miller, 1953.)*

manner. $H(s)$ is the information generated by the stimulus, or the input information; $H(o)$ is the information in the perceptual process, or the output information; and T is the transmitted information. The greater the overlap between $H(s)$ and $H(o)$, the greater the amount of transmitted information, T. $Ho(s)$ is information which is put in at the senses but not recovered by the organism, O. $Hs(o)$ is information added by the organism. T will thus be reduced by the presence of $Ho(s)$, which is called *equivocation,* and by $Hs(o)$, which is called *noise.* Equivocation can be regarded as information which the organism cannot discriminate reliably, and noise as irrelevant perceptual or "mental" sets. We can thus measure transmitted information by the formula

$$T = H\ (s,o) - [Ho(s) + Hs(o)]$$
Total transmitted information = input information − equivocation − noise

In other words, the amount of transmitted information depends on the amount of input information which can be reliably coded by the organism, aided by relevant organismic sets.

We shall now present an actual example of measuring $T,$ before we proceed to a discussion of the problems involved in discovering the factors which determine the transmission of information in form perception, i.e., before discussing the factors influencing the content of the information discriminated in form perception.

In Attneave's (1957b) study, seventy-two shapes were judged for complexity by 168 subjects. The shapes were constructed so that certain physical characteristics were symmetrically varied and the remainder were randomly determined. Those who are interested in the mechanics of the construction of these shapes should consult an article by Attneave and Arnoult (1956). The forms were constructed by connecting a certain number of points according to specified rules. Some of the variables used in the forms were the number of points, turns, symmetry, and the factor of whether the forms were angular or a mixture of angles. Attneave's analysis of his data led him to conclude that 90 percent of the variability in the ratings of complexity of the shapes was accounted for by a weighting of three factors: (1) the number of *independent terms* (angles, curves, or sides in the contour); (2) *symmetry*—symmetrical shapes were judged less complex but were judged more complex when the total number of turns was constant (four- and six-point symmetrical shapes were equivalent to four- and six-point asymmetrical shapes with respect to the number of independent turns but equivalent to eight- and twelve-point asymmetrical shapes with respect to the total number of turns); (3) the arithmetic mean of algebraic differences in degrees between successive turns in the contrast. A similar relationship is expressed by the mathematical equation p^2/A, where p is perimeter and A is the area of the figure.

We particularly want to emphasize the third rule, p^2/A, because this deals with not only the complexity of the shape in terms of the number of turns, but also the overall *relationship between the total perimeter and the number of sides or turns,* which leads into the second important aspect of form which we described above—namely, the relationships between various elements or various sides. In a study related to the work of Attneave, Casperson (1950) used geometric shapes rather than random shapes and measured recognition thresholds and the total number of correct identifications, instead of judged complexity for his standard of form determination. His stimulus shapes consisted of six basic classes: ellipses, rectangles, triangles, diamonds, crosses, and stars. There were five figures in each class, constructed by varying the three dimensions of area, maximum dimension, and perimeter. On the basis of the shortest recognition and the greatest number of correct identifications, the following results were obtained:

1 *Area* produced the best measure of discriminability for ellipses and triangles.
2 *Maximum dimension* was the best for rectangles and diamonds.
3 *Perimeter* was the best for stars and crosses.

It is evident that the same dimensions do not always determine the matrix for the discrimination of the form. Evidently the subject relies on the best dimension available for making the most reliable discrimination. What this dimension is depends on the *overall constellation* involved, and to state that the rule is to follow the law of simplicity is to obscure the problem.

In addition to the work of Attneave (and similar work of Hochberg already reviewed in the last chapter), the researching of Michaels and Zusne, Brown and Owens, and Garner also deals with the question of the matrix determining the complexity and the relational aspect of form perception.

The application of information measurements to the analysis of form, pioneered by the psychologists mentioned above, makes it necessary to determine or specify the dimensions which constitute the informational components. This is precisely what Attneave and the other investigators have done. However, it is important to note carefully that we cannot determine the informational measure of a particular dimension unless we know something about the distribution of the values on this dimensional scale in the general population. Stated another way, what we are saying is that a dimensional value does not have an absolute informational value, but its informational value will depend on the population of values from which it comes. This fact had been stated by Wendell Garner, another user of the informational approach, in the following way.

> How the single stimulus is perceived is a function not so much of what it is but is rather a function of what the total set and particular subset are. The properties of the total set and the subset are also the properties of a single stimulus, so we cannot understand the knowing of the single stimulus without understanding the properties of sets within which it is contained (1966, p. 11).

One of the most conscientious and complete attempts to sample this range of population scores was conducted by Brown and Owens (1967). It is rather difficult to summarize the contents of their article, but we shall attempt to present a brief outline. They constructed 1,000 random shapes, using the technique of Attneave and Arnoult (1956), previously described. There were five samples, and each sample contained shapes of one complexity level only. Shapes of four, eight, twelve, sixteen, and twenty sizes were used. These shapes were then physically measured with respect to eighty dimensions which their complete review of literature indicated were considered to be important determiners of form. These measures consisted of the number of sides, the angularity, its perimeter, the number of terms, and other complicated statistical factors, not unlike but far more numerous than the ones used by Attneave which we described earlier in this chapter. Having made the measures on all the forms, they prepared an eighty-by-eighty table, the essential aspect of which was to determine the extent of the relationship (which the statistician calls the correlation between the various measures). Then, by using a complicated statistical technique, they analyzed all these correlations to see which of them shared common qualities. This technique, which is called *factor analysis,* allows us to group elements into broader relationships. They found that there were twelve factors, although five of them accounted for most of the relationships shown in the table. These five factors were named compactness, jaggedness, skewness related to the y-axis, skewness related to the x-axis, and the dominant axis.

Let us say a little bit about each factor. *Compactness,* which could just as well be called *elongation,* refers to the relative thickness or relative thinness of a figure. For example, in a rectangle and a square of comparable areas, the rectangle is more compact than the square. *Jaggedness* refers to the relative number of acute angles the form contains, the number of its interior angles. The greater the number of acute interior angles, the more jagged a form will appear. While *skewness on the x-axis* and *skewness on the y-axis* are rather difficult to describe, they essentially refer to the degree of symmetry that the figures have. The *dominant axis* refers to the major orientation (e.g., horizontal or vertical) which takes precedence.

Two aspects of the work of Brown and Owens are of particular interest to us. (1) Showing that one can reduce eighty relationships to a basic twelve is helpful in reducing uncertainty. To specify further that five factors account for most of the relationship helps even more. We mentioned earlier in this chapter that when, for example, we want to define a unique face, it is not sufficient to know the hairline, nose shape, curvature of the face, lips and so on. What is more important is to know how these components relate to one another. Using a factor-analysis approach, the way these investigators have, is a step in that direction. (2) Finding that much of the variance these five factors account for depends on the number of sides or turns in the figure is of *central importance*. We recall that Attneave and Arnoult found that this was one of the most important measures that they used. Specifically, Brown and Owens found that, as the number of sides increased from four to twenty, the percentage of the relationships which could be accounted for by the five variables decreased. For example, in the four-sided figure, 87 percent of the total relationships were accounted for, while in the twelve-sided figure, only 78 percent were accounted for. While this still represents a high percentage, it is important to note that we have this relational factor. Brown and Owens conclude, of course, that Attneave and Arnoult's work, particularly their designation of the number of sides and turns, probably should be used as a guide to designing other research. To augment this, we would say that there probably exists a dominant or super principle, or higher hierarchical order, so that effects of these submeasures would be conditional upon the magnitude of the dominant measure. Perhaps it would represent closure to end this section by saying that we might, in the case of complex form, come up with a principle as dominant in this area as *Prägnanz* was in the gestalt laws of organization. Would it be number of turns?

We may ask why the factor of the number of independent sides or turns seems to be so dominant. One answer has been suggested in an article by Arnoult (1960), describing research in which 80 percent of the variance in response could be accounted for by the number of independent sides, angular variability, symmetry, and the ratio p^2/A; it was suggested that the number of independent sides had to do with the *information load*. Thus, in general, increased information load leads to increased difficulty in performance, although this may not follow invariably. One word of caution is in order. Information *content* as a perimeter is a fundamental property, but the information conveyed is only of a "how much" kind. It does not tell us about the manner of the organization, but only about the degree of organization. If, for example, we say that a sixteen-sided figure has four bits of information, it tells us something about the degree, but tells us nothing about the infinite number of ways in which sixteen points can define the contour of the figure and how the contour can be arranged. In order to know more about the form, we need to know the information load and other form parameters. In this regard the work of Brown and Owens and others, while again indicating that the information load is the most important measure, is beginning to tell us what other submeasures exist which are partially correlated with the dominant measure. These submeasures are also important in determining the complexity and organization of the form.

It is interesting to consider why *Prägnanz* or simplicity should be dominant in the gestalt principles of grouping and why the *load* should be dominant in the question of form definition. In a sense these are two sides of the same coin. *Prägnanz,* dealing as it does with redundancy, tells us about the way the perceptual system ensures reliability and minimization of errors but tells us very little about what constitutes the variation or uniqueness of a particular form. Information load, on the other hand, tells us precisely about the number of variations; it does, indeed, tell us about the number of elements or factors which go into the definition of form. The task then becomes finding out what these measures are, and this is precisely what Brown and Owens and Gardner are attempting. For reviews by others who are performing similar services, see Michaels and Zusne (1965) and Zusne (1970).

CODING MECHANISMS FOR FORM

The relational or organizational aspects of form raise the question of how these relations are coded by the perceptual system. Some views follow.

Theory of Feature Analysis

This theory has been advanced by three different groups. Among them, Eleanor J. Gibson and J. J. Gibson have probably been the most influential. In Chapter 12, where it is more appropriate, we refer to some classic experiments by Gibson and Gibson on the recognition of nonsense figures which resemble fingerprints. Although we do not wish to repeat the essence of the experimental outline here, we should perhaps repeat the major finding. While the younger and older children did not differ from the adults in identifying the figures which differed in many dimensions, the younger children did differ from the adults in discriminating those fingerprint-like scribbles which varied only in three dimensions, and these dimensions were not that obvious to the viewer. Moreover, the young children never learned to achieve the high rate of expertness or specificity that the older adults reached.

On the basis of these kinds of data, the Gibsons rejected theories of perceptual learning and form perception which are founded on the development of association or organization. They proposed instead that persons are able, over time, to progressively elaborate certain qualities, features, and dimensional variations of the stimuli. Over time, in other words, the response becomes more specific or differentiated, and the person also learns to attend to the invariant stimulus information.

Other experiments which verify this distinctive feature interpretation of the Gibsons', also reviewed in Chapter 12, are the experiments by Anne Pick and the one by Gibson, Schapiro, and Yonas (1968). In the latter experiment, two sets of nine letters each were used as a test, and the test criteria consisted of the amount of time which was required by the subject to decide whether two simultaneously presented letters were the same or different. Subjects consisted of adults and 7-year-old children.

The results indicated that the time needed to say that two letters were different depended upon which distinct features were shared by the letters. Thus, letters which had similar orientations of lines, such as horizontal and vertical, took a longer time to discriminate than letters which had different orientations, e.g., vertical and horizontal in one letter, as G, and diagonal in other letters, as W. Adults require an average of 571 msec to respond that p and r were different letters, but only 458 msec to respond that G and W were different. The reaction times for children, while much longer, also showed a wide range of variation, depending on the features which the letters shared or did not share.

The data were further subjected to a cluster analysis to determine whether the reaction times could be causally related to the concept of distinctive feature. This analysis revealed that certain key features were important in determining which letters were grouped together. These features were the following: closed versus open lines; curved versus straight lines; diagonality; horizontal versus vertical lines; and intersection. Furthermore, these distinctive features had a far more important influence on discriminating which letters were different than in saying which were the same. In general, judgments of sameness took less time than judgments of difference, and "same" judgments for some pairs were reliably shorter than "same" judgments for other pairs. Gibson and co-workers concluded that, in some cases, the judgment of sameness was based on a direct perception of the replication without an analysis of distinct features.

All the research of Eleanor J. Gibson and her associates reported in this section and also in the next chapter has led her to postulate that learning to perceive more specified and distinct forms progresses, over developmental age, according to a cognitive hierarchy. This hierarchy is presented in Figure 10-4.

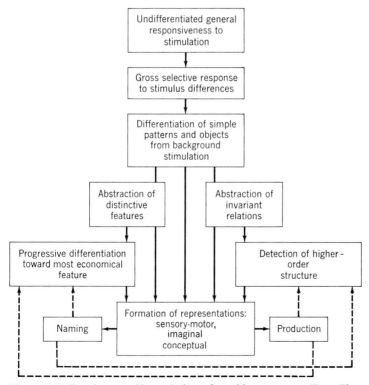

Figure 10-4   Developmental interrelations of cognitive processes. (*From Eleanor J. Gibson,* Principles of Perceptual Learning and Development, © 1967. *Reprinted by permission of Prentice-Hall, Inc., Englewood Cliffs, N.J.*)

The most important part of this diagram for the present purpose is that, at the third stage, the learning of form involves the abstraction of distinctive features and the abstraction of invariant relationships. While we have said much about the perception of distinctive features in this section, and a little about invariant relationships in the previous section, much work still needs to be done before we clearly understand what relationships are involved in perception and recognition of a distinctive form. Furthermore, while Gibson merely describes certain kinds of features which go into the definition of a form, she does not tell us what underlying mechanism might exist which performs such feature extraction. How these features might be extracted will also be discussed toward the middle and end of this chapter.

Schemata or Prototype Theory

While feature theory emphasizes that the individual seeks features on the basis of which he discriminates the form, the theory of schemata learning proposes instead that the individual has developed a model or a standard as a frame upon which other forms are tested or compared. These two different points of view, as we emphasize in the next chapter, differ with respect to their emphasis about what perceptual learning consists of. While feature theory emphasizes that we learn to be increasingly discriminating and differentiated or specific, schemata theory asserts that learning consists of the building up of a standard. A little reflection, however, makes it evident that these two kinds of learning cannot be antagonistic but are, in fact, probably complementary. The very process of building up a standard or model as a frame of reference must mean, in part, that the individual is learning not only more feature elements but also how to put the features together.

A recent definition of schema is advanced by S. H. Evans (1967): "A schema is a set of rules which would serve as instructions for producing in essential aspects a population prototype, an object typical of the population. Furthermore, a schema family is a population of objects all of which can be efficiently described by the same schema rules." Modern research seems to have concluded that the prototype is represented internally as a *central tendency*. The prototype which is a standard or central tendency serves as useful reference for discriminating among the patterns within each category, for learning which patterns belong to the particular category, or for classifying patterns into other categories.

A study in which both the generalization and discrimination (thus integrating the schemata and the feature approach) were present was conducted in a rather ingenious experiment by Posner, Goldsmith, and Welton (1967). In this experiment the prototype consisted of a pattern which could be made by arranging nine dots in a thirteen-by-thirteen matrix. Four different prototypes were used, namely, a triangle, an M, an F, and a random pattern. In addition to the original figure the subject could also be exposed to five distortions. These distortions could be placed on a scale from 1 to 12, where 1 represented a very low degree

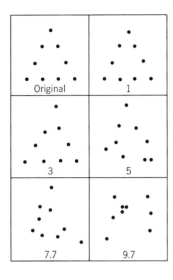

Figure 10-5 Original and five levels of distortion for set of triangles. *(After Posner* et al., 1967 *Copyright 1967 by the American Psychological Association. Reprinted by permission.)*

of distortion and 12 a very high degree of distortion, with 5 representing a moderate degree of distortion. An example of the triangular case with five distortions is presented in Figure 10-5. There were five groups of subjects in the experiment. Group-1 members learned a list of low-variability distortions, while group-5 learned a list of moderate-variability distortions. Following this, both groups were presented with a transfer task in which the list consisted of high-variability distortions. The results were that Group-5 made fewer errors on the transfer task, revealing that the greater variation of patterns during previous learning was more beneficial in transferring to a task consisting of higher-variable patterns.

Research which we reviewed in this section as well as additional research presented in the next chapter seems to indicate that both feature and schemata learning contribute to the growth of perception. There has been much debate as to which of these two is more dominant. The following three experiments will lend a perspective to answering this question. The first experiment, conducted by Anne Pick (1965), utilized a design very similar to the one used by Eleanor Gibson and her associates. Subjects who consisted of children were required to discriminate each of a set of three standard designs from three transformations of each taken from the set of six in Figure 10-6. Group E1, which was called the prototype group, was supposed to show the extent to which learning of the standard had occurred during training. This group received the same standards from training, but three new transformations of the standard during the transfer task. It was reasoned that, if the children had formed an adequate representation of the standard in the pretraining, it would be relatively easy for them to locate the standards among the rest of stimuli, that is, three new transformations. Group E2, the feature group, was supposed to indicate the extent to which distinctive-

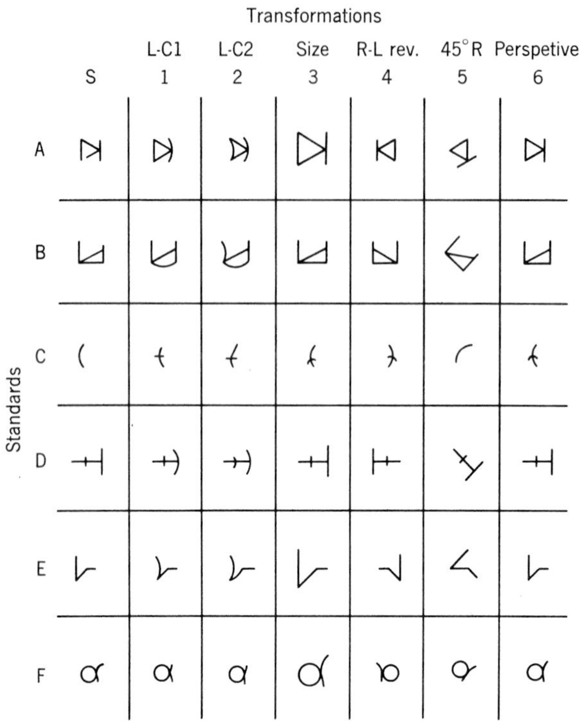

Figure 10-6 Standard and transformations of letter-like stimuli. *(After Pick, 1965, p. 19. Copyright 1965 by the American Psychological Association. Reprinted by permission.)*

feature learning had occurred during pre-training. They received three new standards but the same three types of transformations during the transfer task. Note that in each experiment the subject received only one standard and three transformations in the pretaining of the other three transformations in the transfer task. To return to group E2, if these children had learned to discriminate between the different transformations by their distinctive features, the transfer task would be relatively easy since the same transformations were used in both tests.

Anne Pick presented the stimuli in both a visual and tactile manner. The results indicated that, with simultaneous presentation, both visual and tactile forms revealed the superiority of group E2, that is, the distinctive feature group. However, with successive presentation of tactile forms, there was no difference, suggesting that the formation of a prototype or representation of a standard during pretraining becomes more important when comparisons cannot be made simultaneously. Somehow, therefore, simultaneous presentation seems to facilitate the learning of distinctive features, whereas during successive presentation this advantage is either lost or else the learning of a standard which can be carried over to the successive presentation helps.

A study by Caldwell and Hall (1970) was conducted by these authors because they believed that Pick had loaded the experiment in favor of E2, the distinctive-feature group. For example, a child in the prototype group who was pretrained on transformations 1, 2, and 3 in Figure 10-6 may not have known that a rotation of the pattern would be called different on the transfer task even though he might have been able to discriminate the rotated patterns from the nonrotated standard. Therefore, these investigators changed the grouping of transformations so that 1, 3, and 4 would be used on one task, and 2, 5, and 6 would be used on the other task. As a result of the new grouping, both the feature and the prototype groups would learn during pretraining that line-to-curve changes make a difference from 1 or 3, size transformations make a difference from 3 or 6, and finally that rotation transformations make a difference from 4 or 5.

Under these conditions, where equal information was given the two groups, no significant difference was obtained between the feature and the prototype groups. Caldwell and Hall therefore concluded that both feature learning and prototype learning were not really in opposition, since the formation of a prototype or representation of central tendency consisted of nothing more, in any case, than storing.

In a third and final experiment which will be reviewed here, Aiken (1969) used a task similar to Pick, but the stimuli were presented through the ears; that is, the stimuli were auditory. There were four standards, but only two standards and two features were varied during the training task. The stimuli could vary in frequency, amplitude, duration, and direction. The prototype group was given the same standard but two new features on the transfer task, whereas the feature group was given the same two features but two new standards on the transfer tasks. For a control group both new standards and features were given. The test task required Navy recruits to learn to discriminate between a standard signal and a comparison stimulus which was presented 1.5 seconds later. The mean number of errors in the transfer test was only 4.56 for the prototype group by comparison with 5.94 for the feature group and 7.75 for the control group. While both experimental groups differ significantly from the control group, the difference between the feature group and the prototype group was also significant.

Thus we have the various findings. Pick's study supposedly reports the superiority of feature learning. Caldwell and Hall's study reports no difference, whereas Aiken's study, using auditory stimulation and fewer transformations, reports the superiority of prototype learning. It is evident that different conditions (such as the number of transformations and whether we are using successive or simultaneous presentation and even whether the sense is vision or auditory) may make a difference in which of these two strategies is used.

Perception as Information Processing

Information processing, the descriptive phrase for an orientation toward exploring certain types of problems in experimental psychology, holds the key for understanding the intellectual origins of this approach. Information analysis has already been discussed with regard to the content of the stimulus in form-perception research. Information in that sense is an abstract quantification (e.g., "bits of information") of the nonredundant features of the stimuli. The joining of the words *processing* and *information* reflects both a different meaning of the word *information* and a different approach to its use in psychological research.

Information is no longer used in the communications network sense. It is more loosely defined, but basically refers to those characteristics of the stimulus that are used by the subject in *processing* that stimulus input. The subject is encoding, modifying, selecting, abstracting, etc., certain characteristics of the stimulus as a natural part of his ongoing activity. This activity may be as mundane as looking at words flashed very briefly on a tachistoscope or as abstract as the visual imagery or verbal associations one gets in listening to a symphony. Certain aspects of the stimulus environment ("information") are being transformed ("processed") into some end result (perhaps an observable response, although not necessarily).

Many psychologists today identify themselves as "cognitive psychologists" and their area of research interest as "cognitive psychology." In one sense, this is a tribute to Ulric Neisser, whose book *Cognitive Psychology* (1967) has been of such importance as an intellectual force in this area. The use of the word *cognitive* also dissociates this area of experimental psychology from the earlier work on information analysis, as in form perception. In this book, the term *information processing* is used because of the generic link of this field to the innovative logic spawned by the computer revolution. Neisser considers the analogy between the cognitive problem and the development of programs or "software" in the computer field an advantageous one. What these programs operate on or transform is best defined as information. It should become apparent that many of the concepts of cognitive psychology (or information processing) are direct parallels of, if not identical with, concepts used in computer science.

A model has been presented in Figure 1-2 that is our schematic representation of human information processing as reflected in the act of perception. This model is really a condensation of the essential elements found in many models of information processing (e.g., Haber & Hershenson, 1973; Lindsay & Norman, 1972). It should be apparent at this point that this approach completely rejects any naive realism in which it is assumed that a perceptual experience (e.g., seeing a particular pattern with clarity) reflects a simple direct sensory representation of the stimulus that is a kind of sensory photograph or copy of the stimulus.

On the other hand, is *perception* being discussed in this chapter? Certainly Neisser's discussion clearly puts perception into a broad, undefined realm of stages and end products of the information-processing act. Perception has traditionally referred to processes that involve some elaboration or transformation of sensory input. Brightness discrimination is ordinarily considered a sensory process, physiologically mediated by subcortical mechanisms, whereas brightness constancy is considered perceptual, involving more elaborate cortical processes. This kind of distinction is made in this book and is considered, although not resolved in the same manner, by such authors as Cornsweet (1970).

Perception, from our point of view, should, in one sense, refer to those particular problems traditionally designated as perceptual, such as the constancies of size, shape, and motion. That the problem is investigated from the information-processing point of view would not be relevant. In another sense, however, perception has always been viewed as a hypothetical construct whether as the end product of a certain stage of processing or a processing stage itself.

When we say that a person perceives a word flashed on a tachistoscope, we are using his verbal report as evidence. Yet when we say "perceive" with the reference to the subject, we are not referring to his verbal report. He "perceives" a certain pattern consisting of specified contours of sufficient clarity. It is the constructed image, which is experienced, that we speak of as perceptual. It is private or subjective data. Its properties can be discerned only by reference to some interpretation of the relationship of the subject's response to the stimulus conditions. *Information processing is simply one approach toward defining the relationship between the subject's response and the stimulus conditions. Perception,* from the present point of view, can then be understood as these *constructed images,* whether they be visual, auditory, tactual, etc. As an example of this approach, visual space perception then consists of constructed visual images with "depth structure" as a feature. This analysis does not negate the influence of higher-order variables, such as language structure stored in memory, as in the tachistoscope example, in the construction of these images. This, of course, was the point of Figure 1-2, that in viewing perception within an information-processing analysis, the stages of this process are not simply sequential. Higher-order stages such as the memory storage can directly influence the manner of processing at lower-order stages.

Sensory Register

A major concern of this chapter will be the manner of information processing at the sensory register. To be discussed is the manner in which stimulus information is stored, transformed, and directed to other processing stages in the very first few hundred milliseconds after presentation of the stimulus. By necessity, the role of memorial processes in perception will be presented only incidentally. The emphasis of this section will be on vision. There are two research areas in visual perception that are concerned to a great extent with information processing at the level of the sensory register. These areas are masking and metacontrast. There are many similarities in the types of investigations performed in these two areas, and both are generally classified under the rubric *masking,* which refers to some change in the phenomenal appearance of a stimulus upon the presentation of a second stimulus within some limited temporal proximity. Metacontrast is distinguished from masking in this section because of the unique characteristics of the experimental paradigms used, as will be discussed shortly, and its generally separate theoretical development.

Before discussing metacontrast and masking, it is necessary to describe the phenomena and introduce the terminology of the fields. In Kahneman's (1968) excellent review of this area, visual masking refers to that "class of situations in which some measure of the effectiveness of a visual stimulus (the test stimulus, TS) is reduced by the presentation of another (the masking stimulus, MS) in close temporal contiguity to it." There are two types of masking, *forward masking,* when the MS precedes TS, and *backward masking,* when the MS follows TS. *Metacontrast* refers to that class of masking paradigms in which the TS and MS are presented to nonoverlapping retinal areas, i.e., they are spatially distinct. When the retinal projections of the TS and MS overlap, the experimental procedure is simply referred to as *masking.* Several types of MS are used in both the metacontrast and masking paradigms, and these will be described later.

The major independent variable in most studies of these phenomena is the time relationship between the TS and MS. Two time parameters can be defined. The interstimulus interval (ISI) refers to the time period between the offset of the TS and the onset of the MS, whereas stimulus-onset asynchrony (SOA) refers to the interval between the onsets of these two stimuli. When the MS precedes the TS, both of these measures are expressed in negative values. A -20 msec SOA refers to the fact that the onset of the MS precedes that of the TS by 20 msec.

Metacontrast   The metacontrast literature is a large one that includes many different types of TS and MS along with several manipulations of the stimulus variables that relate the two. In metacontrast the TS and MS are presented to two nonoverlapping retinal areas. At appropriate ISIs or SOAs, the MS produces a "phenomenal suppression" (Lefton, 1973) of the TS so that the subjects are not able to report its occurrence. Two primary experimental procedures are used in investigating metacontrast phenomena. In one procedure, the TS is flanked on both sides by masking stimuli of the same form. Both the TS and MS may simply be patches of light, as in the classic study of Alpern (1953), or both may be triangles, rectangles, etc. The second metacontrast procedure commonly involves a TS that is a disk and an MS that is a ring that surrounds the disk when both are superimposed. In an important study by Weisstein and Haber (1965), the TS was the letter D or O, and the MS was a ring that surrounded the letter.

The data for a metacontrast study are ordinarily plotted with some measure of the degree of metacontrast, e.g., percentage of trials on which the TS is correctly reported, on the ordinate of the graph, and either ISI or SOA on the abscissa. Two types of metacontrast functions may be obtained. One involves a "monotonic" or linear relationship between degree of metacontrast and the temporal spacing of the TS and MS. Often, however, an inverted U-shaped function is obtained. In this case, the greatest amount of metacontrast occurs at some intermediate SOA. Short and long time periods between the TS and MS lead to much less metacontrast.

By now it should already be apparent that it is difficult to organize and summarize the metacontrast literature. Not only are there many procedures and types of results, there are also many manipulations of stimulus variables, which, along with the many response measures used, compound the problem. It is not surprising, therefore, that many studies lead to conflicting results. In this section, only a few of the major findings will be presented to highlight the issues in this very active research area. Comprehensive reviews of this literature can be found in Kahneman (1968) and Lefton (1973).

The early study by Alpern (1953) is an appropriate starting point because the procedures (and findings) have been reproduced in numerous studies. Alpern used a brightness-matching design in which subjects matched the brightness of a TS presented to one eye with that of a comparison or reference stimulus in the other. The subject's specific task was to adjust the brightness of the TS to match that of the comparison stimulus. Metacontrast was induced by presenting two adjacent patches of light on either side of the TS. The TS-MS SOAs varied from −100 to +300 msec. Metacontrast was revealed by increases in the amount of energy that had to be added to the TS to match the reference stimulus; i.e., metacontrast decreased the apparent brightness of the TS. When the test flash luminance was plotted as a function of the SOA, Alpern found maximum metacontrast decreasing as the SOA was decreased or increased from this point; i.e., an inverted U-shaped metacontrast function was obtained.

Alpern did find a relationship between the luminance of the MS, its duration, its proximity to the TS, and the degree of metacontrast produced. Metacontrast could not be obtained when the TS and MS were of equal luminance. It was obtained as the luminance of the MS was increased over that of the TS. Metacontrast decreased as the duration of the TS was increased, but it increased when the duration of the MS was increased. Finally, Alpern found that the angular *intercontour distance* (the visual angle related to the distance between the outside of the TS and the closest boundary of the MS) was an important variable in determining the degree of metacontrast. Maximum metacontrast occurred when the intercontour distance was zero, and it decreased as the spatial separation between the TS and MS was increased up to a visual angle of 2°.

Of the studies using a ring as the MS, that of Weisstein and Haber (1965) has created considerable interest. Numerous investigators have attempted to replicate their findings and have offered theoretical and methodological critiques of the original study. The data reported here are those of Weisstein (1966) who replicated and extended Weisstein and Haber's (1965) study.

Since the methodology of this study is complex and is important in interpreting the results, it will be presented in detail. Weisstein had subjects judge whether an O or a D was present at a particular position along an array (or row) of these letters that was shown for 20 msec on a tachistoscope. Metacontrast influenced the ability of subjects to make these judgments in that a ring MS was presented at various ISIs after the TS array was flashed. The subject was to identify the stimulus that was surrounded by the ring. The ring was thus an "indicator" as well as an MS. The ISIs varied from −20 to +120 msec. In the more extensive of the two studies reported by Weisstein, she had arrays that consisted of one, two, four, and eight letters. For the multiletter arrays, the letter position that was ringed by the MS varied from trial to trial. As can be seen in Figure 10-7, the stimulus conditions further contained situations when only one

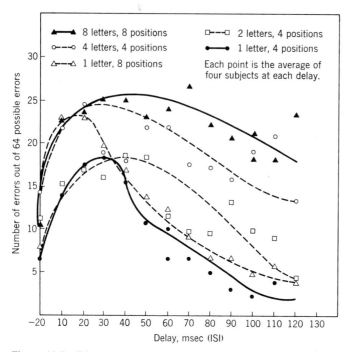

Figure 10-7 The U-shaped masking functions representing the errors made with ring masks as a function of ISI for each array size separately, averaged over subjects. *(From Weisstein, 1966. Copyright 1966 by the American Psychological Association. Reprinted by permission.)*

or two letters were presented in the array, but these letters could be placed at any of the four or eight positions that defined the array.

The data in Figure 10-7 appear complex, but it should be noted that inverted U-shaped functions were obtained in all the experimental conditions. The maximum amount of metacontrast, defined here by errors in identifying the letter O and D, occurred approximately between 15 and 60 msec of ISI, depending on the condition. Although there was a tendency for the range of ISIs for which the MS was effective to increase as the number of letters in the array increased, such differences were not consistent across the four subjects. There were also no differences for any subject in this range when comparing the one-letter, four- and eight-position conditions.

Eriksen and his co-workers (Eriksen, Collins, & Greenspon, 1967; Eriksen, Becker, & Hoffman, 1970) have failed to replicate Weisstein's finding of an inverted U-shaped function relating degree of masking to ISI. Eriksen et al. (1967) obtained monotonic functions such that the amount of masking steadily decreased as the ISI increased. They were also able to show that part of the increased range of ISIs for which metacontrast is found as the number of stimulus letters was increased in Weisstein (1966) could be attributed to using the MS, the ring, as both an indicator and as an MS. It was an indicator in the sense that it informed the subject as to which of the several letter positions he was to report about. Eriksen et al. used separate forms to indicate the stimulus and to mask it, and found less of a range effect than Weisstein. There were some procedural differences between Eriksen et al. (1967) and Weisstein (1966) that are of interest. Eriksen et al. used the letters A, T, and U rather than D and O. There are less confusions of the former stimuli when surrounded by a masking ring than for D and O. The stimuli were presented in a circular arrangement to ensure that all retinal (foveal) positions used were of equal sensitivity. Weisstein had used a linear array of letter positions with less control of the sensitivity of the retinal areas involved.

Failures in replicating particular findings are not unusual in the metacontrast literature. It should be pointed out, therefore, that methodological criticisms, such as those of the Weisstein (1966) study, serve possibly to point out the complexity of the metacontrast phenomena, and how dependent they are on the characteristics of the TS and MS and on the response procedures used in evaluating metaconctrast. Kolers (1962) has summarized the stimulus characteristics that lead to either monotonic masking functions (type A) or U-shaped ones (type B). When the TS and MS are comparable in physical characteristics, such as contrast or luminance, U-shaped masking functions are produced. Monotonic functions result from greater contrast, or luminance, etc., for the MS as opposed to the TS. With regard to response procedures, one must first consider whether identification or simply detection of the TS is required in an experiment. The kind of criteria used by the subject in making identifications must, of necessity, be more complex and stringent than in the detection condition. The meaningfulness of the TS used by Weisstein would be expected to influence the type of masking function obtained.

Lefton (1973) lists several theories about determinants of the shape of the metacontrast function. There is some indication that inverted U-shaped metacontrast functions are obtained in stimulus situations that give rise to the experience of apparent motion between the TS and MS. Kahneman (1967) suggests that metacontrast may result from a failure of "perceptual synthesis" resulting from cues for impossible motion. In the paradigm in which the TS is flanked on both sides by the MS, the TS appears to move laterally, in *both* directions at once. In the disk-ring procedure, the disk appears to grow and disappear at the same time.

However, the largest number of the theories of metacontrast are those that attempt a physiological explanation of the phenomena. These theories or, more accurately, models rely on the current findings in sensory neurophysiology for specification of structure. Therefore, there are several models in which *lateral inhibition* is the key element in metacontrast as it is in the mach band phenomena. Other models refer to the findings on coding cells in the visual cortex by Hubel and Wiesel. Still other models are models per se; i.e., they use hypothetical neural nets or sets of neurons with associated properties and parameters to reproduce the metacontrast phenomena. These models and an evaluation of such models, in general, in the area of information processing, will be discussed in a later section of this chapter. The only point to be made here is that metacontrast does appear to be a central process, i.e., occurs at or beyond the lateral geniculate nuclei (which are located in the highest part of the subcortex). It can be produced with a dichoptic stimulus presentation in which the TS is presented to one eye, the MS to the other (Schiller & Smith, 1968).

It is very difficult to evaluate metacontrast within the structure of an information-processing approach to perception. In the Alpern (1953) study, in which the subject is presented with patches of light as both the TS and MS, the U-shaped metacontrast function most likely indicates processing that involves the operation of the sensory register, the construction of the visual image, with little if any memorial processing. The subject's reports, even if they include apparent movement, can be taken as "perceptual reports" as opposed to "cognitive reports" (Natsoulas, 1967). Consider, however, the Weisstein (1966) study which also resulted in an inverted U-shaped masking function. The TS were the letters O and D. The subject must process those features of the stimulus that allow him to make a discrimination between these two stimuli. This is especially difficult with a ring as the MS. This is one point Eriksen et al. (1967) make in evaluating this study. In this difficult judgment task, it would be expected that some sort of memorial process would be involved that influenced both the types of features or characteristics of the letters processed from the sensory register and any evaluation of them.

Several questions come to mind at this point that directly concern the sensory register and how it may be reflected in the function obtained by Weisstein. Why should the maximum masking effect by the ring take place at some interval of time after its presentation? In what manner is the information from the TS maintained in the sensory register during this interval, if at all? Where does the information go from here if it must be processed rather complexly for features that discriminate between the two test stimuli? As stimulus information is "synthesized" at some later stage of processing (memorial?), does it arrive in some serial sequence or all at once?

Questions such as these are very fundamental to the information-processing approach to perception. The next section of this chapter reviews research on the *iconic storage*, a name Neisser (1967) has given to what has been termed here as the *sensory register*. The term should be taken to represent a very brief, initial, visual memory or storage within which the initial TS in a masking experiment is held and from which information is sent to later stages of the processing sequence. The emphasis on storage and transfer of information from the "icon" makes this a concept of more specific applicability than that of sensory register.

Iconic Storage   The initial concern in reviewing the literature on iconic storage must consider evidence which supports the concept itself. Simply stated, what evidence exists to indicate that the visual information is maintained for a brief duration, on the order of about 300 msec, after the stimulus is terminated? Primary data come from a study by Sperling (1960). Letters were very briefly exposed to the subject via a tachistoscope. The exposure period, 50 msec, was too brief for directed eye movements to aid the subject in identifying the stimuli. Sperling presented his stimuli in a unique manner in that rectangular arrays of letters were presented, e.g., four letters in each of three rows. A "partial-report" technique was used in which subjects were cued as to which row of the array they were to report on. The cuing was accomplished by the presentation of a low-, middle-, or high-frequency tone. This cue was presented at various time delays *after* the presentation of the stimulus array.

In evaluating the results obtained by Sperling, it must be kept in mind that without the use of the partial-report technique, a subject could, at most, report four or five letters accurately. On the other hand, using the partial-report method, Sperling found that subjects had approximately nine letters available when the cue tone was presented *immediately* after the letter array. This was determined by calculating the average percentage of letters of the cue row correctly identified and then multiplying it times the total number of letters in the array. The figure 9 reflects the 76-percent accuracy level of subjects for the zero-delay cue condition. Further evidence for a brief visual memory (icon) was found in the progressive decline in the percentage of correctly identified letters in cued rows as the delay of the cue was increased. Most subjects were able to estimate six or more letters when the cue was delayed about 150 msec. However, a 1-second delay in the cue found subjects at the chance level, i.e., with about four or five letters available as calculated for the whole array.

There are a number of studies in which the persistence of the visual image of a stimulus is considered as evidence for iconic storage. In one such study, Eriksen and Collins (1968) presented two dot patterns in succession. These patterns were such that, independently, they appeared to be a random array of dots, but when superimposed, they joined in producing a recognizable three-letter nonsense syllable. If there was short-term visual storage (a persisting visual image) of the first pattern presented, it would be expected that a direct relationship would be found between the percentage recognition of the nonsense syllables and the amount of time delay between presentation of the first and second pattern in a tachistoscope. Eriksen and Collins found that for several luminance levels of these dot stimuli, the percent of correct recognitions of the nonsense syllables decreased fairly steadily as the ISI of the dot pattern increased up to the maximum value of 100 msec.

EXTRACTION OF STIMULUS INFORMATION FROM THE ICON

At this point, it can be assumed that stimulus information is maintained for a few hundred milliseconds after *termination* of its exposure. The relevant questions now are: (1) In what form is this information encoded or stored in the icon? (2) In what manner is this stimulus information transferred to the memorial stages of processing (a short-term memory?) for further analysis and transformation? (3) Is the transfer of this information a serial or parallel transfer process; i.e., is stimulus information, in whatever form, transferred sequentially, or is all information sent on at once, in a parallel manner?

Once these questions have been addressed, two further problems remain to be discussed for a more complete understanding of the contributions of the information-processing approach to understanding "perceptual problems." The first concerns *figural synthesis* (Neisser, 1967), the manner in which the stimulus information transferred from the icon is assembled or synthesized into a representation of the stimulus form. The second problem is that of *pattern recognition*. Once the stimulus information is transferred to memory, pattern recognition processes ensue such that a stimulus consistently produces a unique response. The major problem for any model of pattern recognition is how one can consistently "recognize" patterns when the same form may be presented in different perspectives, sizes, retinal locations, and even in degraded or schematic form, such as in cartoon drawings of well-known personages.

In order to answer such questions as those posed at the beginning of this section, an experimental methodology has evolved in which the processing of information from the icon is interfered with by the use of a masking stimulus. The paradigm used is that of an ordinary masking study where a TS is presented and is to be identified. Some sort of indicator may be present to direct the subject toward a part of the stimulus display as in the study by Eriksen et al. (1967) in the section on metacontrast. The MS may be a simple illuminated visual field in a tachistoscope or a more complicated pattern or a noise mask. Some of the types of pattern masks that have been used will be introduced in the following discussion. Before reviewing studies on information processing from the icon, some discussion will be necessary on the nature of the role of the types of MS on the information-extraction process itself, i.e., how these MS interfere with processing.

The most straightforward approach to the role of the MS in forward and backward masking is the luminance summation–contrast reduction hypothesis of Eriksen (1966). According to this theory, the ability to identify forms that are presented for brief exposures, as in a tachistoscope, is a function of the contrast ratio between the luminance of the ground upon which the form is superimposed and that of the form itself. Up to a point, the greater the luminance of the ground in relationship to that of the form, the greater should be the percentage of correct identification. Eriksen was able to demonstrate this empirically. The second part of his hypothesis was that the visual system sums or integrates the luminances presented to it within a brief time interval, on the order of 100 msec. The closer the two stimuli, the greater the integration.

A second hypothesis is directly linked to the luminance summation–contrast reduction hypothesis. It concerns summation of the luminance of the MS and TS. Consider a backward-masking situation in which the TS precedes the MS by a short time interval, for example, 20 msec. For an MS, a simple, blank, illuminated field is presented on the tachistoscope. The TS, on the other hand, is a letter such as T, presented on a blank (white) illuminated background. A dark field of view is presented to the subject before the TS and during the ISI that occurs before the MS is presented. If the luminance of the MS sums with that of the TS, a reduction of the contrast ratio between the figure (T) and the ground of the TS occurs. This happens because the luminance of the MS adds to *both* the figure and the ground. It thus reduces the ratio of their luminances. If the figure was 1 ml and ground 10 ml in the TS, a 10-ml mask will now sum with the TS to have a "total stimulus" with a 1-ml figure and a 20-ml ground. To the extent that such summing takes place, it should reduce the percentage of correct identifications of the TS by the subject, which is what Eriksen found. As would be expected, the degree of interference was dependent upon the temporal proximity of the TS and MS; it decreased as the ISI increased.

Erikson's theory on the role of the MS is clearly that it summates or integrates with the TS. This is an "integration" theory for simple (blank) masks. When a noise or pattern MS is used, e.g., a field of overlapping X's, the controversy concerning the function of this mask is whether it again interferes with processing from the icon by integrating with its contents or by "interrupting" the processing itself, perhaps by "erasing" the contents of the icon. The integration hypothesis argues for a degraded, harder-to-process icon, the interruption approach for an end to processing or wiping out of the icon.

Sperling (1963) has conducted a study that addresses itself to this controversy. He presented letter arrays of from two to six letters as the TS. An MS followed the TS (backward masking) by 20 to 60 msec. A noise mask was used that consisted of densely scattered pieces of letters. The data consisted of the number of letters correctly reported after the various SOAs. These data are presented in Figure 10-8. There was a fairly constant relationship—10 msec per letter—between increases in the delay of the MS and the number of letters correctly reported. Sperling interprets these data as indicating that the MS disrupts the cortical representation of the TS. Until it *arrives* in the cortex, the subject can process the TS and report the letters.

Spencer (1969) argues against Sperling's interpretation of the role of the noise mask in Sperling's experiment. Luminance summation could have been occurring because of the relationship between the length of time the TS was presented and the delay interval before the MS was presented. Data of Liss (1968) support an erasure hypothesis and also provide evidence on the prepro-

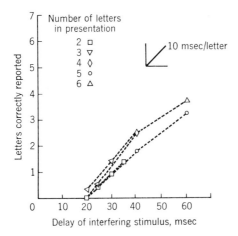

Figure 10-8 The number of letters correctly reported as a function of the SOA between the MS and TS. *(From Sperling, 1963.)*

cessed contents of the icon. Liss found that letters (the TS) followed closely by a noise MS (backward masking) appeared bright and of high contrast to his subjects. The subjects also reported that they did not have time to identify them. The visual image was constructed but could not be used. With longer delays before the MS, the identification could be made. The mask in this study appears, therefore, to have interrupted, interferred with, or erased the contents of the icon rather than to have degraded or summed with it. This is further attested to by the degraded appearance of the TS to the subjects when the TS and MS were presented concurrently, rather than with the delay that allows icon formation of the TS alone.

The study by Spencer further clarifies the role of the MS in processing from the icon. In this study, both blank white masks and pattern masks were used. Backward-masking functions were obtained for TS displays composed of single letters or twelve-letter circular displays. The blank mask had an effect on letter identification for SOAs only up to 75 to 100 msec, whereas the pattern mask was effective for considerably longer delay intervals, e.g., up to 400 msec in one condition. Spencer argues that these data indicate that a blank mask operates at a more peripheral level in the nervous system than the pattern mask.

Spencer and Shuntich (1970) used more than one level of pattern mask energy in a backward-masking paradigm. When a twelve-letter TS was used, a low-energy mask had a progressively greater effect on the subject's ability to identify the letters as the SOA increased, with a maximum effect at 150 msec. Note that in the other studies reviewed, the MS has its greatest effect at zero SOA. These findings are clearly not supported by a strict integration or summation theory in which the greatest effect of the MS would be expected at the zero SOA. Summation, as Eriksen (1966) showed, becomes less likely as the time between the MS and TS increases. On the other hand, these data would support the argument that the low-energy pattern mask becomes more effective in erasing the icon as the icon fades in some manner, with time.

Up to this point studies have been reviewed that indicate that an icon exists, that it may consist of an at least partially constructed representation (visual image) of the stimulus, that it lasts for a few hundred milliseconds, and that information is being processed from it in a serial or sequential order that may be interrupted by a pattern mask. Not all studies agree on this last conclusion. In fact, Sperling (1967) presents evidence that the processing from the icon may proceed in a parallel fashion, i.e., that all the stimulus information is transmitted at the same time to the later (memory) processing stages.

In the Sperling study, five letters were presented in a linear array as the TS. A pattern mask MS was used in a backward-masking procedure. The data of interest are the masking function presented in Figure 10-9. Interestingly, the subjects showed a preference in this order of identifying the five letters in the array that follows the formal coding structure of English; i.e., they reported letters in a left-to-right fashion. Looking at the masking function for the leftmost letter in Figure 10-9, the letter I, we see that 100 percent correct identification is reached at a masking interval of approximately 25 msec. If we look at letters in

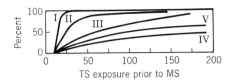

Figure 10-9 The percent of letters reported correctly at various exposure durations for stimulus positions I (leftmost) to V. *(From Sperling, 1967.)*

positions III to V, it is obvious that their identification began to increase with increasing delays of the MS, well before the preceding letter in the left-to-right sequence reached 100 percent identification. Thus letter III is above chance identification well before letter II (more to the left) reaches 100 percent.

These data of Sperling can be interpreted as indicating a parallel transfer function for information leaving the icon. A serial process would argue for 100 percent identification at position I before II is reported at a greater-than-chance level, and II should be identified at 100 percent before III was above chance, etc. Sperling suggested a parallel transfer function with different processing rates at the different letter positions. In other words, the data argue that more than one letter is transferred at a time.

There are several studies that argue for a parallel transfer function. Thus Wolford, Wessel, and Estes (1968) presented sixteen letters in a four-by-four array to their subjects who were to press a key labeled B or F when the array contained one or the other of these letters. The target letters, B and F, were presented more than once in the letter arrays. Although this is not a masking paradigm, the data directly indicate parallel processing from the icon. The subject's reaction time, his time until pressing the button when perceiving the B or F, did *not* reflect the number of times the target letter was presented in the display. If processing of it from the icon was serial or sequential, the subject's reaction time would be expected to decrease as the frequency of appearance of the target letter in the array increased.

Pattern Synthesis and Pattern Recognition   When discussing the transfer of stimulus information from the icon to later processing stages, we indicated that the letters were transferred in parallel. The use of the term *letters* should not be taken to imply that certain patterns in their entirety, synonymous with the stimuli, were the elements of the icon and constituted the information transferred. Although there is evidence for a fairly well defined visual image represented by the icon (Liss, 1968), this does not mean that the stimulus is encoded as a unified gestalt, i.e., as some simple representational structure. The pattern could be stored or encoded in this short-term visual storage or icon as a collection of features, e.g., linear extensions, intersections, that, as a code, represent the stimulus.

Although there is a large literature on the memory or posticon stages of processing in the information-processing literature, this topic is beyond the scope of this chapter. A portion of this research concerns the role of such factors as attention, familiarities, and meaning of the processed stimuli on the subject's ability to search for and identify certain target elements in the stimulus array.

Sperling's study shows the influence of the structure of the English language on processing from the icon.

The general focus of this chapter is on form perception as a perceptual process. For a subject to report on his experience of form, two general processes must occur. A form must be derived from the encoded input of the icon and a unique recognition of the figure must take place.

Neisser (1967) speaks of the role of attention in the development of the percept of a form. He speaks of *focal attention,* the selective allocation of the processing mechanisms to portions of the visual field. "To pay attention to a figure is to make certain analyses of, or certain constructions in, the corresponding part of the icon" (pp. 88–89). Focal attention becomes operational after other "preliminary operations" have segregated the "figural units" of interest. These latter processed are the sort, as described by Neisser, that allow one to segregate a letter on a page and keep it intact and distinct as a unit while it is further explored and discriminated from other units. "Analysis by synthesis" follows in which these features are synthesized into a form that can be recognized as a pattern in memory. With a degraded form, several syntheses may take place to try to "recognize" the stimulus. The direction of these preliminary analyses by the result or mismatch (nonrecognition) of previous synthesis defines the feedback-type role of analysis by synthesis in the recognition process.

The problem of pattern recognition is a very difficult one. Many models, not a small number involving abstract probability theory, have been evolved to handle one or more facets of this problem. Computer simulations of pattern recognition and pattern-recognizing devices have been created. Two general orientations to pattern recognition are those that postulate some sort of *feature-extracting mechanism* within the pattern-recognition process and those that concern themselves with a *template-matching device.* Most current models employ the feature-extracting device. Two reasons for this are (1) the current findings in sensory neurophysiology where feature-extracting-type cells have been found at both cortical and subcortical visual areas in animals, and (2) the inherent difficulties with the template approach. As an example of one of these difficulties, we can ask how one is to recognize a pattern through matching it with an organized template or general model at some memory stage, when the pattern to be recognized can be of any size, placed at any retinal location, be oriented in numerous ways, and distorted selectively. Think of the problems in building a machine to recognize handwritten messages. We can all "read" most handwriting, although the structural aspects of the letters vary widely from individual to individual. How could we have sufficient templates in memory to match all the variations, indicated above, that could be imposed on common patterns such as handwriting? How would we know which template to use? Some mechanism would have to be postulated that selectively changes the patterns or templates stored in memory to sequentially match them to some input for recognition. A parallel application of a class of templates seems unlikely because it would have to be so large. On the other hand, selectively distorting some "basic template" sounds suspiciously like feature analysis.

For feature analysis, our device to recognize handwriting would have to store in memory some collections of features or pattern elements that uniquely identify a letter. Presumably, this would be an exhaustive or closed set. Some device at the icon level would be sensitive to the number of linear elements and transmit this information to some higher center, where it could be synthesized into a "best" pattern for the recognition stage of our device. To the extent that unique features exist for letters and can be abstracted at any retinal location, this device would be much more efficient than one following the template-matching scheme.

Sutherland (1973) has noted several aspects of pattern recognition in human beings and animals for which any theory of pattern recognition or simulation device would have to account. Such factors include being able to recognize a pattern as unique although stimulus size and retinal location may vary from trial to trial. Some more subtle aspects of pattern recognition which Sutherland discusses are that certain rotations of a shape will *not* be treated as equivalent to the original; that some shapes are more easily confused than others; that ambiguous figures can be seen in several ways; and that redundancy in patterns is used in recognizing them.

In a recent book, Reed (1973) has very comprehensively summarized and interpreted the variety of approaches and problems in the field of pattern recognition. Figure 10-10 is Reed's general conceptual model of the various stages in the process of pattern recognition taking into account the current experimental and theoretical trends in this field. His model is clearly of the feature-extraction variety and uses analysis by synthesis as an important aspect of the recognition process. In this model, the stimulus is examined, and both features and their relationship (e.g., "parallel") are extracted. A pattern "description" is produced to represent the stimulus. Sutherland (1968) had

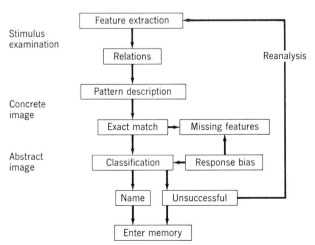

Figure 10-10 A general conceptual framework showing different stages of pattern recognition. *(From Reed, 1973.)*

suggested the efficacy of the description approach in handling a variety of research findings in this area. The description would be synonymous with a concrete image of the stimulus if it completely describes the pattern. The actual matching portion of the recognition process involves an "abstract image" that consists of some sort of visual image or description stored and now retrieved from memory. Reed points out that this would not involve a name for the to-be-recognized pattern because a name would be attached, if at all, after a match with the memory content occurs. From the model it can be seen that reanalysis occurs when matches are unsuccessful. This is the process of analysis by synthesis described earlier where a new feature extraction or analysis occurs as the result of an unsuccessful synthesis or putting together of the currently abstracted features. It is a feedback loop that efficiently keeps the process going until a resolution occurs. There would have to be some criteria for defining a resolution or "successful enough" match addended to this model. This model is really a heroic integration of a very difficult and complex research area.

Neurophysiology and Information Processing in Perception

It is rather easy to think of "features" that could serve as the elements of patterns, e.g., independent lines, linear intersections, rate of angular change in a portion of a pattern's contour. These are the types of stimulus elements Attneave (1957a) explored in discussing the complexity of patterns. Although the dimensions that may underlie patterns are not clear at present, it is nevertheless easy to see a parallel between the relatively simple visual features described above and the kinds of stimuli that seem to be encoded by neurons at various levels in the visual system. In this light, some of the important neurophysiological findings discussed in Chapter 4 will be reviewed here.

The evidence for receptive fields with mutually antagonistic (excitatory-inhibitory) areas is solid and pervasive at all levels of the visual system. Kuffler's (1953) early study has led to a virtual explosion of important data. All these findings indicate that very selective stimulus properties are being encoded within receptive fields at all levels of the visual system. As Uttal (1973) points out, just how selective these systems are did not become apparent until more complex stimuli than flashes of light and clicks were used.

The primary building blocks used by those who apply neurophysiological findings to perceptual phenomena are lateral inhibition and the hierarchical arrangement of cell types found in the cortex by Hubel and Wiesel (see Chapter 4).

A necessary question at this point is what the implications are of these neurophysiological findings for the fields of form perception and pattern recognition. There is no doubt that many investigators have felt that physiological operators, similar in function to Hubel and Wiesel's cortical cells, are appropriate if not essential elements in their explanatory models for various human perceptual phenomena. Some of this material will be reviewed later in this section. Several books on pattern recognition are available today, and a new view seems to be emerging which argues that there has been an overreliance on physiological data that, in themselves, are not of sufficient comprehensiveness or complexity to be of much aid in formulating what might be termed neuropsychological models of perceptual phenomena.

In keeping with this latter view, Dodwell (1970) suggests that it may be "wrong to think of the receptive field organization as being the basis for anything but a 'primary receptive' of local property detectors . . . and that a model for shape recognition and perceptual learning should not at present expect more support from the neurophysiological findings" (pp. 90-91). Uttal (1973) is more sharply critical:

> Someday, future psychobiologists may consider this current trend in 'explanations' exactly as we now look upon the computer models, the telephonic models, or the even more ancient hydraulic and pneumatic models of brain function, as simply the subsequent stage in a series of reductionistic fads. . . . The communication of information patterns through the ascending pathways does seem amenable to some types of single cell analysis. The explanation of complex perceptual phenomena, however, may lie at a level of complexity with which no current neurophysiology can deal. It may also be true that we shall have a difficult time distinguishing between processes which, superficially, seem closely related by experimental designs, but which may have quite different underlying mechanisms. (p. 457)

What specifically do we know about information processing in human beings, as a neurophysiological event? Consider lateral inhibition. The major findings are those summarized in Ratliff (1965). The organism studied was *Limulus,* the horseshoe crab, an invertebrate. Very fine patterns of interactions have been recorded between fibers of the optic nerve in this organism. The apparent sharpening of the spatial features of the information being processed within this primitive visual system has been well documented. Particularly relevant seems the application of the resulting models of lateral inhibition to contour coding in human vision. In Chapter 5, the application of such a model to the mach band problem was undertaken. That these bands of lightness and darkness occur at points of the stimulus pattern where intensity changes are most rapid seems to make a physiological model based on lateral inhibition most appropriate. Uttal finds this application in vertebrate neurophysiology to human illusions acceptable primarily because it does not seem to involve a central process and seems entirely dependent upon the geometry of the stimulus.

It should be stressed at this point that there is no direct physiological evidence implicating lateral inhibition in higher-order organisms. The assumption seems plausible, but there is no reason why neural sharpening of borders and contours could not be resolved by some more abstract process even at the peripheral level in mammals. Recall the controversy concerning the place theory of von Békésy (Chapter 6). Pitch is spatially coded according to this theory, but the areas of the basilar membrane displaced by any pure tone are quite broad. Some neural sharpening at the local level is necessary for this theory, and von Békésy invoked lateral inhibition in his "funneling" concept. There is more behavioral evidence for funneling, especially for the tactile sense, but there is no physiological data and thus no way of evaluating a physiological model implicating direct lateral interactions within the associated neural plexus.

Lateral inhibition has been used as an explanatory mechanism for many models of masking and metacontrast. Bridgeman (1971) has metacontrast as an "artifact" of the operation of lateral inhibition. His model used in a computer simulation of human neuronal activity draws upon the *Limulus* studies directly for functional relationships in this neural activity. In developing a model for backward masking, Purcell, Stewart, and Dember (1968) have generated a number of hypotheses about lateral inhibition in human beings that also follow directly from the work on *Limulus*.

Weisstein (1968), on the other hand, uses neural network theory to explain metacontrast findings. The five neurons involved in this network are not those involved in the peripheral coding of stimulus features. Thus one neuron is a "decision" neuron. Two other neurons, individually, contain the integrated inputs from the peripheral sensory fibers on the target and mask. Many assumptions about the properties of these cells are necessary to explain the complicated findings that are characteristic of the metacontrast literature. As Lefton (1973), in his review of metacontrast studies, points out, Weisstein's model has demonstrated predictive validity in matching the outcomes of several metacontrast studies.

The level of physiological processing proposed by the various models, as well as its form, forces the pertinent question here. Which of these models is most accurate vis-à-vis sensory physiology? Although all these models are concerned with human behavioral (perceptual) data, they are really physiological models. In a real sense, their validity cannot be determined by how well they fit the behavioral data but remains to be determined as future findings in neurophysiology become available. Neurophysiological models of these phenomena may be less productive than an information-processing model that systematically explores the manner but *not* the mechanism by which the spatial and temporal features of the masking and metacontrast stimuli are encoded.

In comparison with lateral inhibition, it would seem that a strong argument can be made that the operation of cortical and lateral geniculate cells of the type explored by Hubel and Wiesel can be used for explanations of certain phenomena in metacontrast, masking, and pattern recognition. Many patterns can easily be expressed as line segments of specific orientations, e.g., letters of the alphabet and numerals. More complicated figures, such as animals and faces, can be schematized in terms of simple features. It is therefore a relatively minor leap to involve Hubel and Wiesel cell types in an analysis of the processing of such stimuli.

One argument that can be brought to bear against the hypothesis that straightforward feature abstraction via cortical cells is the fundamental process in pattern recognition is the importance of the entire stimulus organization in determining the subject's response. Recall the centrality of figural organization in the gestalt theory of perception. This theory proposed that certain innate cortical processes operated to produce the "best" form given the structural aspects of the stimulus. A good or "best" figure ordinarily had a minimum of irregularities, many redundant or repeated features, and was symmetrical. Examples of gestalt-like processes in everyday perceptual experiences are extrememly numerous. Consider the number of times we fail to notice the use of the word *the* when it occurs twice in succession in a sentence. We do not notice such irregularities although our English professors might.

Royer and Garner (1966, 1970) have examined the types of organization that subjects impose on auditory patterns consisting of repetitions of two tones. If X represents one tone and O another, a typical nine-element tonal pattern would be XXOXXOXXO. When presented at sufficiently slow interstimulus intervals, such patterns are clearly discerned by the subjects. Since these stimuli do not have recognizable beginnings and endings, the organizations that are imposed by the subject on the repetitive presentations of these stimuli can be examined. These organizations have gestalt-like properties. A "temporal gestalt" is important. Meaningful units in the organizations are applied by the subjects, e.g., the rhythm of XXO in the examples above. Further, the judged organizations usually have a symmetry or balance. Royer and Garner (1970) conclude:

> In the process of perceiving, the organism selects an organization already inherent in the stimulus. The limited organizations possible with a given pattern are made known to the organism, which then selects the one most suited to his preferred organizing principles. Thus, the concept of his perceiving it as an accumulation of directional associations between sequential elements or, ever more so, as associations between the elements and possible responses is quite inadequate. (p. 120)

Uttal (1969) uses a unique character-recognition task that directly implicates a central, organizationally selective encoding process rather than some more peripheral feature-abstracting mechanism. The stimuli were letters of the alphabet formed by various arrangements of dots (Figure 10-11*a*). These stimuli were masked by dynamic visual noise (DVN) patterns. The latter were produced by the random placement of dots on the screen of an oscilloscope at some specified interdot time interval. Given the fact that the visual system integrates images over a set time period and with the various interdot intervals used, several different noise masks can be produced. Three of these masks are given in Figure 10-11b.

Uttal performed three different masking studies in which the subjects judged the identity of letters when the DVN was presented (1) for an extended interval within which the letter stimuli were presented, (2) before the letter stimuli, and (3) after the characters. The results of the first experiment showed, as would be expected, that there is an inverse relationship between the percentage of correctly identified letters and the density of the DVN. However, identification is approximately 60 percent, even with the very dense DVN that occurs when dots of the DVN are produced every 3 msec.

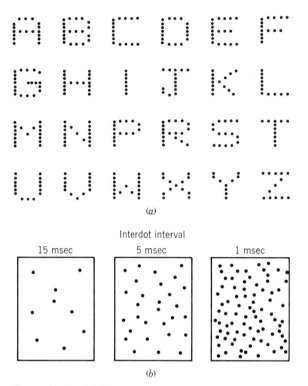

Figure 10-11 *(a)* The set of characters used as test stimuli. *(b)* A representation of three levels of dynamic visual noise (DVN). *(From Uttal, 1969.)*

Consider Figure 10-12, which shows the percent of correctly identified letters for the leading and trailing noise experiments at the various delay intervals used between the presentation of the DVN and the letter stimuli. What is remarkable is the greater than 80 percent recognition scores for the 3-msec interdot interval DVN for both these experiments at the smallest DVN-letter interval.

Both these data and those of the first experiment would indicate that subjects can readily distinguish the noise and letters even when presented simultaneously. As in Royer and Garner's study described above, subjects are apparently responding to organization as organization and not to isolated features of the stimuli. If the latter were the case in Uttal's study, it is hard to imagine what criteria could be used by the subject to separate local sections of the dot display (both the DVN and letters are dots) into the DVN and letter components. The temporal and spatial assocations of the dots at single location would not suffice.

In short, to the extent that overall stimulus organization can be shown to be an element in the processing of patterned stimuli, an analysis of pattern recognition via physiological feature detectors of the sort associated with certain cells of the visual cortex would not be adequate. Some higher-order integration of the coded outputs of such cells would have to be involved. The integrating principle

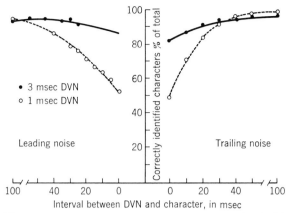

Figure 10-12   The effect of either leading or trailing DVN, of two levels, on the identification of the alphabetic characters presented at various ISIs. *(From Uttal, 1969.)*

would have to be sufficiently abstract to include the meaningfulness of these letter stimuli. Such organizing operations are the substance of the gestalt approach to perception.

SUMMARY

Chapter 10 started with a description of the problems of form perception. An adequate theory of form needs to specify at least three things: (1) what determines the relative complexity of form; (2) what determines its relational quality; (3) what the coding or processing mechanisms are which the perceptual system utilizes for extracting both the complexity and relational aspects.

After we described work dealing with complexity, the matrix of form, and theories dealing with how the relational quality is extracted, we presented an extensive discussion of the general information-processing approach to perception, up to and including the form stage in the perceptual hierarchy.

Chapter 11

Information Processing
Part Two: Attention
and Illusions

While describing the information-processing approach, we referred to Neisser's distinction between preattentive attention and focal attention. We did this to show that attention is an important aspect of the perceptual system. In this chapter we shall describe its relationship to past experience, and end by showing the dependence of illusion on the latter two variables.

ATTENTION

Attention can be defined as the selective aspect of perception and response. Any theory of attention presupposes some general framework to fix the nature of processing in the perceptual system—such as the model presented in the previous chapter and in Chapter 1.

All of us can think of many examples when we had to decide about attending to one of two competing events or to attend to one of two competing responses coming from within us. Perhaps the example of the party phenomenon is a good one to illustrate what we have in mind. You are at a party and someone is talking to you. You are, however, attracted by some characteristic about a person who is standing near you in a neighboring group. As you pretend to be listening to the individual who is talking to you, your eyes drift in the direction of the other

It is important that the subject man be car pushed house slightly boy beyond hat his shoe normal candy limits horse of tree competence pen for be only in phone this cow way book can hot one tape be pin certain stand that shops he with is his paying teeth attention in to the the empty relevant air task and hat minimal shoe attention candy to horse the tree second or peripheral task.

(a)

In performing an experiment like this one on man attention car it house is boy critically hat important shoe that candy the old material horse that tree is pen being phone read cow by book the hot subject tape for pin the stand relevant view task sky be read cohesive man and car gramatically house complete boy but hat without shoe either candy being horse so tree easy pen that phone full cow attention book is hot not tape required pin in stand order view to sky read red it nor too difficult.

(b)

Figure 11-1 After Lindsay & Norman, 1973, p. 357.

person, and perhaps you even try to listen to what is being said in the next group. Even though you cannot hear anything coming from the other group, the fact that your visual attention is directed in that direction blocks out most of what is being said to you. If anyone were then to ask you what the person talking had said, you would remember embarrassingly little.

The task outlined in Figure 11-1 demonstrates the two aspects which affect the direction of attention. You are asked to read the two passages but attend to the shaded part of the paragraph only. Try doing it in Figure 11-1a and 11-1b. You will probably find that you have no difficulty reading only the shaded message in Figure 11-1a and 11-1b, but when you get to line three in Figure 11-1a, you will find that suddenly you are tempted to read the nonshaded parts as well. Why the difference? In Figure 11-1b the shaded message makes sense or has meaning, whereas in Figure 11-1a the shaded part does not make sense. In order to get meaning, you have to read the nonshaded part after that.

The above demonstration highlights the two aspects of attention: (1) Attention is first of all attracted by some characteristic of the stimulus which catches our eye, such as the shading in this particular demonstration; (2) the far more important part of attention comes from some internal direction on the part of the subject. We shall now concern ourselves with an examination of these two determiners of perception.

Stimulus and Eye-Movement Factors in Attention

Most of us are aware of the fact that such aspects of the stimulus as motion, contrast, and change or novelty will attract our attention to that object (Berlyne, 1951 & 1973).

One of the major ways in which attention is engaged is through the direction and control of eye movements to find stimuli of potential interest. Eye movements, however, always depend on the context of the information that we are seeking. The movement between eye fixations is not independent of the information we extract during the fixations. That is to say, what we do with our eyes when they are not focused depends on the task which engages our eyes in the first place.

Another important factor to consider in eye movement is the difference between foveal and peripheral vision. During the former we can identify in detail what exists in the stimulus. Pattern acuity then drops 50 percent when an object is located only 1° from the center of the fovea and an additional 35 percent when it is 8° from the center (Riggs, 1965, pp. 81–131). However, we do get some kinds of cues from the periphery. For example, objects in motion or which have high contrast may nevertheless shift our eye movement even when these stimulus objects occur on the periphery of our visual field.

The above considerations suggest that two tasks seem to be involved in attention. The first is *identification,* which requires foveal vision, while the other concerns a *decision* about the direction of the next eye movement, depending on information located on the periphery. Neisser (1967) suggests one way of understanding what happens when we shift from peripheral to central vision. He reasons that an object cannot be identified until it is first separated from a background. He called this segregation a *"pre-attentive* process." This preattentive process is global and allows the figure to be focused upon so that its features can be analyzed for more specific aspects. When the figure has become segregated, focal attention can occur, usually by a shift in the position of the eyes. The preattentive process gives rise to focal attention. During preattentive attention a part of the field is separated into a figure, whereas during focal attention this figure is analyzed for its specific informational aspects.

Some interesting work on the difference between foveal and peripheral vision, and its relation to the preattentive process, has been conducted by Sanders (1963). Sanders conceptualized that there are three different attentional fields, each varying in the number of degrees that it covers. The first, the *display field,* covers the central and peripheral vision during a single fixation or a glance; the second, the *eye field,* extends to include the area that is covered by saccadic eye movements; finally, the *head field,* in addition to the first two, covers the amount of space included by head movements. Figure 11-2 shows the extent of the fields during free head movement and when the head is fixed. Sanders believes that the two dips in the curve indicate the breaking points between the

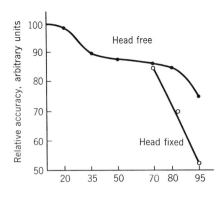

Figure 11-2 Accuracy in reporting the number of lights in two columns as a function of the distance between them, when the head is free to move and when it is fixed. *(After Sanders, 1963.)*

display and eye fields and between the eye and head fields; thus eye movement extends the display field from 30 to 80°, while head movement extends the field beyond 80°.

Sanders' distinction between the three fields is relevant to the preattentive process postulated by Neisser. Thus, within the display field, preattentive processes are capable of finding and segregating all figures. However, when the visual angle between the objects and the field is greater than the limits of the preattentive process, the parallel nature of processing will be lost, and eye movements will be needed to complete testing, or if it gets very far out, head movements will be necessary. The important contribution of Sanders is his discovery that, even out to 80°, some information can be available to help direct eye movements.

Central or Internal Factors

We come now to the internal or organismic factors which direct attention. This is by far the most important factor. The phenomenon to be explained by some theory of internal direction of attention is the fact the most of us find it extremely difficult to attend to more than one incoming message. The question concerns what the nature and determination of this selectivity in perception are all about.

One of the earliest theories developed to explain selective attention was the *filter* model of D. E. Broadbent (1958). The essential notion was that physical features of two stimuli were considered as channels which had limited channel capacity, and that there was a complete gating of the unattended channel. This view was supported by the fact that, if you send two separate messages to the two ears through earphones and ask the subject to pay attention only to one ear, he cannot recall what was sent into the unattended ear. For example, in split-span experiments, when digit pairs are presented dichotically to the two ears, the subject reports one ear and then the other.

However, research has indicated that, if the unattended ear contains information which can be meaningfully related to the attended ear, the subject will be able to report that information to the unattended ear. Moreover, it has been noted that subjects will report their own name 30 percent of the time when it is delivered to the unattended ear (Moray, 1959).

There are a number of other problems which Broadbent's model had difficulty in explaining. While it is true that the subject can follow a message sent only into one ear, if a single passage is given at twice the normal rate, it is almost as intelligible as before. Furthermore, if the information content of the passage is doubled by using a low-order approximation to English, subjects achieve shadowing scores considerably higher than 50 percent of their original performance. (*Shadowing* means following the information coming into one channel or one ear.) The limit does not seem to lie in the overall information level but rather in the number of physically separate inputs we can handle or in the number of separate sequences of interdependent items we can follow. This obviously gives trouble to the limited-channel theory. When subjects are asked to repeat one of the dichotic auditory messages, the other produces negligible interference. However, if asked to name the colors of printed words which themselves name other colors, they find it extremely difficult to attend selectively to the colors, and the words cause severe interference.

The above evidence as well as much other evidence is reviewed by Anne M. Treisman (1969). She also points out that in attention there is selection of perception as well as response. Broadbent (1970, pp. 51–60) presents data which show that the selective aspect of perception is far more important than that of response. In any case, any theory about attention must presuppose some general model about the nature of perceptual processing similar to ones we discussed in Chapter 1 and have used throughout this book. Mechanisms of perceptual transformation of physical stimuli into psychological perceptions which we have described in various parts of the book, for example, motion systems, suggest that there are a number of different perceptual *analyzers,* each of which provides a set of mutually exclusive descriptions for a stimulus. Judgments about the different dimensions appear to be made independently, with little or no interaction. These independent dimensions suggest the existence of separate analyzers. However, such a model does not explain perception of complex or multidimensional patterns. Perception of shape, for example, may depend on two or more levels of analyzers, those at the higher level grouping which classify the outputs of those at the lower level to give another mutually exclusive set of complex percepts. Our *hierarchy of perceptual organization* is consistent with this notion.

If there are different perceptual analyzers, they may be arranged *in series, in parallel, or in hierarchy*. The outputs of analyzers at any one level, or any combination of outputs, may potentially be both stored *in memory* and used to control the overt response.

One theory, a very contemporary one, which attempts to take account of the role of memory and all these active processing aspects of attention, has been advanced by Norman (1968). His theory is diagramed in Figure 11-3. This model of Norman's, which is far more extensive than Broadbent's, has the following essential characteristics. Channel 1 is the attended one, while channel 2 is not. The notion is that, after sensory analysis and feature analysis, some kind of passive process is actually going on in both channels and in memory. The major impact of attention is that, from memory to active synthesis, there is a comparison between the expectations and the actual imput. And it is during this active processing that the synthesis takes place.

Note that, in the Norman model, after sensory analysis, feature analysis and memory are located in time sequence where our registration and perception processing is going on. He, at this point, is not making a distinction between memory and short-term memory. Furthermore, his memory in active-synthesis stage represents the highest stage in the model which we produced in Chapter 1.

Treisman and Riley, modifying Broadbent's model since the filter is too simple, also suggested that there is an *attenuation* of the message in the non-attended channel. In their 1969 article, they try to present detailed analyses of the elements which go into this complex attentional selectivity suggested by Norman.

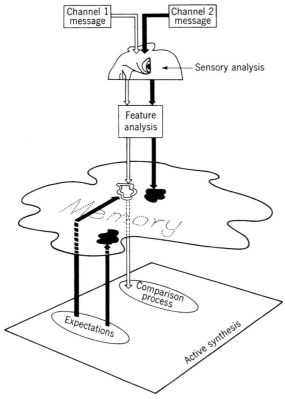

Figure 11-3 The attentional model. *(After Lindsay & Norman, 1968, p. 369.)*

Treisman reasons that there are four functionally different types of selection which determine attention, one affecting only response and memory while the other three restrict perception. The four types are: (1) output selection; (2) input selection; (3) analyzer selection; and (4) test or target selection.

Output selection assumes some limit to the response we can make and to the information we can store, and that simultaneous aspects of perceptual analysis compete for access to the limited-capacity motor system and memory.

During *input selection,* perception is restricted by selecting which sets of sensory data to analyze. This type of attention implies at least two successive stages of analysis so that the dimension taken by the first analyzer can be used to label the sensory data wanted for analysis by the second analyzer. Input selection defines the data we *look at* and *listen to,* but not the properties we look or listen for.

Analyzer selection, on the other hand, selects one or more dimensions or properties of stimuli to analyze and ignores other dimensional properties.

Finally, *test* or *target selection* collects the particular items we wish to identify where the items are defined by one feature or specified sets of critical features.

Two different measures have been used to investigate to what extent perceptual processing can be done in parallel when attention is directed and to what extent it must be done serially, requiring focused attention. The first method compares the *accuracy* of responses with tasks requiring attention to two inputs, dimensions, or targets with those requiring attention to only one. The second method measures the difference in *reaction time* which results from different numbers of inputs, dimensions, or targets to be matched or identified. We now go into a summary of typical experiments using these methods.

Two experiments suggest that the main limit on dividing attention is set by the sharing of a single analyzer. Thus, Treisman and Riley (1969) asked subjects to repeat a string of digits heard in one ear while listening with either ear for a letter, which was sometimes in the same voice as the digits and sometimes in a different voice. The targets (letters) were detected much less in the nonshadowed message, suggesting that the main difficulty arises in the sharing of a single analyzer for two inputs.

In an experiment by Lawson (1966) subjects were asked to make a discriminative response to one of two possible tones embedded in a shadowed and a nonshadowed message. Their performance was worse than with a single tone and showed a greater decrement on the nonshadowed message. It may thus be harder to use different analyzers on different inputs than on the same input, at least when the two inputs must be distinguished from each other. Part of overloading in divided-attention tasks may therefore be due to the reception and labeling of inputs from two different sources, as well as to the double use of a single analyzer.

Lappin (1967) compared the reports of tachistoscopically presented circles, varying in size, color, and angle of line through the center, when subjects were asked to report the three dimensions of one item, one dimension of three items, or a different dimension of three different items. The particular stimuli and the responses made were directly comparable, since the experimental conditions changed only the relations between them. The first condition was easiest, and the last condition slightly harder than the second. The first required the use of *three analyzers on one input,* the second the use of *one analyzer on three inputs,* and the third the use of *three analyzers on three different inputs.* Division of attention between different inputs was again the main source of difficulty. Specifically, the use of three inputs was much more difficult than the use of one input, and limits on the use of different analyzers appeared only when they were used for different inputs which the subject has to distinguish by the spatial location. It was also found that the responses to the three dimensions were essentially uncorrelated and independent, which would support the suggestion of *parallel analysis.*

The data and the experiments reviewed above suggest that inputs are processed serially, that analyzers can be used in parallel, and that it is only when the analyzers have to be shared between more than one input that it is difficult for the analyzers to be used in parallel. The difficulty with more than one input has been verified in an experiment by Treisman and Geffen (1967) where more clear-cut limits to the division of attention were shown. They found that the accuracy of monitoring in a selective-listening task decreases as the range of targets increase. In sixty test targets, the subjects detected fewer targets in *both* shadowed and nonshadowed passages when they were defined as "any digit" or "any color" than when they were defined as specific single words like "night" or "hot."

The reaction-time method has been used primarily to determine whether tests or targets are processed in series or in parallel. The clearest example of this task is the one used by Sternberg (1967) in which subjects were asked to search through a visual display of varying size for a particular target letter. The reaction time increased linearly with the number of items in the display, strongly suggesting that visual items in different spatial locations must be *identified serially.* Furthermore, experiments by Kristofferson (1967) on judgments of successiveness suggest some *minimum time* for identifying one stimulus before another can be accepted by the perceptual system.

Finally, Sternberg found strong evidence for serial search through a set of memorized targets. He measured reaction times to match one or more visual digits with a varying number of memorized digits, and found that the response latency increased linearly with the number of comparisons to be made, suggesting that looking *for* and looking *at* an additional target letter required equal processing capacity.

We see that there is quite strong evidence that true division of attention is difficult or impossible, that serial processing is necessary, both with two or more inputs and with tests for two or more targets. Thus, inputs and targets are processed in series, whereas analyzers may be used in parallel. Nevertheless, there is evidence to suggest that *it is difficult to focus on an analyzer* while filtering out others at the same time. Thus, Biederman (1966) found that irrelevant dimensions are analyzed and cause delays in reaction time. He compared response latencies in a contingent task, a filtering task, and a condensation task where the values on all three dimensions were relevant to the response. Intertrial changes on the irrelevant dimension delayed the response in both filtering and contingent tasks, the delay varying with discriminability. His main aim was to demonstrate that selective and serial processing of different dimensions are possible. He argued that this is demonstrated by the facts that (1) reaction time was faster in the contingent than the condensation task, (2) intertrial repetitions and discriminability had both more effect when they involve the primary dimensions than the secondary, and (3) errors were more frequent on the secondary dimension. However, some of these findings could be explained on the assumption that all dimensions were analyzed in parallel, but response was initiated as soon as the relevant information had been obtained. Then the slowest dimension would determine reaction times only when it was relevant to the tasks in the contingent condition, but would always be completed for the condensation task.

It does seem that focusing particular perceptual analyzers while excluding others might be difficult or impossible. There are two possible sources of interference, other than a direct perceptual limit on the number of analyzers which can operate simultaneously. (1) Interference may arise at the response level when the output of analyzers evokes conflicting responses. Using the Stroop test, Klein (1964) found that subjects did better if they were allowed to first read the words; he suggested that allowing subjects first to "unload" the competing response facilitated their performance on the color-naming task. Another test would be to see if one could reduce the interference by using a nonverbal response, which should conflict less with the irrelevant but dominant reading response. (2) Irrelevant analyzers may indirectly produce perceptual as well as response interference by effectively increasing the number of irrelevant inputs to be rejected. Treisman (1964) gives an example of this. Two irrelevant messages in different voices or different positions interfered more with attention to a third than two irrelevant messages which did not differ in voice quality or position. If subjects had been able to "switch out" the analyzers distinguishing the man's from the woman's voice, the two irrelevant messages which differed only in voice tone quality would have acted as a single competing input to the speech analyzers, instead of as two competing inputs.

In this section on attention we showed first that there were certain external factors which could direct attention by attracting eye movements. Then we discussed a variety of research which showed that the division of internal attention is limited by the nature of the processing in the perceptual system. It seems that, while the analyzers can be processed in parallel, sensory inputs or stimulus inputs and targets can be analyzed only in serial. Finally, we showed further that focusing on one analyzer while ignoring others seems to be rather difficult. All these findings seem to be consistent with the model of attention suggested by Norman and the attenuator model of Treisman.

ILLUSIONS

The preceding section considered the internal direction of attention. One factor we did not investigate is the effect of past or sensory experiences on attentional direction. This variable—namely, past experiential effects—has been studied extensively with illusions, to an examination of which we now turn, beginning with figural aftereffects.

Figural Aftereffects

Work on figural aftereffects goes back to J. J. Gibson (1933), who reported the following set of experimental facts. An observer is presented with a slightly curved line in the vertical position, which he has to inspect steadily for 5 to 10 minutes. Toward the end of the inspection period the observer reports that the line appears to be less curved; adaptation has occurred. The effect of this adaptation to curvature is so strong that, if a straight line is now presented to the observer, it appears to be curved in the opposite direction. The adaptation has led to a negative aftereffect. Apparently, this is not a case of pure sensory (retinal) adaptation, for if the lines are inspected monocularly, the effect is only about half as strong. Evidently, summation occurs in the brain, the most likely area being the cerebral cortex.

J.J. Gibson (1937a, 1937b) and Gibson and Radner (1937) continued study-ing figural aftereffects with subjects who adapted to wearing goggles which contained distorting lenses. They found that, after subjects had worn such goggles for a period of time, the distortions which occurred apparently disap-peared for a time, or were greatly reduced. Chapter 13 goes into a detailed analysis of these spatial adaptive effects. Furthermore, when the subjects viewed the world without these goggles, straight lines then appeared to be distorted in the opposite direction until the perceptual system readjusted to its former state.

Other researchers have reported some more specific facts about the nature of these aftereffects. For example, Bales and Folansbee (1935) reported that the maximum effect occurred with a tilt of 10 percent and with curves, gentle curves giving the greatest effect. Furthermore, Morant and Mikaelin (1960) showed that exact spatial location of the inspection and test figure was not necessary for the effect to take place. Thus an aftereffect was still found if the inspection figure was tilted in the vertical plane and the test figure was presented in the horizontal plane. Furthermore, it has also been reported that aftereffects occur in the third dimension. For example, Bergman and Gibson (1959) found that the effect existed for textured surfaces, sloping away from the subject. Further, Ikeda and Obonai (1953) showed a relationship between the length of inspection and the temporal duration of the aftereffect. Thus, an inspection of 1 second gave rise to an aftereffect which reduced to zero after 10 seconds, whereas an inspection time of 4 minutes gave rise to an aftereffect which did not diminish to zero until after 80 seconds. The effect of the inspection period did not affect the size of the aftereffect, only its duration before extinction.

While Gibson explained these aftereffects in terms of sensory adaptation, Wolfgang Köhler saw in them the prototype of a theory of the physiological mechanism underlying all form perception. This theory was first introduced in a paper by Köhler and Wallach (1944) in which they also report a number of experiments on figural aftereffects. The experimental paradigm for their demon-stration is presented in Figure 11-4. The inspection figure is exposed to the observer, who fixates the X. The test figure is so arranged that the left squares fall symmetrically above and below the area where the left inspection square had been located. Similarly, the right squares of the test figure fall in the area between the positions where the right inspection figures had been located. The reported result is that the observer typically sees the *two right squares pushed together, whereas the two left squares are pushed farther apart.*

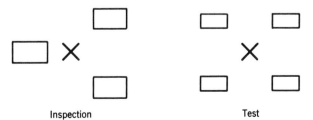

Inspection   Test

Figure 11-4 Demonstration of figural aftereffects. *(From Köhler and Wallach, 1944.)*

Köhler and Wallach advanced the *satiation theory* of cortical conduction to explain these effects. They asserted first that "only things, figures, lines, patches, dots—that is, particular visual entities cause such after-effects" (1944, p. 315). Any segregated entity in the visual field is associated with an electric current in the visual sector of the nervous system, and they stated that this "figure current polarizes the tissue through which it flows, causing higher resistance to current; when later the current of a T-figure spreads in the effective medium, it is dispersed away from this area causing the figural after-effects."

What Köhler and Wallach are saying is that the part of the brain which is polarized becomes satiated with the flow of direct current as a result of prolonged stimulation; its resistance is consequently increased. When the test figures are presented, the current which flows from the test figure is spread away from the associated medium and is dispersed. The current will flow from the area of highest resistance to that of lowest resistance, that is from highly satiated areas to less satiated areas. Notice that current will flow only as a result of the stimulation of specific entities, and will flow only from one area of current to another area of current. If we apply this theory to the results of the above experiment, the results are not hard to understand. The visual area of the cortex which became satiated as a result of polarization is the part which was stimulated by the contours of the inspection figures. Now when the test figures are shown, the stimulated areas of the brain become polarized, and a current will flow from the satiated region to these neighboring stimulated areas. Thus it will flow outward on the left and inward on the right of the figure. The result is that the left square is spread apart and the right squares are pushed together. The demonstration can be verified in many other ways. For example, the inspection figure would merely consist of one outlined square. If the test square is located outside the inspection figure, it will appear even bigger: its size will be pushed out. Similar results have been reported with the third dimension by Köhler and Emery (1947), verifying the work of Gibson and his followers who also found the third-dimensional figural aftereffects.

Temporal Factors   The relationship between the duration of the inspection of the figure and the duration of the aftereffect as well as the interaction between the inspection time and interval between removal of the inspection figure and presentation of the test figure has been, by now, thoroughly investigated. Hammer (1949), using plain bar figures, found that the magnitude of the displacement increased with the increase in the inspection period up to durations of 50 to 100 seconds, at which point the displacement remained approximately constant. We already mentioned that Ikeda and Obonai (1953) found that the aftereffects decreased with delay in measurement after the end of the inspection period, with the rate of decay varying directly with the length of inspection period. That is, the decay was extremely fast with short inspection periods and very slow for long periods. This result was also verified by Oyama (1953). However, both studies found that, in apparent contrast to Hammer's results, the length of inspection period had little effect on the magnitude of displacement.

The difference in the results of Hammer and the Japanese psychologists may be partially or wholly due to different methodologies. Hammer, following the work of Köhler and his co-workers, used the method of average error or adjustment, in which the subject merely adjusted the test figure to show the magnitude of the aftereffect. The Japanese used the method of constant stimuli. Furthermore, concentric circles were their inspection figures; one of the circles was presented as the test figure, and the subject reported whether the other circle (of the same size as the inspection figure) was equal, smaller, or larger in size. Further work by Oyama (1956), Obonai and Suto (1952), and Fujiwara and Obonai (1953) was not so definite as to the effect of the length of inspection. It appears, however, that the effect of the inspection periods alone has a greater influence upon the rate of decay of displacement than upon the magnitude of displacement which is present immediately following the inspection period. Furthermore, prolonged inspection of the figure is not necessary for the aftereffect to occur; but again, the delay between the inspection and test does influence the measured result of the effect. Duncan (1962) also confirmed the results of the increase in decay time for increased inspection time and the relatively small effect of the latter on the size of the initial aftereffect.

Central (Brain) Factors   The fact that figural aftereffect lasts for a long time (months?) and also the fact that maximum displacement occurs when the test and inspection figures are in slightly different spatial areas although contiguous, rather than if they completely coincide, led Köhler to theorize that the effect is produced centrally. Definitive evidence that central areas are involved in the production of the aftereffect, however, was obtained by McEwan (1959) and Sutherland (1961). Both sets of investigators found that the figural aftereffect was produced by the *apparent* size of the figure rather than its retinal size. Thus, for example, when distance cues were provided, the aftereffect was appropriate to the apparent size of the figure rather than to its retinal size. This was accomplished in the McEwan study by presenting inspection and test figures which were retinally equal, but when some inspection figures were apparently larger and some apparently smaller than the test figures because of the distance variable, the aftereffects were related to the apparent sizes; thus there were differences between the same inspection figures depending on the apparent size as determined by the distance variant.

Another demonstration of central factors used the apparent meaning of the inspection stimulus to the subject. In an experiment by Weitman (1963) the inspection figure was a square which was divided down the middle by a contour resembling the profile of a human face, similar to the ambiguous figures described in Chapter 9. The test figure was a pair of dashes placed one each immediately below one-half of the square. In the two conditions the profile was facing in either direction (left or right), and in each presentation, one side of the square was the figure and the other the background, and vice versa.

The results indicated that a greater figural aftereffect was always reported on the part of the square that was seen as a figure—that is, a greater displacement of the dash was reported for the figural side. These results indicate, of course, that there are gestalt or configurational factors related to figure-ground effect, and, since we already saw in Chapter 9 that the figure is most strongly determined by central attention, we have here another verification of the fact that central factors are involved in the determination of figural aftereffects.

Other Theoretical Explanations of Figural Aftereffects Some important difficulties encountered by the satiation theory will now be briefly described. The most important difficulty is that some researchers have found just the opposite effect from those predicted by Köhler and Wallach—that is, rather than the currents being displaced away from the satiated areas, they seem to be attracted toward it. In such figures attraction rather than repulsion occurs. A general review of these attraction findings was presented by Malhotra (1968). Typical of such findings is the experiment of Smith (1954), who used the figures presented in Figure 11-5.

Following inspection of the figure shown on the left, the subjects were required to look at and report the sizes of the two figures appearing on the right which were presented in such a way that the left test figure coincided with the inspection figure. Rather than the left square appearing to be bigger, as predicted by the satiation theory, it in fact was seen as being *smaller*. Ganz and Day (1965) also report attraction effects when the figures were exposed at low intensities and when the distance between the figures was very small. A second major difficulty has to do with the fact that the satiation theory seems to ignore the anatomy and physiology of the brain. Thus, Lashley, Chow, and Semmes (1951) imbedded gold pins in the cortex of one monkey and placed sheets of gold foil in the occipital surface of another. The monkeys showed no impairment in visual pattern discrimination in postoperative tests. The authors had reasoned that the gold should short-circuit the current and destroy the pattern set up by the stimulation of the forms. However, the reasoning that gold would short-circuit the current ignores one important axiom of the theory—namely, that figures are distorted only because the current flows from highly satiated areas to less satiated areas. In the experiment mentioned above, when the form stimulates the cortex, figure current flows in that area of the cortex. Anyone who then claims that metal conductors would short-circuit the figure current must first prove that the metal has a resistance lower than any part of the brain, since the current flows

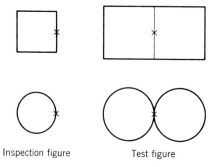

Inspection figure   Test figure

Figure 11-5 The figures used by Smith. *(After Smith, 1954.)*

in the medium offering the lowest resistance. To prove that a metal is a better conductor than any part of the cortex would be almost impossible. This state of affairs indicates very potently how difficult it is, in fact, to put satiation theory to a crucial test at all.

Finally, a more serious criticism of satiation theory arises from the data which have steadily been collected since the early 1950s, which say something about how forms are built up from lines and contours. We shall describe this difficulty from the perspective of one perception theory later. In the present context we note the view of Sutherland (1961), who reasons that, since the displacement effect reaches its maximum with small interfigural distances, inspection and test lines which are not parallel should appear to be best. The actually observed distortion, however, is much smaller than satiation theory would predict. Sutherland argues, instead, that the observed findings fit in more with the proposition that the perceived orientation of a line is built up by the firing of a large population of directionally sensitive *analyzers*. These analyzers are capable of becoming fatigued. Therefore, after the viewing of the inspection figure, the perceived orientation of the test figure will be derived from a biased population of analyzers, those which are less fatigued. The important difference here is that the effects are described as a direct result of what happens to physiological properties of the cell and also its coding properties—a view more consistent with modern neurophysiology and neuropsychology as we saw when we described the work of Hubel and Wiesel in earlier chapters.

Another theory which deals with what happens in the cell, a theory which described these phenomena as a function of inhibition, is presented by Ganz (1966a, 1966b). We shall not go into this theory here because it requires direct knowledge of physiology which is beyond the scope of this book. However, we shall go into one theory which has competed strongly with that of Köhler and Wallach, namely, the statistical theory of Osgood and Heyer (1952).

Statistical Theory   The theory of Osgood and Heyer is based on the theory of visual acuity of Marshall and Talbot (1942, pp. 117–164), well reviewed by Osgood in 1953.

Day has stated that "an enormous objection to such a hypothesis [of Köhler] can be found in the lack of correspondence between the alleged diffusion and satiation processes and the established evidence regarding neurophysiological evidence at the cortex" (1956, p. 139).

Day was specifically referring to the interpretation of the experiment by Bitterman, Krauskopf, and Hochberg (1954) which was discussed in Chapter 2. It will be remembered that various illuminated forms were presented against dark backgrounds to the observers for 0.5 second after they had been dark-adapted for 10 minutes; exposures were repeated every 2 seconds. During the indefinite state the forms were confused; a square was seen as a circle, a triangle as a circle, a cross as a diamond, and an X as a square. The same confusions occurred consistently. To explain these findings, Bitterman et al. suggested a (diffusion model) chemical analogy of the satiation theory which hypothesizes that chemical diffusion occurs at satiated points; the diffusion process thereupon reduces the accuracy of the perception. It is easy to see how they could theorize that satiation around the contour area would lead to the diffusion of current which would push the lines in or out and thus lead to the misperceptions reported. Results in keeping the diffusion model were obtained by Gaito (1959b), and it was reported that short-duration exposure straight lines were misperceived as curved lines more frequently than when the reverse misperception occurred. While this would be predicted by the diffusion model, it would probably also be predicted by the satiation model.

The satiation theory, however, is not necessarily the most satisfactory way of explaining these results. We noted in Chapter 2 that many experimentalists have found that there is an order effect in the emergence of various perceptual segregations. Thus, the stage of indefinite form is followed by the stage of definite form after the information in stimulus energy has been increased. It seems more plausible, therefore, to suggest that the incorrect perceptions noted by Bitterman et al. are the results of inadequate stimulation for extracting the necessary information. This explanation is more consistent with all the experimental facts reported in Chapter 2. Incidentally, it was observed above that the order effect did appear with many of the subjects.

Having misgivings similar to that noted above, Day advanced a *statistical theory of form determination* as an alternative explanation to the satiation theory. He argued that this theory, based on the work of W. A. Marshall and Talbot (1942) on the neurophysiology of vision, is in much closer and realistic agreement with neurological theory. This reinterpretation "has as its central notion a cortical representation of a perceived contour in the form of a gaussian distribution of neural excitation in area 17" (Day, 1956, p. 139). This theory essentially states that neural impulses resulting from form stimulation are at their maximum along contours and taper off in the areas around the contours. This tapering of neural excitation, however, follows the normal probability curve of distribution, with the contour as the peak of excitation. If the physical stimulus is not strong enough, the peak of neural excitation will be below the threshold required for clear perception of the contour. Since the distribution of neural energy around each contour will be rather flat, the combined effect results in a fairly even distribution of excitation. The somewhat high level of excitation around the contour is not above the threshold required for clear detection of contour, and the form qualities are confused. A graphical picture of what supposedly happens is presented in Figure 11-6.

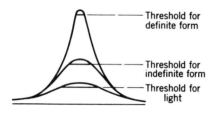

Threshold for
definite form

Threshold for
indefinite form

Threshold for
light

Figure 11-6 The distribution of cortical excitation about the edge between stimulus figure and surround at three stages of form perception. *(After Day, 1956, p. 143.)*

A similar statistical theory has also been suggested by Osgood and Heyer (1952) to explain figural aftereffects. They maintain that the contours of the test and inspection figures produce a normal curve of excitation, with the maximum being at the contour point. The excitation curve for stimulation during the inspection period flattens with the removal of the inspection figure, but is still present during the presentation of the test figure, and the contour of the latter falls to one side or the other of the previously inspected contour. The curve that would normally appear for the test figure is then modified by the residual inspection figure excitation at the curve so that the maximum of the modified curve (at the contour point) is to the right or left of the test-figure curve. The latter aspect accounts for the displacement effect. A weakness of the statistical theory is that it is based on the theory of Marshall and Talbot, who assume that the magnitude of neural excitation is related to optic nystagmus, which causes movement of the retinal image. Ratliff (1952), however, found instead that nystagmus acts to prevent total adaptation of receptors. Complete adaptation blots out vision completely. His result has been verified by Pritchard, Heron, and Hebb (1960), as reported in the next chapter.

At present there is little choice between the statistical and satiation theories, except that the former is closer to the more accepted view of neurological functioning. A crucial experiment has not been performed, since unfortunately both theories appear to predict similar results.

Relation to Other Illusions A similarity between the concentric-circle illusion, shown in Figure 11-7, and the figural aftereffects has been pointed out by Ikeda and Obonai (1955a, 1955b). The small circle on the right is the same size as the inner one on the left, but is perceived as being larger. Ikeda and Obonai have shown that the aftereffect, a consecutive event, approaches the illusory effect, a simultaneous event, as a time interval between the inspection and test periods is reduced to zero. This relationship suggests that both the illusion and the aftereffects probably belong to the same class of events, with time as the important variable. This effect is also related to the fusion of successively exposed lights into continuous movement as reported by J. L. Brown and Voth (1937), reported in a later chapter, which is part of a larger class of spatiotemporal organizations in perception. Earlier in this section we have also referred to other work by Japanese psychologists, relating figural aftereffects to illusions.

The results of the work discussed above could be handled by the satiation theory. Furthermore, Köhler and Fishback (1950) have applied this approach to

Figure 11-7 Concentric-circle illusion.

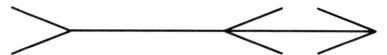

Figure 11-8 Müller-Lyer illusion.

the destruction of the Müller-Lyer illusion, presented in Figure 11-8. Although the two lines are equal, the right one looks shorter than the left one. The arrows at the ends obviously have some effect in producing this illusion. It has been found that the illusion can be decreased by practice with the figure (Judd, 1902). Köhler and Fishback discovered that it can be decreased by about the same amount if only the end of the line (with the arrows) is presented for continuous inspection. The authors concluded that it must be the effect of satiation in the area inscribed by the arrows and not the result of direct comparisons of the lines which lowers the illusion. The effect is explained as follows: Since there is more satiation between the open part of the arrows than at its point, the arrow is pushed toward the point. This explanation accounts for the lengthening or shortening of the two lines which represents the decrease in the illusion. It is a challenge to the usual explanation of learning, but Köhler and Fishback did find certain similarities to the results of normal learning, such as the fact that distributed practice of inspection led to greater decrease in the illusion than did mass practice.

An experiment which attempted to test some of the implications of Köhler's theory about practice, satiation, and reduced illusory effect was performed by Moed (1959). He deduced from Köhler's theory that repetitive stimulation of the brain in the same way leads to fast satiation, and hence to faster destruction of the illusion than repetitive stimulation in different ways. Thus, referring to the left part of the figure in Figure 11-5 as A and the right part as B, we have the following situation. If we always present sections A and B in the same orientation, the illusion would eventually disappear. This is called *asymmetrical association*. On the other hand, we can present A on the left half of the time and B on the left half of the time, and vice versa. In this way the association effects cancel out. This is called *symmetrical satiation*. Moed's experiment used the following conditions of satiation: (1) completely asymmetrical; (2) partly symmetrical; (3) completely symmetrical. In Köhler's theory we expect that condition 1 should show the greatest reduction in illusion, with condition 2 next and condition 3 least. In fact, all conditions showed reduction in illusion after a period of exposure; there were no significant differences between the three conditions. It would be difficult for Köhler to handle these results, especially given the controls used by Moed. Since the satiation theory and the effect of practice have led us to illusions, it would be appropriate to present a description of some of the other well-known illusions at this point.

Geometric Illusions

Figure 11-9 gives us an example of other well-known illusions. Their causes are not well understood, and little would be accomplished here by giving a thorough description of all the work and hypothesizing which is taking place. An excellent summary and analytic discussion are provided by J. O. Robinson (1973, p. 253).

To give an idea, however, of the kinds of existing views, we shall present a brief description of two of them, one a peripheral theory and the other a central theory of the causes of illusions.

Eye-Movement Theory   A good example of a peripheral explanation is the eye-movement theory. The best formulation of this point of view was probably advanced by Harvey Carr (1935). While he did not believe that eye movement was a sufficient explanation of illusions, he did suggest that it contributed to the production of illusions. The proposition was that, in the perception of any figure, the eyes will also react to accompanying lines and will pass more easily over unfilled than filled lines; that is, eye movement will be interrupted by figures which have other lines, as in the case of the illusion presented in the last figure. For example, in the Müller-Lyer illusion, the eyes move more freely over the figure with the fins pointing inward than the one with the fins pointing outward. It is as if the lines coming inward on the inward fins interfere with the perception of the middle line. Similarly, in the Poggendorf and Zöllner illusions, deflections and hesitations of eye movements occur at the junction of the oblique line, when the subject is instructed to move his eyes along the lines of the figure. In the case of the Poggendorf and Zöllner illusion as well as the Müller-Lyer illusion, practice which reduces the illusion reduces the deflection and, furthermore, hesitation and less easy movement are also reduced in the case of the Müller-Lyer illusion.

Major difficulties for the eye-movement theory are provided by the studies on stabilized retinal images. Thus, Pritchard (1958) found that the Zöllner illusion was not affected by stabilizing the retinal image; Evans and Marsden (1966) found that illusions persisted under stabilized retinal-image conditions for the Müller-Lyer, Poggendorf, Hering, and Zöllner figures. It seems clear that, while eye movements are not necessary for illusions, they probably have some influence on them.

Gregory's Theory of Central Correction   In a manner similar to that of the transactionalists, which we described in the chapter on space perception, Gregory accounts for the illusions on the basis of correction which the perceiver makes in response to cues to distance and depth perception. Thus, his argument is that the individual perceives the illusory figure as a three-dimensional figure projected on a two-dimensional plane. Various cues to depth would make parts of the figure appear to be farther away than others and, since the retinal sizes of all parts are the same, those which appear to be farther away would be corrected to appear as larger; hence the illusion. Gregory refers to this enlargement of the more distant (line) as *constancy scaling*. Moreover, this constancy scaling is caused by two different mechanisms, according to Gregory.

The first way that constancy scaling is achieved, which he calls *primary constancy* scaling, results from perspective features in the illusory display itself.

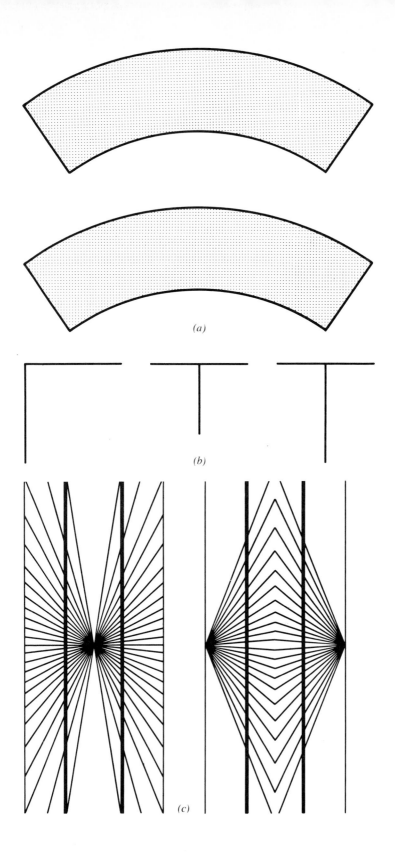

(a)

(b)

(c)

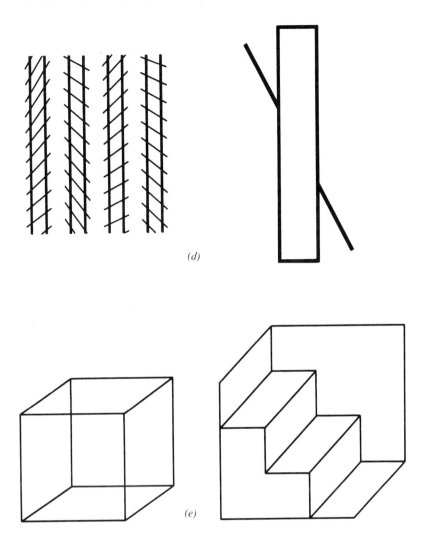

(d)

(e)

Figure 11-9 Varieties of illusory effects. *(a)* Jastrow illusion. The lower figure appears larger than the upper. *(b)* The vertical-horizontal illusion. In the figure on the right the vertical line appears larger even though the lines are of equal length. In the middle figure the vertical line is shorter. The perception of equality on the left shows that the illusions in the other two figures are related, at least in part, to the intersections of the lines. How might satiation theory explain these facts? In a study by Gregory and Wallace (1963) on the perception of a congenitally blind person who was given surgery (see Chapter 9), interesting data were reported. The normal reporting of curved lines in the Hering illusion *(c)*, nonparallel lines in the Zölner illusion and displacement of the slanted line in the Poggendorf illusion *(d)*, and the perception of depth and reversal in the Necker cube and staircase illusion *(e)* were all absent. Instead, the subject reported these lines as straight and saw no depth or reversal. The problem of choosing between satiation theory and a learning interpretation is aggravated by data such as these.

Thus, the Ponzo illusion has the same perspective changes as does a railway track; that is, as the lines approach one another, distance recedes. Consequently, a line of the same retinal shape which is located closer to the two converging lines will be seen as being farther away, and vice versa. The second mechanism, called *secondary* constancy scaling, is created when the typical cues to distance, such as binocular disparity, size, position, and the various gradients, give rise to changes in apparent distance. Again, the more distant-appearing line, having the same visual image, is seen as larger.

Gregory theorizes that primary constancy scaling is a mechanical mechanism and quite primitive, whereas secondary constancy scaling is a higher process, is more deliberate, involves judgment, and utilizes the various cues to distance. His work and ingenious demonstrations are contained in Gregory (1966, 1968a, 1968b, 1970).

While Gregory's theory had generated the most enthusiasm in the experimental literature, difficulties have been experienced in attempts at empirical verification. For example, Hotopf (1966) created figures where there were no perspective changes or phenomenological cues with respect to distance. Yet the illusion was obtained. The figure used by Hotopf is presented in Figure 11-10*a*.

Another similar example comes from the work of Fisher (1970), who exposed the figure represented in Figure 11-10*b*. Notice that the figure can be seen as a receding passage or as an approaching pyramid. Also, the lines in between represent four Ponzo illusions. Whether the line closer to the approaching lines is seen as bigger would depend on whether the figure is seen as a passage or as a pyramid. Irrespective of whether the viewers saw a passage or a pyramid, they always reported that the lines closest to the center were seen as bigger.

It is no doubt true that the cues to distance and perspective will influence the illusions, as indeed do eye movements. Toward the end of the chapter on space perception we, in fact, present figures which indicate how artificial cues to distance can give exaggerated impressions of size. However, data reviewed here as well as other evidence support the view of Hotopf, who suggests that illusions are determined by multiple variables such as perspective corrections, contrast,

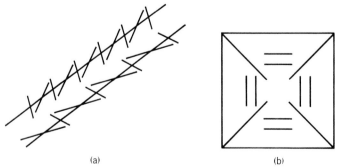

(a)   (b)

Figure 11-10 *(a) After Hotopf, 1966. (b)* Figure used by Fisher (1970) to study illusions in depth perception.

orientation, and probably certain other kinds of hypotheses generated from past experience. For a more recent theory based on constancy, see Day (1972).

Whatever may turn out to be true, we shall probably always find that the way perceptual constancies are related to illusions, like most other perceptions, depends on the kinds of models, sets, and coding devices that the individual brings to the perceptual scene from his past experience. As we shall see in Chapter 15, Segall, Campbell, and Herskovits (1966) found that the presence, absence, or exaggeration of illusions depends very much on the kind of world in which individuals have been brought up. As J. O. Robinson (1973) points out in his very comprehensive book, "an interesting attitude toward illusions is that which regards them as the debt which the visual system pays for other advantages in the process of seeing" (p. 253). He goes on to say that "the visual system is developed in such a way that, under normal circumstances, the maximum amount of information is gained from the visual field. The specific tricks that it plays usually serves this end remarkably well, but there are other situations, usually ones which could not possibly have been important to primitive man, in which the tricks are turned against the system" (p. 253). He ends his book with the somewhat pessimistic statement that "at this moment (the illusions) seem little less mysterious to us than they were in the middle of the nineteenth century, to Helmholtz" (p. 253).

SUMMARY

To continue from Chapter 10, the first major section of the present chapter considered the way selective attention operates in the information-processing system. First we considered the effect of peripheral factors which attracted eye movements, or attention. Next we analyzed four ways in which attention can be regulated in internal information processing. They involve: (1) attention-response selection, (2) input, (3) analyzers, and (4) targets. The last three involve perception. We say data which indicate that analyzers can be processed in parallel while inputs and targets are processed in series.

The second major section of the chapter described various kinds of illusions, relating them to peripheral factors, internal factors, memory, and past experience. We saw again that the last two variables are the most important.

Chapter 12

Perceptual Learning and Development

The question about the extent to which perception is innate and the extent to which it is learned has a long intellectual history which the interested reader can follow in Boring (1942, 1950). In general, the Platonists, Kant, and German idealists, Hering, the phenomenologists, and the gestalt psychologists represent the nativistic line. Conversely, the Aristotelians, the British empiricists, Helmholtz, Hebb, and most contemporary information-processing theorists represent the empiricist line. Our own view was stated in Chapters 1 and 2. It postulates that perception begins, at birth, with wired-in programs which become modified as a result of stimulus experience (which permits learning during development).

THEORETICAL PERSPECTIVE

Before examining the wealth of research relevant to the nature-nurture question, it would help to give a brief description of what seem to us to be the major theoretical orientations. Our treatment is uneven in length because some views have generated more influence, or are older. There are five major theoretical views.

Gestalt Theory This is extensively discussed in Chapter 9, so does not need repeating here. The central hypothesis is that the intrinsic laws of perceptual organization produce innate organization—in the direction of *Prägnanz*.

Hebb's Theory of Structural Changes Hebb's (1949, 1960) three-stage theory of perceptual organization-unity, nonsensory unity, and identity was already described and discussed in Chapter 2. The important theorem is that, through sensory experience and stimulation, stimulus elements are combined into cell assemblies which, through associative experience, build superordinate assemblies, called *phase sequences*. "A phase sequence is an 'ideational series' with its motor elements" (Hebb, 1949, p. 98). Thus, an identity (e.g., a triangle, t) is part of a phase sequence such that one sequence might be a-b-t-a-c-t-b-. Another sequence could be a-b-c-t-d-e-t-a-b. In sum, the basis of the perception of a complex is called a phase sequence and the experience of *t* is one part of the sequence. Notice that the genesis of the triangle requires more than peripheral stimulation. It requires the recruitment of an ideational source, as well—which is the phase sequence consisting of learned structural organizations in the central nervous system.

Gibson's Response-Specificity Theory This theoretical perspective represents the joint venture of James J. and Eleanor J. Gibson. J. J. Gibson (1966) postulates that there is permanent stimulus information in the ambient optic array—that is, in the stimulus array reaching the retina. More specifically, the stimulus information exists in the *textured* optic array and the spatial and temporal transformations to which they give rise. These ordinal patterns of stimulation consist of higher-order families of relationships. During experience or perceptual learning the activity of the organism is crucial, and perceptual learning consists of feature detection, that is, in the stimulus becoming more specific and differentiated (E. J. Gibson, 1969).

Fantz: Acquisition of Knowledge For Fantz (1967) perceptual development consists of the acquisition of knowledge. This knowledge acquisition or storage of perceptual information is directed by the selection capacities of the organism. Moreover, knowledge acquisition takes place independently of specific changes in response, a distinction not apparently made by the Gibsons.

Kagan: Schemata Development For Kagan (1967, 1970) perceptual development gives rise to the formation of schemata. *Schemata* refer to the internal representation of the stimulus identity. The child's attention depends on the relationship of the stimulus to the child's schemata. Attention will maximally be attracted by newly emerging schemata and by stimuli which consist of moderate discrepancy from existing schemata. Later in life the individual's attention is also attracted by stimuli which activate *hypotheses*.

The five theories have focused on particular aspects. Perhaps if we first concentrate on their characteristic perspective focus and attempt to put them together in some fashion, we shall arrive at a more complete picture.

PLASTICITY OF INNATE PERCEPTUAL CAPACITIES

Gestalt theory postulated the existence of innate perceptual capacities and organizations. Here follow some major facts.

According to an extensive review by Hershenson (1967), the basic visual capacities are present in the human infant. However, there is considerable question about how well certain functions are performed. For example, binocular fusion is probably incomplete. Furthermore, accommodation is not sufficiently accurate. This acuity improves during the early months.

In addition to the *plasticity* described above, it has also been shown that fixation patterns and the size of the field change during the early months of life. We shall discuss fixation patterns later with the work of Fantz. With respect to increases in the field with age, the data of Tronick (1972) in Figure 12-1 are self-explanatory.

Research findings reveal change with respect to gestalt grouping, as well, during the first few months of life. Thus, Bower (1965), in testing three gestalt laws, found that only common fate (probably related to movement) was evident at 4 weeks of age, with proximity and good continuation not showing up until 20 to 30 weeks of age.

To end this introduction, we recall Bower's work on shape and size constancy and spatial vision capacities of infants in Chapter 8. It was argued then

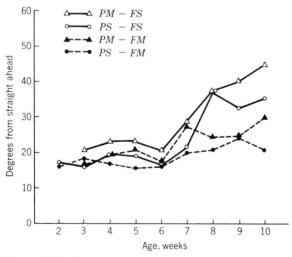

Figure 12-1 The growth in the effective visual field for each week and each stimulus condition. Each point is an average of the limens for all subjects in that condition. Note how the growth in the size of the effective visual field is related to the stimulus conditions (*P*—peripheral object; *F*—fixation object; *S*—object stationary; *M*—object in motion). *(After Tronick, 1972, p. 374.)*

that movement parallax and other aspects of motion are probably the cause of the effective cues; these were considered part of the reafferent mechanisms. In other work Bower also uncovered the fact that the tendency toward closure-like responses also requires a mobil organism viewing a three-dimensional array— slides of stimuli did not give rise to closure. Again, we see the importance of movement and the use of solid objects.

Innate Structural Organization in the Cortex

Conclusive evidence that capacities for coding specific informational aspects exist in cortical-cell organization has been disclosed by Hubel and Wiesel (1959, 1962, 1968) in single-cell recording. In their painstaking research very small electrodes were implanted in single cells of the visual cortex of both cats and monkeys so that recordings could be taken from these electrodes, while various kinds of stimuli were presented to the eye of the intact animal. The differential pattern of responsiveness indicated that the visual cortex consists of different categories of neural cells, each category being specifically sensitive to a particular kind of stimulus dimension. Thus, some cells respond to both location and orientation, some to only one of these, others to edge, still others to movement, and so on. Furthermore, within the class orientation, the cells are specific with respect to one direction of orientation. For example, a "vertical" cell will respond maximally if a line or bar is presented in a vertical orientation, but will respond very weakly if the line is presented in the horizontal position. In further studies of receptive fields in experienced kittens, Hubel and Wiesel (1963a) used four kittens whose characteristics were as follows: One was tested following its eighth day of age at which time its eyes began to open; a second had translucent contact occluders over both lenses from day 9 until day 16, at which time it was tested; a third had the occluder over only one eye while the other eye was exposed to normal patterned lights, and this kitten was tested at age 19 days; a fourth was raised in normal patterned light until tested at the age of 20 days.

Except for sluggishness of reaction, the cortical cells of the visually inexperienced kittens (1 and 2) strongly resembled cells of mature cats in their responses to patterned stimuli. The cells responded poorly, and often not at all to changes in diffuse retinal illumination. They responded best to straight-line stimuli (i.e., slits, dark bars, or edges) but only when these were appropriately oriented within the receptive fields, which averaged about 2 to 5° in diameter.

The cells of the two experienced kittens were active, even in the absence of patterned stimulation. Responses to restricted stimuli were brisker and showed little of the fatigue that was apparent in the 8-day-old kitten. As a rule, the specific stimulus aspect which specific receptive fields reported were more precisely defined in the experienced patterns.

In the cortical recordings there were, on the whole, no obvious differences between the two eyes of the experienced cats. In fact, the cell giving the larger spikes was far more evident in the eye that had been occluded in the case of the third cat. There was no tendency for cells dominated by the occluded eye to have less maintained activity or to respond less briskly and precisely than the other cells. The researchers therefore concluded that the sluggishness of maintained activity and responses in the first two kittens was related to age rather than to visual experiences.

Thus we see that, with the exception of the low activity level and whether the cell is activated contralaterally or ipsilaterally, even as late as 19 days of age a cell need not have had previous patterned stimulation from an eye in order to respond normally to it. (*Contralateral* means located on the opposite side; *ipsilateral* means located on the same side.)

What about longer periods of deprivation? This question was investigated in other research studies of Wiesel and Hubel (1963a, 1965). In these two experiments, single-cell recordings from monocularly deprived kittens were compared with those from binocularly deprived kittens. Six kittens had one eye sutured from 8 days until about 3 months of age, while four other kittens had both eyes so sutured. Then when the eye(s) were opened, both groups were tested. The surprising result was that there was practically no cortical response from stimulation to the deprived eye in the monocularly deprived kittens, while most cells from the eyes of the binocularly deprived kittens not only responded to visual stimuli, but over half of the ones that responded did so normally. It was as if the ill effects from closing one eye had been averted by closing the other. Taken together, the two sets of experiments seem to suggest that early in life the functional integrity of the pathway may depend not only on the *amount* of different impulse activity, but also on the *interrelationships* between the various sets of afferents. Why this should be so we simply do not know at present, but the finding is fascinating.

The plasticity of reactions of these cortical receptive fields is further revealed in an insightful study of Hirsch and Spinelli (1970). Kittens were raised with hoods over their eyes (for 8 hours daily) between the ages of 3 and 10 to 12 weeks. It is important to note that the hoods did not produce complete occlusion. Rather, they were so constructed that horizontal openings appeared in one and vertical in the other. Then they were tested through each eye with a variety of stimuli. It was found that the different eyes revealed different distributions of orientations of these cortical unit receptive fields. Moreover, the masking of an eye gave rise to *no* diagonally oriented receptive fields. This is not true in control animals. The authors conclude that functional neural corrections can be "selectively and predictably" modified by environmental stimulation. In their study they showed this by raising kittens with their eyes viewing different patterns.

In review of this area Ganz (1970) summarizes the difference between recovery in binocularly and monocularly deprived cats, in research similar to Hubel and Wiesel's (1965). Recovery is fairly adequate in the monocularly deprived (or binocularly deprived) animal with respect to depth, surfaces, and large moving arrays, and in cells responsible for the orientation of the organism to visual stimulation. Recovery was poor (as revealed by inability) in guiding limits toward small visual objects and in the identification of visual form. The first function has to do with orientation, and the second with the recognition of form.

Ganz thus concludes, in agreement with the position and research presented

so far in this book and with Held (1967), that there are two basic mechanisms—
one innate and one more subject to learning. The second mechanism involves a
stage of analysis which apparently is mediated by the visual cortex cells with
selective receptive fields (feature detectors and extractors). When an animal uses
an eye that has greatly attenuated access to those feature analyzers (e.g.,
monocularly deprived animals) "it cannot readily form visual discriminations,
nor can it readily retrieve memory traces established through the feature analyzers controlled by the other eye" (Ganz, 1970, p. 19).

Sensory-Deprivation Effects

Another interesting group of experiments which are pertinent to the effects of
sensory experiences on perception in general consists of the sensory-deprivation
studies. In these experiments the quantity and quality of the sensory input of
subjects are decreased. Usually the subjects are placed in small spaces, isolated
from other individuals as depicted in Figure 12-2. Men have survived long-term
confinement in relatively small spaces with a reduction in quantity and variability
of sensory input (e.g., prisoners in solitary confinement, shipwrecked mariners,
hermits) and in many cases with little adverse effect on behavior.

In Heron's technique the subjects' sensory environment is reduced through
placing them in isolated chambers, with diffuse lighting, white noise, and cardboard cylinders over their limbs. Two other techniques are to use a tank-type
respirator (Wexler, Mendelson, Leiderman, & Solomon, 1958) or complete
immersion in a tank of water with only the face with a mask above the water
(Shurley, 1963). The submersion has a most severe and rapid negative effect on
psychological functioning. Subjects usually want to leave it after ten hours.
Isolation effects can be tolerated up to twenty-four hours by most subjects
(Zuckerman, 1969).

Since Zubek (1969) has provided an excellent review, we shall list only the

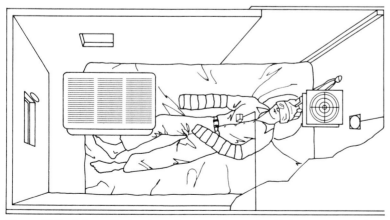

Figure 12-2 Schematic drawing of an experimental cubicle for research in sensory deprivation. The ceiling has been removed and the subject is viewed from above. (From Heron, in
Solomon et al., 1961.)

findings which have held up. (1) The McGill studies, using Heron's isolation chamber (Bexton, Heron & Scott, 1954; Heron, 1957; Heron, Doane, & Scott, 1956), found that ability to concentrate and to carry out organized thinking and various intellectual tasks was adversely affected. Visual, aural, and tactual hallucinations occurred. Reductions in size constancy and depth perception plus fewer reversals in reversible figures were also reported by Zubek. (2) The tank-type respirator isolation also produces pseudosomatic delusions, illusions, and hallucinations (Wexler, Mendelson, Leiderman, & Solomon, 1958). (3) Vernon, McGill, and Schiffman (1958), Doane, Mahut, Heron, and Scott (1959), and Zubek, Pushkar, Sansom, and Gowing (1961) have shown conclusively that complete darkness does not produce these effects. It is reduction to homogeneity, not absence of stimulation, that produces impairment of intellectual, motor, and perceptual functioning (Zubek et al., 1962). (4) Hebb (1968), Cameron, Levy, Ban, and Rubenstein (1961), Zubek and MacNeill (1966, 1967) have all emphasized that it is a reduction which produces cognitive dysfunction and hallucinations, accompanied by slowing the EEG patterns, because the brainstem arousal mechanism is reduced. Thus, the conclusion is that optimal arousal of the cortex is necessary for adequate brain function and perceptual learning (Hebb, 1960, 1968; Fuster, 1958).

Form Discrimination from Stabilized Retinal Images

Optic nystagmus, the rapid movement of the eyeball, leads to a shifting of the image to different cells. These continuous small movements of the eyeballs (saccades) are necessary for good visual acuity. If the image is stabilized, i.e., keeps stimulating the same cells, acuity is decreased and form discrimination becomes less effective, until finally the perceptual object fades out. Among others, Riggs, Cornsweet, and Lewis, (1957) and Pritchard, Heron, and Hebb (1960) have developed a technique for stabilizing the retinal image, thus providing an excellent method for studying the temporal development course for the perceptual process and also for determining the basic units making up the total form. They also showed the necessity of heterogeneity and stimulus change for adequate perception.

Examples of the stimuli used by Pritchard et al. are shown in Figure 12-3. Employing the technique of stabilizing retinal images developed by Pritchard, the authors presented these visual stimuli to four experienced subjects. The reported phenomena have been confirmed. The figures would eventually begin to fade, come back, and fade again. The time before fading and the percentage of the time that the figure would remain intact depended on its complexity. Thus a simple figure like a line was visible about 10 percent of the viewing time, whereas a complex figure like an unconnected set of curlicues or a facial profile (items 2 and 3) maintained at least one of its parts for as much as 80 percent of viewing time. The authors state that "chaotic as the activity of the figure may seem at first, it still obeys some rules which relate to the form of the figure itself" (Pritchard et al., p. 71). They conclude that gestalt and elementaristic conceptions of percep-

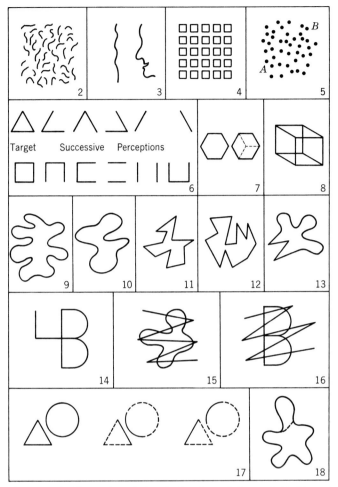

Figure 12-3 Examples of visual stimuli used (items 6, 7, 17, and 18 also show successive perceptions). *(After Pritchard, Heron, & Hebb, 1960, p. 71.)*

tion are not as antithetical as was once thought. This complementarity is summed up in the following propositions:

1 Perceptual elements, as distinct from sensory elements in Hebb's sense, exist in their own right, but the wholes are simpler than usually conceived and consist of straight lines or short segments of curves.

2 "More complex wholes, such as squares or circles, are syntheses of simpler ones though they may also function as genuine single entities" (Pritchard et al., pp. 67–76).

They conclude that these phenomena and others "are intelligible in terms of a semi-autonomous activity of closed systems in perception but *unintelligible when perception is regarded as a simple input system"* (Pritchard et al., p. 76; italics added). Probable ways of accomplishing this are described at the end of the chapter.

Experiential Deprivation Studies

A wide range of studies with a variety of species supports Hebb's hypothesis that learning or early experience affects the growth of form perception. Since all these studies have similar results, we shall only summarize them. In all of them there was absence of light or patterned light for a significant period during infancy and childhood. This deprivation had selective deleterious effects in perceptual discrimination. Von Senden (1932, 1960) reports that congenitally blind human beings, given vision surgically, have little difficulty in color perception but considerable difficulty in space and form perception which improves with learning.

Hebb (1937a, 1937b) and Woodruff and Slovak (1965) all report that animals raised in the dark are as good as light-reared animals in brightness discrimination. Discrimination between horizontal and vertical striations indicated a strain difference, but, in form discrimination, the dark-reared were significantly inferior. After showing that this difference also existed in chimpanzees (Riesen, 1947), Riesen (1961) and Siegel (1953) demonstrated that chimpanzees and ring doves, respectively, who are raised in diffuse light, are also inferior to light-reared animals in form discrimination.

Finally, Tees (1968) found that dark-reared rats were inferior only in a discrimination of N from X. On three tests of striations (horizontal versus vertical or oblique) they were as good as normally reared animals. They, as well as McCleary (1960), therefore, believe it is the difficulty of the task, and not pattern perception per se, which is affected by experience. The latter has also studied the effect of learning on the act or *response* the organism makes to the stimulus, rather than "seeing" as such.

One such study was performed by Meyers and McCleary (1964). McCleary and Longfellow (1961) had already established that binocular transfer can occur without prior sensory experience, i.e., even when cats were raised without the benefit of patterned light.

In the Meyers and McCleary experiment, the experimental group of cats was raised without visual light until 7 weeks of age. From then until the testing began at 35 weeks of age, they were given 1 hour of diffuse-light experience a day and allowed free play. The control group of cats was raised under the normal light-dark daily cycle during the same period.

Following preliminary training to accustom the cats to the test situation, they were monocularly trained in a shock-avoidance situation. The cat was in a harness. A form (cross or circle) was presented. If he would flex his right leg, a shock would be avoided. If he did not flex the leg after the form was presented, a shock would be delivered to the right leg. After the avoidance flex was learned to perfection, the cat was tested through presentation of the stimulus to the other, untrained eye. In other words, an interocular transfer test was conducted. The five experimental cats gave 50, 50, 70, 95, and 95 percent correct responses on the transfer test, while the control gave 60, 75, 75, and 95 percent correct responses. The differences are not significant.

From these findings the authors conclude, plausibly, that binocular sensory equivalence does not require prior experience with patterned light. They reason further that previous reports that lack of experience interferes with perceptual discrimination might, in fact, depend on what kind of response the organism has to make to indicate his discrimination. That is, early visual experience might be necessary to build *visuomotor equivalence* into various parts of the visual system. This view is lent credence by the empirical findings from their experiment that on the initial monocularly trained avoidance task, the experimental cats required significantly longer number of trials (480 to 2,240) than the control cats (120 to 200). If this is so with a response as simple as leg flexion, it might be even more so in more complicated visuomotor responses such as jumping or running into one chamber rather than into another.

There is other research which shows the importance of early visual experience in building visuomotor capacities. The work of Held is exemplary in this regard.

Visuomotor Integration   Following the conceptualization of Erich von Holst on the difference between *reafferent* and *exafferent stimulation,* Held and Hein (1963), in a very ingenious experiment, studied the difference in the effects of *active* and *passive* movement. The notion of reafferent stimulation postulates that the brain has some way of compensating for active movement so that the world remains stable; conversely, passive movement, as when something else moves, creates no such compensating movement, and hence, the world moves. In the study of Held and Hein the differential effects of these kinds of movements were studied developmentally.

Ten pairs of kittens were divided into two groups. Group X, consisting of eight pairs, was reared in the dark for approximately 10 weeks. Group T, consisting of two pairs, was exposed to the pattern interior of the laboratory from age 2 weeks until age 10 weeks. At approximately 10 weeks of age, both groups were given three hours daily exposure in a motion apparatus. This apparatus was so constructed that a member of each pair of kittens (A, the active member) was allowed to move through three axes. When A moved, the passive member, P, which was connected by a yoke, would go through equivalent sensory movement. The difference was that A moved while P was moved. See Figure 12-4 (page 258).

After a number of such daily experiences and following certain preliminary perceptual tests, the cats were put through the crucial test of spatial (depth) discrimination. For this test they used the visual cliff of Gibson and Walk which is discussed in Chapter 13.

The results were quite startling. *All* (that is, 100 percent) of the active members of the pair *always* chose the "shallow" end to descend in twelve trials. On the other hand, in one-third to one-half of the times the passive member

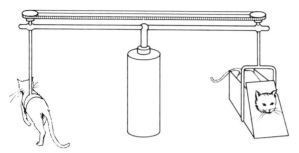

Figure 12-4 Apparatus for equating motion and consequent visual feedback for an actively moving *(A)* and a passively moving *(P)* subject. *(Richard Held and A. Hein, 1963.)*

chose the "deep" end. From this result Held and Hein conclude plausibly that active movement (not just sensory experience) is necessary for the development of the kind of visuomotor integration which is required for adaptive spatial perception and locomotion, and perceptual-motor coordination.

Other investigators who have shown the importance of early experience (although they emphasized sensory instead of motor) are Riesen (1958, pp. 57–80) and Riesen and Aarons (1959). Of course, motor experience, working as it must through the kinesthetic sense, is also a kind of sensory experience.

Differential Perceptual Sets and Differential Experience

The studies just reviewed show that learning affects the growth of form. Learning can also affect differential reaction sets toward already perceived forms. This has been shown by Forgus (1955a, 1955b), among others. Also, Hess (1950) showed that if rats are raised with light from only above, or only below, they will peck at photographs of grain illuminated from only above, or only below. Hess interprets this as a kind of perceptual set of "assumption."

The origin of these sets is seen in a study (Forgus, 1958a) in which litters of rats were randomly split into four groups after they had been weaned. The animals were then individually reared in separate cages. The cages of group T contained outlined triangles and circles on their walls. The walls of the cages of group A also contained circles, but the *sides of the triangles contained a gap in the middle,* although the angles were continuous. The cage walls of groups S had the same circles, but the *"triangle" had no angles.* Group C, the control group, had no forms in its cages. The forms are shown in Figure 12-5.

The rats were reared in these cages until maturity, at which time they were tested on a form-discrimination problem. The two forms which they had to discriminate were identical to the triangle and circle contained in the cages of group T. (Of course, the three experimental groups had seen the same circle.) The results showed that group S was highly superior to all other groups, the only other difference being that group T was somewhat superior to the control group. We should mention here that Eleanor J. Gibson and Walk (1956) also found that rats reared with forms in their living cages were better able to discriminate them than rats raised without the presence of these forms. But the striking difference was the superiority of group S.

  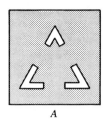

| T | S | A |

Figure 12-5 Triangles *T*, *S*, and *A*, which were located next to the circle in the cages of group *T*, group *S*, and group *A*, respectively. The outlines of the forms were white, and the backgrounds were black. *(Forgus, 1958a, p. 76.)*

Our interpretation of this experiment is that the differential sensitivity to triangle versus circle was greater for the side-form group S than for any of the other groups. To explain this, we must specify what the differences in the relationships between the forms were in the test situation as opposed to the rearing situation. It has been reasoned that rats respond to differences in form on the basis of differential cues from the *bottom* part of the figures (Lashley, 1938). To ascertain the differences between the test and the rearing, we must therefore ask how the relationship between the bases of the two figures changed from the home cage to the test maze. Let us examine this question for the three experimental groups. In their home cages, the members of the side-form group were exposed to a triangle whose base was clearly demarcated. This resulted from the lack of angles, which led to discontinuity of both brightness and contour, while the circle was continuous. When these rats were placed in the test situation, however, they were faced with a triangle whose base was continuous in both brightness and contour. The marked change in the stimulus relationship focused the animals' attention on the stimulus cards, which in turn led to a faster rate of discrimination learning. In other words, the side-form animals were more sensitive to the actual problem situation because the change in the stimulus relationship from rearing to test was greater for them than it was for members of the other groups. This inference is tenable when we contrast the rearing and the test situations of the side-form group with those of the other groups.

In the case of the true-form group T the relationship between the triangle and the circle was identical in the rearing and the test situations. As contrasted with the experience of the first group, both forms were equally familiar; therefore it was more difficult to develop a differential response to the situation.

The angle-form group A, like the side-form group, faced a new situation. But let us examine this statement more closely. The change from the home triangle to the test triangle was not nearly so great for this group as for the side-form group. Whereas side-form group faced a change in the discontinuity of both brightness and contour, the angle-form group faced a change in brightness only. The continuity at the angles remained the same.

The control group was presented a situation which was completely the reverse of that of the true-form group. Whereas the true-form group faced two equally familiar forms in the test siutation, the control group faced two forms which were equally unfamiliar. Therefore, the animals of this group, too, would have great difficulty in developing a differential response between the two test forms.

In summary, the transfer from previous experience to test problems is based not so much on familiarity with the test stimuli as on the *extent to which previously learned relationships aid an animal in developing differential responses to the relevant cues in the problem situation.* It is true that familiarity made the true-form group superior to the control group, but the former was grossly inferior to the side-form group. It appears that such principles as frequency may be influential, but they do not tell the whole story.

Perhaps the major contribution Hebb has made is to point our attention to looking at the need of varied stimulation for the growth and adequate functioning of perception. The foregoing review on sensory deprivation and enriched experience has amply demonstrated this importance. Another way to study the effect of perceptual experience is to investigate the normal course of perceptual development, rather than to vary (experimentally) the variety of experience.

DEVELOPMENTAL STUDIES

Fantz (1961a, 1961b) and Fantz & Nevis (1967) have been concerned primarily with the developmental sequence in perceptual growth in order to determine the relative role of maturation and experience. In this program change in selective processes was studied and then related to knowledge acquisition.

Fantz (1961a) studied the development of form perception in young chicks, chimpanzees, and human infants. The chicks, whose behavior is visually dominated, were presented with a number of different shapes, each enclosed in a clear plastic container to eliminate the influence of smell, taste, or touch. The number of pecks made on each shape was recorded by an electrical circuit attached to each container. More than 1,000 chicks, hatched in darkness to preclude visual learning and withheld from exposure to real food, were tested upon their first exposure to light. Some of the results follow for 112 chicks. During the first 10 minutes they pecked at a sphere 1,000 times, a cube-like shape 300 times, and a pyramid 100 times. Not only did the chicks peck at the sphere 10 times more frequently than at the pyramid, but they also consistently "preferred" a sphere to a flat disk. What appears to be a strong evolutionary development of form discrimination in chicks might not be true of higher animals. Consequently, Fantz tried to tease out the roles of innate ability, maturation, and learning in monkeys, chimpanzees, and man. Taking off from Riesen's study, previously mentioned, he raised monkeys in darkness from 1 to 11 weeks of age. The monkeys reared under these conditions for the shorter period generally exhibited good spatial orientation after a few hours or days when brought into a normal environment, and they also showed a normal interest in patterned objects. Those left in the dark for the longer periods, however, exhibited almost complete spatial disorientation when brought into the light for the first time. "The older infant monkeys bumped into things, fell off tables, could not locate objects visually—for all practical purposes they were blind" (Fantz, 1961a, p. 5). He reports that it sometimes took weeks for them to "learn to see." As contrasted with the younger ones, who preferred patterned objects, the older infant monkeys appeared to be more interested in color, brightness, and size.

From these results with the monkeys Fantz reasons in the following manner. Obviously innate ability cannot be the whole answer; otherwise the dark-reared animals would not be so highly disoriented. Maturation cannot stand alone, either; otherwise the younger animals would not be superior to the older ones. Similarly, learning alone is inadequate as an explanation; otherwise the older animals would not require a longer time to learn to perceive than the younger ones. Evidently, following the wired-in reaction to certain stimuli, chimpanzees reared in darkness, except when brought into a testing situation, exhibited a definite preference for certain objects. There is an interesting interaction between maturation and learning in the development of pattern discrimination. The amount of training interacts with the time at which it takes place to produce the effect. Early learning is superior to late learning (given maturational readiness, presumably).

While practical limitations preclude the use of experimental controls as adequate as those employed with the other animals, Fantz presents some interesting data on human infants. Infants between the ages of 1 and 15 weeks were tested at weekly intervals in a "looking chamber." The infant was placed on his back, and looked up at a chamber of uniform color and lighting. The experimenter placed two objects, slightly separated, at the top of the chamber. The positions of the objects were randomly varied. By looking through a peephole in the top cover of the chamber, the experimenter could see which object was reflected in the infant's eyes. In this way *visual fixation,* which was taken as an index of visual interest, was measured (see Figure 12-6). The results for various patterns follow.

1 The infants preferred heterogeneous patterns over homogeneous ones. Thus, while no choice was shown between a large triangle and a small one or between a circle and a triangle, a checkerboard pattern was preferred over a homogeneously colored rectangle. Moreover, during a 1-minute test, the infants would, on the average, fixate a bull's-eye pattern for almost 20 seconds, while they would look at a horizontally striped pattern for only 10 seconds. Although there was a preference for the stripes in infants under 2 weeks old, the preference gradually shifted to a bull's-eye, until the experimenter found a marked preference for the latter in the 8-week-old infants.

2 The infants preferred looking at the pattern of a human face over printed matter and a bull's-eye over homogeneously colored disks (red, white, yellow), in that order. The pattern, not color or brightness, is important. *The preference for a face is age-dependent,* showing consistency from 8 weeks of age.

3 Finally, the adaptive significance of the form is indicated by the fact that the infant preferred a human-face pattern to a scrambled-face pattern to an oval which was black at the top and reddish at the bottom, in that order.

Fantz' work provides some fascinating insights into the complex interaction between innate, maturational, and learning variables in the development of form

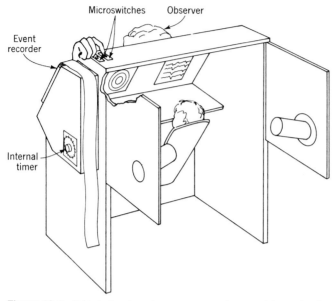

Figure 12-6 Infant visual-preference apparatus used for paired comparison test of infants, who were in semiupright position in a baby seat on the lap of a seated person. The view of subject was restricted by adjustable head pads to the inside of the chamber, which was lined with blue felt and illuminated by a shaded lamp on either side of the chamber, giving about 10 to 15 footcandles of reflected light. The targets were attached to the back of a "stage"; when pivoted upward, the bottom of the stage covered the opening. Inside dimensions of chamber are 32 inches high, 28 inches across, and 19 inches deep (excluding wings for lights). *(Fantz, 1961a.)*

perception and its adaptive significance. One word of caution, however, seems in order. The fact *that the infants prefer certain kinds of complex patterns to others does not necessarily mean that they can freely and completely discriminate their identity.* It may very well be that the kinds of visual exploration revealed in such interest provide the very kinds of neural excitations which lead to the cortical organization or structural transformation of cells, which then make the complete identification of forms possible. In this regard it is instructive to note that Gollin (1960) found that a greater amount of completeness was required for younger children to recognize incomplete forms than for older children to perform the same task.

Relevant to Fantz' data, Eleanor Gibson (1969, pp. 347–356), in reflecting on the development of perception of the human face, after summarizing a number of studies, abstracts the following highlights:

1 There is preferential eye fixation as early as 2 to 6 days of age, although we do not know what information is extracted. The emerging importance of the fixating on the eyes at 3½ weeks, however, suggests the beginning of feature differentiation.

2 After the age of 2 months there are indications that real facial features begin to be differentiated.

3 By 4 months realistically portrayed sculptured faces are differentiated from scrambled portrayals of weird faces. The social smile has been present for about four weeks.

4 By 5 months of age several features of the human face have been perceptually differentiated.

5 By 6 months of age infants distinguish between an unfamiliar and a familiar smiling face and figure.

6 After 8 months of age the differentiation of faces had become greatly refined and specified.

Research by some other investigators is related to the work of Fantz (and the theorizing of Hebb). One such study was conducted by Salapatek and Kessen (1966). Using an apparatus setup similar to that of Fantz, the eye-fixation patterns of a number of infants were studied while they were looking at a triangle. The infants were less than 8 days of age. During a 20-minute period, 100 pictures were taken, then the triangle was rotated through 180° and 600 pictures taken. The results were interesting. Unlike the situation while viewing a homogeneous stimulus when eye movements showed much dispersing, the infants tended to fixate at the vertex of a triangle. Moreover, each infant seemed to show a preference for a particular vertex, and there was little evidence of moving from one vertex to the other two.

The attentional focus on angle and medium complexity is consistent with Hebb's development theory of form perception. It might very well be that relatively heterogeneous sensory experiences give rise to the kinds of coding-cell patterns postulated by Hebb.

Schemata Mechanism Kagan, as we have said, believes that these fixation patterns contribute to and reveal the kinds of schemata—internal representations—that the child posesses. Additional work by Salapatek (1968) found that 50 to 70 percent of human newborns chose 50 percent of the figure for prolonged fixation or investigation. Moreover, the parts of the figure selected were angular, arcual, or line contour.

Karmel (1969) verified the finding that contour seemed to attract attention. Furthermore, Karmel, Hoffman, and Fegy (1974) related fixation function to visually evoked potentials (VEP) in the occipital cortex. Both studies found that 13- to 20-week old infants preferred contour with moderate thickness. (Checkerboard patterns were used.) The magnitude of VEPs co-varied with the time of fixation—both gave an inverted U-curve when related to thickness of contour. With older infants the curve shifted upward to denser contours.

It is of course plausible that the attraction to lines and vertices found by Salapatek and Karmel is directed by the receptive coding cells in the cortex. Keep in mind also that the organization of these receptive fields changes with experience.

Other research has indicated that there is also a shift to increasing complexity with age development during infancy. Thus Brennan, Ames, and Moore (1966) found that preference for complexity was age-related. Their 3-week-olds preferred two-by-two checks, 8-week-olds eight-by-eight checks, and 14-week-olds twenty-four-by-twenty-four checks.

Again, to lend strength to the view relating fixation pattern to VEPs, Harter and Smitt (1970) found that, as infants grew from 21 to 155 days, the magnitude of VEPs shifted from relatively large checks to progressively smaller (finer) checks.

Finally, we shall briefly refer to Kagan's notion that these shifts in fixation patterns (and presumably in concomitant brain mechanisms) include a development of schemata. McCall and Kagan (1967) showed that cardiac deceleration (an index of attention) was larger for moderate discrepancy from a learned standard than for large discrepancies. The subjects were 4-month-old girls, and they used a long-term familiarization procedure. Similar results were obtained by McCall and Melson (1969). McCall and Kagan (1970) showed, again in 4-month-olds, that fixation time is an increasing monotonic function about amount of change (replacement of parts) in the standard.

Finally, turning to more significant identities, Kagan and his associates report that evidence that a stimulus matches or is discrepant from an internal (schema) will not always show up in fixation time but will show up in other response measures. Thus Kagan (1967) found that 4-month-old infants had an equal score for first and total fixations to a photo of a man's face and schematic drawing thereof. However, the photo produced *more smiling and cardiac deceleration*. Also, at 6 months of age a female face is differentiated from a male face in terms of vocalization.

While Kagan believed that the development of schemata preceded the differential response to faces, Eleanor J. Gibson's (1969) view relates to increased differentiation feature detection, to which we now turn.

RESPONSE SPECIFICITY AND FEATURE DIFFERENTIATION

We come now to a fourth effect of practice, namely, an increase in response differentiation in addition to structure, selection, and schema. Theorizing in this area has been led by J. J. and Eleanor J. Gibson (1955, 1956) and Eleanor J. Gibson (1959). These authors contend that all existing theories of the perceptual process, including those based on association, "take for granted a discrepancy between the sensory input and the finished percept and they aim to explain the difference. . . . The development of perception must necessarily be one of supplementing or interpreting or organizing" (Gibson & Gibson, 1955, p. 33).

They propose an opposing view by presenting the results of an experiment. Human subjects were confronted with nonsense figures which looked like parts of human fingerprints. These can be seen in Figure 12-7. The figures could differ in three dimensions of variation: (1) number of coils (three, four, or five), (2) horizontal compression or stretching, and (3) orientation or right-left reversal. In all, eighteen such items were printed photographically on cards and shuffled with twelve other cards which included some that differed in many dimensions. Each subject was first shown a critical item, another nonsense figure, exposed for 5

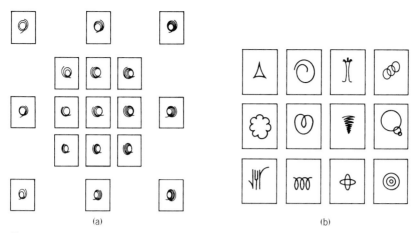

Figure 12-7 *(a)* Nonsense items differing in three dimensions of variation. *(b)* Nonsense items differing in many dimensions of variation. *(Gibson & Gibson, 1955.)*

seconds. Then the pack of thirty cards was exposed individually for 3 seconds, and the subject was told to report which of them had the critical figure.

The authors found that *there were generally no incorrect recognitions of the figures differing in many dimensions* but the other eighteen figures were sometimes misperceived. The mean number of trials required to reach the correct response ranged from 3.1 in adults to 6.7 in young children. Moreover, there was a difference in the magnitude of erroneous recognition, depending on whether the eighteen figures differed in one, two, or three dimensions. Those differing in one quality led to a greater percentage of erroneous recognitions than those differing in two qualities, which, in turn, led to more numerous errors than those differing in three qualities. From this experiment and other evidence, particularly noting the shorter number of trials needed by adults and the fewer errors made about forms differing in many dimensions, Gibson and Gibson concluded that perceptual learning leads to increased specificity or differentiation of the perceptual act; i.e., the individual becomes more attentive to the variables of the stimulus array.

Further support for this view comes from the data of Ryan and Schwartz (1965) who showed that accentuation of a feature, through cartoon-like drawings, speeded up discrimination, and from Fraisse and Elkin (1963) who found that an accented drawing produces a lower recognition threshold than a real object, photograph, or outline drawing.

After presenting an excellent review of the studies dealing with the effect of practice on perceptual judgment, including studies (Fehrer, 1935; Gilliland, 1925; Lawrence, 1949, 1950, 1952; Seward, 1931) on pattern discrimination which support their own results, Eleanor J. Gibson (1953) offers a theoretical suggestion as to how this increased specificity or differentiation of the perceptual response might take place. A schematic representation of that theory is presented in Figure 12-8.

A central discriminative feature between a theory like Hebb's and a theory

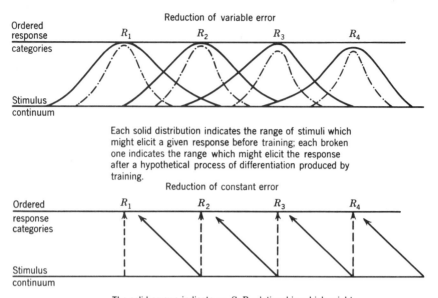

Ordered response categories

R_1 R_2 R_3 R_4

Reduction of variable error

Stimulus continuum

Each solid distribution indicates the range of stimuli which might elicit a given response before training; each broken one indicates the range which might elicit the response after a hypothetical process of differentiation produced by training.

Reduction of constant error

Ordered response categories

R_1 R_2 R_3 R_4

Stimulus continuum

The solid arrows indicate an S–R relationship which might exist before training; the broken arrows, a relationship which might exist after hypothetical correction of a constant error.

Figure 12-8 Schematic formulation of changes which may occur in improvement of perceptual judgments. *(After Eleanor J. Gibson, 1953, p. 424.)*

like that of the Gibsons is that Hebb considers sensory stimulation to have invariant consequences, whereas perceptual consequences are variables and derive their stability from cortical sets resulting from learning; conversely, the Gibsons believe that sensory stimulation produces the changeable consequences, while the perceptual consequences contain invariant relationships which result from the properties of objects and which do not have to be learned. In other words, for Hebb sensory stimulation has constant effects. It is the perception which is variable and has to be made stable by learning. The Gibsons believe instead that sensory stimulation is variable and the perceptual relationships are constant. In one article J. J. Gibson states: "I submit to Hebb the suggestion that the first problem in perceptual physiology is not how the brain responds to form as such, unvarying form, but instead how it responds to the *invariant variables of changing form.* I think we should attempt a direct physiological theory of object perception without waiting for a successful theory of picture perception" (1963, p. 14; italics added). What Gibson is saying is that it is not the unchanging form stimulus (such as in a picture) but the changing patterns of an object (as when the perceiver moves) that constitute the stimulus for form. There are certain *invariant relationships,* e.g., a family of perspective changes, which provide the information that defines the form. One of the central tasks in perceptual learning is learning to pay attention to those higher-order invariances.

    An interesting attempt to assess the relative weights of the two kinds of processes postulated by Hebb and the Gibsons—the building up of schemata and the development of increased distinctiveness—was performed by Anne Pick (1965), a student of the Gibsons at Cornell University.

In this experiment sixty kindergarten pupils were divided into three groups of twenty each, with an equal number of boys and girls in each group. The training procedure was the same for all groups. Three standard letter-like forms were placed on a stand, and a pack of cards containing two copies of each standard and *three transformations* of each standard was spread out in front of the subject on the table. The task of the subject was to look at each of the fifteen cards and decide whether it was exactly like one of the standards or different. When the subject had made a judgment about every card in the pack, the procedure was repeated until he reached a criterion of one perfect trial.

The three groups differed on the transfer test. Group C, a kind of control, provided a base line with which to compare the transfer performance of the other two groups. This group received three standards and three transformations which were different from the ones used in training. Group EI reflected the extent to which *standard, prototype, or schemata* learning had occurred during training. This group received the same standard as in training, but three new transformations of these standards. Group EII reflected the extent to which distinctive-feature learning had occurred during training. Members of this group received three new standards, but the same three types of transformations of these standards with which they dealt during training.

The number of confusion errors during the transfer trial was recorded. The means were 101 for group C, 69 for group EI, and 39 for group EII. The differences are statistically significant.

The subjects who in the transfer trial dealt with forms which they had never seen before but which varied from each other in familiar ways (the EII group) made the fewest errors. This suggested to the researcher that during the training trials subjects were learning how the forms varied from each other as they improved in their ability to discriminate among them. She also concluded, from the result that EI was superior to C, that prototype learning also occurred during training. She thought, however, that the clear superiority of group EII implied that such learning may not be essential to improvements in discrimination of this sort. For other research studies and theoretical conceptualizations which support this view, see Gibson, Gibson, Pick, and Osser (1962) and E. J. Gibson (1969, pp. 75–118).

The conclusions of Anne Pick and compatible views stated above are probably correct. However, these studies cannot unequivocally be used to say that prototype, schemata, or enrichment learning is not essential to pattern discrimination. In a theory such as Hebb's this kind of enrichment is slow and occurs very early in life, not in a few days at age 5 years. For a review of the issues in the development of form perception, see Elizabeth Bond (1972).

Five Trends in Perceptual Development

While there is much controversy, some debate, and considerable equivocation, and a lot of evidence still is required, we can probably deduce the five general trends from the research that has been described in this chapter.

1 Maturational Emergence of Innate Structures It seems fairly safe to conclude from the work of Hubel and Wiesel, McCleary and his co-workers, and to some extent from the work of Robert Fantz, that there are certain innate structures which enable the discrimination of at least the rudimentary elements of form. What other work has shown, including the work of McCleary and Riesen, is that deprivation does not prevent so much the development of the structures as their emergence in actual behavior. Furthermore, the very significant research of such investigations as Hirsch and Spinelli (1970) and Held and Hein (1963) indicates the tremendous plasticity of the perceptual system and its cortical mechanisms at length.

2 Growth of Schemata or Models The theorizing of Hebb, Kagan, Fantz, and others, as well as some of the research generated from these ideas, suggests that learning and practice do lead to the development of form schemata. Moreover, other studies which support this point of view show that more of the elements for form discrimination are necessary in younger children than in children who are older. Motor experience (active) is also influential.

3 Decrease in Stimulus Generalization This position, of course, has primarily been championed by Eleanor and James Gibson. On the basis of their 1955 experiments and other data, Gibson and Gibson have concluded that the younger children are unable to master a set of features which defined, for example, the standard scribble and, therefore, are unable to discover the uniqueness of each scribble. But, as greater specificity is achieved, verbal statements spontaneously occur, indicating that some of the distinct features are being detected.

This ability to detect features and to develop greater ability to discover uniqueness and, therefore, to achieve improved specificity and discrimination has been verified in other experiments. One having to do with electrodermal stimulation and response showed that the gradient in the generalization (electrical stimulation to the skin) became steeper with age.

Riess (1946), and then Mednick and Lehtinen (1957), also compared generalization in children of various ages, the youngest being 7 years old. When the children were shown a group of eleven lamps which were placed in a row, they were told that they should press a key when the middle light came on. They were also told that sometimes, when other lights came on, they should not press the key. With practice, of course, the children primarily would press the middle key. However, the children who were 8½ years of age showed a higher proportion of responses to the standard lamps. On the other hand, the children who were 7 years of age gave a higher percentage of incorrect responses, that is, responding to the other lamps, than was true in the children who were 8½ years of age. Thus, typical generalization curves were shown for the two groups, with the gradient being steeper and narrower for the 8½-year-old child.

4 Reduction of Variability Earlier in this chapter we presented the graph for variable error and constant error and Eleanor Gibson's conceptualization of this change over age. In addition to a decrease in stimulus generalization there is also marked reduction in variability with age. For example, Piaget and his students have shown that, from age 5 to age 12 years, there is a dramatic drop in a variable error from almost 60 to about 10 percent. At the beginning the youngest age group accept an equivalent height to a standard rod, a group of rods varying over more than half of the height of the standard. The width of the area of uncertainty was about six times as great as the mean constant error, and it narrows progressively with age. While there is a drop in the constant error also, it decreases from a high of about 10 percent to a low of about 2 percent. For additional data on how the variable error decreases relative to the constant error, see E. J. Gibson and Olum (1960, pp. 311–373).

5   Reduction in Discrimination Time   Finally, the work of Gibson also shows that discrimination time or reaction time decreases with age. For example, in a disjunctive reaction-time experiment, conducted by Yonas and Gibson (1967), the subject pushed a lever in one direction if a letter exposed before him was a letter that had been designated by the experimenter; he pushed it in the other direction if it was any other letter. There were three groups of subjects; children from the second grade and the sixth grade, and college students. In all cases, of course, reaction time for the correct letter was lower than for the incorrect letter. However, for the incorrect letter, the average reaction time was 0.90 second for the second grade, 0.65 second for the sixth grade, and less than 0.50 second for college sophomores. Over a period of more than a hundred trials, these disjunctive reaction times decreased for all subjects. There is no significant difference in the slope of the reduction curve. Analysis indicated that it was not the difficulty of the task, lack of understanding the task, or inattention on the part of the younger children that accounted for these results. The authors reasoned *that there may be a shift with age in the set of distinctive features used in discrimination of the forms;* either there was reduction of the set to a more economical one, or pickup of tied features (high-ordered structures) that reduced the number of comparisons required for discrimination of sameness or difference.

These are trends in perceptual-learning research. Data generated so far do not allow us to choose between a schemata or feature—specificity theory. We do know that some innate coding ability exists. We also know that it is plastic and changes with specific experience. We know, further, that attention and selective capacities direct the growth of perception. We still do not know how attention functions to filter out the irrelevant and preserve the critical information, nor what the relative importance of associative representations (schemata) and invariant higher-order invariables are in perception. As of now we see them as valuable perspectives in form perception and peripheral learning, in general.

As Eleanor Gibson ends her 1969 book, "We know something about the laws and what experiments we can be doing to improve our knowledge of them, but the 'strategy in the middle' leaves us a great deal to think about."

SUMMARY

This chapter reviewed the studies and conceptualizations dealing with the relationship between experience and perceptual ability. First, we reviewed studies which show clearly that there are certain innate perceptual structures which provide for at least the elementary basis of form or pattern perception. These structures, however, are plastic and change significantly with differential experience. Next, we reviewed a number of studies on sense deprivation, stabilized retinal image, experiential deprivation of sensory experience and motor activity, and varied experience which indicated influence of experience on the development of perception. Third, we analyzed research on the normal development of perception. Fourth, we reviewed the views and research which favor the position that experience gives rise to development of improved discrimination and filtering, providing the capacity to perceive increased specificity and uniqueness. Our concluding section listed current trends in perceptual learning research and put our existing knowledge in perspective.

Chapter 13

Space Perception

In our introduction to Chapter 1 we emphasized the central role perception plays in man's adaptation to his environment. The world of spatial behavior affords many examples of the adaptive aspects of perception. In the preceding chapter we saw how important active spatial movement is for the development of visuomotor integration. In Chapter 8 we analyzed the relationship between distance and size perception. In this chapter we shall examine such adaptive aspects of space perception as the interaction between visual and proprioceptive references in determining spatial location; the contribution of organismic variables to the growth of depth perception; and the remarkable plasticity of the adaptation to varying spatial environments. The attitude adopted by the perceiver is a central determiner in many of these functions. The perception of space can be broken down into two areas:

    1 *Two-dimensional space.* Here we are concerned with the fact that we can locate things in space—that is, to the left or right and up or down.
    2 *Three-dimensional space.* We can also perceive the distance an object is away from us; i.e., we can tell, within limits, whether it is near or far along the line of sight. This is the third dimension, which itself consists of two somewhat separate, although related, aspects. The first is the perception of the *depth* of an

object like a cube or anything which has volume. In addition to the object's height and width, which bound its two-dimensional area, we can perceive its depth or thickness. The second aspect is the perception of the *relative distance* of objects from us along the third dimension.

When we consider the phenomena of space perception, as outlined above, we must examine the way the individual locates objects not only with respect to one another but also with respect to his own bodily orientation. So we become concerned not only with the spatial location of external entities but also with where we are, in what position (upright, to the side, etc.), and in which direction or directions we must go to get from here to there.

TWO-DIMENSIONAL SPACE: EXPERIMENTS AND PRINCIPLES

The main coordinates of two-dimensional space are the gravitational *vertical* and the *horizontal,* which is perpendicular to it. These two planes constitute the main frame of reference against which we ordinarily judge spatial direction that is located in two dimensions. Emphasizing the importance of the visual mechanism, the gestalt psychologists have traditionally argued that space is not located with reference to our bodies but with reference to the vertical and horizontal as perceived "out there." The two-dimensional field can be represented essentially by a right angle. When Wertheimer said that the lines which contain this right angle are *Prägnanzstufen* (pregnant steps), he meant that the lines provide a consistent anchor for judging the direction of other angles. When Koffka invoked the principles of "invariance" to account for the accuracy of spatial perception, he was reasoning in a similar way. They suggested that we perceive spatial direction of objects correctly because the angles made by these objects with the framework remain invariant or consistent. If one axis of the framework is tilted without the observer's realizing it, equilibrium is upset; consequently, a compensatory force will be generated to restore the balance. Under such conditions the observer usually perceives a compensatory tilt, in the opposite direction, of other objects located in the field.

Since gestalt research does not fully explain the nature of this force or what generates it, it should be used cautiously as a hypothetical descriptive concept.

Both Carr and Gibson have argued that the placement of parts of the body in relation to external objects is an important aspect of perceiving direction. Carr has asserted that the visual detection by an individual of parts of his eyebrows, nose, cheek, trunk, arms, and legs is a necessary component of accurately localizing an object in space, while Gibson has stated that the inclusion of his own body in the perceptual process permits the individual to infer that he is "here" and the object is "there." Other investigators referred to below have insisted on including the contribution of proprioceptive mechanisms—i.e., vestibular (concerned with balance) and kinesthetic (concerned with bodily reaction) sensation—to give a more complete understanding of spatial perception. Much research has investigated visual and proprioceptive interaction.

Interaction between Visual and Proprioceptive Determiners of the Perceived Vertical and Horizontal

The results of an experiment by J. J. Gibson (1933), which were verified by M. D. Vernon (1934) and Radner and Gibson (1935), suggested the conditions under which the perceived spatial direction remains invariant with respect to the vertical coordinate. The first two experiments showed that if an inclined line or shape is fixated for a long time and no other visual surround is present, the line eventually appears to be less steeply inclined; i.e., it begins to "approach" the true vertical. The third experiment, however, showed that if the tilt is very strongly perceived and verbalized as such, the inclination may even be exaggerated. Nevertheless, in all these conditions, after the perceived inclination has been diminished, a vertical line subsequently introduced appears to have *an equivalent tilt in the opposite direction.* (We note, in passing, the similarity of these findings with those of Köhler et al. on figural aftereffects, discussed in Chapter 10.) The above data support the gestalt notion of invariance.

As early as 1912 Wertheimer performed an experiment which, he believed, also supported gestalt theory. In this experiment observers were required to look at the reflection of a room in an inclined mirror through a tube which eliminated the rest of the surround. The observers reported that the room (not the mirror) appeared to be inclined and that the objects in the room were arranged in a disorderly fashion. During the early part of the observation the subjects were quite disoriented in space, but as time elapsed, the room was seen to recover its usual spatial framework, and the subjects regained their orientation. The gestalt psychologists would argue that since the visual framework tends to remain constant, the inclined plane produces a compensatory force to right itself.

Individual Differences in Visual Proprioceptive Determination

In an experimental task similar to that of Wertheimer—i.e., the observer had to look at the reflection of a room in an inclined mirror through a tube which prevented direct vision of the room—Asch and Witkin (1948a) concluded that their experiment verified Wertheimer's results and supported Koffka's theory. In this experiment the subjects were blindfolded when they were brought into the room. After the blindfolds had been removed, the subjects immediately looked through the tube while they were in an upright position. Once this experiment had been completed, they were again brought into the room, this time without blindfolds, and were permitted to look at the scene in the mirror with free vision. In both conditions the subjects were required to adjust a line to their judgment of the vertical plane. Although five different effects, showing individual differences between subjects, were observed, one result occurred most frequently. This dominant effect was that most subjects set the vertical relative to the tilted plane in the mirror and not relative to the postural or gravitational vertical. Quite a few observers reported that the tilt was seen at the beginning but that it gradually disappeared in the perception. Asch and Witkin were impressed by the *tremendous stability,* or tendency toward stability, of the *visual spatial framework.*

The findings of Gibson and Mowrer (1938) and Mann (1952) suggest caution before we completely accept any theory which emphasizes the visual determiners of two-dimensional space to the exclusion of postural determiners. For example, in the experiment of Gibson and Mowrer, which was similar to that of Wertheimer, they found that, while the room scene became less steeply inclined with continued inspection, the tilt was not eliminated completely. It appeared to them that the observers adapted themselves to the fact that the two main coordinates of space were distorted, which led to the disappearance of the feeling of disorientation. After reviewing the relevant data, J. J. Gibson (1952) urged that we do not argue over whether the visual or the proprioceptive factors are more important but emphasize instead the *joint interaction* of the factors in the visual-proprioceptive complex which determine perceived direction of two-dimensional space. The following sections elaborate this joint determination.

Dominant Visual Framework

In a second experiment, Asch and Witkin (1948b) varied both visual and proprioceptive conditions of stimulation. This time the subjects were brought into a room which was actually tilted through 22°. As before, they were first brought in blindfolded and asked to adjust a rod to the vertical immediately after the blindfolds had been removed. They were then brought into the room with free vision, and the experiment was repeated. The results of this experiment, in general, verified those of the tilted-mirror experiment. While individual differences similar to those observed in the first experiment were obtained, the majority of the subjects again estimated the vertical to be roughly parallel to the walls of the inclined room rather than parallel to their upright bodies. Furthermore, when the subject was making his judgment from a tilted chair, the visual framework became an even stronger determiner of the estimated vertical. This was particularly true when the subject's body was tilted in a direction opposite that of the room. This tendency appears to be so strong that *when the visual coordinates are distorted, the perceived vertical undergoes a comparable distortion.*

In another experiment Witkin (1950a, 1950b) studied the effect of postural distortion on perceived space when the visual framework was in its usual position. Blindfolded subjects were placed in a cubicle which was moved around a circular track at various speeds. Proprioceptive stimulation was thus produced by the gravitational force and the centrifugal force caused by the rotation. When his blindfold was removed, each subject was required to adjust a rod to the vertical and horizontal positions. He was able to do this with a very high degree of accuracy when the cubicle was lit, but he made a much greater error when adjusting an illuminated rod when the cubicle was dark (thus with most of the visual framework removed). This was especially true after the cubicle had been moving at high speeds of rotation. The error of estimation, however, was smaller than the angle of the resultant force (gravitational and centrifugal). As usual, a great deal of variability was observed between subjects in the dark-cubicle condition. Some subjects saw the walls of the cubicle as vertical, while others thought that they were tilted. Although visual cues were dominant, postural forces became more important when visual cues were reduced or removed.

Increasing Importance of Proprioceptive Stimulation in a Reduced Visual Framework

A number of studies (Witkin & Asch, 1948a, 1948b) have demonstrated that it is only when there is no visual framework (e.g., darkness with no luminescence) that the subject would set the vertical to his body position, even if the latter is tilted.

That vision is dominant over other spatial senses as well has been clearly demonstrated in studies by Rock and Harris (1967) and Hay, Pick, and Ikeda (1965). Rock and Harris produced a conflict between the size information provided by vision and that provided by tactile-kinesthetic information for a small plastic square. The subject viewed the square through a lens that made it appear smaller than its objective size. At the same time he felt it from beneath the cloth upon which it rested. The subject later made size judgments of the square by drawing it or selecting the appropriate squares from a series of comparison stimuli. The dominance of vision over the tactile-kinesthetic sense was clearly revealed by the subject's repeated choice of a square smaller than the objective size of the one used in the experiment. Hay, Pick, and Ikeda were able to show "visual capture" of the proprioceptive sense by having subjects judge both the "felt" and viewed position of their fingers as observed through a prism that displaced the image of the fingers laterally. The felt position of the fingers, its proprioceptive location, was significantly shifted toward its visual location. (We repeat that it is only when visual cues are removed that other senses replace sight as a frame of reference.)

Sensoritonic Theory   Related to visual interaction with other senses is sensoritonic theory, developed by Werner and his co-workers at Clark University. The major tenet is that bodily (tonic) and sensory stimulation interact to determine spatial orientation. A number of studies (Werner & Wapner, 1949, 1952, 1955; Wapner, Werner, & Chandler, 1951) have shown, for example, that a tap on the right shoulder or input to the right ear will displace the vertical to the left.

The fact that sometimes there is an equilibrial shift and at other times there is not leads Glick (1968) to invoke Koffka's principle of *egocentric* and *objective* localization to account for the two effects, with children having a greater tendency to the former.

Field independence is considered more desirable, and yet Werner considers paying attention to the body as an egocentric and a developmentally more primitive level of development. This apparent paradox can be resolved if we realize that the demands of the task should be the criterion. Thus, under some conditions, paying more attention to external stimuli would be more adaptive, while under others, relying on bodily cues would be more effective. Therefore egocentric and field-independent constructs are here considered as parts of a larger class—namely, organismic field articulation. The more articulated or differentiated this organization, the greater the likelihood that the appropriate locus will be retrieved when desirable. There is more on this in the last chapter, in the section on cognitive-style differentiation.

Related to sensoritonic theory is further evidence that proprioceptive kinesthetic processes are involved in the adaptation. Mack and Rock (1968) found conclusively, in four different experiments, that movement was both necessary and sufficient for adaptation to take place.

Adaptation to an Optically Rearranged Spatial Environment

One of the simplest procedures for altering the sensory-motor behavior of individuals is to place such devices as prisms, mirrors, or lenses before their eyes. Such devices can invert, reverse, curve, tilt, or laterally displace the retinal image of objects—and thus the visual world as it appears to the observer. The most often discussed of the early studies in *visual* or *prism adaptation,* as this research area is commonly called, are those conducted by George Stratton, an American psychologist trained by Wundt. Stratton intended to determine whether the inversion of the retinal image was necessary for the perception of objects as upright. It had been known since at least the sixteenth century that the normal retinal image is inverted.

By attacking the problem directly—i.e., by viewing the world entirely through a lens system that inverted the visual field and thus righted the retinal image—Stratton became godfather to the modern field of visual adaptation. His inverting system was composed of an adjustable tube with two double convex lenses at either end. The tubes were inserted into a goggle-like plaster cast worn about the eyes. Monocular viewing was obtained by occluding the left tube with black paper. The monocular field of view was about 45°.

The experiences of Stratton summarized here come from his second experiment (1897) in which he wore his lens device for seven days. The first of Stratton's findings that can be delineated concerns motor movements. Stratton's visual-motor coordination was so poor initially that he often resorted to closing his eyes and getting about by touch and memory. By the fifth day, however, ''In walking I did not so often run into obstacles in the very effort to avoid them. I usually took the right direction without reflecting and without the need any longer of constantly watching my feet. When the doors were open I could walk through them and the entire house by visual guidance alone . . .'' (p. 355). On the seventh day, Stratton was primarily troubled by finer discriminations such as extent of movement.

The second type of finding reported by Stratton concerns changes in the various proprioceptive systems of the observer. *Proprioception,* as used here, refers to the felt or subjective position of the various parts of the body. This may concern the relative positions of two systems—e.g., the felt position of the arm with respect to the head—or the felt position of one system—e.g., the right arm with respect to the observer's estimation of the general or egocentric spatial position of his body.

After several days of wearing his inverting lenses, Stratton reported quite vivid changes in proprioception: "I felt that my legs were where I saw them. . . . If I tapped my knee in plain sight, the contact was localized only where sight reported it to be" (p. 358). Note that given the optical inversion produced by the lens system, this meant that Stratton felt his legs to be above his head.

The third type of finding reported by Stratton concerns the visual changes he might have experienced in the spatial orientation of objects. Certainly, the primary question to ask about Stratton's experiment is whether or not the visual world eventually appeared upright—i.e., did it ever look the same as it did before the lenses were put on? What Stratton has to say about this is never clear. Many articles have been written over the past several decades interpreting his findings, but the studies themselves have never been replicated. Early in the experiment, Stratton felt that the room was upside down. On the fifth day he mentions that when he looked at his legs or arms, what he saw "seemed rather upright than inverted" (p. 354). On the other hand, he accepts a harmony between touch and sight as the definition of upright: "a harmony between touch and sight, which, in the final analysis, is the real meaning of upright vision" (pp. 475–476).

When Stratton removed the optical device on the eighth day, "The reversal of everything from the order to which I had grown accustomed during the past week, gave the scene a surprising, bewildering air which lasted for several hours. It was hardly the feeling, though, that things were upside down" (p. 476). With respect to motor movements, Stratton found that he continually reached in the direction appropriate to the inverted world and thus inappropriately to the now restored visual world. These movements and perceptual experiences, occurring upon removal of the lenses, that are inappropriate to the noninverted visual input, are called *aftereffects*.

Köhler's Work Although Stratton's studies indicated that a rearranged visual input produced interesting changes in the observer's sensorimotor and proprioceptive systems, very little follow-up research into the adaptation mechanisms occurred until the work of Ivo Köhler in Austria (1951, trans. 1964). The surge of interest in prism adaptation of the last two decades can be directly linked to Köhler's publication.

Perhaps Köhler's best-known prism experiment is the one in which his subjects wore half-prism spectacles for a period of fifty days. The spectacles were so constructed that upward vision had to pass through a prism with a 10° displacement angle. The base of the prism was to the left. Since in viewing through prisms the visual image is laterally displaced in the direction *opposite* to the base (or thick part) of the prism, Köhler's subjects when looking up saw objects in a position that was actually 10° to the *right* of their true position. Downward vision passed through clear glass and was therefore normal.

During the first ten days of wearing these spectacles, when the subject looked straight ahead through the center of the glasses, the upper part of the image was curved and suspended above and to the right of the lower part. By the tenth day, when the subject looked *down* through the clear glass, he began to notice the image displaced in the opposite direction from which it would have been displaced when viewed through the prism—i.e., it was shifted to the left. A *negative aftereffect* had occurred in the sense that this aftereffect was in the direction opposite to the prism distortion. At this point, when the subject looked up through the prism half, the image was less displaced, almost normal.

The adaptive changes from the eleventh to the fiftieth days were even more interesting. Eventually, when the subject was looking down, the world began to appear normal. When he was looking up, the world also appeared normal. The subject's vision had become differentially adapted to each condition. After removal of the glasses, the subject perceived a negative aftereffect only when looking up. Thus, depending on eye or head position, the same stimulus would appear distorted or veridical even though the retinal pattern was precisely the same for both eye-head positions.

In summary, Köhler found adaptation to be variable even though the visual stimulus was constant and always presented to the same retinal area. The adaptive changes were directly linked to one specific situation, the direction of gaze, as produced by either the subject's eye movements or a change in his head position. Köhler refers to the resulting aftereffects as *situational aftereffects*. For Köhler, these results served as evidence for some type of central type of adaptation (i.e., some adaptation in the central nervous system) in that differential motor movements of the eyes or head were directly associated with different sensory experiences.

Whether or not Köhler's situational aftereffects reflect a visual change as part of the adaptive process has been a point of controversy. It is necessary to point out that Köhler's subject did learn to move his eyes in such a manner as to compensate for the effect of the prism. A continuation of this activity upon removal of the prisms could account for Köhler's findings. Pick and Hay (1966) and Hay and Pick (1966b) have investigated these gaze-dependent situational aftereffects and have found evidence that they occur, but only in a limited manner. Their subjects showed negative aftereffects that were gaze-contingent but could counteract only a small proportion of the distortion produced by the prisms.

Reafference Theory   The current era of intensive experimental investigations into the nature and mechanisms of prism adaptation began with the early work of Richard Held and his co-workers on the reafference model. The use of the term *experimental* here implies a manipulation, control, and statistical evaluation of the factors proposed as essential to the occurrence of adaptation.

The concept of reafference was developed by Von Holst (1954). Neural messages from sensory receptors traveling to the central nervous system (CNS) are called *afference*. Motor impulses which originate in the CNS and produce contractions in the skeletal musculature are called *efference*. According to Von

Holst, there are two different sources of afferent stimuli: (1) stimuli produced by self-initiated muscular activity, *reafference;* and (2) stimuli produced by external factors, *exafference*. This distinction is clarified in the following quotation from Von Holst: "If I shake the branch of a tree, various receptors of my skin and joints produce a reafference, but if I place my hand on a branch shaken by the wind, the stimuli of the same receptors produce an ex-afference" (1954, p. 161).

Since the same receptors conduct reafferent and exafferent information, the CNS must distinguish one from the other in order to regulate the body's motor movements. The mechanism by which this is accomplished is the *efferent copy*, a reproduction of the efferent signal that produces reafferent feedback. It is supposedly canceled out by this feedback. Exafference has no efferent copy to cancel and thus can lead to distortions in motor movement or at least to unregulated movement.

Held has taken Von Holst's concept of reafference and extended it to account for the acquisition of adaptive changes in visual-motor coordination in situations in which the visual field has been optically distorted by prisms and the like. The major change imparted by Held is that reafference is broadly defined as sensory feedback. Visual feedback from any self-induced ("active") motor movement serves as reafference. Visual feedback from movements which are not self-induced ("passive") would be exafferent. Only reafferent feedback from active movement leads to adaptation in Held's model. Only in this circumstance is there an efferent copy of the efferent signal producing the movement. Therefore, only in this case can the visual *feedback* from the movement (reafference) and thus the movement itself be evaluated in terms of its adequacy given the initiating efference.

A study by Held and Hein (1958) will be considered here to clarify Held's model and present some representative data. Both before and after wearing prisms, subjects performed the same task—pointing to a target when the hand was not visible. During an intermediate prism-viewing condition, independent groups of subjects either (1) simply watched their hand on a shelf in front of them (no-movement group), (2) watched their hand as they themselves moved it (active-movement group), or (3) watched their hand as the experimenter moved it for them (passive-movement group).

Adaptation in this study would be reflected in a shift in the target-pointing behavior of the subjects on the posttest in comparison to the pretest. Negative aftereffects in target pointing should occur such that subjects on postexposure trials err in pointing at the targets in the direction of the base of the prism. This would show that they have learned while wearing the prisms that the true position of the object (the hand) is in the direction opposite to the displacement produced by the prism. Since the displacement is away from the base, the true position is toward the base of the prism. They would show sensory-motor compensation for the prism effect.

Held and Hein found that only the active-movement group showed statistically significant differences between the pretest and posttest in pointing to the target. These were negative aftereffects in the direction of the base of the prism.

These data directly support the reafference model. Only the active-movement group would be expected to adapt in that this was the only group that had to initiate efferent signals to control arm movement. For these subjects, the hand, under prism viewing, was not seen (reafference) to coincide with its expected location (a memory trace associated with the efferent copy), given the particular movement imposed by the current efferent signal. The passive and no-movement groups had no mechanism by which to correct their movements in that there was no retrieval of a reafferent trace from memory to compare with the current visual feedback.

Held's reafference theory came under attack almost from its inception. The principal sources of evidence against it came from studies in which passive-movement or no-movement subjects adapt. Wallach, Kravitz, and Lindauer (1963) obtained significant aftereffects in target pointing following an exposure condition in which their subjects regarded their feet from a bent-over position while wearing 11° displacing prisms for 10 minutes. Howard, Craske, and Templeton (1965) argued that Held and Hein's procedure did not provide subjects with sufficient exafferent information. They provided exafferent information by having subjects watch a wooden rod with lights on it approach one cheek but instead strike them on the mouth. The trick was accomplished through the use of mirrors. Aftereffects in target pointing were obtained that compensated for the mirror's displacement of the image. The subject's head was always in a fixed position in this study and no part of the body was visible.

Melamed, Halay, and Gildow (1973) have shown that even in an exposure condition comparable to that used by Held and Hein, in which a subject merely views his prismatically displaced hand on a homogeneous background, passive movement can lead to adaptation equivalent to that for active movement. This result was obtained by simply adding vertical lines along the background upon which the subject viewed his hand movement. The argument is that active-movement subjects have to track their own movements, while passive-movement subjects are ordinarily specifically instructed to operate at a lower attentional level, i.e., to remain passive and let the experimenter control the movement of their arms. The addition of the lines gives the passive subjects reference points for evaluating the location of their arms, i.e., an ability to locate or trace the arm without controlling its movement, such that they show the same adaptive shifts as the active-movement subjects.

Proprioceptive Consequences of Adaptation The work of Held has been presented in some detail because it represents the starting point of the "modern" empirical studies of visual adaptation. Without disregarding the obvious problems of reafference theory discussed previously, we may still say that it is the most complete attempt to explain the *process* of visual-motor change that underlies adaptation.

Current approaches to prism adaptation focus primarily on the results of the adaptive process, whatever its characteristics. These results are generally considered proprioceptive, i.e., they involve changes in the apparent position of a body member. From the work of Harris (1963, 1965) and Hay and Pick (1966a), it is fairly well established that the changes in visual-motor coordination revealed in target-pointing behavior, represent, as a minimum, shifts in the felt position of the arm with respect to the median plane of the body. With the use of some exposure procedures described later, a second change, that of the visual direction of the target, is said to occur. The latter change may also be proprioceptive, representing a change in the felt position of the eyes with respect to the head. This explanation is problematical because of the lack of convincing evidence for feedback from the appropriate muscles to the CNS.

In order to demonstrate the importance of the findings concerning proprioception, Harris' (1963) study will be presented here in detail. Harris employed a 3-minute exposure period in which the subjects actively pointed several times at a rod in the true straight-ahead position. The subject's arm was visible. Both the hand used in the exposure conditions and the unexposed hand were tested in the pre- and postexposure tests. The most important of these tests were (1) pointing at target rods with the hand not visible and (2) pointing straight ahead of the nose with the eyes closed.

Harris obtained equivalent significant aftereffects in *both* pointing tasks for the hand used in the exposure task. The significance of this finding is in the result for the task of pointing straight ahead. Since vision was not employed, it indicates that the subject's judgment of the position of his arm had changed rather than arguing for some recorrelation of visual feedback and movement (reafference theory). Following exposure with base-right prisms that shift the visual image to the *left* of the object's true position, the subject would now position his arm, on the posttest, to the *right* of his pretest estimate of the straight ahead. The subjects apparently learned the correspondence between the true and apparent position of objects.

The fact that the amount of the aftereffect in pointing straight ahead was not different from that found for the task of pointing at the target led Harris to conclude that the latter result was due to the same proprioceptive shift in arm position. It was the only explanation that fitted both findings.

Harris' (1963) second finding concerns the lack of aftereffects for the previously unexposed arm, i.e., the lack of *intermanual transfer* of prism adaptation. This finding rules out a visual explanation for the adaptive shifts found in the target-pointing procedures for the exposed hand. Any aftereffect in pointing at targets that was produced by changes in the visual position of the target would be expected for *both* hands. As will be discussed later, intermanual transfer has been found for certain exposure conditions, and the amount of such transfer does appear to be related to the degree to which an aftereffect in the *visual* positioning of the apparent straight-ahead occurs.

Information Discordance Theories   Up to this point two general theories— or, better, orientations—to adaptation have been presented. Held's reafference theory deals with a process explanation of adaptation; Harris' theory deals with the end results or sites of adaptation. A large number of investigators, typified by Freedman (1968b pp. 63–76), take an informational approach. Freedman reasons that the use of an optical device such as a prism introduces a discrepancy between channels of information about the spatial characteristics of the subject's environment that were concordant previously. For an observer who is reaching for targets through laterally displacing prisms, the visual and proprioceptive feedback received about arm position is no longer congruent. Adaptation results to the extent that the observer can compensate for this discrepancy—e.g., by letting vision dominate his localization of arm position, as Harris proposes.

It should be clear that the informational-discrepancy hypothesis in actuality is only a framework for evolving a theory of the process of adaptation. Exactly what information is necessary and how it is used in compensating for the disarrangement is never spelled out, although there are some indications at present. Thus, Cannon (1970, 1971) and Uhlarik and Cannon (1970, 1971) argue that when inconsistency of information is between two sensory channels, the unattended channel is the one that undergoes an adaptive shift. From this viewpoint, Harris' (1963) evidence for a change in felt arm position comes from the fact that the subject attends to the visual location of his prismatically (visually) displaced hand. Thus, the hand comes to feel to be, spatially, where it looks to be.

Melamed, Halay, and Gildow, in a study described earlier, found that the addition of background lines to the exposure field allowed passive-movement subjects to adapt. The explanation that this allows these subjects to track their arm movements implies that they are processing a discrepancy between the visual and proprioceptive location of their hands, and that this is the necessary condition for visual-motor adaptation to occur, whether movement is active or passive.

Further evidence for the discordance hypothesis comes from evaluations of the various prism-exposure methodologies used (Howard, 1968, pp. 19–36; Freedman, 1968a, pp. 231–240; Wilkinson, 1971). The smallest aftereffects in pointing at a visual target occur with Held's exposure condition where the subject simply views his hand on a homogeneous background. Much larger aftereffects (Uhlarik, 1973; Melamed & Moore, 1973) occur with a procedure developed by Howard (1968). In Howard's procedure, the subject cannot see his hand as he moves it toward a target in the exposure task until the end of the movement; i.e., he sees his fingertip and the target location at the end of the movement. It can be argued, as Uhlarik does argue, that there are two sources of discordant information in this exposure condition, whereas Held's contains only one. Both procedures, according to this view, give the subject discordant visual and proprioceptive information about the location of the arm. On the other hand, the subject also receives *target-error information* in Howard's procedure.

Another indication that more information, however defined, leads to more "complete" adaptation is that the transfer of adaptation to the unexposed hand typically can be found with Howard's procedure but never with Held's. This transfer has been found to occur to an extent equivalent to the visual change or change in felt-eye position (Hay & Pick, 1966a) which also can be found when Howard's procedure is used but not Held's.

At this point it is necessary to introduce a final set of findings into this discussion. These concern the so-called "linear model" of prism adaptation, which states that the target-pointing aftereffects of prism exposure are equivalent to the sum of change in felt arm position and the change in the visual judgment of the apparent straight-ahead. Wilkinson (1971) found such a relationship using Howard's procedure.

More recent data have raised some important questions concerning the generality of such a model even when restricting it to Howard's procedure. One question concerns the effect of the spacing of the subject's responses during the exposure period (i.e., while wearing the prisms). For example, Welch and his associates (Choe & Welch, 1974; Welch, Choe, & Heinrich, 1974) allowed subjects to view their errors while pointing at targets during the exposure period and found that when responding was massed, the two-component additive model held quite well. However, when exposure responses were distributed, a third component seemed to be elicited.

The important issue of individual differences has also been raised in the study by Templeton, Howard, and Wilkinson (1974) in which a direct recording of eye position while directing the gaze toward an unseen toe was used to measure the visual aftereffects. In this study, the researchers found that a number of subjects failed to show adaptive visual aftereffects and in these subjects the target-pointing aftereffects were larger than the sum of the proprioceptive and visual aftereffects, the additive model holding only for those subjects who did show adaptive visual aftereffects.

The importance of an individual-differences approach to the study of adaptation has been advanced in a recent study by Warren and Platt (1975), who found that the amount of adaptation was positively correlated with indices of eye ability and negatively correlated with indices of hand ability. These findings led Warren and Platt to the conclusion that the strength of the various components of adaptation depend at least in part on the different abilities of subjects to make use of available information on which these components depend.

It should be apparent that this last discussion on the informational-discordance approach is the most general of all approaches to adaptation. Although it does not greatly advance knowledge on the process of adaptation, it does tie together certain diverse findings; these include the greater efficacy of certain exposure conditions, the occurrence of visual changes, and the circumstances under which the linear model on the sites of adaptation can predict target-pointing behavior.

The preceding review has shown us that spatial orientation, including the perception of the vertical, is a complex affair, involving the interaction of visual and proprioceptive stimulation. When there are transformations in sensory stimuli, the visual framework appears to be most stable or dominant. However, there are individual differences, and the proprioceptive (organismic) factors become more influential with age. The most general explanation would be one which formulates the problem of spatial adaptation in informational-expectancy terms—that is, spatial adaptation involves the effort on the part of the subject to rectify any discrepancy between the expectancy and the outcome of his spatial balance, since the attitude he adopted is of primary importance.

THREE-DIMENSIONAL SPACE

We saw in the introduction to this chapter that there are two major emphases in three-dimensional space as well. One, stressing memory and the perceiver's attitude, is most strongly represented today by transactional theory (e.g., Kilpatrick, 1961, pp. 13–32). The demonstrations presented in Figures 13-3 to 13-5 and 13-8 are examples of what the approach has produced. This view essentially is that information in the physical stimuli is equivocal—that is, the same pattern can be produced by many different objects, located at different distances or in different perspectives. The only way a particular dimension can thus be specified is through definitive information produced by the subject's memory and inferences. This is, indeed, an empiristic position.

The alternative position, the psychophysical theory, represented most influentially by J. J. Gibson (1966), argues, indeed, that the reliable information for any pattern is located precisely in the change in stimulation which accompanies changes in distance and perspective. Certain *invariant* higher-order relationships exist within these optical transformations, and they contain the reliable information for a stable definition of a dimension of form.

Rather than organize our treatment around these two theories, we must, instead, organize it in the context of the relative distances at which cues to space and distance are effective. It turns out, perhaps coincidentially, that the transactional demonstrations cover relatively short distances, whereas Gibson's analysis has also been applied to longer distances.

The traditional list of visual depth determiners has been classified into primary and secondary cues. The primary cues are effective in direct sensory perception, while the secondary cues are used principally, although not exclusively, to create depth effects in drawings and paintings. This distinction may have led to an unfortunate connotation since the so-called secondary cues, which must also have actual psychological effects in the real world, have been neglected in research. Yet they are necessary in the perception of especially large distances.

Primary Cues

We shall classify the cues into groups according to the relative distances at which they cease to be effective, i.e., distances where successive changes become too small (falling below the difference limen) to produce a change in discriminable depth. The distances still need to be more precisely determined, but some evidence exists to permit the classification of an ordinal hierarchy at least. The distances reported are thus intended as guides and are not to be regarded as firmly established.

Eye-Muscle Adjustments   These are the cues of *accommodation* and *convergence* which operate at distances up to 25 and 80 feet or less, respectively. Accommodation, which is the change in the shape of the crystalline lens to bring the object into clear focus as distance varies, was established as an experimental fact by Scheiner and thought to be a depth cue by Helmholtz. Since each eye has its own lens and since one eye can accommodate while the other, for example, is closed, accommodation is called a *monocular cue*. There are many other monocular cues, most of which are listed under the secondary cues, but accommodation and the principles of perspective geometry (visual angle and linear perspective) are the basic cues in the direct sensory perception of depth. Of course, the laws of perspective geometry are not limited to distances up to 80 feet, but work for much greater distances. While the accommodation cue refers to the feedback from apparent tension in the lens muscle as it accommodates, the convergence cue (which is binocular) refers to the apparent tension in the muscles which pull the eye to converge as objects approach the perceiver.

The power of monocular cues in creating impressions of certain spatial arrangements as illustrated in the Ames demonstrations (Ames is a proponent of transactional theory) is presented in Figures 13-1 and 13-2. If brought to these

Figure 13-1   A monocular distorted room based on a 4-foot x 4-foot reference room. When viewed with one eye with the chin in the hollow place on the horizontal crossbar, the room is perceived as shown in Figure 13-2. *(After Kilpatrick, 1961, p. 165.)*

Figure 13-2 The large monocular distorted room. *(After Kilpatrick, 1961, p. 166.)*

rooms blindfolded, the subject immediately, upon opening *one* eye and playing his head in the correct position, sees rectangular rooms. If the subject starts to look with both eyes and then closes one eye, the room is first seen according to its distortion but gradually turns into a rectangular room after inspection periods up to 30 seconds or more. Presumably, memory and inference contribute to the adaptation. The reason the effect does not work with two eyes is because each retina receives a different image.

Chalmers (1952) studied the relative distances at which accommodation and convergence were effective. In this experiment perceived size, instead of judged distance, was the dependent variable. The subject was seated in a dark room, and a luminescent strip (the standard) was presented to him at distances between 10 and 120 feet. He had to equate the size of a comparison strip with that of the standard under four conditions: when the comparison was at 10 feet and at 120 feet, and under monocular and binocular observation. Under the monocular conditions size constancy held up to 25 feet, while under the binocular conditions it held up to 80 feet. Since other cues could have little effect in this experimental situation, it is concluded that accommodation has a limit of 25 feet and convergence, 80 feet, as effective cues.

Some very interesting work that links oculomotor cues to adaptation, which we discussed in the last section, has more recently been reported by Wallach and his co-workers. In most of this work the dependent variables are judged size and judged distance. The independent variables are accommodation and convergence, since in all cases the perception experiments are done in total darkness with the exception of the stimulus being illuminated. So, no other cues can play a role. Sometimes accommodation and convergence are also artificially interfered with. That size matching is a reliable way of demonstrating the effectiveness of accommodation and convergence had previously been established by Leibowitz and Moore (1966) and by Wallach and Floor (1971). Wallach and Frey (1972a) then went on to experiment with the relationship between these oculomotor cues and adaptation, by letting the subject wear lenses which artificially altered both the accommodation and convergence while, of course, leaving the objective distance the same.

Specifically, the lenses acted to make the accommodation and convergence distances look closer. The effective results of this experiment was that the subject therefore perceived the size to be smaller. Why is this the case? Obviously since the retinal size is the same and the distances tend to be closer because of accommodation, if we apply the size-distance invariance hypothesis, the perceived size will be smaller. In other work, Wallach, Frey, and Bode (1972) verified that oculomotor adaptation produced adaptive changes in perceived size and *larger* ones in perceived stereoscopic depth.

Finally, Wallach and Frey (1972b) were able to show similar kinds of processes operating without the use of apparatus, such as lenses which distort the normal operation of cues. The subjects observed in the dark for 20 minutes a luminous figure that objectively expanded as it moved toward the subjects and contracted as it moved away from them. This was the adaptation task. However, instead of testing for changes in size perception, the authors tested for a change in the relationship between accommodation and convergence on the one hand, and registered distance on the other. In one experiment, such a change was measured by obtaining estimates of perceived size and depth before and after the adaptation period. Highly significant changes of size and *significantly greater* changes of stereoscopic depth were obtained. The authors concluded that the change in stereoscopic depth that was larger than the size change could be ascribed to a change in the registered distance.

In a second experiment, they tested for change in distance by having the subject point from the side to a vertical line before, and again after, the adaptation period, under conditions where only accommodation and convergence could serve as distance cues. Significant changes in the pointing distance were measured, indicating more directly a change in the relationship between these oculomotor adjustments and perceived distance. It is indeed interesting that such phenomena exist. In the experiments of Wallach and Frey, the natural fluctuation of visual angle with distance was exaggerated by the expansion and contraction phenomena. These authors are concluding that, in order to correct for this, a counteradaptation process is taking place, which carries over to a posttest, such that there is an alteration in the perceived distance.

These observations have been verified by Wallach and Frey (1972a) and Wallach, Frey, and Bode (1972). Particularly instructive is the final experiment of Wallach and Frey (1972b). It showed that, under natural conditions rather than distorting lenses, adaptation can also result with respect to accommodation and convergence. Perhaps the finding is consistent with transactional theory. The subjects viewed a luminous object in the dark for 20 minutes while it expanded and contracted as it approached and receded from the subject, respectively. Estimates were made of both size and distance, with changes in accommodation and convergence, both before and after adaptation. It was found that, after adaptation there was an increase in size and an even larger increase in distance. The authors reason that this exaggeration of subjective distance is a result of counteradaptation—that is, correction for the artificial changes of the size of the object. This discussion of the effect of oculomotor cues on registered distance leads neatly into the discussion of binocular disparity, which also has a profound effect on depth perception.

Binocular Disparity   Binocular disparity is effective up to medium ranges of 800 to 1,900 feet. Since the time of Helmholtz a complicated conception called the *horopter* has been discussed in the literature. An understanding of this conception is important for a detailed mathematical analysis of certain aspects of depth perception, but for a psychological understanding of the general phenomena of depth and distance perception a definitive statement is sufficient. If an observer fixates a certain point in space, stimulation from certain other points produces clear corresponding images on the two retinas. These are called *corresponding retinal points* since stimulation from them does not produce double images. Theoretically, light proceeds from a point on the horopter to identical geometrical locations in the two retinas. If one retina could be slipped over the other to produce a "cyclopean" eye in the middle of the forehead, the two corresponding retinal points would be coincident (see Julesz, 1970). The horopter is a theoretical line which connects corresponding points. It can be induced geometrically that "the *theoretical* shape of the horopter is a circle which passes through the point of fixation and the centers of rotation of the two eyes" (Woodworth & Schlosberg, 1954, p. 461). Stimuli coming from points on either side of the horopter produce disparate images on the retinas, and it is this disparity between the two images, called *binocular disparity,* which is considered a cue to relative depth or distance.

Ogle has stressed that the horopter is theoretical and deviates from the Vieth-Müller circle defining the theoretical horopter described by Woodworth and Schlosberg. This deviation results from Panum's areas which define the areas where we get fusion of double images falling on noncorresponding points and from physiological nystagmus. Evidently the horopter is not just a line.

Furthermore, the asymmetry in function between the two retinas increases as visual distance decreases (Ogle, 1950, pp. 13–39). Presumably the tendency to fusion increases as distance increases, and hence the cue of disparity eventually breaks down. Fusion demands that disparity be suppressed, but when we

Figure 13-3 Basic random stereo pair. When the two fields are viewed stereoscopically, the center square appears in front of the background. *(After Julesz, 1964, p. 357.)*

measure stereoscopic acuity, we have a situation in which binocular vision with stereopsis demands fusion of disparate patterns from the retinas while information about their disparity is maintained.

Extensive, more contemporary reviews of the horopter are provided in rather technical articles by Shipley and Rawlings (1970a, 1970b). An important point they make is that the innate cerebral coordinate system need not be evoked by actual horizontal retinal disparities; it is there in the cortex to begin with and need only be locked in (1970a, p. 1237).

Binocular depth perception can be considered a "pattern-matching" process in which the noncorrespondence in the retinal patterns of the eyes is the source of the depth effect. Julesz (1964) has used computer-generated random-dot stereo images to produce stimuli that are completely devoid of any monocular depth cues or convergence. Presenting these stimulus pairs for 1 msec raises the experimental question: Will depth still be experienced by the viewer when the only information available to use is spatial disparity in the *two stereo patterns?* Figure 13-3 presents a pair of random stereo images used by Julesz in his research. The basic pattern, e.g., the one on the right for right-eye viewing through a stereoscope, actually is formed by filling in the cells of a 100-by-100 matrix (10,000) with a random assortment of a number of brightness levels. The retinal disparity is produced by shifting a portion of the basic pattern by a number of pattern elements. In the figure, a central square area is shifted by six picture elements for the left-eye view, and, virtually instantaneously, when viewed through a stereoscope, a square in front of its background can be seen. This research leaves little doubt that binocular disparity is a very effective and self-sufficient cue to depth.

In addition to showing that accommodation, convergence, and binocular disparity are subject to adaptation and experiental effects, we have also tried to reason that two binocular cues are effective over a wide range of distances. In fact, evidence from Gogel and Sturm (1972) suggests that convergence is a stronger cue than accommodation in a more general context. Subjects were dark-adapted for 5 minutes, then presented with a *small* and a *large* luminous frame in a counterbalanced design with respect to size. Presentations were made monocularly and binocularly, with these also counterbalanced with respect to presentations. When looking at wheels, subjects experienced a change in perceived distance in the second presentation. It was found that this was so only in the monocular condition—that is, for the monocular condition, the larger frame appeared nearer and the smaller frame appeared smaller (when they were presented the second time). Under binocular viewing the perceived distance was not significantly different. Instead, the frames seemed to be their objective size, large or small. Under these conditions, the cues were, in descending order by strength, convergence, relative size, and accommodation.

Subjective Space   The above demonstrations of the transactionalists provide a good lead to considering more of the subjective aspects of space and distance.

Luneberg (1948, pp. 215–240) deduces that the relation of sensory (psychological) distance to the physical distance is hyperbolic, i.e., curved and negatively accelerated. There is no infinity in sensory distance. These curves, which are called *Luneberg's circles,* differ for different observers and at different ages for the same observer. There are two subjective constants. One is related to the interpupillary distance of the eyes and determines sensitivity of depth perception which is greater than sensitivity of size perception. The other constant relates sensory judgment of size to actual physical size.

Luneberg's attempt to relate physical and subjective space, which has qualitative support in the evidence discussed although it awaits quantitative verification, brings to mind Gilinsky's attempt to relate physical distance to psychological distance, which we discussed in Chapter 8. She also stated that the function relating the two was negatively accelerated and approached an asymptote at rather short distances. Her conclusion had been challenged by Gruber (1956) in connection with his work which we also discussed in Chapter 8.

Gruber's data indicate that perceived distance d does not approach a maximum asymptotic function as physical distance increases since he failed to produce the negative constant error which would be expected if $d/D < 1$ for all values of D. Thus, while these attempts to develop mathematical relationships for distance perception are admirable, specification of the nature of the function awaits more empirical data.

More definitive evidence on attitudinal influence relates to the well-known concern between size-distance relationships. One study that again points out the complexity of the size-distance invariance relationship was performed by Landauer and Epstein (1969); it was also mentioned in Chapter 8. All subjects in this study were brought blindfolded into a dark room where they were allowed to be dark-adapted before the experiment was begun. They were then shown a dimly illuminated disk and were asked to judge both the size and the distance of the disk. These judgments were made in terms of well-known objects which were then translated into millimeters for size and centimeters for distance. Half of the subjects gave size judgments first and distance judgments second, while the other half gave them in the reverse order. Four different groups of subjects were used for different visual angles (different distances) of 8°, 4°, 2°, and 1°, respectively, for the size of the same disk. The results of the experiment revealed that judged size tended to vary directly with visual angle, whereas judged distance tended to vary inversely with visual angle. Since clearly the subject was able to translate visual angle into distance, one would have thought that he would see the stimulus as the same-sized object getting further away from him or at other times coming closer to him. Indeed, it is curious that he saw it both as getting smaller and getting further away (and vice versa), which is a clear violation of the size-distance variance hypothesis. It would seem, therefore, that the subject was making independent judgments of size and distance. On the one hand he was using visual angle to judge distance, and on the other hand he was using visual angle to give a "retinal size" match, similar to what was found in one of Gilinsky's experiments discussed in Chapter 8.

Other variables influencing the judgment of distance are *familiarity* and past experience. These variables were investigated by Ono (1969). In two different conditions, photographs of a golf ball and a baseball were placed on pieces of cardboard in front of the subject. In one condiiton, both pictures had the diameter of an actual golf ball, whereas in the other condition, the pictures had the actual diameter of a baseball. The subject was asked to indicate, by pressing buttons, which of the two balls, the left or the right one, was closer to him. Examination of the results indicated that the golf ball appeared closer for a greater proportion of the time than the baseball. In other words, since the visual angle is always the same, the subject compensated for this conflict by saying the golf ball was closer, since he knew from past experience that a golf ball is smaller than a baseball.

Other evidence showing that the size-distance relationship is indeed dependent on the assumed attitude of the subject is provided by an interesting study conducted by Coltheart (1970), who created the set experimentally. In this experiment, the subjects viewed a black triangle of light under completely reduced conditions. One set of instructions told the subjects that the triangle was 4 inches, whereas another set of instructions said that it was 8 inches. They were then asked to estimate the distance of the triangles in feet; amazingly, the mean for the first set of instructions was 7.70, while for the second set of instructions it was 13.72. In other words, given the same visual angle, subjects judged that if a triangle twice as large projected the same visual angle, it had to be twice as far away.

Secondary Cues: Gradients

The cues which are traditionally called *secondary* are effective at distances up to and beyond 600 yards. The upper limit at which these cues are useful has not been established, but studies have used distances exceeding 1,000 yards and, in some cases, as high as 10,000 feet. More work needs to be done on these cues to determine thresholds and the distances at which gradients approach their effective limits.

1   Upward Angular Location of Grounded Objects   As the angle of displacement of grounded objects measured from the horizontal line of sight appears to decrease, the objects appear farther away from the observer. Objects which appear to be vertically closer to the horizon are also farther away, given level ground, and this fact (i.e., differences in the upward angular location) can be used as a cue to distance. Artists employ this cue very effectively. When they want to create the impression that something is farther away, they locate it higher on the canvas in the picture.

This cue is probably the most reasonable explanation of the moon illusion—the well-known observation that the moon looks bigger the closer it is to the horizon and smaller the closer it is to the zenith of the sky (see Kaufman & Rock, 1962). Relative to this point, Galanter and Galanter (1973) did a series of very illuminating experiments. They measured estimates of range magnitude, up to distances of almost 10,000 feet, as a function of angle of regard. In keeping with previous findings (Künnapas, 1960; Teghtsoonian & Teghtsoonian, 1969, 1970), they found a nonlinear but power function relating perceived distance to actual distance, such that perceived distance equals actual distance, n. Their most revealing discovery was that the exponent, n, varied with angle of regard, such that

$n = 1.25$ for targets near the ground
$n = 0.80$ for targets (aircraft) in zenith
$n = 1.00$ for targets midway between

So we have here a mathematical verification that objects close to the horizon are seen as farther away (by a power of 1.25).

2   Perceived Size of Familiar Objects   We have stated many times in this chapter and in Chapter 8 that the relative retinal-image sizes (visual angle) of familiar objects can be used as a cue to distance. The object appears to be getting farther away the smaller its retinal image. As we discuss in Chapter 8 and in the last section of this chapter, this cue has to compete with the other cues to distance.

3   Texture and Density Gradients   If we look across a landscape (a patch of grass, a field of daisies, shrubs, or trees), we observe that the texture of the ground becomes finer (denser) as distance increases. Consequently objects located on a ground with finer texture appear to be farther away than objects located on coarser ground of the same type of texture. J. J. Gibson (1950, 1966) has stressed the importance of this gradient underlying the perception of relative distance, but the precision of this cue has not been established. Dusek, Teichner, and Kobrick (1955), for example, found that the variability of relative-distance discrimination is not significantly different for terrain of pavement, sand, or snow. They used distances up to 500 yards. However, Clark,

Smith, and Rabe (1956) found that under monocular conditions outline gradients and texture gradients in a form lead to more accurate judgments of slant of the form than when the form is homogeneous.

Gradient Theory of Space Perception

As Gibson has stated, "The word *gradient* means nothing more complex than an increase or decrease of something along a given axis or dimension" (1950). An example is given: The gradient of a highway is its change in altitude with distance. The gradient may be zero, when the road is level or when it increases or decreases at a constant rate; positive, when the inclination increases with distance; or negative, when it decreases with distance. Furthermore, the change (gradient) may be moderate or rapid, or it may change along the way, as is true when the road passes over a hilly terrain. If the change is very abrupt, as it is when an inclination terminates at a cliff or an edge, it is called a *step*.

The concept of gradient thus defined is used by Gibson to develop a theory of space perception. In essence, the kinds of gradients he specifies are based on the two rules of perspective previously discussed. The first rule, the law of visual angle, states that frontal dimension is projected as a size S which is inversely proportional to distance D; algebraically this means that S is proportional to $1/D$. The second rule states that the longitudinal dimension is projected as an altitude A which is inversely proportional to the square of the distance. The algebraic equivalent of this rule states that A is proportional to $1/D^2$. Thus it is the longitudinal dimension which is compressed relative to the frontal dimension. Gibson has applied these perspective techniques to the *texture of a surface* instead of to the edges of a surface, as is usual. By so doing he has demonstrated that these perspective techniques can be used to construct such patterns as texture gradients and density gradients, which often underlie our perception of depth and distance.

This is another example of his psychophysical theory—his notion that the information for a pattern is located in the invariant relationship among changes, in this case the invariant in the size of gradient. Examples of different gradients, and steps of stimulation and the corresponding impressions of receding, continuous, or abrupt changes in surface they give, are presented in Figure 13-4.

Gibson (1960a) emphasizes his belief that every phenomenal aspect of the visual world is represented by a corresponding aspect in the physical energy which influences the receptors. Instead of discussing inference, we should be looking for the determination of ability to discriminate these higher-order patterns of stimulation.

In a manner similar to that of Attneave and Frost (1969), discussed in Chapter 8, Vickers (1971) discusses an alternative interpretation to the creation of depth effect, using the principle of *Prägnanz*—i.e., perceptual economy of information processing. In fact, what Vickers is suggesting is that the gradient explanation can probably be subsumed under the perceptual economy hypothesis—that is, gradients would be a special application of the more major variable,

Figure 13-4 Texture and density gradients and steps of stimulation giving impressions of receding, continuous, or abrupt changes in surface and distance.

perceptual economy. By use of the patterns presented in Figure 13-5 and the various ways of measuring relative depth, it was found that the later figures always produced more depth—that is, 4 had more depth than 3, 2, and 1.

The experiment of Vickers showed that the greater the number of variables and the greater the difference within a variable, the greater the depth effect. A third experiment showed that judged slants increased as a function of the number of gradient invariables in each pattern.

Vickers reasons that his experiments show that the subject attempts to balance economy with adaptiveness—that is, the subject perceives the variables in the patterns as invariant, but adjusts the slope at which the hypothetical plane containing them must lie according to the amount of conforming evidence. He reasons further that it might be worthwhile to consider the possibility that the perceptual system does not "simply tend to reduce redundancy in the decoding of visual data to a minimum, but seeks to balance the advantage gained by this against the possible cost of making an error, or introducing some distortion into the data by more efficient recoding" (Vickers, 1971, p. 27). Thus, moderate reduction in redundancy might warrant a moderate distance or slant estimate whereas the high reduction might justify a bolder or increased estimate. While further work is needed, Vickers believes that his theory may be an advance over Gibson's theory. First, he reasons, it provides a broader base, and, second, it can account for incorrect as well as correct perception. Gradients are there because the perceptions of invariance would be an economy necessitated by the enor-

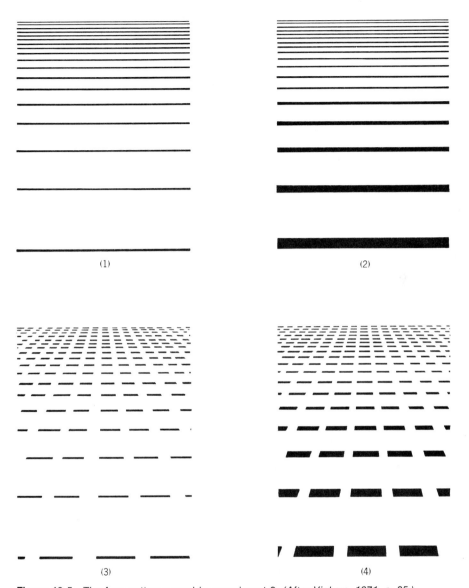

Figure 13-5   The four patterns used in experiment 2. *(After Vickers, 1971, p. 25.)*

mous information potential of the visual array and the limited cognitive capacity or channel capacity of the infant.

While Gibson has probably had the greatest impact of modern theorists in the study of space perception, we would not give a representative position if we did not point out that his position has been seriously challenged. We have already referred to the alternative perspective of Attneave and Vickers. Here follow other alternative interpretations. Ericksson (1973) had pointed out that a surface with a coarser texture located farther away from the subject could present a texture gradient of the same magnitude as a surface with a finer texture located closer to the subject. (Of course, Gibson usually considers the *continuous* surface.) Nevertheless, in the stationary subject, with monocular viewing, texture-gradient cues can be ambiguous. Similar reasoning, with experimental data to back it up, has been provided by Newman (1972) about gradients of binocular disparity and by Gyr (1972) about optical transformation accompanying movement. The last-mentioned reviewer utilizes most of von Holst's work and theorizing about reafference, which we have already discussed on other occasions.

The net effect of these other perspectives is the suggestion that we must supplement information about relations and transformations in the optic array with information coming from one's own movement and from memory. Gibson's emphasis on optical relationships is perhaps one of *strategy,* and it certainly has paid off in data genesis. Since his view also concerns the ecology of stimulus patterns, one would not think that he would argue, on principle, against the inclusion of other sources of information, like bodily movement information, in the ecological matrix.

Other Secondary Cues

1 Superposition (Interposition)   This term means that a near object may partially obscure far objects. Such an interruption of the surface of one object by the boundaries of the nearer object is a cue to relative distance of the two objects. All of us have observed this interruption when looking at a distant mountain range. Data from two experiments of Chapanis and McCleary (1953) suggest that these cues cannot come from the relative continuity of the contour alone but also from the *relative sizes* of the elements in the pattern.

2 Aerial Perspective   As we look at objects in the distance, we frequently notice that the more-distant objects appear to be bluer or more violet in color. Thus the green vegetation on a mountain nearer the horizon looks more bluish than the vegetation of a mountain closer to us. This observation of the change in color, which has not been measured, is a probable cue, called aerial perspective, and depends on the amount of haze in the atmosphere and the level of illumination.

3 Filled and Empty Space   It has been noted that a distance which is filled with objects looks farther away than one which is relatively empty.

4 Light and Shade   It has been shown that the appearance of spatial depth of an object is lost when it completely lacks shadow. Thus, light and shade patterns provide cues not to distance but to the depth or relief of a single solid object. An illustration of the use of lighting in producing a greater depth effect is shown in Figure 13-6a and *b.*

(a)

(b)

Figure 13-6 The effect of lighting contrast on the impression of depth. Notice that low contrast reduces depth significantly.

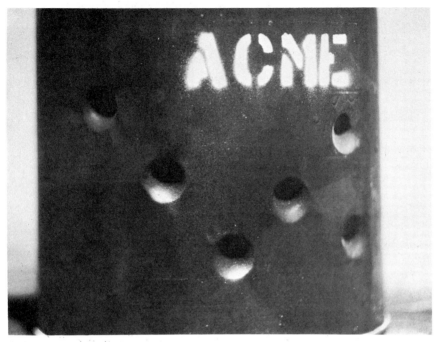

Figure 13-7 Light-shade effects on depth. Turn the illustration upside down and notice the reversal of depth effect.

Another example which not only illustrates the light-shade effect on depth but also shows that the depth effect is reversed when the image is inverted is presented in Figure 13-7. In order to get the reversal of depth relationship, turn the page upside down (Evans, 1948).

5 Relative Brightness If two equidistant bright surfaces are presented (one to each eye) and a dark filter is interposed between one eye and its corresponding surface, the latter surface appears to be farther away. It is sometimes mistakenly believed that the more distant an object, the lower the intensity of its retinal image. Gibson has reminded us that relative brightness is only a cue of distance of point sources of light; it does not apply to reflection surfaces.

6 Linear Perspective This cue is similar to the cue of relative sizes but applies to longitudinal rather than frontal dimensions. The law of linear perspective states that the retinal size of a longitudinal dimension is inversely proportional to the square of the distance from the observer. We have all witnessed the operation of this cue when looking at a straight highway or railroad and noticing the sides or rails converge in the distance.

7 Motion Parallax   This cue is defined as the relative apparent motion of objects as an individual moves his head or opens and shuts each eye in succession. Generally the nearer object appears to move faster than the more distant one.

Interaction and Utilization of Cues

All these cues interact. Sometimes they compete. Often, however, when many of these cues are operating simultaneously, they facilitate greater accuracy of depth discrimination since they transmit a certain amount of redundant information (signs) about depth. When we look at a spatial scene with both eyes and through an unobstructed visual field, depth perception is usually more accurate. If we look at a distant range of mountains, we can detect at least five cues—interposition, aerial perspective, linear perspective, relative size, and upward angular location—working together. We can gradually reduce the accuracy of depth perception by systematically reducing the cues until we reach the condition of monocular perception in the dark, in which depth perception is almost nonexistent. A good indication of how, for example, the light-contrast cue can strengthen the texture cue is illustrated in Figures 13-8 and 13-9.

In Figure 13-10 we see how the cue of linear perspective, which gives the impression of receding distance and thus makes the higher man of the two look bigger, can be in conflict with the cue of upward location. When this picture is turned upside down, the illusion is decreased; i.e., the man no longer looks that much bigger since he is now lower on the page.

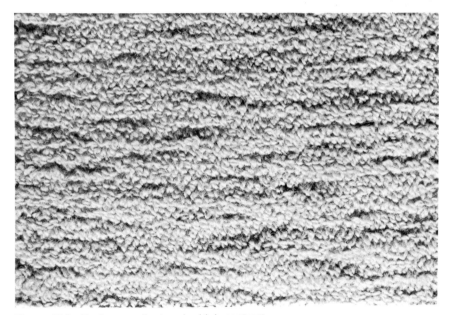

Figure 13-8   Texture gradient under high contrast.

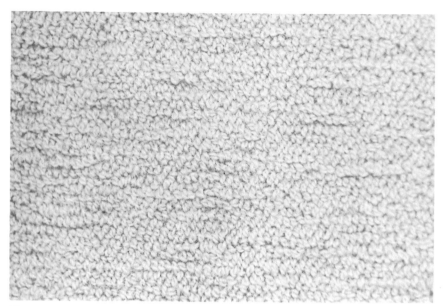

Figure 13-9 The same surface as in Figure 13-8 under low contrast. Notice the diminishing of texture gradient.

Depth in Reproductions An interesting description of the pattern of cues which make a considerable amount of depth perceivable in a picture was provided by Schlosberg (1941). He was referring to the "plastic" depth that can be obtained monocularly and is most striking when the viewing lens has the same focal length as the camera lens with which the picture was taken.

The perception of depth cues determines whether we see a picture as *representing* depth or as actual objects deployed in depth. Depth cues may include shading, clearness of outline, perspective, and superposition. Depth is immediately a way of perceiving, not merely the addition of something to a picture in varying amounts.

Cues for "flatness" include identity of binocular fields, surface glare, the absence of monocular parallax changes when the picture is moved, cues from accommodation, and others. The flatness cues, which cause normal binocular inspection of a picture to force the observer to see a flat picture, may be eliminated (thus permitting the plastic effect) by looking at the picture from a distance, by monocular viewing (looking through a tube or a lens, or looking at the picture monocularly in a mirror), partial binocular vision (blurring the image in one eye during binocular vision or using prisms to displace or rotate the image in one eye), full binocular vision through a large lens, and the use of the iconoscope. The plastic effect has, according to Schlosberg, an "all-or-none" character: the effect is usually either clearly present or absent.

In a similar analysis, Evans (1948, pp. 141–142) shows that for good depth effects the visual angle or magnification should be high, the contrast high, the

Figure 13-10 Interaction between linear perspective and upward angular location. If we turn the page upside down, we notice that the illusion of size is diminished.

image sharp rather than diffuse, the tone continuous rather than grainy, and the surface glossy rather than matted. Furthermore, he points out how important viewing distance is as a determiner of good depth impression from a photograph. He states that the correct viewing distance for a print is the focal length of the lens multiplied by the number of times the print will be magnified. For example, if the focal length is 2 inches and the print will be magnified four times, then the correct viewing distance is 8 inches. A comparison of the two photographs in Figure 13-11 shows how a reduction of the viewing distance drastically diminishes the depth effect.

Discrimination of Space and Experience From the evidence examined in this chapter we may reasonably conclude that there exists an innate potential to

(a)

(b)

Figure 13-11 *(a)* Wide viewing distance. *(b)* Same scene as in *a*, but with a narrower viewing distance. Notice the reduction in impression of distance.

respond to the various relationships which lead to our perception of space. Which of these factors becomes more functional to an individual as he develops probably depends to a large extent on experience and learning. Moreover, it has been shown that the accuracy of space perception can be greatly improved by training, even in adults. Thus, Horowitz and Kappauf (1946) reported that a constant range error of 30 to 40 percent was reduced to 20 percent by training in serial range estimation. Other reports show that a probable error of 30 percent was reduced to 17 percent and that constant errors as well as variability of range estimation were reduced through training. Also, Eleanor J. Gibson (1953) has concluded that the most effective and general method of improving absolute judgment of distance is through a technique she calls *scale training*. In this experiment the subjects had to learn to discriminate distances on a 300-yard grassy field. One reference point was located near the subject; the other was a hedge at the end of the field. Using the technique of fractionation, the experimenter required the subject to divide the 300 yards into successive halves, i.e., 150 yards, 75 yards, and so on. After repeated trials, the subject's accuracy improved to such an extent that it even showed transfer of improved distance judgments to completely different grassy fields. It would seem that the subjects' difference threshold to the texture gradient had probably been lowered through training.

A thorough investigation of the development of depth perception was undertaken by Eleanor J. Gibson and her associates (Gibson, Tighe, & Walk, 1957; Gibson & Walk, 1960). They constructed an apparatus called a *visual cliff,* which is depicted together with an explanation in the photographs in Figure 13-12. A number of species, including chicks, turtles, rats, lambs, kids, pigs, kittens, dogs, and human infants, were tested on this apparatus. Depth discrimination seemed to be present in all these animals, and the kinds of emergent behavioral patterns were characteristic of the way the particular species had adapted to its environment. Thus, chicks less than 24 hours old always hopped off the board on the "shallow" side. Kids and lambs 1 day of age never stepped into the glass on the "deep" side.

To eliminate the effect of spurious variables, kids and goats were tested at the Cornell Behavior Farm in a modified experiment. The pattern was attached to plywood which could be moved from a distance just under the glass to distances farther beneath the glass. When the pattern was just beneath the glass, the animal would move around freely, but when the optical floor was more than 1 foot below the glass, the visual cliff was apparently too great: the animal would immediately freeze into a crouching, defensive position. "Despite repeated experience of the tactual solidity of the glass, the animals never learned to function without optical support. Their sense of security or danger continued to depend upon the visual cues that give them their perception of depth" (Gibson & Walk, p. 4).

Human beings are, of course, highly dependent on vision. In one experiment Gibson and Walk tested thirty-six infants, ranging in age from 6 to 14 months, on

(a)

(b)

Figure 13-12   The visual cliff. Note the baby crawling toward the mother on the shallow side and staying away from the mother on the deep side. *(After Gibson and Walk, 1960. Reprinted with permission. Copyright 1960, 1961 by Scientific American, Inc. All rights reserved. Photograph courtesy of William Vandivert.)*

the visual cliff. Of the twenty-seven infants who moved off the board, all crawled out on the shallow side at least once. Only three moved off the edge of the board to the glass on the deep side.

The data presented thus far do not tell us whether certain kinds of experience with light stimulation are necessary before these abilities to discriminate depth emerge. Therefore Gibson and Walk performed an experiment to test the variable of experience. One group of rats was reared in darkness, and another under normal conditions. When tested on the visual cliff at 90 days of age, the animals from both groups chose the shallow side. Then the experimenters manipulated two cues to depth perception. When the density gradient cue was iliminated, the dark-reared animals still preferred the shallow side, but when the motion parallax cue was eliminated, allowing only the pattern density to operate as a cue, no preference was elicited. Evidently motion parallax as a cue is innate, but pattern density is not. (See also T. Bower in Chapter 8.)

We need more information about the course of development of these other experientially affected cues. We do know that Benson and Yonas found cues of shading and linear perspective in the 3-year-old but found that the position cue could not operate by itself. Chapter 12 has extensive discussions on perceptual development.

SUMMARY

In this chapter we saw how the perception of space is determined by the information carried in relational stimulation. Thus the perception of two dimensions and bodily orientation are affected by both external (e.g., visual) and internal (proprioceptive) referents.

The fascinating interaction between visual and bodily stimulation is indicated by such studies as sensoritonic investigations. These and other experiments also reveal the amazing adaptability of human beings to space orientation when the formal frameworks are distorted. An informational analysis seems to be the most general way of formulating these effects.

In the case of three-dimensional space, we saw how a variety of cues produce a "field" effect which makes the perception of depth inevitable and not, for example, merely something added to a picture. These cues or their combinational effect must be destroyed or reduced for the impression of depth to be reduced or confused. We considered a psychophysical-gradient, learning and combinational theory of space perception.

For adaptive behavior to take place, there must be an innate reaction to some aspect in the energy flux carried to the receptor. With learning, experience, or training, however, the organism's sensitivity to a greater variety of these cues and to their interacting effects improves greatly. In rats, for example, the cue of motion parallax is innate, whereas density gradient does not become a cue until experience has taught the organism the "significance" of this variable. Training also leads to increased specificity or differentiation within a particular cue, or to striking a balance between redundancy and information discrimination.

Chapter 14

The Perception of Movement
and Events

In Chapter 9 we learned that spatial segregations in groupings are based on brightness gradients and configurational principles. Moreover, as Beck demonstrated, these configurational principles are probably based on orientation aspects. We shall see in this chapter that configurational principles and spatiotemporal relationships are the determiners of the visual perception of motion as well. We shall analyze both real and apparent motion, and also configurational events. We shall begin with a transitional case between depth and movement perception—that is, one of the Ames demonstrations which we referred to in Chapter 13.

PERSPECTIVE REVERSAL AND ROTARY MOTION

The Ames demonstration of the trapezoidal window provides a good opportunity to analyze the role of perspective reversal in the perception of movement. The demonstration is diagramed in Figure 14-1. In this demonstration, a trapezoid, cut from flat cardboard, shaped and painted to resemble a window frame, is mounted on a rod. The subject stands about 20 feet from this trapezoid while it rotates through a complete 360° arc. Instead of seeing a rotating trapezoid, the

306

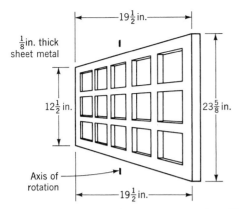

Figure 14-1 The Ames trapezoidal window. This is a view of the trapezoid perpendicular to the line of sight. Both sides are painted alike, the frame white, the shadows gray, the panes cut out. When rotated, the frame appears to oscillate. *(After Ames, 1951.)*

subject sees a window sash which oscillates through an arc of 90° to 100°. It is important to note that the sash will even seem to be slanted when in the frontal-parallel plane, and that it will swing from this line to the opposite as it rotates. Since the long end always appears nearer, *the subject will see a rectangle which appears to be oscillating.* Thus, not only is the shape distorted, but during half of the oscillation the apparent motion is opposite to the actual physical motion. Even more striking is the fact that, if a single object such as a ball, a tube, or a card is attached to the window, this object will appear to make a complete arc, traveling through the window as the latter oscillates. If the trapezoid is replaced by a right angle, the true complete arc motion will be seen.

Although Ames interprets the illusion as caused by past experience, others have questioned this. For example, Pastore (1952) and Canestrari and Farne (1969) report observing the illusion even when the trapezoid is not a simulated window. A very useful analysis of this phenomenon is presented by Hochberg (1972). The following is a discussion of the questions he raises.

Parallel versus Polar Projections Figure 14-2 contains diagrams illustrating polar and parallel projections. Images coming from polar projections tend to be stable, whereas images coming from parallel projections are not stable, and frequently give rise to perspective reversals. When the trapezoid demonstration is viewed from a relatively large distance, the image on the retina represents parallel projection. Consequently, it will be ambiguous, and there will be perspective reversal. In this case, one tends to see oscillation rather than rotation. Braunstein and Payne (1968) have also shown that with parallel projections right angles as well as trapezoid forms appear to reverse directions, whereas with polar projection both shapes seem to rotate completely and

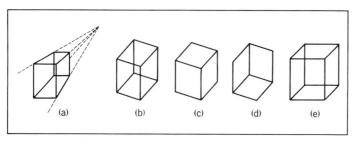

Figure 14-2 The same object in different perspectives. *(a)* Polar projection: *(b–e)* Parallel projection; *b–d* are in isometric perspective. *(After Hochberg, 1972, p. 499.)*

continuously. Moreover, Zegers (1965), in confirming results, demonstrated that the reversal rate will increase as the viewing distance increases. In such a case the retinal size of the trapezoid decreases, and hence the image changes from polar to parallel projection.

Cross (1969) has advanced the thesis that the illusion consists essentially of a nonveridical perception of depth. He reasons that circular motion in a plane parallel to the line of sight must be mediated by depth cues, and that in such illusions as the Ames trapezoid demonstration there is a confounding of cues to depth perception. Thus, the long edge is seen as nearer both when it truly is and when the short side is nearer during half of each rotation. Then the relative distance of parts of the object is perceived incorrectly.

To demonstrate his view that it is linear perspective and not the shape that makes the difference, Cross performed an interesting little experiment. He rotated two pairs of lines through a common point. However, these lines were not connected to form a shape. What varied was the ratio of the lengths of the lines. The stimulus line pairs provided length ratios of 3:3, 3:2, 3:1, and 3:0. The results indicated that as we go from lines of equal length to ratios of 3:2 and 3:1, the number of reversals increases from between 100 and 200 to 400. The number drops slightly only when we go to a 3:0 ratio. The conclusion is self-evident: As linear perspective is exaggerated, making the smaller line seem farther away, the larger line will more likely be seen to remain in front, increasing the tendency to produce the illusion of oscillation.

To show further the effect of depth cues on the production of the oscillation illusion, Cross and Cross (1969) presented various figures, one at a time, in rotation to their subject. They reasoned that (1) shadowed and/or perspectived objects (e.g., trapezoids) would be more multidirective than comparable plane figures because the former incorporate confounding depth cues; (2) shadowed and perspectived objects would give rise to more multidirective illusions than comparable figures incorporating either shadow or perspective alone; (3) circular objects would be more productive of illusion than rectilinear objects. These predictions were based on the fact that circular objects provide less cues to depth information to counter a confounding cue than do rectilinear objects of compara-

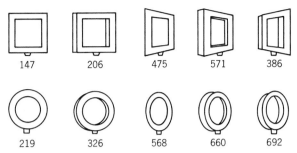

Figure 14-3 The stimulus objects were patterned identically on both sides and rotated on a vertical shaft with the axis of rotation bisecting the figures. From left to right the objects incorporate: no confounding cues, shadow interposition, linear perspective, shadow interposition and perspective, and antagonistic confounding cues. The total number of illusory reveals or rotary motion reported out of a possible 1,000 is shown for each object. *(After Cross, 1969, p. 95.)*

ble dimensions. The figures that they used as well as the number of reversals given by ten subjects are presented in Figure 14-3. It is evident that all their predictions were verified. For example, shadowed rectangles gave more reversals than plane figures, trapezoids gave more than right angles, shadowed trapezoids were even higher, with shadowed circles giving the greatest number of reversals.

Finally Canestrari and Farne (1969) found that the depth cues of interposition and texture density, which intensify the depth effect, just as linear perspective in the Cross demonstration, will increase the probability that continuous rotation will be perceived as oscillation. It appears that the visual system fits erroneous assumptions about the object's three-dimensional orientation to the changing stimulus patterns that arise as the object rotates. It is quite clear now that this reversal in motion is related to the exaggeration of depth cues. The precise nature of the specific transformation requires further research, but *that oscillation is coupled with depth perspective is quite certain.*

The discussion of real and illusory motion leads us to a consideration of real and apparent motion.

REAL AND APPARENT MOTION

In an insightful analysis, followed by some compelling experiments, Kolers (1964) advances some penetrating arguments in favor of separating the dynamics of real movement from those of apparent movement. He used the technique of visual masking described in Chapter 10. As a target he used a small luminous line flashed in the path of a larger moving line. He found that *when the moving line is closest to the target and when it is brighter, it will have the effect of increasing the threshold of the target,* i.e., increasing the amount of light required for the target to be seen.

Kolers then investigated whether the phi phenomena would mask a probe presented between the two exposed stimuli. The first and most important result is that a generalized inhibitory effect occurs; that is, the probability of perceiving the probe for all conditions of interstimulus interval was always less than 0.9 which, incidentally, is its minimum value in the absence of A and B. Thus, when time intervals of 5, 25, 50, 75, and 95 msec were used between successive exposures of A and B, the probability of seeing the probe was generally around 0.6. Second, the highest probability occurs at a time, 25 msec, which does not correspond to the least effect obtained with real movement.

A third finding is that the probability that the probe would be seen is almost independent of the time between the probe and the stimulus that precedes it, but *varies markedly with the time between the probe and stimulus that follows it*— that is, a strong inhibitory effect is exerted upon the probe by the line following it temporally, rather than by the line preceding it.

Kolers concluded that the masking effect is due principally to the effects of the alternated termini of the apparent movement upon the probe. *This is quite different from real movement where there is an interaction.* An important fact for Kolers seems to be the inference that the *apparent movement* is perceived as the direct result of a given order and timing of stimulation, and that it is coded at some level of the visual system at which no interaction occurs between nervous events reporting movement and those reporting other elements in the visual field.

Organization of the Perception of Real Movement

Movement is perceived under the following conditions:

1 When the image of an object moves across the retina.
2 When the image of an object remains stationary on the retina and the eye pursues the object.
3 Under certain conditions to be described below, when both the eye and its retinal image are stationary.

A central problem in the understanding of perceived motion is the threshold for detecting movement across space. There are actually two kinds of thresholds: (1) *velocity threshold,* which is the minimum velocity of the amount of space traversed in a time that can be detected, and (2) *displacement threshold,* which is the minimum distance over which movement can be detected. A number of interesting findings have been reported concerning threshold phenomena, and to these we now turn.

THRESHOLDS OF VELOCITY AND DISPLACEMENT AND VELOCITY CONSTANCY

In the data reported below, the abbreviation min/sec refers to the minutes of visual angle of displacement divided by seconds of time. A higher ratio means that greater velocity is required for movement to be detected. Conversely, a lower ratio means that the subject is seeing motion at a slower speed.

The first set of findings concerns the difference between threshold for absolute and relative movement. The threshold for a single moving target is much higher than when there is a framework against which a particular target's movement is judged. For example, investigators have reported that while the threshold, when only the moving stimulus is presented, is 10 to 20 min/sec, the threshold is only between 1 and 2 min/sec when a moving target is fixated against a stationary visual field (Aubert, 1886; Bourdon, 1902; Grim, 1911). Moreover, Aubert also found that the threshold is lower in foveal vision than in peripheral vision.

Increasing the informational energy also seems to lower the threshold. Thus, R. H. Brown (1955) reported that increasing the luminance and the duration of the target's exposure decreases its velocity threshold, and Leibowitz (1955a) also reported that increased luminance produces decreased velocity thresholds.

These findings regarding different velocity thresholds—that is, that the velocity thresholds for perceiving a single moving object is about 10 times as great as it is for viewing against a reference stimulus—might be related to the difference between detecting a stimulus (level I of the hierarchy) and detecting a figure emerging from a background (level II). Other investigators have also theorized that there are probably different processes involved in the perception of absolute and relative movement. Leibowitz (1955b) suggests that it is only with longer exposures (60 msec) that velocity thresholds are improved by the stationary framework, and Gregory (1964) presents supporting data. However, Shaffer and Wallach (1966) show that, with a framework that closely surrounded the target, displacement thresholds, even at short exposure durations, are lower with the framework than without it. The important thing to note is that anything which can articulate the background is likely to improve the ability to detect a movement and, therefore, has the effect of lowering the velocity threshold.

Additional evidence that perception of absolute movement (movement in an otherwise homogeneous field) is different from perception of relative movement (movement when there is some framework) was provided by Kinchla (1971), who showed that the perception of light in an otherwise dark room is more accurate when there is another reference light in its proximity, provided the reference light is within approximately 15° of the target light.

There have also been a number of interesting studies concerning what might be called *velocity constancy*. In one study, J. J. Gibson (1954) reports that when a patterned surface on a moving belt is presented, the speed and direction of the linear motion are perceived with some degree of accuracy. The same observation holds in the perception of the locomotion of the surface of a disk. Moreover, the perceived velocity of the moving surface tends to remain constant, even at different distances from the eye, despite the fact that the retinal velocity of its image varies inversely with the distance from the eye. A fact to remember, however, is that the retinal image of the distance through which the surface is moving also varies inversely with the distance from the eye. In other words, the *ratio between the retinal image of the distance and the angular velocity of the retinal image remains constant*. The resulting constant velocity, then, is in agreement with our hypothesis that motion perception is relational.

In a similar finding, Brown (1931c) presented a repetitive pattern of moving targets behind windows of variable size. Targets could, for example, be a band of black squares on a white background. He found that if the field of movement is increased in length, the stimulus velocity must also be increased proportionally, if the perceived motion of the two fields are to be judged as equal. Again, we can see that this *transposition effect,* which gives rise to velocity constancy, might exist in normal viewing conditions, since again the *ratio* of retinal displacement would remain constant, regardless of the distance of the target from the observer. Other experiments which confirm and verify the existence of speed constancy are discussed and analyzed by Wallach (1959).

A very informative study, which tested and analyzed the nature of speed constancy and which also related to its size constancy, was published by Rock, Hill, and Fineman (1968). These psychologists developed the following points. First, if perceived speed were solely a function of speed of retinal-image displacement, the farther away the object, the slower it would move. We know now that this is not so. Second, if perceived velocity were a function of phenomenal displacement, speed constancy would be derivable from size constancy. For example, an object moving at the speed of 1 ft/sec would be perceived at proper velocity, provided the subject perceived the 1 foot as 1 foot even when the visual angle became smaller as distance increased. This deduction is compounded, however, by the transposition phenomena of Brown which we described above. Rock et al. remind us that the transposition principle states that perceived speed is a function of rate of displacement of an object relative to a frame of reference. Thus, if point A moves from top to bottom of a rectangle, then, in order to be seen moving at the same speed, point B in the rectangle of a different size must move, not the same physical distance A moved in that same time, but rather from top to bottom of its own rectangle. This finding is related to a previously described principle which stated that, if the extent of the background changes, the physical rate of movement has to change proportionally in order for phenomenal velocity to remain constant.

While two principles appear to be at work, Rock and Ebenholtz (1959), following additional experiments, reasoned that the *speed transposition effect* may, in itself, be based, in part, on a *size transposition effect.* Therefore, Rock and his associates (1968) decided to test whether there was any relationship between speed constancy and size constancy.

The task of the experiment required the subject to compare the speeds of two vertical moving luminous circles in an otherwise dark room. The standard circle to the subject's right was 8 inches from his eyes, whereas the variable circle to his left was 72 inches from his eyes. The subject was required to compare both the speed of the moving circles and the sizes of two identical triangles at the 8 and 72 inch distances. These comparisons were made under both binocular and monocular vision though an artificial pupil. The assumption was that *size constancy would be present in the first condition because of the cues of accommodation and convergence, whereas it should be essentially absent in the second condition.* The method of adjustment was used to measure the speed of the circle and the size of the triangles.

For the binocular conditions, the judged movements of the standard and the variable circles were not significantly different. That is, the speed of the standard circle was set at 3 in/sec, while that of the variable was set at 4 in/sec. Under this condition, the size of the variable triangle was set at an average of 2.4 inches. On the other hand, under the monocular condition, while the speed of the standard was still set at about 3 in/sec, the speed of the variable circle, in order to be seen as equal, was raised to 11.6 in/sec. Correspondingly, the size of the variable triangle was set at 8.2 inches. These differences are significant. In other words, the variable circle is now set at about four times the speed of the standard, and, similarly, the variable triangle is set at about four times the height of the standard. That is exactly what we would expect with no size constancy, since the variable is four times as far away.

Rock et al. therefore conclude that, *wherever size constancy prevails and to whatever degree, speed constancy will always prevail to the same degree.* However, since speed constancy can also be explained in terms of a transposition principle, it appears to be a case "that there are two bases of speed constancy in daily life" (p. 39).

The factors which underlie the principles described above involve such variables as time duration, spatial aspects, and figure-ground relationships. The aspect of figure-ground is sufficiently important to merit further discussion.

Duncker (1939) found that when the subject fixated one light, it was seen as moving, even when the other light was actually in physical motion, the fixated light being stationary. Duncker suggested that the fixated light was seen as moving because it stood out as a figure, the other light becoming part of the ground.

In the same study a stationary light was enclosed by a moving luminescent-outlined rectangle, in an otherwise dark room. Again Duncker found that the light was seen as moving while the rectangle appeared to be stationary. Evidently we *perceive not absolute but relative motion.* We do not see one point moving absolutely in space, but rather *something moving relative to something else.* Ostensibly the emergence of figure (which is what is seen as moving) is determined by the same kind of principle, such as eye focus, which determines the emergence of figure discussed in Chapter 9.

Tests of Three Hypotheses of Motion

A very important study which relates the perception of induced movement to certain aspects of space perception, already referred to earlier in this chapter and in Chapter 13, was performed by Gogel and Koslow (1971). Taking their clue from earlier work, these investigators subjected three hypotheses to a controlled experimental analysis. The first hypothesis, advanced by Wallach (1959, 1965, pp. 52–59) and Wallach and Schaffer (1966), called the *object-relative* hypothesis, suggests that induced movement is the result of a misperception associated with object-relative displacements. Although the direction of movement is correctly perceived, the motion is attributed to the wrong object. The essential aspect of this hypothesis is that *movement between two objects is relative to the two objects* and is not related to any distance or spatial effects with respect to the observer. Consequently, object-relative motion would remain invariant with respect to distance, as viewed from the observer.

The second hypothesis, the *subject-relative* hypothesis, advanced by Brosgole (1966) and Brosgole, Cristal, and Carpenter (1968), ascribed induced motion to a misperception of perceived direction. Perceived direction will depend on perceived distance and spatial factors relative to the subject. Thus, *any data influenced by egocentric perception will be considered to support the subject-relative hypothesis.*

The third hypothesis, called the *adjacency hypothesis,* has already been referred to (although not by this name) in earlier parts of this chapter when we reported that, in real movement, the effects of masking are greatest the closer the target and the masking stimulus are to one another in space.

In bare outline, the essential tests of these three hypotheses were conducted as follows. In the experimental conditions three combinations of Duncker's dot and frame device were used. In experiment 1, the frame was presented at a relatively *near* position; in experiment 2, the frame was presented at a *middle* position, and in experiment 3, the frame was presented at the *far* position. All these positions were directly in front of the observer. Under each experimental condition, the dot would be presented in either the *near,* the *middle,* or the *far* position. These positions of the dot are labeled N, M, and F, respectively, in Figure 14-4. In the experimental conditions it was always the frame which was in actual physical motion while the dot was stationary. Three control conditions were also set up, identical to the experimental conditions except that the dot was moving and the frame was stationary.

The results of the experiment with respect to extent of perceived movement and perceived distance are diagrammatically presented in Figure 14-4. The data, which are complex, indicate the following:

1   In all cases it can be seen that the subjects in both conditions perceived the relative position of the dot correctly—that is, they always saw the near one as being nearer, the middle one as being in between, and the far dot as being the farthest away.

2   As far as perceived movement is concerned, consider the control situation first. In all cases since the dot was actually moving, and since the physical angle of this placement was the same, one would expect motion to be seen as greatest when the distance was perceived as farthest away. This is in keeping with the size-distance invariancy hypothesis and data reported earlier in this chapter by Rock. Quite clearly, in all three control conditions this was so. When the dot was perceived at the farthest point, it gave the greatest extent of lateral movement.

3   The picture in the experimental conditions with respect to movement is

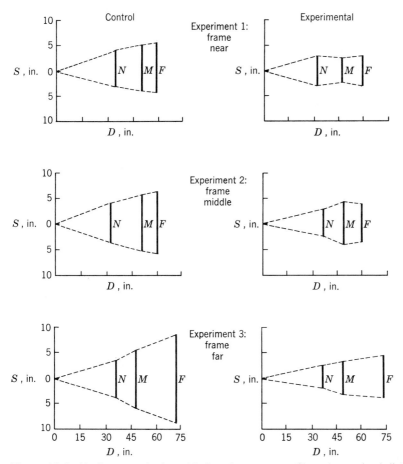

Figure 14-4 Median magnitudes of induced movement, *S'*, and perceived distance, *D'*, of the point of light for the three distance positions of the light *(N, M, F)* in the control and experimental conditions. *(After Gogel & Koslow, 1971, p. 145.)*

quite different. Here we should keep in mind that it is in fact the frame that is moving and not the dot, and hence the perceived motion of the dot would be induced rather than real, and we would therefore have to invoke the *adjacency hypothesis* in addition to either of the other two hypotheses. In experiment 1, with the frame in the near experimental position, positioning of the point of light increasingly behind the frame should result in a decreased magnitude of linear induced motion according to the adjacency hypothesis, and an increased magnitude of induced movement according to the subject-relative hypothesis. Thus in the N, M, and F positions of the dot, the effects of adjacency and subject-relative distance could cancel out, and there should essentially be no difference in the perceived induced movement in the N, M, and F positions. That is essentially what the first graph in the experimental conditions shows us.

With the frame in the middle position (experiment 2), the dot in front would produce minimal movement according to both the adjacency and the subject-relative hypotheses. Hence in that case we would expect the least amount of linear induced movement, and that is what was found. With the dot in the far position we should get a great movement according to the subject-relative hypothesis, but less movement according to the adjacency hypothesis. Thus it should be a little bit more than in the N position. That again is found. With the dot in the middle position, we should get moderate movement according to the subject-relative hypothesis, and greatest movement according to the adjacency hypothesis, and these two should sum. The prediction is that this position of the dot, namely, M, should give the greatest magnitude of linear induced movement; that was found. With the frame at the farthest position (experiment 3), the greatest movement should be in the F position, and this result was also obtained.

In a follow-up experiment, Gogel and Koslow (1972) presented two frames, a large and a small one, in different positions in relation to a dot. The frames moved in opposite directions. It was found that when the frame was closer and small, it had a greater motion-inducing effect. We have here an interaction between space and motion perception, again in agreement with the adjacency principle. Gogel and Tietz (1974) also demonstrated the effect of perceived slant (manipulated by perspective cues) and apparent relative motion.

APPARENT MOVEMENT

Spatiotemporal Relationships and Interresponse Interval

In Wertheimer's study on phi movement, one kind of apparent movement, two lines, spatially separated in the frontal plane, were exposed successively to the subject, who was sitting in an otherwise dark room. The time interval between successive exposures of the two lights turned out to be a crucial factor.

Korte (1915) carried out a more extended and parametric study of the phi phenomenon. He found that *if the distance between the lights was increased, the time interval had to be increased for optimum phi movement to be maintained.* By varying the distance between the lights, the time interval of successive exposures, and the intensity of the lights in his experiments, Korte obtained certain relationships for phi movement on the basis of which he formulated four laws which govern the perception of optimal phi: (1) The distance between lights varies directly with the time interval between successive exposures; (2) the distance varies directly with the intensity of the light stimuli; (3) the intensity varies inversely with the time interval; and (4) the optimal interstimulus interval (ISI) for motion decreases as the duration of the stimulus (t) is increased.

The first law seems to hold up well, but the effect of intensity is controversial. For example, Neuhaus (1930) reported results which conflicted with Korte's second law. This is not the place to repeat a review of this problem, which has been covered very well by Neff (1936), but one thing seems fairly certain, and that is the reported *relationship* which is necessary *between the spatial distance and the time interval* for the perception of optimal motion. See also Sgro's (1963) revision of Korte's data and Graham's (1965) reference to the need to consider modifying Korte's laws.

Neuhaus (1930) and Kolers (1964) both confirmed Korte's fourth law, but they disagreed on the shape of the function that relates the optimal ISI to t. Kahneman and Wolman's (1970) study throws light on this uncertainty. Their results suggest two rules: (1) For stimulus durations (t) shorter than 100 msec, optimal motion occurs when the stimulus *onsets* differ by about 120 msec—that is, have an ISI of 20 msec; (2) for stimulus durations longer than 100 msec, optimal motion occurs when the second stimulus begins at the termination of the first stimulus, that is, when the ISI = 0.

From these rules, Kahneman and Wolman advance the theory that the quality of motion depends solely on the interresponse-interval (IRI) rather than the ISI—that is, optimal motion depends on the *interval between the responses to the two stimuli.* The theory assumes that, up to 100 msec, the duration of the response to the stimuli, T, is constant (Ta) but is always greater than ta, the duration of the stimulus, because of response persistence. Thus $Ta > ta$. For $ta > 100$ msec, $T = t + (Ta - ta)$. This hypothesized difference in the duration of the response as a function of t is graphed in Figure 14-5.

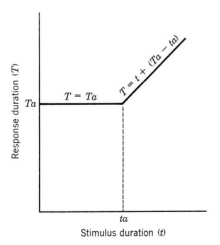

Figure 14-5 Hypothetical function relating the duration of the visual response to the duration of the stimulus. *(After Kahneman & Wolman, 1970, p. 161.)*

Other Varieties of Apparent Movement   Most of the following kinds of apparent movement have been described by Kenkel (1913). The first mode of apparent movement, *alpha* movement, designates that class of an apparent movement where the object appears to change size. *Gamma* movement designates the phenomena where apparent expansion and contraction take place under conditions when the stimulus object's luminance is increased and decreased, respectively. *Delta* movement occurs when the second stimulus is more luminous than the first one: the subject sees apparent reversal in the direction of movement.

Configurational Effects

In addition to space-time relation (for example, IRI), configurational principles are also influential in perceived apparent movement. Some of the earliest work on the configurational nature of motion perception was performed by J. F. Brown (1931a) and Metzger (1926), who studied the thresholds of velocity between the perception of change of position and movement, and the perception of movement and of partial fusion of moving illuminated objects. Their moving objects consisted of such illuminated designs as a row of squares. They reported that two transformations in motion were evident: first, a change from shift of position to steady movement; second, a change from steady movement to a continuous circular path. The same "shrinkage" was reported when subjects observed four lights arranged as if at the ends of the two sides of a cross (J. F. Brown & Voth, 1937).

An interesting fact uncovered by this study was that the shrinkage depended upon the time interval between successive exposures. It was only at particular time intervals (corresponding to the time required for optimum phi) that a band of light moving in a circle was seen. At time intervals lower or greater than this value, either simultaneous or successive flickering was seen. The results are summarized in Figure 14-6.

That the nature of the phenomenal motion is not fully understood is apparent from subsequent experiments. Sylvester (1960) attempted to replicate the experiment of Brown and Voth. After successively energizing the lights at the four corners (of a cross or diamond), as described by Brown and Voth, he did not

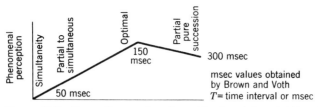

Figure 14-6   Perception as a function of the time interval. *(After J. F. Brown & Voth, 1937.)*

obtain the reported movement of light in a circular path lying within the perimeter of lights. Data of Christian and Weizacker (1943), who extended the first experiment of Brown and Voth, may throw some light on what possibly is happening. The latter investigators found that sometimes shrinkage occurs, sometimes "expansion," and sometimes a fluctuation between the two. It would thus seem that the forces operating to pull a "circle of light" in or out depend on the relationship between the speed of movement and the circumference of the circle. Unfortunately, the exact relationships have not been determined. In our laboratory we found that *instructions* play a crucial role.

An attempt to relate these organizational effects to the gestalt laws of configuration was made by Ternus (1926), who presented three points of light, *a, b,* and *c,* which were slightly separated along a straight line. This stimulus was shortly followed by three other light points, *b, c,* and *d.* The position of the *b*'s and *c*'s in the first and second stimuli were identical, and the distance separating contiguous points was constant. The subject reported seeing, *a, b,* and *c* moving to the right despite the fact that the stimuli were not moving physically. This result is in agreement with the law of uniform direction, uniform density, and common fate which was referred to in Chapter 9. In a similar experiment the first stimulus consisted of three dots exposed as above, but in a vertical plane, while the second consisted of three dots arranged in a straight line which formed an acute angle with the "line" of the first stimulus. The subjects reported that the three dots had moved through an arc. Ternus (1926) called these demonstrations the perceived movement of *phenomenal identity.* The reason for his choice of this term is self-evident. Spatial position of the dots *(proximity)* was obviously important in his experiment.

The identity that a point appears to maintain is determined not by whether it falls on the same retinal region, but where it fits in the overall pattern. The path of apparent movement selected seems to be the one which will preserve the identity of two successively viewed patterns.

Other studies have given us some additional information about these configurational factors. Thus, if the two stimuli are alike, a simple sliding movement on a straight or curved path is usually seen (Hall, Earle, & Crookes, 1952).

Other investigators have described three-dimensional apparent movement. Fernberger (1934) described the situation in which the law of similarity can be considered to counteract the law of proximity in determining the perception of motion of phenomenal identity. He exposed a pair of lines, a thin line and a thick one, which were shortly followed by a similar pair of lines, but in the second exposure, the thin line was on the opposite side of the thick one. The subject reported that the thin line was jumping over and under the thick line—that is, three-dimensional motion was perceived. It would seem that this kind of third-dimensional movement offers a good "simple" solution. In a similar way, Steinig (1929) showed that when an inverted V is followed by a V right side up and slightly lower in the field, the V will be seen to be undergoing translatory motion in space.

Before leaving this section we note here, in passing, that apparent motion and metacontrast, discussed fully in Chapter 10, might be related. The *perceptual-moment hypothesis* put forth by Stroud (1956, pp. 174–207) affords an integrating concept for the two phenomena. The hypothesis asserts that before information reaches the cortex, temporal events are quantitized into temporal units of about 100 msec. Thus, if a second stimulus, spatially *contiguous,* is presented 100 msec after a first stimulus was presented, there would be a *fusion* between them. This could account not only for the general fact of metacontrast, but also for the continuous apparent motion since the separate impulses (*a* and *b*) will fall in the same time frames. Rather than seeing two separate stimuli, we see fusion with motion (the latter because of spatial contiguity rather than identity).

THE MECHANICS OF CODING INFORMATION FOR MOVEMENT

So far in this chapter we have tried to systematize the phenomenology and stimulus relationships concerned with movement and certain spatiotemporal events. It is now necessary to consider the psychophysiological mechanisms which enable the nervous system to code effectively the information relevant to the perception of movement and nonmovement. The complexity of this process becomes evident when we consider the significant adjustments that the organism has to make in order to react adaptively to movement-related stimulation. The various tasks consist of the following: (1) Perceive the motion of an object which is moving and the counterpart in apparent motion; (2) perceive the environment as stationary even though the eyes move continuously (saccadic eye movements and visual nystagmus); (3) respond to movement(s) of one's own body; (4) distinguish between movement resulting from head and eye movement and that resulting from object movement. Three orientations have been developed to explain the mechanisms involved which permit the organism to perform these four tasks.

The first approach, championed by J. J. Gibson (1968), reasons that it is not the image of the external object that is displaced across the retina, but the active retina in constant motion that is displaced across the image. Thus, the source of information is not displacement of the retinal image but actual displacement of the external object.

The second viewpoint, backed with the work of Hubel and Wiesel (1962) and Sekuler and Ganz (1963) who uncovered motion-detection systems, regards the source of information as successive stimulation of adjacent retinal points.

The third orientation, based on the work and theorizing of von Holst (1954), argues that visual information, the concern of the first two approaches, must be integrated with information coming from our own movement—either reafferent visual information or exafferent nonvisual information.

We have discussed, earlier in this book, the major works and theories on which these approaches are based. We need now to describe their explanations of the sources of movement information listed above, beginning with Gibson and the first approach.

Gibson's Theory of Relative Transformation of the Ambient Array

J. J. Gibson (1968) theorizes that the information for movement is contained in the changes in the ambient array of reflected light which accompany relative motion between the observer and objects in his environment. He specifically describes five kinds of transformations in the ambient array coming from the environment which give rise, through retinal correlates, to five kinds of perceived motion. We now list these kinds of motion, together with a brief description of the ambient-array transformation or change containing the information for the particular kind of motion.

1 Movement of an External Object Several transformations in the ambient array occur as the object moves against its stable environment. These include transformation in occlusion, brightness, perspective, and texture. For example, as an object moves closer to the observer, increased occlusion of other objects in the environment occurs on all sides. Conversely, as the object recedes from the observer, there is corresponding disocclusion. From the *pattern* of occlusion and the *gradient* of transformation, the direction and velocity of motion can be judged. There are similar patterns and gradients of transformations connected with brightness, perspective, and texture relationships, as we described in the preceding chapter.

2 Movement of the Observer When the observer moves, or even when the surround moves, such as when one is sitting in a stationary train while another train moves, the *entire ambient* array is transformed. This gives rise to the perception that one is moving in the opposite direction.

3 Object Movement While the Observer Moves This perception is brought about by an interaction of the transformation described for the two classes above.

4 Movement of the Observer's Head Transformation in occlusion occurs. For example, as the observer moves his head from right to left, there is gradual occlusion of the right edge and corresponding disocclusion of the left edge, producing gradual fading of the right side of the field and gradual bringing into view of the left side.

5 Movement of Observer's Bodily Extremities in Field of View In addition to the transformations listed in (1) above for any external object, information from kinesthetic feedback provides the source for this kind of movement.

Motion-Detection System of Successive Retinal Stimulation

The second theory explains movement perception as resulting from some kind of coding of successive stimulation of adjacent retinal points. This sequence of successive stimulation would be the necessary information to signal to the motion-detection system that objects were moving, provided that there were a *coding* mechanism that could detect this change.

The work of Hubel and Wiesel (1962) on the single-cell recording in the cat's cortex lends strong support to the belief that such coding mechanisms exist. As part of their results on specific-cell reaction, they found a relatively large receptive field where cells were responsive only to objects which were in movement. For example, if a stationary bar were presented, these cells would not respond. Moreover, specific cells were responsive to stimuli of certain orientation, length, width, direction, and velocity. However, most of these cells were not specific to all these dimensions simultaneously.

The other supportive line of evidence comes from research on motion aftereffects. It has long been known that such effects exist. For example, in the classic waterfall illusion, if the observer looks at a waterfall for some time, and then moves his eyes to a stationary ground, the latter will appear to move upward—i.e., in the reverse direction. In the laboratory study of this phenomenon, viewing of a rotating spiral disk will be followed by the disk appearing to rotate in the opposite direction, when it is stopped (e.g., Spiegel, 1962).

In an application of movement aftereffect, which generated data relevant to the existence of a motion-detection system, Sekuler and Ganz (1963) obtained the luminance threshold for the movement of stripes which were moving in the same or reverse directions. The moving stripes were viewed under stabilized retinal conditions (see Chapter 12) so that any perceived movement would not be attributed to eye movements but had to come from the stripes moving across the retina. In a temporal sequence successive stripe patterns were moving in either reverse or the same direction. The hypothesis was that, if motion was coded by a cortical motion detector, watching movement in one direction should decrease the sensitivity of that detector, thus elevating the threshold for detecting that pattern of movement.

The results clearly show that there is, indeed, a much higher luminance threshold for same direction (NR) than for reversed direction (R). The data supports strongly the contention that, in human beings there are unitary motion-detecting systems, whose sensitivities are temporarily inhibited during a refractory period following stimulation.

One word of caution is needed about the above findings. Under ordinary circumstances we do not view moving objects under stabilized retinal conditions, and movement stimuli would thus fall on different motion-detection units. However, to the extent that motion afterimages occur, and they would be quite common, some decrease in sensitivity would always follow.

Frisby (1972) has argued that the existence of cortical motion-detection systems would also help explain the existence of such apparent motion as the phi phenomenon. Thus, if a light first stimulated one cell, *a,* and subsequently another cell, *b,* then movement would be seen to move from *a* to *b* without the intervening space being traversed. Provided that the *a* and *b* cells, respectively, were the same for real and phi motion, these two classes would be similarly coded. Frisby's explanation is useful, but it must contend with the differences noted by Kolers, especially his suggestion that the perception of apparent motion seems to be organized more peripherally than the perception of real motion.

Research on the motion-detection system adds valuable knowledge about how movement-coding mechanisms might work but has not dealt with the problem of how a distinction between observer and object movement is coded. In this respect, Gibson's theorizing, which goes beyond point-for-point (or narrow region) stimulation of the retina to encompass relational patterns and transformation, does, at least, attempt to specify the informational differences which provide the source for this distinction. But Gibson does not concern himself with the neurophysiological mechanisms which code these informational differences. The third theory does.

Integration of Motor and Visual Information

Von Holst (1954) applied reafference theory to motion perception. In the first experiment he temporarily paralyzed the eye muscle so that it could not move in one direction—e.g., to the left. He then instructed the observer to move his eye to the left. This instruction alone was sufficient to give rise to the perception that the visual field was moving to the left. In the second experiment he mechanically moved the eye to the left, and the observer, as expected, "saw" the visual world moving in the opposite direction (to the right). In the final experiment, he instructed the observer to move his eye to the left while at the same time mechanically moving it to the left. The observer reported a stationary world.

It is this third result, particularly, that can be extended to induce what might go on in natural perception. The reasoning proceeds as follows. When the observer initiates eye movement (efference), the information of that command is stored in the cortex. After the eye movement the information from the receptor reaches the cortex. If this information matches the stored information (reafference), the observer knows that he initiated the movement (motor). If not (exafference), he perceives the movement as coming from the external object. It is, furthermore, plausible that this kind of efferent mechanism and the occurrence of reafference could work just as easily for other movements of the observer, not just his eyes.

For an analysis of some of the problems described, see Hochberg (1972, pp. 530–532), and for further evidence on efferent-afferent factors, see Gyr (1972). Finally Spiegel (1965) provides a general review of motion perception.

MOTION AND EVENT PERCEPTION

J. J. Gibson (1957) extended his theory described above to analyze the organization of the phenomenon of the *kinetic depth effect*—what is seen when an object rotating in the third dimension casts a shadow on a translucent screen. The problem is to explain how two-dimensional projections are seen in three dimensions. The transformations through which the shadow goes are called the *kinetic depth effect* and are diagramed in Figure 14-7. Before we describe this figure, let us set the theoretical framework, as Gibson sees it.

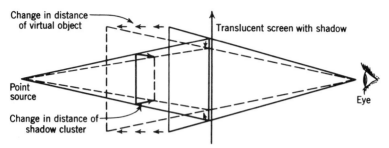

Figure 14-7 The shadow transformer. The variables of form and transformation are thus isolated for study. *(After J. J. Gibson, 1957, p. 291.)*

Gibson's analysis, which is polar rather than analytical, begins by accepting the moving pattern as given and then uses the operations of defining perspective transformations in geometry to describe a family of changes. This is how he attempts to define or measure the projection in two dimensions of a physical motion in three dimensions. As we have seen at the beginning of this chapter, there are two kinds of projections, parallel and polar. Since the former results in similar projections which differ only in size, they give rise to ambiguous depth perception. Polar (also called central) projection on the other hand results in foreshortening (as can be seen in Figure 14-7). This is what we do when we draw scenes and objects in perspective, as the architect draws a view of a house for a client. Although both kinds of projection lead to a perspective transformation in geometry, the ordinary usage of the term, perspective transformation, is limited to the latter case.

In this theory Gibson proposes that motion can be described as a continuous *series of perspective transformations*. This series, which is a family of static forms of a temporal series, can be analyzed by six parameters: (1) vertical translation of the pattern in a plane; (2) horizontal translation of the pattern; (3) enlargement or reduction of the pattern (the first three are transformations of translation); (4) horizontal foreshortening of the pattern; (5) vertical foreshortening of the pattern; (6) rotation of the pattern in the plane.

In one experiment J. J. Gibson and Eleanor J. Gibson (1957) applied this theory to analyze the results of an experiment on the perception of rigid motion. The experimental arrangement is diagramed in Figure 14-7. The mount containing the shadow caster could be rotated on any one of three axes or translated in any of three dimensions. The shadow was actually cast by opaque figures which were painted on a transparent screen on the mount. It was found that the size and shape of the moving image, the "virtual object" seen behind the translucent screen, changed as the mount moved—that is, the order of transformation followed the spatial order of movement.

Similar empirical demonstrations were performed with nonrigid, elastic motion by von Fieandt and Gibson (1959). In their experiment 940 changes from motion to rotation to motion of compression or the reverse were detected by any observer. Only once was there a false-positive—that is, seeing a change when no actual physical change took place. Unsophisticated observers could distinguish this nonperspective transformation from continuous perspective transformation as described above.

Kinetic Depth Effect

Gibson's analysis and demonstrations are related to the kinetic depth effect. For example, in one of his demonstrations, a shadow is cast on a screen through several parallel sheets of glass, each of which has been sprinkled with talcum powder. When the sheets of glass are stationary, a "Milky Way" effect is perceived, but, if the sandwich of mounts is moved, a *depth effect* is produced, with each layer of nebulous material appearing to stand in front of its neighbor.

Although the term *kinetic depth effect* was recommended by Wallach and O'Connell (1953), the demonstration of the phenomenon goes back to Metzger (1934) who used, as a stimulus, a light pattern reflected from a turntable. When the turntable was at rest, the light reflected on the translucent screen was seen as a two-dimensional pattern. However, when the turntable rotated, most observers reported that the rods projected on the screen were moving in the third dimension.

In further analysis of the kinetic depth effect, Wallach and O'Connell produced the image by using various wire forms which projected shadows on the screen. In one such experiment the shadow's projection was produced by a rotating form of three rods connected at their ends and diverging at angles of 110°. It was only when the observers could see the ends of the rods that the two-dimensional projection was seen in depth. The conclusion of the authors that, for kinetic depth, changes in direction are not enough but must be accompanied by *changes in apparent size* concurs with Gibson's position previously stated. We see, in other words, that organizational complexity and the kinds of relational transformation that Gibson describes underlie the informational base for perceiving kinetic depth.

Investigation of configurations in event perception has also been pioneered by the Swedish psychologist Johannsen (1950). His apparatus consisted of a series of mechanically controlled celluloid disks which could be rotated and otherwise moved in the frontal and horizontal planes. Figures painted on these disks were projected on a translucent screen from which the observer could see the phenomenal movements of these events.

One of the most interesting studies by Johannsen was *motion synthesis,* which is illustrated by the following demonstration. By painting appropriate dots on the disk, the following pattern is projected on the screen: two points are viewed simultaneously, one, *a,* moving up and down at a constant rate, while the other, *b,* subscribes a circle, also moving at a constant rate. The observer reported seeing two separate up-and-down motions, with *b* having a slight sideways motion as well. Johannsen called *a* the *influencing* element and *b* the *affected* element. We see in his work that configurational movement can be produced by arranging elements in certain ways; the elements thus affect one another.

(a)   (b)

Figure 14-8 *(a)* Outline contours of a walking and a running subject and *(b)* the corresponding dot configurations. *(After Johannsen, 1973, p. 202.)*

The Swedish psychologists are currently carrying on a very creative analysis of the combinational motion effect, with depth aspects. They use the technique of vector analysis (see, for example, Borjesson & von Hofsten, 1972). Examples of this work are the application of vector analysis to the perception of organismic (biological) motion like walking and running. By presenting a pattern of moving dots, without the form contour as in B of Figure 14-8, Johannsen (1973) has been able to create the impression of walking and running. His paper presents a vector analysis of why this is so.

We have come full circle from polar projection through configurational analysis back to the configurational aspects of families of transformations in polar projection.

SUMMARY

Linking space to motion perception, this chapter began with an analysis of illusory movement—namely, rotary motion or oscillation. In this case parallel rather than polar projection creates exaggerated perspective, giving rise to ambiguous depth.

Illusory motion led us to a consideration of the distinction between real and apparent movement, one of which seems to be that the latter is more peripherally organized than the former.

We then moved on to a description of the relationship between velocity thresholds and size constancy and transformation phenomena. An analysis of real movement in terms of figure-ground, spatiotemporal configurations, and the adjacency and subject-relative hypotheses followed. Apparent movement was similarly analyzed and also related to the interresponse-interval (IRI), perceptual moment construct, and larger organizational effects, such as metacontrast and quantification of time. The latter naturally led to a consideration of time perception.

An important analysis of possible mechanisms for coding movement, such as motion-detection systems, was finally followed by a description of phenomenal events, such as kinetic depth.

Chapter 15

Social Perception, Motives,
and Personality

Throughout this book we have concerned ourselves with attempts to find ways of specifying the sources of information which are extracted at various levels of the perceptual hierarchy. We saw repeatedly that sources of information located within the perceiver come more and more into play as we move from level III to level IV. This is even more true, however, in the organization of level V—where perception extracts information related to emotions, motives, values, personal meanings, and social events. Our analysis will be couched in terms of the information-processing model we presented in Chapter 2.

In the present chapter we shall focus on the following phenomena: (1) the perception of interpersonal events such as causality, intentionality, and motives; (2) the dynamics of person and interpersonal perception; (3) the influence of personality dynamics and sociocultural experience on perception; (4) value, attitudinal, and personality aspects of perception.

A good bridge with the last chapter is, in effect, an extension of the kind of space-time relationships which deal with movement events pioneered by the European psychologists, especially Michotte in Belgium.

PERCEPTION OF SOCIAL EVENTS: CAUSALITY, INTENTIONALITY, AND MOTIVES

This area of inquiry received its greatest impact from Michotte (1946, 1963), whose research represents the first concerted attack on the problem of assessing another's personality through experimenting with the perception of kinetic structures. He started by studying the dynamics of how cause is attributed, then progressed to a consideration of how human beings attribute motives and emotionality.

Michotte's Work on Phenomenal Causality

Johannsen's (1973) recent work, mentioned in the last chapter, showed that certain patterns of human motor behavior, e.g., running, can be created in perception by movement combinations. Michotte (1963) has shown that other kinds of perception—e.g., seeing one element causing a particular event to happen to another element—can also be created by certain movement combinations which he calls *kinetic structures*. There is no doubt that human beings do perceive cause and effect relationships. It is therefore a legitimate question for the psychology of perception to ask what the informational sources of these relationships are. Using special technical equipment, such as that depicted in Figure 15-1, Michotte (1946) was able to make two (or more) small colored rectangles, 1 centimeter long and 0.5 centimeter wide, move along a horizontal slot, 15 centimeters long and 0.5 centimeter wide. These rectangles could be stopped at any position on the slot, or made to move at any moment. The direction, speed, and extent of movement of the objects could also be changed whenever desired. Thus an infinite variety of combinations of movements could be obtained.

Using this ingenious technique, Michotte found that certain combinations of visual stimuli produce certain specific causal impressions. The effect of these combinations depends on such relational factors as (1) the initial distance

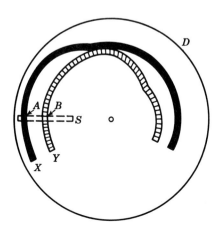

Figure 15-1 The causality phenomenon. As the disk *D* rotates *A* and *B* are seen as the rectangles through the slot *S*. *(From Michotte, 1946.)*

between the objects, (2) the time they begin to move, (3) their speed, (4) the time interval between the movement when the first object comes into contact with the second and the time the second object moves, (5) the nature and effect of the contact, (6) the direction of movement, and (7) the distance moved.

For example, in the "billiard ball" effect, A moves rapidly to B and propels it forward, then comes to rest: A is seen as causing B to move. Similarly, in the "pushcart" effect, A moves more slowly to B and carries the latter off with it: A is seen as uniting with B. Notice that in these perceptions (gestalt principle of common fate) of phenomenal causality, the speed of approach and separation, the length of contact, and the effect following contact are the important space-time or kinetic relationships which determine what is perceived.

There were other elaborations. Thus, if, after being touched by A, B moves through too great a distance, the impression of a causal connection is absent. Michotte interprets this by saying that the impact has a certain *radius of action* within which it is effective. If B moves too far, it goes beyond this radius of action and thus appears to have its own power of motion. *But increasing the length of B's path does not increase the number of reports of B's being released by A* (Boyle, 1960). If we increase the velocity of both A and B, the radius of action increases.

While Michotte asserts that the impression of causality arises spontaneously, experience merely serving to define more precisely the conditions under which mechanical causality is perceived, other investigators have found an important *experiential* determiner of phenomenal causality. For example, Gruber and his associates (Gruber, Fink, & Damn, 1957) and Powesland (1959) studied the influence of practice on attributing the collapse of a model "bridge" to the prior removal of one of its vertical supports. The "temporal threshold of causality" was defined as the maximum value of delay (between removal of the vertical support and collapse of the bridge) consistent with reliable reports by the subject of an impression of causality. It was found that practice trials with longer delays increased this threshold value, whereas practice with shorter delays decreased this threshold value. See also Olum (1956) for developmental differences.

Other investigators have uncovered ways of inhibiting the perception of causality. Thus, Gemelli and Capellini (1958), requiring their subjects to adopt an analytic attitude, obtained a reduction in the number of reports of phenomenal causality. In addition, Houssiadas (1964) was also able to reduce the number of causal responses by inducing a set, toward the stimulus situation, which was inappropriate to "inferring" causality.

The reader probably noted that some of the combinations reported earlier gave rise to the impression of intentionality. Thus we find such reports as "momentary agreements between A and B," "A carrying off B by brute force," "A and B go together," and "B runs away from A." All these statements imply that A or B, or both, wanted to do something; i.e., they had intentions. This, of course, takes us into the area dealing with the perception of motives, which is involved in social perception. We discuss this in the next section.

Attribution of Emotionality   The uniting and repulsing phenomena are like emotions, which can be divided roughly into two classes, depending on whether they present an integrative or a segregative relationship between the individual experiencing them and the thing, person, or event which is their object. Examples of integrative emotions are sympathy, friendship, and love, whereas antipathy, disgust, anger, hate, and fear are segregative types. The motor reactions corresponding to an integrative emotion usually result in an approach, which may manifest itself in the positioning of an individual close to another or by establishing a contact more or less pronounced or more or less prolonged—a handshake or an embrace. The motor reactions corresponding to segregative emotions on the other hand reveal themselves in withdrawal behavior, such as running away from something we dislike or fear. Michotte's thesis is that the *physical reactions* in the target subject create similar kinetic structures in the perceiver (e.g., approach or withdrawal).

Heider and Simmel (1944), by presenting subjects with inanimate objects, did propose to determine the dependence of the individual's response on certain stimulus configurations. The subjects were asked to interpret a motion-picture film (an animated cartoon) in which three geometric figures (a large triangle, a small triangle, and a circle) were shown moving in different directions and at various speeds. As shown in Figure 15-2, the figures were moving around or in and out of a rectangle, a section of which periodically opened or closed like a door.

Of interest to us here are the results obtained from two fairly large groups of female college students. The first group was merely asked to describe the film as a motion picture, while the second group was asked to interpret it as if the objects were human beings. Despite the difference in the instructions, all but one subject in the first group also attributed human characteristics to the objects. We may thus treat the results of the two groups together.

The phenomenal relationship between the objects was determined by temporal succession, spatial proximity, and good continuation. For example, in one scene the big triangle was following the small triangle around until it touched the small triangle, which then changed its direction and came to rest. This scene was interpreted in general as follows: The big man was chasing the little man, and

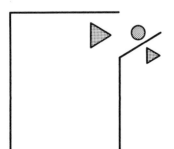

Figure 15-2 Exposure objects displayed in various positions and configurations from the moving film. The small triangle (hero) is seen as opening the door for the circle (girl), who is escaping from the large triangle (villain). *(After Heider and Simmel, 1944.)*

when he caught him, he hit the little man until the latter reeled back under the impact of his blow. This interpretation illustrated the principle of temporal succession and good continuation. The principle of spatial proximity determined "interpersonal" relationships between the three objects. Thus the little triangle and the circle, which were seen together frequently, stood out as a pair that was opposed to the big triangle. This pair was seen as a man and a girl in love. The big triangle was seen as a villain who fought with the little man and who chased or pursued the girl.

The work discussed in this section suggests that such configurational principles as good continuation, proximity, and figure-ground effects play a significant role in organizing the perception of motivational and emotional expressions under certain experimental conditions. We see in the work of Heider and Simmel and of Michotte an interesting approach to causality and intentionality.

Evaluation, Implication, and Extension of Phenomenal Causality Studies

While Michotte and Heider have given us some of the phenomenological variables related to the perception of interpersonal relationships, the quantitative function of these relationships awaits further work. Moreover, once these relationships have been established, the question of whether these expressive behaviors operate independently of experience still arises. For example, recall Gruber et al. (1957) who found that the time interval (threshold) for seeing the "bridge" collapse could be altered by experience. Thus, if the practice trials interpolated between two estimates of causality consisted of long time intervals, the threshold was increased on the second trial, whereas it was reduced if the practice trials consisted of near-zero delays. Similar findings were reported by Powesland (1959).

Olum (1956) has approached the possible role of experience in phenomenal causality indirectly by studying the developmental aspects of the perception of causality. Using Michotte's techniques, she studied the pushing and releasing phenomena in 7-year-old children and adults. Two results of interest are relevant to us. First, the children frequently saw A passing B, although this did not in fact happen. Second, B was often seen to come and meet A. Olum interprets these results as possibly related to developmental aspects of perceiving configuration and stroboscopic motion. The reader should also consult Lacey and Dallenbach (1939) for informative treatment of how children learn causal relations.

PERSON PERCEPTION OR SOCIAL COGNITION

The experiential aspects of the perception of personal attributes are of crucial importance since they are conceivably related to the nature of interpersonal relationships. Heider (1958), in fact, extended his research and thinking on phenomenal events into a general inquiry concerning the psychology and perception of interpersonal relationships. Tagiuri (1960, pp. 175–193), in findings consistent with those of Heider and Michotte, also reports that movement patterns are used as cues in person perception.

Person perception concerns itself with how we perceive and know the psychological characteristics of other persons. Tagiuri (1969, pp. 395–449), in the revised edition of the original review of Bruner and Tagiuri (1954) on person perception, reasons plausibly that we could also refer to this process as *social cognition.*

In spite of many valiant attempts to study the process of social cognizing, and the accumulation of extensive literature since the 1950s, we, lamentably, still know very little in a substantive way about the principles underlying this process. For example, many hypotheses have been generated about the sources of information and the possible cues used to determine knowledge about peoples' intentions and inner feelings, but few positive data have been verified. Moreover, some of our intuitive, "commonsense" impressions have not been supported by research findings. For example, Fiedler (1953) and Steiner (1959a, 1959b) have found that it is an oversimplification to believe that individuals who are most accurate in the perception of others also get along best with others. Tagiuri (1969) points out that a complex determination is probably made by higher-order relationships of the stimulus, situation, temporal sequence, and the interval representation of the perceiver. Some of these relationships have been studied in nonverbal communication.

Nonverbal Communication

Mehrabian (1972), in his treatise on this subject, specifies that cues for nonverbal communication come from four categories: facial and vocal expression; hand gestures; posture and position; movement and the implicit aspects of vocalization. Most of the informative data concern the last two categories, and they contribute to the *positiveness* (or negativeness) of the feelings of the person observed, the *potency* or status of that individual, and his *responsiveness* to the communication.

Two classes of principles, which bear revealing resemblance to the laws of configuration described by Michotte and the gestalt psychologists, appear to organize the above dimensions into cues of postural and implicit vocalization. These principles are immediacy and relaxation.

Immediacy   In the category of posture and position, immediacy cues are transmitted through more touching, closer position, forward lean, smaller distance, more direct and longer eye contact, and proximity in the direction of body orientation. All these cues, which are related to proximity and radius of action, reveal the degree of positiveness of feeling.

Immediacy is also reflected in the implicit aspects of verbalization. Thus, spatiotemporal indicators in the first word of the following pairs transmit more positive (affiliative) feelings than the second word: Here-there; this-that; there-those. For example, Here (there) is John; I know this (that) person; these (those) people need help. This information is all the more important when we realize that untrained people can make these judgments reliably.

In one very interesting and illuminating study Mehrabian uncovered, further, that there was a combined effect of verbal and *contextual* immediacy. Thus, in addition to cues implicit in verbalization designated in the last paragraph, he found that contextual immediacy was transmitted by obsessional qualifications, duration, temporal order of occurrence, and dissociated categories. More specifically, frequency of obsessional qualifications reveals negative attitudes, longer duration or hesitation suggests unwillingness, delaying the evocation of certain subjects indicates uneasiness, while insertion of dissociated categories probably conveys anxiety or threat. In other words, if people display obsessive mannerisms, hesitate, take a long time to speak and also block, then their attitude to the person is negative. Changing the subject probably reveals threat or anxiety.

Relaxation   In the dimension of relaxation, asymmetrical rather than symmetrical position of the posture and the limbs reveals a more relaxed attitude. More specifically, relaxation is measured by asymmetrical arm position, sideways lean, openness of arm position, asymmetrical leg position, and reclining body position. Furthermore, Mehrabian also found that we are moderately relaxed with those we like, very relaxed with those we dislike or disrespect, and tense with those who are threatening to us. Finally, besides positiveness, relaxation also reveals status or potency. Thus, individuals in positions that are more potent or of a higher status generally reveal more relaxed positions. Other authors who emphasize the cue value of asymmetrical bodily orientation are Cook (1971, pp. 70–80) and Sommer (1967), both of whom also provide general reviews of work in this area.

We have referred to positiveness and potency. As far as responsiveness is concerned, there is some suggestion that persuasiveness on the part of the transmitter is likely to increase his responsiveness as well as that of the receiver of the message.

Facial and Bodily Cues   Expressions of the face and other parts of the body also provide some interesting revelations about our feelings. A number of investigators, including Kendon (1972) as well as Cook and Mehrabian, have emphasized that it is the duration of gaze, not frequency of shifts in gaze, which reveals positive intent. (This might be the basis of the expression "shifty eyes.") Moreover, Argyle and Dean (1965) add the importance of considering mutual gaze. Thus, if a person wants to convey a desire for friendship or greater intimacy, he will gaze directly and for a relatively prolonged time. If the recipient has compatible intent, he will reciprocate the gaze; if not, he will probably look away.

Comparing and contrasting facial and bodily expressions, one finds that the former are more reliable at conveying attitudes of liking. On the other hand, implicit cues are more reliable than verbal statements for conveying negative attitudes since the latter are not sanctioned in society. (See Zaidel & Mehrabian, 1969).

Finally, Mehrabian (1971), following the lead of Ekman and Friesen (1969), studied the saliency of facial, hand, and leg gestures as cues in conveying honesty and deception. In this study college students were asked to write about their attitudes on abortion. Two groups, expressing the most extreme attitudes (positive and negative), were used. Individuals of each group were given two messages, consistent and opposite to their true beliefs, and were instructed to convince another individual of these views. While these subjects were interacting, judges were observing and coding their nonverbal gestures. It was found that when the communication revealed honest belief, the face, hands, and legs were equally communicative. However, when the transmitters were deceiving, leg and foot movement were more revealing than hand movement, which, in turn, was more revealing than facial expression. More specifically when honestly communicating, there is more foot and leg movement than when deceiving—almost as if the leg were "frozen" under the latter condition. The point is that we are usually conscious of transmitting feelings through the face. Thus, when we are deceiving, we might smile falsely. But the parts of our bodies under less conscious control, like the legs, will betray our true feelings. Note that in usual communication, our face is monitored the most.

RECOGNITION OF FACIAL EXPRESSION OF EMOTIONS: CLINICAL AND CULTURAL ASPECTS

Most reviews support a social learning interpretation or social perception of data that reveals few universal patterns of emotional expression (Hunt, 1941; Bruner & Tagiuri, 1954; Tagiuri, 1968). However, very thoughtful analysis of the issues involved in this debate, together with some careful experiments, has been presented by Ekman (1972). He points out that the absence of universal patterns of emotional expression in past studies is inconclusive because of equivocation in the research designs. This equivocation comes from two sources. The first concerns the nature of the stimulus eliciting the particular emotion. It is a mistake to believe that "objectively" similar stimuli mean the same thing to different peoples. For example, a death might be the occasion for sadness in one culture but for rejoicing in another. Thus, merely to study the facial reaction to a death proves nothing about the underlying emotional experience since the latter might in fact be different in different cultures. Therefore, finding different facial reactions does not show that the same emotion is expressed differently in different cultures. In order to come to this conclusion, we must have independent knowledge that the actual emotions were, in fact, the same.

The second source of difficulty comes from the fact that the expression of emotions is not a single but a multidetermined process. Some of the stages in the process might be universal, whereas others might be influenced by customs of a particular culture. To elaborate on this stage process, Ekman suggests a model for describing the organization of the facial expressions of emotions which we have diagrammed in Figure 15-3.

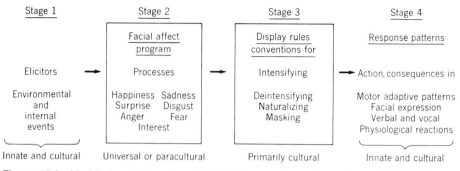

Figure 15-3 Model describing stages in facial expression of emotions. *(Modified from Ekman, 1972, p. 213.)*

The term *elicitor* refers to any stimulus which is effective in arousing one or more of the emotions listed in the box under stage 1. Ever since the time of Darwin, and especially since the data and insights of modern ethology, it has become rather obvious that certain classes of stimuli—for example, those connected with threat to survival—are innate and, therefore, universal in calling up specific emotional reactions. On the other hand, comparative anthropology has also indicated that the kinds of emotions aroused by apparently "identical elicitors" are culturally conditioned. Thus, for example, there are cultures like the Zuni in New Mexico where the kinds of events which generally elicit anger in most cultures will call up a more "benign" emotion.

Stage 2, the *facial affect program* is the most significant postulation of Ekman's model. It is enlightening to fit this construct into the general context which we have used throughout this text. This context concerns the question of the nature of the process which codes the information that is necessary for effective perception. An example, from the last chapter, was the hypothesized motion-detection system. In the present case it is the facial affect program which is postulated as a system that both codes the relevant information in a specific elicitor and also sends down signals "*triggering* a set of muscular movements" or a "patterned set of neural impulses to facial muscles" (Ekman, 1972, p. 216, italics ours).

It is rather interesting to contemplate the implications of the suggestion that the facial affect program is a link between the experiencing of a specific emotion and the innervations of a particular set of facial muscles. What this means is that this program, presumably organized in the brain, has stored rules for not only "reading" the appropriate messages in an eliciting stimulus, but also for instructing the mechanism controlling the facial musculature about the specific reaction patterns to that emotionally provoking stimulus.

The survival and adaptive value of such a program is, of course, quite evident. For example, the knotting of the forehead, the bringing together and lowering of the eyebrows and eyes, and the gritting and tension in the mouth and lower face may all be signs that the individual is getting ready to strike out as a reaction to anger. It is not only adaptive because appropriate preparatory actions are mastered, but also because the facial pattern, when recognized, might remove the target object, a consequence advantageous to both individuals in the transaction. Similarly, the recognition of the facial patterns connected with happiness, fear, and sadness are more likely to lead to feelings (and probably appropriate action) of friendliness, protection, and sympathy, respectively.

The designation, in the model, that there is a *triggering* or *innervation* of neural impulses to facial muscles rather than simply specifying facial muscle reactions separates stage 2 from stage 3. Thus the universal or innate program causes these triggering or innervating neural impulses. What kind of facial pattern is actively displayed can obviously be limited or constrained (through rules of prescription and proscription) by culture.

Finally, it is rather evident, with a little reflective imagination, that the varieties of consequences (stage 4) of an experienced emotion can also result from cultural modification of biologically appropriate action.

Ekman (1972) and his co-workers, in a number of separate studies, collected interesting data which lend support to the plausibility of the existence of some such universal program underlying the perception and expression of emotion in the face. This research was based on theory developed, in part, by Tomkins (1963) and Ekman and his co-workers. The theory has, among its postulates, the assertion that the primary information for distinguishing emotions is contained in cues in three areas of the face—namely, brows-forehead, eyes-lids, and mouth-lower face. Elaborate descriptions and rules for coding different patterns in these areas, as well as the whole face, were developed and could be used with high "inter-rater" reliability by more than one judge (e.g., four in some "experiments").

In one experiment 3,000 photographs collected, in part, by Ekman and his co-workers and Tomkins and McCarter (1964) were inspected by the researchers on the basis of the theory and sorted into groups corresponding to one of six emotions. Thirty photographs could be sorted reliably and unequivocally to meet these criteria. These pictures were then shown one at a time (usually for 10 seconds each) to a number of subjects from five literature cultures: Argentina, Brazil, Chile, Japan, and the United States. The subjects were asked to categorize each photograph into *one* of the six emotions listed under stage 2 in Figure 15-3.

By means of a number of careful controls and sound statistical analysis, it was found that there was a high and significant correlation between the individuals from the different cultures with respect to the perceived emotions in the photographs. That is to say, most individuals, irrespective of culture, saw the same emotion in the same photograph of the face. Further verification that this correlation is not simply contributed to by contact between these cultures came from an independent study in which it was found that individuals from two preliterate cultures, the Fore and the Dani, also recognize and express the emotions in like ways, with respect to facial patterns. Since these cultures are preliterate, more difficult problems of measurement arose. For example, three photographs would be shown, a particular story told, and the subject asked to pick out one of the three photographs which depicted the facial reaction to that story.

Ekman's work provides strong support for the position that there is an innate (universal or pancultural) foundation for the perception of emotions through facial expressions. One might wonder whether the close match across the cultures would have been obtained if the emotional categories were not limited in number to six. Ekman states that from prior analysis, however, the six categories exhaust all the primary emotions experienced by human beings. Be that as it may, the research is impressive and raises the question of how this universal tendency and similarity in perceiving emotions from facial expressions might come about.

We have already discussed the adaptive value of being able to express certain facial muscular patterns in reaction to specific emotional expressions. It occurs to the present authors that this expressive ability could conceivably lead to the perception of these patterns through the following development. After repetitive experience in such expressive patterns, with the inevitable *feedback* from the muscles to *long-term brain storage,* the brain would presumably have models for each emotional-expressive pattern. These models become the frame of reference against which the visual perception of other people's facial patterns are judged. This theory is admittedly speculative and specifies cross-modal (muscle and visual sense) interaction, but is consistent with what we have learned in other sections of this book about how perceptual programs become modified through experience. While testing this theory on human beings might present mammoth practical difficulties, a beginning could be made by interfering with the specified temporal stage on other forms of expressive behavior in animals.

The model in Figure 15-3 also states that some elicitors of emotions and their perception can also come from internal organismic sets. This proposition is related to the more general question of the origin and differential effect of long-term organismic sets, already discussed in an earlier chapter. One such source of differentiating sets comes from the effect of particular cultural and subcultural expression, to a discussion of which we now turn.

Cultural Influences

Although this issue has been controversial among social scientists for quite some time, there have been a number of proponents of the view that culture influences the direction of perception. In addition to scholars mentioned in Chapter 12, other leading proponents of this view include Kluckholn (1954), French (1963, pp. 388–428) and Triandis (1964, pp. 2–48). Informative reviews of the literature and issues have been provided by Dennis (1951, pp. 148–169) and Miller (1973).

As early as the beginning of the present century Rivers (1901, pp. 15–20, 1905), following research with the British expedition to the Torres Straits, reported that the Toda and Papuan of New Guinea have significantly less susceptibility to the Müller-Lyer illusion but correspondingly greater susceptibility to horizontal-vertical line illusion by comparison with the English (see also

Seligman, 1901). We shall return to why this may be so later. But the finding, if reliable, is fascinating because of the bidirectional effect on culture. This report received corroboration in that black South Africans also showed greater tendency to the horizontal-vertical illusion but less tendency to the Müller-Lyer illusion than white controls.

Segall, Campbell, and Hershkovitz (1966) have warned that certain peoples, when looking at a picture, pay more attention to edges and other more salient aspects than to the picture itself. They note astutely that irrelevant contours and the wide borders which Westerners ignore, because of their broader experience with pictures, are focused on by members of some other cultures. Thus, use of cutout photographs, color, line drawings, and movies produces better results. Similarly, we should separate verbal responses into what the subject actually sees and what he thinks he might be expected to see.

Following a brilliant analysis and systemization of these cautions, Segall et al. offer a helpful theoretical explanation of how cultural experience can influence differences in perceptual selectivity. Among anthropologists they favor the kind of approach of Hallowell, who has stated that "the human organism becomes *selectively sensitized* to certain arrays of stimuli rather than others (as) a function of the individual's membership in one cultural group rather than another, whatever other factors are involved" (Hallowell, 1951, p. 168, italics ours). This quotation bears remarkable agreement with the data and theory we advanced earlier when discussing the differential reactive sets which result from experience in animals and man.

Segall et al. utilize the conceptualization of Egon Brunswik, also described previously in this book, to throw light on how these selective sensitizations may develop during socialization experiences. Their assertion is "if human groups differ in their visual inference tendencies, it is because their visual environments differ" (1966, p. 78). This conclusion is deduced from Brunswik's theory of "ecological cue validity" which is based on probabilistic functionalism. The central thesis is that as a result of ecological sampling in experience, the individual comes to apprehend the probable significance of cues. That is how the particular operations come about.

Segall et al. apply this conceptualization specifically to explain the causes of illusions. While the process of apprehending cue validity is, in general, functional, they are "misleading" in the case of illusionary perception. We are reminded here of the report of Gregory and Wallace (1963) who, testing a congenitally blind individual 48 days after corneal transplant to give vision, found that normal visual inference habits were lacking. The subject could make nothing of pictures and facial expressions. Since he could not interpret two-dimensional representations, no constancy scaling could be evoked. Hence he showed marked absence of illusions.

For individuals who grow up with the appropriate visual-environmental experience, there will be the evoking of constancy scaling which is inappropriate to the flat plane (visible as a textured surface). Segall et al. show how this is so in some well-known illusions.

In an exceptionally well-designed study they showed various examples of four illusions (see Chapter 11 for examples)—the Müller-Lyer, the Sander, and two examples of the vertical-horizontal—to members from a variety of African, Pacific, and New World cultures, including students at Northwestern University, which was the center from which this massive cross-cultural study in perception emanated. Each variation of the illusion was placed on a separate page in a booklet with detailed instructions. To make sure that the subjects understood the instructions, since some were from preliterate peoples, check items were given as preliminary exercises. In this way base lines were established. Through these and other cautions and checks it could reliably be determined that any expressions of a perceptual illusion could not be because of experimental or measurement error. These booklets were mailed to fellow researchers in these various countries who collected the data and mailed them back to Northwestern University for analysis.

The results were analyzed with respect to frequency of or tendency to illusions—e.g., seeing one line longer in the Müller-Lyer, the vertical line longer than the horizontal in the vertical-horizontal, and the diagonal longer in the "wider" parallelogram in the Sander illusion.

The results suggest that cultural experiences differentiate in either direction. Specifically, rural cultures, used to receding furrows, experienced more foreshortening—thus they exaggerate the vertical-horizontal illusion. We, living in a geometric world, exaggerate the Müller-Lyer illusion. See Tajfel (1969, pp. 315–394) and Gomrich (1962) about how experiential set directs perception in artists.

PROCESSING OF PERSONALITY-RELEVANT INFORMATION

In this section we want to analyze the value of interpreting the relationship between personality variables and perception in the context of the kind of information-processing model we presented in Chapter 2. This is a position similar to the one taken by Erdelyi (1974).

Ever since the awareness of the psychoanalytic theories of Freud there has been a popular belief in clinical circles that emotions and motives distort human perception. In 1948 this belief was boosted by research reports of Bruner and Goodman (1947). Although publication of their findings had tremendous impact, we shall review its effects only very briefly since current knowledge in perception makes most of the issues dated. Those interested in the historical development can read Erdelyi.

Bruner and Goodman's report, which ushered in the so-called "new look" approach to perception, stated that poor children overestimated the size of a 25-cent coin to a significantly greater extent than rich children. The researchers believed that this overestimation came about because the poor children valued the coin more than the rich children did. However, it should be noted that *all* children overestimated, poorer children overestimating more. We cannot ignore that all the children tested had a constant positive error of overestimation. Moreover, Carter and Schooler, who used the same children to estimate both coins and disks (for comparison) whereas different children estimated coins and disks in the earlier study, found that it was only in the *recollection* that poor children's overestimation was significantly greater.

The constant error and suggestion of memory influence suggest that we might be dealing with a cognitive (see Chapter 1) rather than a motivational variable. If this were so, it would be more consistent with our information-processing approach. The possibility of this kind of explanation suggested itself to the present authors from the work of Gardner and Long on *perceptual scanning*. We need to go into this work in some detail. First, Gardner (1961) had found that the apparent magnitude of the diameter of a circle was related to how extensively the individual scanned. Using Piaget's construct of centration, he simply counted each focusing look at the stimulus as a centration. The total number of looks per unit time was considered to be the scanning score. It was found that the magnitude of error (overestimating the circle diameter) was negatively related to the *extensiveness* of scanning. This cognitive-style ability is related to other perceptual phenomena. Thus, using the concentric-circle illusion, Gardner and Long (1962a) found that the magnitude of judging the smaller circle is correlated with judging the size of the larger circle when both appear alone, and is also related to the size of the illusion—all signs of consistency in some perceptual ability or cognitive style.

Gardner and Long (1962b) theorized that the extensiveness of scanning is a cognitive (style) variable which determines, in part, *ego control of affect* (a control command).

Since values are related to affect, we can apply the cognitive-style difference to account for the coin experiment, in which case we would have to postulate that poorer children are narrower scanners than rich children. There is reason to believe that individuals raised in affluent environments have more varied perceptual experience than children from impoverished homes. This difference presumably leads to differences in perceptual and cognitive ability—and, therefore, in cognitive control of affect, impulses, and needs. This reasoning, which requires experimental verification, would say that poor children overestimated the coin more because they did not scan as extensively as richer children. This narrowing of scanning would result both from *less varied perceptual experience* and also *"motivational or need" fixation*.

It is revealing to note that Bruner's (1951) prediction that structural and functional explanations of perception will converge seems to have come true. Thus Gardner and Long's work suggests a structural (cognitive control) explanation of a functional variable (values), whereas the work to which we now turn deals with the effect of a functional variable (emotions) on a structural event (recognition thresholds and perceptual discriminations).

The formal position of the new-look approach was introduced in a theoretical article by Bruner and Goodman (1947). Emphasizing the creative aspects of perception, they specified the three functions of selection, accentuation, and fixation—all of which deal with the ways the perceptual process selectively codes or attends to stimulus information. One support for this position was the report by Postman, Bruner, and McGinnies (1948) that words which are congruent with the perceiver's values (previously measured by the Allport-Vernon test of values) have lower recognition thresholds, whereas words that are not have higher recognition thresholds; values selectively sensitize the perceptions toward certain semantic content and defend against low-value meanings.

The effect of perceptual defense was reported in another study which had tremendous impact. McGinnies (1949) found that eight emotionally provocative words (e.g., whore, bitch) had a significantly higher recognition threshold and galvanic skin response (GSR), an indicator of emotional arousal, than eleven neutral words.

Some investigators have criticized McGinnies' study on the ground that it did not control for the frequency with which the critical or the neutral words occur in the common literature. Thus, Solomon and Howes (1951) present data which they claim can account for McGinnies' effect by controlling for words through the Thorndike-Lorge (1944) word count. However, Eriksen (1963, pp. 31–62) reports that the correlation between the Thorndike-Lorge frequencies over the number of correct definitions given by the subject for neutral words is 0.57, and only 0.03 for the taboo words. Therefore using this control in the recognition threshold studies is misleading. Moreover, as Eriksen pointed out, in the inspection of the scatter plots of Solomon and Howes, all the threshold difference would have to be caused by extremely infrequent and very frequent words.

Other investigators have reasoned that the perceptual defense effect was caused by a response bias—that is, suppression of perceived meaning—as if the perceiver did not believe what he saw. (For example, see Aronfreed, Messick, and Diggory, 1953.) Diggory (1956) found more of the effect if the experimenter was male and the subjects were female. Goldiamond (1962) reasons that the subject is using a stricter criterion for taboo words than neutral words; that is an application of detection theory, reported in Chapter 3 (e.g., Green & Swets, 1966).

It appears, however, that these criteria have wide variations; sometimes suppression (defense) seems to occur, at other times vigilance (see Deese, 1955). There is also controversy about whether emotional words give higher or lower thresholds (Nothman 1962; Broadbent & Gregory, 1967; Chapman & Feather, 1972; Dorfman, 1967). Eriksen (1951a, 1951b; 1954) provides a theory with a clinical and methodological perspective.

There are experiments which show that the frequency is not a sufficient condition to account for the threshold phenomena. Many investigators (Eriksen & Brown, 1956; Postman & Solomon, 1950; Spence, 1957a, 1957b) have found that stimuli have been associated with success or failure or with the relative values of the stimuli. With this type of data in mind, Eriksen goes on to offer a learning (reinforcement) interpretation of these clinical phenomena.

What is the case for linking these experimental findings to general defense mechanisms? First, we must remember that repression theory does not state that all aggressive or sex-like stimuli are automatically repressed by all or even a majority of subjects. There are wide individual differences in what kinds of stimuli are anxiety-provoking and in whether a person withdraws from or attacks anxiety-provoking situations. These differences are probably tied to the effects of the individual's past learning experiences in such situations.

Actually, as Eriksen points out, there are two broad classes of defense mechanisms, namely, repression, which should be accompanied by avoidance or higher recognition thresholds, and the group consisting of intellectualization, reaction formation, and projection, which should be accompanied by vigilance or lowered recognition thresholds. Here are some relevant experiments. In one study, Eriksen (1951a) found that psychiatric patients who exhibited a high degree of disturbance and avoidance in *word association* to words in the emotional categories of aggression, homosexuality, and dependence also showed higher recognition thresholds for the corresponding pictures as opposed to neutral pictures. As a further clarification, other studies (Eriksen, 1951b; Lazarus, Eriksen, & Fonda, 1951) found subjects who were able to interpret freely aggressive and sexual content in the Thematic Apperception Test (TAT) stories or who, in sentence completion tests, showed heightened sensitivity to hostile and sexual stimuli which were either visual or auditory. So it is not the nature of the stimulus per se which counts but the subject's characteristic mode of responding to it—whether the stimulus is a *sensitizer* or a *represser*. Furthermore, other investigators (Stein, 1953) have indicated that these characteristic modes of responding are reliable and repeatable from one set of stimuli to another.

In summing up his explanation of perceptual defense, Eriksen points out that most of these experiments present the subject with a situation which is more like a guessing game than a perceptual task. The subject has to "guess" or discriminate from inadequate cues. What the subject is likely to call up depends on relative habit strengths of various categories. Thus Eriksen is making a distinction between the *perceptual process* and the response resulting from that process. He attributes the perceptual defense data to the response variable primarily because of the lack of evidence showing the effect of learning on the perceptual process per se in these phenomena. Moreover, various studies (for example, Goldiamond & Hawkins, 1958; Goldstein, 1962) indicate that the frequency effect of Solomon and Howes (which these authors presumably thought influences the perceptual process itself) upon the recognition threshold can be obtained in the absence of any perceptual stimuli. The case is strong to attribute these phenomena to response set. "which in turn is probably due to conditioned avoidance response to the anxiety-provoking stimuli" (Eriksen, 1963, p. 57).

Cognitive Congruence Explanation of Defense

The theorizing of Bruner and Postman, Deese, and Eriksen deals with the nature of perceptual selectivity and accentuation and the functional utility of these processes in motivation and adaptive behavior. One might ask the question, as Deese did, whether it is necessary to speak of both vigilance (accentuation) and defense, or whether the postulation of one process would be sufficient and, indeed, even more correct. Whatever our theoretical explanation of perceptual selectivity is, it must be *consistent* with our general conceptualization of the perceptual process. The model we have adopted, described in Chapter 1 and emphasized consistently throughout this work, has been an *outflow* process. This model, postulating as it does that we can code only identities for which we have sets or models in central long-term storage, would have to choose the accentuation process, subsuming "defensive" phenomena under it.

It was in the context of this outflow theory that an experiment was conducted by Forgus and DeWolfe (1969). The research was designed to determine whether what has been labeled *perceptual defense* is in fact a special case of perceptual accentuation. In this study one of the present authors (Forgus) interviewed forty-nine actively hallucinating male and female schizophrenic hospital patients. The interviews were tape-recorded verbatim so that the themes of the hallucinations could be content-analyzed. A reliable scoring manual for categorizing the hallucinatory themes was constructed using the hallucinations of a representative ten males and seven females. (Interjudge reliability correlation coefficient was 0.93.)

Twenty-seven (out of the remaining thirty) patients who were still in the hospital at this stage of the study heard a short taped story which contained a composite of the themes (four) present in the hallucinations of the entire sample. In eighteen of the twenty-three subjects on whose dominant recall themes the two judges agreed, the major hallucinatory theme category predicted the dominant recall themes. Adequate controls indicated that this was not a spurious correlation.

What the study showed was that we could measure the dominant perceptual sets (or schemata) of the subjects and that these sets, in fact, *directed* perceptual selectivity. Thus selectivity was a result of active processing or sensitization rather than repression or defense. It is not so much that we have blocking but that stimulus material is categorized into the schemata existing in long-term memory. Forgus and DeWolfe (1974) cross-validated with delusional patients. That is, they found that delusional material can also be scored to predict selective perception and categorization.

While equivocation exists in much of the data, few would argue, presumably, that value or cognitive set does not play a directional role in perception. In fact, the influence of emotional salience of certain dimensions generalizes from interpersonal perception to group and ethnic perception, such as in the operation of stereotypes. We have already reported in this chapter that anti-Semitic individuals are more accurate in discriminating "Semitic" features and that South African Afrikaners exaggerate differences between white and black South Africans. In a similar way Secord, Bevan, and Katz (1956) found that prejudiced subjects, compared with less prejudiced subjects, exaggerated differences in skin color and other physical characteristics between black and white Americans.

The explanation of these perceptual accentuations of emotionally salient factors, favored here, which has also been emphasized by Tajfel (1957) with empirical support from research by Tajfel and Wilkes (1963), is that only differences of relevant criteria are accentuated. How this might work can be induced from an experiment on nonpersonal relevant stimuli conducted by Davidon (1962).

In Davidon's experiment subjects were required to judge the brightness and height of a series of gray blocks. After adaptation levels were established in the judgments of these brightnesses and heights, a tall, light block was introduced. Half of the subjects were told to reject all *lighter* blocks, while the other half were told to reject all the taller blocks. Then both groups were told to categorize heights and brightness again. Shifts in scale were associated with differences in the *relative* attributes of the standard—i.e., subjects who were given instructions to "unbalance" brightness did so while those instructed to do the same with height also acquiesced.

In Davidon's work exaggeration was induced; in the course of development it arises experientially. These kinds of response sets can be produced in a variety of ways. One powerful way, through experience, is by conditioning responses to certain stimulus dimensions—as Eriksen theorized about perceptual sensitization and inhibition. The next section deals with a dramatic demonstration, controversial as it is, of such emotional conditioning.

A very penetrating analysis by Erdelyi (1974) discusses how the perceptual defense (or vigilance) phenomena can be explained by the kind of stage-informational model we present in Chapter 1. He emphasizes that the major advantage of such a model is that it specifies multi-loci for selectivity (see also Shiffrin & Geister, 1973). His major belief is that storage is achieved through *control commands* from the central system. This control command signals whether processing should stop at a particular stage or continue.

Erdelyi then described various stages—such as eye fixation and sensory transduction—at which these commands can operate. He believes, however, that the most important stage for selection is the transition between iconic and short-term memory. Visual research by Haber (1966) has suggested that this is the major locus of the effect of instruction-produced selective sets in the encoding stage of processing. He reasons plausibly that there are also "chronic" sets from LTM which can have these selective functions. An experiment by Erdelyi and Appelbaum (1973) supports this notion. Subjects who were members of a Jewish organization were asked to look at a circular array of neutral pictures, under three different conditions. In two of them either the Star of David or the swastika was at the center of the array. In the third array a picture of a window was at the center. It was found that there was a lower rate of processing in the first two emotionally charged arrays—that is, when viewing these arrays, subjects mentioned seeing fewer neutral pictures during the single fixation time of 200 msec. Interestingly enough, reactions to the two emotional arrays (with the Star of David or the swastika) did not differ from one another. Thus, the presence of an emotional stimulus can disrupt (i.e., selectively inhibit) the processing of other information. This study is also congruent with the results of Forgus and DeWolfe (1974) concerning the selective-coding model of delusional patients.

Subception and Subliminal Events   Lazarus and McCleary (1951) conducted a fascinating study which, like studies of Eriksen mentioned in the last
section, attempted to determine how association to perceptual stimuli develops. But their explanation was quite different from Eriksen's. In their study of
subception they started with nonsense syllables so as to control as completely
as possible for past experience. The researchers conditioned five out of ten of
these nonsense syllables to a GSR by shocking the subject after the five
syllables had been presented visually. Then the authors tachistoscopically
exposed each nonsense syllable at duration levels such that the verbal recognitions were 50 percent correct. The complete results are presented in Figure
15-4.

The result of greatest interest is the difference between the two mean wrong
(mw) categories. In every case the shock syllable gave a significantly greater
GSR than the nonshock syllable, suggesting "subception" and a perceptual
defense.

Much debate has centered on the problem of perceptual defense and subception. Eriksen (1956a) has probably made the strongest criticism. For him, the
subception phenomenon results because one of the variations (the verbal-report
range) is held constant while variables in the other system (the GSR) are
measured. Eriksen reasons statistically that if two response systems are correlated with the same stimulus and with each other, holding one constant will lead
to the remaining responses being correlated with the stimulus. (This is usually the
case but is not necessarily so.)

Ranken (1956) put the alternative hypotheses of Eriksen and Lazarus to a
critical experimental test. After thresholds were determined, some of the three-
letter nonsense syllables used were conditioned to the GSR. The criterion for conditioning was that the average amplitude of the GSR for the shock syllables had to
be three times as great as the average GSR for nonshock syllables. Then the
standard subception experiment was essentially repeated with the syllables
presented for varying exposure times, from subliminal to supraliminal. GSR and
verbal reports were recorded. As shown in Figure 15-5, the results indicated,
first, that there was heightened GSR for the shock syllables. Second, the GSR for
shock syllables was much greater than the GSR for nonshock syllables as the
duration of exposure was increased. We might say that with increasing duration
of exposure the subjects were able to extract more information from the stimulus. Third, it seems that the GSR was related to the actual reporting of shock
syllables and not to the probability of shock syllables occurring (this is seen in
Figure 15-6). Thus we see that the correct reporting of shock syllables gave the
greatest GSR for all exposure durations.

The debate as to what causes the so-called subception effect has not been
settled. Eriksen (1960) points out that there are three possibilities:

A Stimulus→perceptual process→verbal response→GSR
B Stimulus→GSR→perceptual process
C Stimulus→perceptual process→GSR

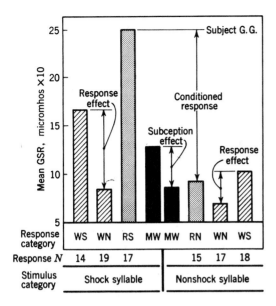

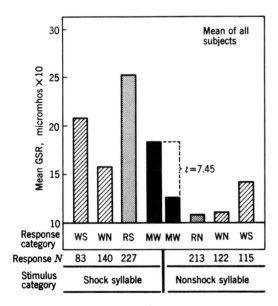

Figure 15-4 GSR data from the final test period. WS = wrong, shock; RS = right, shock; RN = right, no shock; WN = wrong, no shock; MW = mean wrong; WS = wrong, shock. *(After Lazarus and McCleary, 1951, p. 119.)*

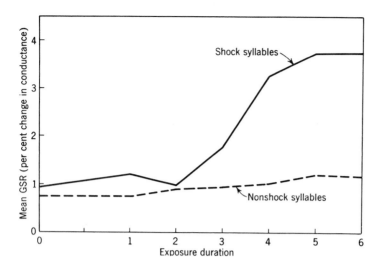

Figure 15-5 Results of a subception experiment. Actual durations were different for each subject. Duration 3 was longest, giving a zero probability of a correct verbal report in preliminary testing; duration 6 was shortest, giving 1.0 probability of report. Durations 1 and 2 were one-half and three-quarters, respectively, of duration 3.

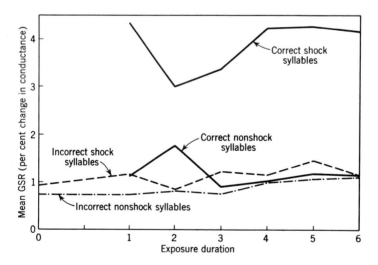

Figure 15-6 Results of subception experiment. *(After Ranken, 1956.)*

Eriksen goes on: If A were the explanation, the subception effect could not have been obtained. If B were true and GSR were held constant, we would not find a correlation between stimulus and verbal report. Eriksen did find such a correlation, and thus alternative C is the most plausible explanation.

Further Considerations   It does seem from the foregoing that the subject can make some kind of discrimination of stimuli even when he does not report them accurately. There must therefore be some basis for this discrimination. The nature of this basis is suggested by an experiment of Bricker and Chapanis (1953), whose work indicates that subliminal presentation of syllables does convey some information to the subjects. By varying the similarity of the nonsense syllables, they found that on the incorrect trials the subjects guessed the correct syllables in fewer than a chance number of trials. Similarity was varied by altering the letters used in the syllables. Syllables which were more similar to the shock syllables also elicited the GSR more frequently than syllables which were less similar.

Dixon (1971) explains the subception phenomenon in terms similar to Erdelyi's explanation of defense and vigilance. That is, only some of the information is coded out of iconic into short-term memory. There is selective obstruction of information processing.

From the perception of intentionality to the perception of personality and emotionally relevant information, we have seen that we can specify both the informational components of the stimulus and the stage at which the processing terminates (or is disrupted) to explain the results.

SUMMARY

As a takeoff from the preceding chapter, this chapter began with a description of phenomenal causality. The relevant principles of spatiotemporal and configurational relationships were theorized by Michotte and Heider to be influential in the perception of integrative and segregative emotions and intents. This led to a more general discussion of person perception or visual cognition, where the variables of movement patterns, temporal sequence, and interpersonal representation were listed. Nonverbal cues of immediacy and relaxation (again related to gestalt principles) were seen as important signs to positiveness, potency, and responsiveness.

From perception of personal characteristics we proceeded to universal and cultural determiners. We described a model, the facial affect program, for accounting for universal discrimination of facial patterns of emotional expression, how different visual environments in different cultures produce different visual inference tendencies, how group experience can produce differences in visual scanning, and how experience in general provides differential sets or schemata against which incoming information is always coded congruently. These are the ways perceptual accentuation subsumes "defensive" phenomena.

Finally, in considering emotional characteristics and stereotypes, we made the point that relevant dimensions are shifted in the direction of the perceiver's bias which might be situationally or (long-term) experientially determined. Our stage-information-processing model, which specifies that information or specific meaning can be terminated or disrupted at different stages (through central control commands), is used to explain these latter phenomena.

Chapter 16

Retrospect and Prospect

In Chapter 1 we discussed the intricate and multidirectional relationships between perception, learning, and thinking. Almost the entire book has provided examples of how the information-extraction process of perception is determined not only by wired-in physiological mechanisms but also by processes which are affected by memory and sets. These, of course, involve learning and the thought process.

In a recent book, Bryant (1974) has brilliantly demonstrated, through sound experiments, how early perceptual abilities guide the growth of the child's conceptual development. Departing somewhat from Piaget, he notes the child's dependence on environmental frameworks for making adequate judgments about his environment. Since the child is limited in his ability to make absolute judgments, he relies on relative judgments for his discriminations. And the way he forms relationships about two objects is to relate each to the environment. This, of course, means that the child (4 to 8 years of age) is capable of making inferences, an ability denied by Piaget. Thus for Bryant, inference from concrete perceptual experience guides the child's development of conceptual, logical, and thinking abilities. Such later developing abilities as the capacity for understanding conservation and reciprocity, described later in this section, are initially founded on the child's dependence of perceiving in the context of environmental framework. It is interesting to restate here our observation in Chapter 13 that spatial perception also develops from field dependence to relative field independence. In both cases internal, symbolic representations become more complex and determining of perceptual and cognitive abilities.

Furthermore, Lindsay and Norman (1972) and Solso (1973) have presented vivid compendiums of the tremendous domain that cognitive psychology now covers. Ten years ago few psychologists were conducting actual experiments on cognition. Now, study of cognition spans the entire field of psychology, from sensory perception to human motivation and clinical psychology. It thus seems fitting to end this book with a description of some work on human motivation, emotion, and cognitive style which ties together so beautifully cognitive and affective processes—two key areas of psychology and adaptive behavior.

COGNITIVE TRANSFORMATION OF NEEDS TO MOTIVES

The major thesis of the cognitive orientation is that the particular developmental level of the cognitive structure will determine the direction and intensity of the individual's motivational action as well as the uniqueness or distinctiveness of his personality pattern. A good example of this principle is the demonstration of L. Kohlberg (1969) that children's goals with respect to moral behavior and causal attribution depend on their level of cognitive development or conceptual understanding. Thus, for example, a child does not develop real feelings of compassion or empathy until he has developed the cognitive principle called *reciprocity,* which in turn requires the understanding of the reversible operations, as specified by Piaget. The research indicates, of course, why there are individual and perhaps even cultural differences with respect to when this ability comes. It is highly unlikely that it comes before the age of 8 years in the average child. Before the development of this understanding, moral concerns are rather self-centered and involve considerations of being caught. It is only after the child understands that other individuals may feel the same way he does, and this does not come until the notion of reciprocity has developed, that the child will have genuine feelings of compassion. Most of us have observed this in our own existence.

Perhaps the most systematic examples of the relationship between cognition and motivation exist in the work on cognitive style. *Cognitive style* is defined as the particular way the individual approaches the environment and copes with the tasks of life as well as with anxiety. Our first example is an extension of Wulf's (1922) work on memory changes.

Sharpeners and Levelers   Individuals who are sharpeners are more *cognitively differentiated* than those who are levelers. As such, they can cope with a wider range of environmental information, and are therefore more adaptive. Not only are these individuals more cognitively *articulated,* but in the setting of their goals, they tend to be more *excitement-oriented.* Conversely, individuals who are levelers tend to seek *security.* They appear to look for the familiar and the predictable; unlike the sharpeners, they have difficulty with uncertainty and tend, therefore, to be more stereotyped, "tribalistic," and closed-minded. Another major distinguishing characteristic is that sharpeners expend more effort in the pursuit of their goals and tend to have more intense energy expenditure and emotional reactions. (See Holzman & Gardner, 1960.)

It is easy to see from the above description that sharpeners probably expose themselves more to situations of insecurity, anxiety, and personal danger. On the other hand, while levelers tend to live a safer life, should they be thrown into a stressful situation which they had not anticipated, they will be more likely to have a "breakdown." In sum, while sharpeners are more creative and sometimes act according to the rubric "creative people are crazy," they will in general present themselves as individuals who are more interesting and more creative and who represent a wider diversity and unpredictability of style. The levelers, by contrast, are probably in certain ways more dependable, more conventional, and therefore more predictable.

Narrow and Extensive Scanners A second major variable in cognitive style, also growing out of research in perception and previously described, is the concept of extensive and narrow scanning. This concept has also been applied again to motivation and ego-coping style by Gardner and Long (1962a, 1962b). Essentially the extensiveness of scanning is measured by the number of *centrations* that an individual exhibits when he looks at a circle. These centrations or fixations, during a period of time, are counted while the individual looks at a circle and are correlated with his accuracy of estimating the diameter of the circle. Extensive scanners will have a higher frequency of centration time, and they are not only more accurate in estimating the diameters of circles, but also show less tendency toward the concentric-circle illusion and toward overestimating the diameter of circular objects. That is, their positive constant error is lower.

Extensive scanners are more accurate and more flexible and show greater differentiation in their extraction of information from the stimulus and environment. In addition, they tend to be less impulsive than the narrow scanners.

Finally, narrow scanners are largely dependent upon stimulation, are more stimulus-bound, and show a narrower range of incentives. Furthermore, since they demand more immediate gratification, they are less likely to expend as much energy as do the extensive scanners. That is to say, narrow scanners have less reserve and are more likely to act out than the extensive scanners. We see in general that extensive scanners have a more effective way of coping both with affective needs and with diverse stimulation.

Field-Independent and Field-Dependent Individuals The final variable in cognitive style that we shall discuss, designated by Witkin et al. (1962) as part of the larger class of psychological differentiations, came out of the work on the perception of the vertical and its relationship to the figure-embedded task.

Field dependence and field independence were described in Chapter 13. Field-independent individuals have more articulated or more differentiated cognitive structure. These individuals also tend to be more analytical, have a frame of reference which has a wide perspective, see the self as being more differentiated, and see other people as being more differentiated as well. Consequently, their interpersonal relationships are characterized by a wider range of goals, their interpersonal perceptions are more likely to be more accurate, they will expend more effort, and, finally, they are less likely to exhibit such primitive defense mechanisms as a repression or denial. Like the extensive scanners and sharpeners, they are more likely to be characterized as information seekers. Furthermore, they will attempt to confront a problem rather than avoid it.

EMOTIONAL COMPONENTS OF COGNITIVE SET

The writings of Schachter (1964, pp. 49–80) and Schachter and Singer (1962) have contributed much to the understanding of how cognition is important not only in the direction of motivation, but also in providing a frame of reference for interpreting emotional behavior.

In their article, Schachter and Singer point out that two variables interact to produce a particular emotional effect, the *cognitive expectancy* and the *physiological arousal*. For example, they have found that when individuals are given either epinephrine or a placebo and then placed in a pleasant situation, the individuals who were given the arouser of the sympathetic nervous system are more likely to display euphoric behavior than those given the placebo. Similarly, when individuals are given either epinephrine or no medication and then placed in a situation which will make them angry, the individuals given epinephrine are more likely to display anger, brought on by frustration, than the individuals given no medication. A third demonstration involved giving individuals barbiturates which depressed the sympathetic nervous system and then putting them in a cheating situation. It was found in this case that the ones who were given the placebo were less likely to cheat than those who were given the barbiturates. In other words, dulling of the sympathetic nervous system is likely to depress one's feelings of anxiety or guilt and, therefore, is likely not to inhibit the tendency to be tempted by a cheating situation—in this case, cheating on an examination.

The most fascinating application of this two-factor theory of cognition and arousal with respect to emotional reaction was conducted by Schachter and Latané (1964). The essential design of their experiment took the following sequence. Inmates of a prison were classified into two groups, *criminally psychopathic* and *nonpsychopathic*. Individuals in each group were required to learn a mental maze. Without being told, subjects were always shocked on specific wrong "choices." The experimenters were really interested in finding out whether there would be increased avoidance of the wrong choices on subsequent trials—that is, whether a typical avoidance-learning curve would be obtained. Such a typical avoidance-learning curve did occur for the nonpsychopathic group, but *not* for psychopathic criminals.

To investigate further why the psychopath did not seem to respond to a shock, which presumably should give rise to some kind of emotional reaction, assuming that a shock is painful, the investigators repeated the foregoing experiment. However, now all subjects performed after being given a significant dose of epinephrine which, as noted above, acts to increase the arousability of the sympathetic branch of the autonomic nervous system. The effect of such chemical treatment is to make the individual more sensitive to emotional stimulation.

There was a rather drastic reversal of the previous results. In this condition the psychopathic criminals showed a decidedly steep reduction of errors. That is, by contrast with the neutral conditions, the psychopaths learned avoidance much faster under epinephrine, while the nonpsychopaths learned avoidance more slowly under epinephrine.

Schachter and Singer (1962), following Schachter's two-factor theory of emotions, had previously shown the interaction between cognitive definition and physiological arousal and lowered arousal. Thus, when individuals are led to expect euphoria, it is more likely to occur when they are given epinephrine than a placebo. Similarly, when they are placed in a situation which frustrates them, anger is more likely to occur in the subjects which have been given epinephrine. Conversely, when subjects (college students) are placed in a cheating-prone situation, those who are given chlorpromazine or barbiturates, which depress the sympathetic activity, are more likely to cheat than those given a placebo. The presumed reason is that awareness of anxiety, which acts as a check to cheating, is decreased by the activation of these drugs which depress emotional reactivity.

To return to the experiment with the psychopathic criminals, the explanation of Schachter and Latané is that under normal circumstances the criminal psychopath has a *constitutionally* hyperactive tendency to experience emotionality. It is, of course, an open question as to what produces this hyperactivity, although the authors tend to favor a genetic explanation. This hyperactivity has led to an inhibition, lest they be overwhelmed by emotional stimulation. When, however, artificial doses of epinephrine are introduced, hyperactivity becomes apparent. Conversely, normal individuals, who are already reactive to optimal emotional stimulation, now have their performance disrupted because they are overaroused.

A somewhat modified interpretation of the above experiment would focus on considering the emotional stimuli as providing *cognitive information* as well. Thus, it might be argued that the psychopaths have either not learned to code the emotional significance of pain, or were exposed to severe pain when they were quite young and, therefore, had to learn to block against the effect of pain. This could occur either in children who, for example, were pampered and therefore never really learned to attend to guilt-provoking situations, or were introduced to severe conditions of anxiety when quite young. The latter situation could occur through severe punishment or emotional deprivation. Thus, a lack of opportunity for learning to process the painful component of emotional stimuli or having to ward off emotional stimuli because of their overwhelming nature could cause inappropriate and maladaptive behavior in the psychopaths.

This cognitive interpretation of emotional reaction is supported by the conceptualizing and data of Valins (1966, 1972). In one experiment subjects were presented with pictures of females; the subjects were male. While the subjects were looking at these pictures, earphones attached to their ears provided them with auditory stimulation as well. The subjects were told that they were listening to their own heart beats. For some of the pictures, the experimenter arbitrarily sent in exaggerated "heart beats." These were not true heart beats, however. Following this experiment, the subjects were asked to rate the pictures with respect to "esthetic" value. The subjects rated the pictures associated with the exaggerated heart rate as being most attractive as if they were justifying their presumed greater arousal in the presence of those pictures. What is even more remarkable is the fact that even after the subjects were told about the deception, they held to their original esthetic opinions. It appears that supposed heightened arousal led the subjects to pay closer attention to those stimuli which were so emphasized and they, therefore, found evidence to support their perceived-feeling state. Once this evidence is obtained, it is likely to remain.

In a somewhat more complicated experiment, Valins and Ray (1967) were able to show that the perception of *decreased* emotional reaction carries significant, cognitive information. Subjects were shown a sequence of slides which depicted snakes. On subsequent slides the snakes were apparently depicted in more menacing postures. Bogus heart rates were again fed back to the subjects' ears. However, dispersed among the slides of the snakes there were slides with the word SHOCKED marked on them. When these slides appeared, the subjects were given an electric shock which increased in intensity upon subsequent presentations. These increased shocks were also accompanied by an apparent increase in the heart rate. However, the subjects' actual heart rates while viewing the subsequent snake slides remained the same. It is as if the subjects could say to themselves, "I was not afraid of snakes," even though the snake posture became more fear-provoking. The subject could check this because his attributed heart rate for the increasing shock, did, in fact, increase. Subjects in the control group, where the increased intensity was attributed to loud noises, did exhibit more fear toward the snakes. This fact was revealed in a test where the experimental subjects were more likely to hold rattlesnakes than the controlled subjects. To summarize the view of Valins and his associates, we can say the following: "If my heart is pounding, I must be angry, afraid, or euphoric." Thus, cognitions appear to be a sufficient condition for an emotional response.

R. S. Lazarus (1966) has also shown how *cognitive intervention* can be used to direct or alter an emotional or feeling state. His idea is that the fear or anxiety reaction to stress can be reduced by the introduction of effective cognitive controls or interventions. It is as if the subject were talking to himself.

Two demonstrations are described by Lazarus and his associates. In the first one, subjects viewed a film during which adolescent youths were shown with their penises cut with rather deep incisions. During the viewing of this movie, the subjects were concurrently exposed to a running commentary (auditory) which denied that the operation was painful. This denial was effective in reducing heart autonomic reaction to this fear-provoking stimulation. Note, however, that providing the denial intervention before the viewing as well as throughout is more effective than just providing the commentary during the viewing. It is as if the cognitive preparation helps the subject to deal with a distressful situation. In a subsequent experiment, subjects were shown a "safety" film during which accidents were depicted. This time intellectualization as well as denial were used as cognitive intervention. During intellectualization there was a rather neutral, unanimated description of the facts, and again we can see that the cognitive controls are effective in reducing anxiety as measured by skin conductance—in this case apparent intellectualization having a stronger effect than denial.

The relationship between cognition and emotions, using more phenomenological, clinical, or projective procedures, has also been described by Maddi (1970) and Breger (1969). Maddi deals with the search for meaning which he contends to be the central problem of human motivation. He reminds us that certain cognitive functions—such as perception, judgment, and imagination—are as much a part of being human as the need for contact and physiological nourishment. He believes, further, that the *core* personality is much the same for all human beings since it is based on these psychophysiological needs and cognitive foundations. People differ because of the peripheral personalities which they develop and which depend primarily on the effects of socialization experiences and practices. Maddi considers that the "ideal" of peripheral personality is one which is effective in dealing with stress because it is congruent with the basic potential core. On the other hand, the "nonideal" peripheral personality, since it is not congruent with the potential core of the personality, tends to be premorbid and becomes pathological in the face of stress. This is so, claims Maddi, because the "nonideal" peripheral personality has had the kind of socialization experience which is more likely to predispose the individual to concerns with security and anxiety (we may also add conflict). We add that there is a greater tendency toward conflict in these individuals because of the existence of noncongruence between psychobiological predisposition and psychosocial actualization. Clearly, there will be less likelihood of conflict if the effects of learning are more congruent with what we may consider to be the inherent nature of the human being.

An implication of Maddi's approach is that experience should produce the kind of cognitive skill which permits the individual to satisfy the basic demands of being human without undue concerns with security and anxiety. The work of Valins and Lazarus shows how this can be effected in a relatively short-term way. What is required is a consideration of ways during the developmental history of the individual in which this kind of cognitive intervention can become a strong internal part of the individual.

Louis Breger, in discussing the information-processing aspects of dreams, also points out that long-term memory contains not only stored facts but meaningful schemata which have emotional components. In attempting to analyze the theme sequences in dreams, and relating them to current concerns of the subject, he gives examples of how the relatively *primary-process* thinking, which is characterized by a relatively loose, surrealistic structure, represents attempts on the part of the subject to integrate current conflicts, anxieties, threats, and other problems into the existing schemata about the world and the subject's relation to it. This does not mean, of course, that the structure remains the same, but, rather, that any slight changes in the structure must be incorporated within the dominant themes and salient beliefs of the existing cognitive structure. In this way the individual continues to get meaning out of his experiences, attempts to cope with new uncertainties or threats, and grows and expands his consciousness.

Finally, in the work already referred to, Forgus and DeWolfe (1969, 1974) have shown how fantasy material from patients in mental hospitals—such as hallucinations and delusions—can be reliably scored to provide valid indices of the dominant cognitive themes the subjects possess with respect to the motives of competence, interpersonal relationships, sex, and self. Moreover, these themes reveal not only the dominant beliefs and the motives, but also environmental presses. In this way we are able to determine what some of the dominant conflicts of the individual are likely to be. For example, quite understandably, we find that the overwhelming majority of patients in mental hospitals view themselves as wanting and liking people (their motives) but perceive most others to be unfriendly toward them (the press). What they probably do not know is that they frequently exhibit unattractive behavior in attempts to get what they want. So, their perception of the press is probably quite accurate. It is also true that patients in mental hospitals generally behave in ways which the public finds unacceptable, or in such ways which lead to nonattainment of personal goals. One way of assisting such individuals, both preventively and therapeutically, would be to teach them to consider alternative ways of formulating their goals and of attempting to satisfy these goals. Clearly, teaching alternative ways of formulating or looking for satisfaction is very much an attempt to broaden the perspective of cognitive structures. This, indeed, may be the very essence of adaptive behavior and mental health.

In Chapter 1 we defined perception as a superset with learning and thinking as subsets. We have just seen that cognition as a superset also interacts within (sub?) sets of motivation and emotion. Are we beginning to integrate human processes scientifically? Where will we be ten years from now? The prospect appears very exciting. Considering perception as a *constructive* process certainly seems to have power to open up other problem areas of psychology.

Bibliography

Adams, O. S., Fitts, P. M., Rappaport, M., & Weinstein, M. Relations among some measures of pattern discriminability. *Journal of Experimental Psychology,* 1954, **48,** 81–85.

Aiken, E. G. Auditory discrimination learning: Prototype storage and distinctive features detection mechanism. *Perception and Psychophysics,* 1969, **6,** 95–96.

Allport, F. *Social psychology,* Boston: Houghton Mifflin, 1924.

Alpern, M. Metacontrast. *Journal of the Optical Society of America,* 1953, **43,** 648–657.

Ames, A. *Some demonstrations concerned with the origin and nature of our sensations: A lab manual.* Hanover, N.H.: Dartmouth Eye Inst., 1946.

Ames, A. Visual perception and the rotating trapezoidal window. *Psychological Monographs,* 1951, No. 324.

Argyle, M., & Dean, J. Eye contact, distance and affiliation. *Sociometry,* 1965, **28,** 289–304.

Arnoult, M. D. Prediction of perceptual responses from structural characteristics of the stimulus. *Perception and Motor Skills,* 1960, **11,** 261–268.

Aronfreed, J. M., Messick, S. A., & Diggory, J. C. Re-examining emotionality and perceptual defense. *Journal of Personality,* 1953, **21,** 517–528.

Asch, S. E., & Witkin, H. A. Studies in space orientation. I: Perception of the upright with displaced visual fields. *Journal of Experimental Psychology,* 1948, **38,** 325–337. (a)

Asch, S. E., & Witkin, H. A. Studies in space orientation. II: Perception of the upright with displaced visual fields and with body tilted. *Journal of Experimental Psychology,* 1948, **38,** 455. (b)

Attneave, F. Some informational aspects of visual perception. *Psychological Review,* 1954, **61,** 183–193.

Attneave, F. Symmetry, information, and memory for patterns. *American Journal of Psychology,* 1955, **68,** 209–222.

Attneave, F. Physical determinants of the judged complexity of shapes. *Journal of Experimental Psychology,* 1957, **53,** 221–227. (a)

Attneave, F. Transfer of experience with a class schema to identification learning of patterns and shapes. *Journal of Experimental Psychology,* 1957, **54,** 81–88. (b)

Attneave, F. Perceptions and related areas. In S. Koch (Ed.), *Psychology: A study of a science.* New York: McGraw-Hill, 1962.

Attneave, F. The determination of perceived tridimensional criteria. *Perception and Psychophysics,* 1969, **6,** 391–396.

Attneave, F., & Arnoult, M. D. The quantitative study of shape and pattern perception. *Psychological Bulletin,* 1956, **53,** 452–471.

Attneave, F., & Frost, R. The discrimination of perceived tridimensional orientation by minimum criteria. *Perception and Psychophysics,* 1969, **6,** 391–396.

Attneave, F., & Reid, K. W. Voluntary control of frame of reference and shape equivalence under head rotation. *Journal of Experimental Psychology,* 1968, **78,** 153–159.

Aubert, H. Die Bewegungsem Findung. *Archiv. für die Gesante Physiologie,* 1886, **39,** 452–471.

Averbach, I., & Coriell, A. S. Short-term memory in vision. *Bell System Technical Journal,* 1961, **40,** 309–328.

Bales, J. F., & Follansbee, G. L., The aftereffect of the perception of curved lines. *Journal of Experimental Psychology,* 1935, **18,** 499–503.

Barlow, H. B. Dark-adaptation: A new hypothesis. *Vision Research,* 1964, **4,** 47–57.

Baron, J., & Thurston, I. An analysis of the word superiority effect. *Cognitive Psychology,* 1973, **4,** 207–228.

Batteau, D. W. The role of the pinna in human localization. *Proceedings of the Royal Society of London,* Series B, 1967, **168,** 158–180.

Bear, G. Figural goodness and the predictability of figural elements. *Perception and Psychophysics,* 1973, **13,** 32–40.

Beck, J. Apparent spatial location and the perception of lightness. *Journal of Experimental Psychology,* 1965, **60,** 170–179.

Beck, J. Contrast and assimilation in lightness judgements. *Perception and Psychophysics,* 1966, **1,** 342–344. (a)

Beck, J. Perceptual grouping produced by change in orientation and shape. *Science,* 1966, **154,** 538–540. (b)

Beck, J. Effect of orientation and of shape similarity on perceptual grouping. *Perception and Psychophysics,* 1966, **1,** 300–302. (c)

Beck, J. Perceptual grouping produced by line figures. *Perception and Psychophysics,* 1967, **2,** 491–495.

Beck, J. Lightness and orientation. *American Journal of Psychology,* 1969, **82,** 359–366.

Beck, J. Surface lightness and cues for the illumination. *American Journal of Psychology,* 1971, **84,** 1–11.

Beck, J., & Gibson, J. J. The relation of apparent shape to apparent slant in the perception of objects. *Journal of Experimental Psychology,* 1955, **50,** 125–133.

Békésy, von, G. The vibration of the cochlear partition in anatomical preparations and in models of the inner ear. *Journal of the Acoustical Society of America,* 1949, **21,** 233–245.

Békésy, von, G. Current status of theories of hearing. *Science,* 1956, **123,** 779–783.

Békésy, von, G. *Experiments in hearing.* New York: McGraw-Hill, 1960.

Békésy, von, G. *Sensory inhibition.* Princeton, N.J.: Princeton University Press, 1967.

Benson, C., & Yonas, A. Development of sensitivity to static pictorial depth information. *Perception and Psychophysics,* 1973, **13,** 361–366.

Bergman, R., & Gibson, J. J. The negative after-effects of the perception of a surface slanted on the third dimension. *American Journal of Psychology,* 1959, **72,** 364.

Berlyne, D. E. Attention to change. *British Journal of Psychology,* 1951, **42,** 269–278.

Berlyne, D. E. Attention. In E. Canterette and M. Friedman (Eds.), *Handbook of perception,* Vol. **1.** *Historical and philosophical roots of perception.* New York: Academic, 1973.

Bexton, W. H., Heron, W., & Scott, T. H. Effects of decrease variation in the sensory environment. *Canadian Journal of Psychology,* 1954, **8,** 70–76.

Bierderman, I. Human performance in contingent information processing tasks. Tech. Rep. No. 3, 1966, Human Performance Center, University of Michigan.

Bitterman, M. E., Krauskopf, J., & Hochberg, J. E. Threshold for visual form: A diffusion model. *American Journal of Psychology,* 1954, **67,** 205–219.

Blessing, W. W., Landauer, A. A., & Coltheart, M. The effect of false perspective cues on distance and size judgements: An examination of the invariance hypothesis. *American Journal of Psychology,* 1967, **60,** 250–256.

Bolles, R. C., & Bailey, D. E. Importance of object recognition in size constancy. *Journal of Experimental Psychology,* 1956, **51,** 222–225.

Bond, E. Form perception in the infant. *Psychological Bulletin,* 1972, **77,** 225–245.

Boring, E. G. *Sensation and perception in the history of experimental psychology.* New York: Appleton-Century-Crofts, 1942.

Boring, E. G. *A history of experimental psychology.* New York: Appleton-Century-Crofts, 1950.

Borjesson, E., & Hofsten, von, C. Spatial determinants of depth perception in two-dot motion patterns. *Perception and Psychophysics,* 1972, **11,** 263–268.

Bourdon, B. *La perception visuelle de l'espace.* Paris: Schleicher, 1902.

Bower, T. G. R. Discrimination of depth in premotor infants. *Science,* 1964, **1,** 368.

Bower, T. G. R. Stimulus variables determining space perception in infants. *Science,* 1965, **149,** 88–89.

Bower, T. G. R. Slant perception and shape constancy in infants. *Science,* 1966, **151,** 832–834. (a)

Bower, T. G. R. The visual world of infants. *Scientific American,* 1966, **215,** 80–92. (b)

Bower, T. G. R. The object in the world of the infant. *Scientific American,* 1971, **225,** 30–35.

Bower, T. G. R., Broughton, J. M., & Moore, M. K. Infant responses to approaching objects: An indicator of response to distance variables. *Perception and Psychophysics,* 1970, **9,** 193–196.

Bower, T. G. R., Broughton, J., & Moore, M. K. The development of the object concept as manifested in the tracking behavior of infants between 7 and 20 weeks of age. *Journal of Experimental Child Psychology,* 1971, **11,** 182–193.

Boyle, D. G. A Contribution to the study of phenomenal causation. *Quarterly Journal of Experimental Psychology,* 1960, **12,** 171–179.

Braunstein, M. L., & Payne, J. W. Perspective and the rotating trapezoid. *Journal of the Optical Society of America,* 1968, **58,** 399–403.

Breese, B. B. On inhibition. *Psychological Monographs,* 1899, **3,** No. 1 (Whole No. 11).

Breger, L. (Ed.) *Cognitive psychology.* Englewood Cliffs, N.J.: Prentice-Hall, 1969.

Brennan, W. M., Ames, E. W., & Moore, R. W. Age differences in infants' attention to patterns of different complexities. *Science,* 1966, **151,** 354–366.

Bricker, P. D., & Chapanis, H. Do incorrectly perceived stimuli convey some information? *Psychological Review,* 1953, **60,** 181–188.

Bridgeman, B. Metacontrast and lateral inhibition. *Psychological Review,* 1971, **78,** 528–539.

Bridgen, R. F. A tachistoscopic study of the differentiation of perception. *Psychological Monographs,* 1933, **44,** (1) 153–166.

Brindley, G. S. *Physiology of the retina and visual pathway.* London: E. Arnold, 1970.

Brindley, G. S., & Merton, T. A. The absence of position in the human eye. *Journal of Physiology,* 1960, **53,** 127–130.

Broadbent, D. E. *Perception and communication.* New York: Pergamon, 1958.

Broadbent, D. E. Stimulus set and response sets: Two kinds of selective attention. In D. I. Mostofsky (Ed.), *Attention: Contemporary theory and analysis.* New York: Appleton-Century-Crofts, 1970.

Broadbent, D. E., & Gregory, M. Perception of emotionally toned words. *Nature,* 1967, **215,** 518–584.

Broota, K. D., & Epstein, W. The time it takes to make vertical size distance judgements. *Perception and Psychophysics,* 1973, **14,** 358–364.

Brosgole, L. An analysis of induced motion. NAVTRADEVCEN, LH-48, U.S. Naval Training Device Center, Port Washington, N.Y., 1966.

Brosgole, L. C., Cristal, L., & Carpenter, O. The role of eye movements in the perception of visually induced motion. *Perception and Psychophysics,* 1968, **3,** 166–168.

Brown, D. R., & Owens, D. H. The metrics of visual form; methodological dispepsin. *Psychological Bulletin,* 1967, **68,** 243–259.

Brown, J. F. The visual perception of velocity. *Psychologische Forschung,* 1931, **14,** 199–232. (a)

Brown, J. F. The thresholds for visual movement. *Psychologische Forschung,* 1931, **14,** 249–269. (b)

Brown, J. F., & Voth, A. C. The path of seen movement as a function of the vector field. *American Journal of Psychiatry,* 1937, **49,** 543–563.

Brown, J. L. Flicker and intermittent stimulation. In C. H. Graham (Ed.), *Vision and visual perception.* New York: Wiley, 1965, 251–320.

Brown, R. H. Velocity discrimination and the intensity time relationship. *Journal of the Optical Society of America,* 1955, **45,** 189–192.

Brugge, J. F., Dubrovsky, N. A., Aitkin, L. M., & Anderson, D. J. Sensitivity of single neurons in auditory cortex of cat to binaural tonal stimulation. Effects of varying interaural time and intensity. *Journal of Neurophysiology,* 1969, **32,** 1005–1024.

Bruner, J. *The process of education.* Cambridge, Mass.: Harvard, 1961.

Bruner, J. S. Personality and perception. In R. R. Blake and G. V. Ramsay (Eds.), *Perception: An approach to personality.* New York: Ronald, 1951.

Bruner, J. S. On perceptual readiness. *Psychological Review,* 1957 *64,* 123–152.

Bruner, J. S., & Goodman, C. C. Value and need as organizing factors in perception. *Journal of Abnormal and Social Psychology,* 1947, **42,** 33–44.

Bruner, J. S., & Tagiuri, R. The perception of people. In G. Lindzey (Ed.), *Handbook of social psychology.* Reading, Mass. Addison-Wesley, 1954.

Brunswik, E. Zur Entwicklung der Albedowahrnehmung. *Zeitschrift für Psychology,* 1929, **109,** 40–115.

Brunswik, E. Distal focusing of perception: Size constancy in a representative sample of situations. *Psychological Monographs,* 1944, No. 254.

Brunswik, E. *Systematic and representative design of psychological experiments, with results in physical and social perception.* Berkeley: Univ. of California Press, 1947.

Brunswik, E. Historical and thematic relations of psychology to other sciences. *Scientific Monographs,* 1956, **83,** 151–161.

Brunswik, E. (Ed.), et al. Untersuchungen über Wahrnehmung Gegenstände. *Archiv für die Gesamte Psychologie,* 1933, **88,** 377–628.

Bryant, P. *Perception and Understanding in Children.* New York: Basic Books, 1974.

Burzlaff, W. Methodologische Beiträge zum Problem der Farbenkonstanz. *Zeitschrift für Psychologie,* 1931, **119,** 177–235.

Caldwell, E. C., & Hall, V. C. Distinctive feature vs. prototype learning re-examined. *Journal of Experimental Psychology,* 1970, **83,** 7–12.

Cameron, D. E., Levy, L., Ban, T., & Rubenstein, L. Sensory deprivation; effects upon the functioning humans in space systems. In B. E. Flahery (Ed.), *Psychophysiological aspects of space flight.* New York: Columbia, 1961, 225–237.

Campbell, D. T., Segall, M. H., & Herskovitz, M. J. Cultural differences in the perception of geometric illusion. *Science,* 1963, **139,** 769–771.

Campbell, F. W., & Rushton, W. A. H. Measurement of the scotopic pigment in the living human eye. *Journal of Physiology,* 1955, **130,** 131–147.

Canestrari, R., & Farne, M. Depth cues and apparent oscillatory motion. *Perception and Motor Skills,* 1969, **29,** 508–510.

Cannon, L. K. Intermodality inconsistency of input and directed attention as determinants of the nature of adaptation. *Journal of Experimental Psychology,* 1970, **84,** 141–147.

Cannon, L. K. Directed attention and maladaptive "adaptation" to displacement of the visual field. *Journal of Experimental Psychology,* 1971, **88,** 405–508.

Carlson, V. R. Overestimation in size constancy judgements. *American Journal of Psychology,* 1960, **73,** 199–213.

Carlson, V. R., & Tassore, E. P. Independent size judgements at different distances. *Journal of Experimental Psychology,* 1967, **73,** 491–497.

Carlson, V. R., & Tassore, E. P. Familiar versus unfamiliar size; a theoretical derivation and test. *Journal of Experimental Psychology,* 1971, **1,** 109–115.

Carr, H. A. *An introduction to space perception.* New York: Longmans, 1935.

Carter, L. F., & Schooler, K. Value need and other factors in perception *Psychological Review,* 1949, **56,** 200–207.

Casperson, R. C. The visual discrimination of geometric forms. *Journal of Experimental Psychology,* 1950, **40,** 668–681.

Chalmers, E. L., Jr. Monocular and binocular cues in the perception of size and distance. *American Journal of Psychology,* 1952, **55,** 415–423.

Chapanis, A., & McCleary, R. A. Interposition as a cue for the perception of relative distance. *Journal of General Psychology,* 1953, **48,** 113–132.

Chapman, R., & Feather, B. W. Modifications of perception by classical conditioning procedures. *Journal of Experimental Psychology,* 1972, **93**, 338–342.

Choe, C. S., & Welch, R. B. Variables affecting the intermanual transfer and decay of prism adaptation. *Journal of Experimental Psychology,* 1974, **102**, 1076–1083.

Christian, P., & Weizacker, V. V. On the vision of figured movement of luminous points. *Zeitschrift für Psychologie,* 1943, **70**, 30–51.

Clark, W. C., Smith, A. H., & Rabe, A. Retinal gradients of outline distortion and binocular disparity as stimulus for slant. *Canadian Journal of Psychology,* 1956, **10**, 77–81.

Cohen, W. Spatial and textural characteristics of the Ganzfeld. *American Journal of Psychology,* 1957, **70**, 403–410.

Cohen, W. Apparent movement of simple figures in the Ganzfeld. *Perception and Motor Skills,* 1958, **8**, 32. (a)

Cohen, W. Color perception in the chromatic Ganzfeld. *American Journal of Psychology,* 1958, **71**, 390–394. (b)

Cole, R. E., & Diamond, A. L. Amount of surround and test-inducing separation in simultaneous brightness contrast. *Perception and Psychophysics,* 1971, **9**, 125–128.

Coltheart, M. The influence of haptic size information upon visual judgments of absolute size. *Perception and Psychophysics,* 1969, **5**, 143–144.

Coltheart, M. The effect of verbal size information upon visual judgements of absolute distance. *Perception and Psychophysics,* 1970, **9**, 222–223.

Cook, M. *Interpersonal perception.* Baltimore: Penguin, 1971.

Cornsweet, T. N. *Visual perception.* New York: Academic, 1970.

Corso, J. F. *The experimental psychology of sensory behavior.* New York: Holt, 1967.

Craik, K. J. W., & Vernon, M. D. *Perception during dark adaptation. British Journal of Psychology,* 1942, **32**, 206–230.

Cross, J. F. Linear perspective as a cue in misperceived rotary motion. *Perception and Psychophysics,* 1969, **6**, 145–146.

Cross, J. F., & Cross, J. The misperception of rotary motion. *Perception and Psychophysics,* 1969, **5**, 94–96.

Cruikshank, R. M. The development of visual size constancy in early infancy. *Journal of Genetic Psychology,* 1941, **58**, 327–351.

Davidon, R. S. Relevance and category scales of judgment. *British Journal of Psychology,* 1962, **53**, 373–379.

Davies, A. E. An analysis of elementary psychic process. *Psychological Review,* 1905, **12**, 166–206.

Davis, H. A model for transducer action in the cochlea. *Cold Springs Harbor Symposium in Quarterly Journal of Biology,* 1965, **30**, 181–190.

Davis, H., & Silverman, S. R. *Hearing and deafness.* New York: Holt, 1960.

Day, R. H. Application of the statistical theory to form perception. *Psychological Review,* 1956, **63**, 139–148.

Day, R. H. Visual spatial illusions: A general explanation. *Science,* 1972, **175**, 1335–1340.

Day, R. H., & Power, R. P. Apparent reversal (oscillation) of rotary motion on depth: An investigation and a general theory. *Psychological Review,* 1965, **72**, 117–127.

Deese, J. Some problems in the theory of vigilance. *Psychological Review,* 1955, **62**, 359–368.

Dennis, W. Cultural and developmental factors on perception. In R. R. Blake & G. V. Ramsay (Eds.), *Perception: An approach to personality.* New York: Ronald, 1951.

Devalois, R. L. Analysis and coding of color vision in the primate visual system. *Cold Spring Harbor Symposia,* 1965, **30,** 567–579.

Devalois, R. L. Studies of the physiology of primate vision. In J. R. Piena & J. R. Lavene (Eds.), *Visual Science,* Bloomington: Indiana University Press, 1971, Vol. 1, 107–124.

DeValois, R. L., Abramov, I., & Jacobs, G. H. Analysis of response patterns of the LGN cells. *Journal of the Optical Society of America,* 1966, **56,** 966–977.

Diamond, A. L. Foveal simultaneous brightness contrast as a function of inducing and test field luminances. *Journal of Experimental Psychology,* 1953, **45,** 304–314.

Diamond, A. L. A theory of depression and enhancement in the brightness response. *Psychological Review,* 1960, **67,** 168–199.

Diamond, A. L. Brightness of a field as a function of its area. *Journal of the Optical Society of America,* 1962, **52,** 700–706.

Dickinson, C. A. Experience and visual perception. *American Journal of Psychology,* 1926, **37,** 330–344.

Dickinson, C. A. The course of experience. *American Journal of Psychology,* 1927, **38,** 266–279.

Diggory, J. C. Personal communication regarding experiment on perceptual defense, 1956.

Dixon, N. F. *Subliminal perception: The nature of a controversy.* New York: McGraw-Hill, 1971.

Djang, S. The role of past experience in the visual perception of masked forms. *Journal of Experimental Psychology,* 1937, **20,** 29–59.

Doane, B. K., Mahut, H., Heron, W., & Scott, T. H. Changes in perceptual function after isolation. *Canadian Journal of Psychology,* 1959, **13,** 210–219.

Dodwell, P. C. *Visual pattern recognition.* New York: Holt, 1970.

Dorfman, D. D. Recognition of taboo words as a function of a priori probability. *Journal of Personality and Social Psychology,* 1967, **7,** 1–10.

Doughty, J. M., & Garner, W. R. Pitch characteristics of short tones. Two kinds of pitch threshold. *Journal of Experimental Psychology,* 1947, **37,** 351–365.

Dowling, J. E. The site of visual adaptation. *Science,* 1967, **155,** 273–279.

Dowling, J. E., & Boycott, B. B. Organization of the primate retina: Electronmicroscopy. *Proceedings of the Royal Society B,* 1966, **166,** 80–111.

Dugger, James A., & Courson, R. W. Effect of angle of retinal vision on rate of fluctuation of the Necker cube. *Perception and Motor Skills,* 1968, **26,** 1239–1242.

Duncan, C. P. Amount and rate of decay of visual aftereffect as function of type of inspection stimulus and inspection time. *American Journal of Psychology,* 1962, **75,** 242–50.

Duncker, K. The influence of past experience upon perceptual properties. *American Journal of Psychology,* 1939, **52,** 225–265.

Dusek, E. R., Teichner, W. H., & Kobrick, J. L. The effects of angular relationship between the observer and the base surround on relative depth discrimination. *American Journal of Psychology,* 1955, **68,** 438–443.

Earhard, B., & Fullerton, R. How much does repetition facilitate perception? *Journal of Experimental Psychology,* 1968, **81,** 101–108.

Eibl-Eibesfeldt, I. *Ethology: The biology of behavior.* New York: Holt, 1970.

Eissler, K. In E. Brunswik (Ed.) et al., Untersuchungen über Wahrnehmung Gegenstände. *Archiv für die Gesamte Psychologie,* 1933, **88,** 377–628.

Ekman, P. Universals and cultural differences in facial expressions of emotion. In J. K.

Cole (Ed.), *Nebraska Symposium on Motivation,* Lincoln, Univ. of Nebraska Press, 1972.

Ekman, P., & Friesen, W. V. Non-verbal leakage and clues to perception. *Psychiatry,* 1969, **32,** 88–106.

Enoch, J. M. Nature of the transmission of energy in the retinal receptors. *Journal of the Optical Society of America,* 1961, **51,** 1122–1126.

Epstein, W. *Varieties of perceptual learning.* New York: McGraw-Hill, 1967.

Epstein, W., & Landauer, A. A. Size and distance judgements under reduced conditions of viewing. *Perception and Psychophysics,* 1969, **6,** 269–272.

Erdelyi, M. H. A new look at the New Look: Perceptual defense and vigilance. *Psychological Review,* 1974, **81, 1,** 1–25.

Erdelyi, M. H., & Appelbaum, G. A. Cognitive masking: The disruptive effect of an emotional stimulus upon the perception of contiguous neutral items. *Bulletin of the Psychonomic Society,* 1973, **1,** 59–61.

Eriksen, C. W. Perceptual defense as a function of unacceptable needs. *Journal of Abnormal and Social Psychology,* 1951, **46,** 557–564 (a)

Eriksen, C. W. Some implications for TAT interpretation arising from need and perception experiments. *Journal of Personality,* 1951, **19,** 283–288. (b)

Eriksen, C. W. Psychological defenses and ego strength in the recall of completed and incompleted tasks. *Journal of Abnormal and Social Psychology,* 1954, **49,** 45–50.

Eriksen, C. W. Subception: Fact or artifact? *Psychological Review,* 1956, **63,** 74–80.

Eriksen, C. W. Discrimination and learning without awareness: A methodological survey and evaluation. *Psychological Review,* 1960, **67,** 279–300.

Eriksen, C. W. Perception and personality. In J. M. Wepman and R. W. Heine (Eds.), *Concepts of personality.* Chicago: Aldine, 1963.

Eriksen, C. W. Temporal luminance summation effects in backward and forward masking. *Perception and Psychophysics,* 1966, **1,** 87–92.

Eriksen, C. W., Becker, B. B., & Hoffman, J. E. Safari to masking land: A hunt for the elusive U. *Perception and Psychophysics,* 1970, **8,** 245–250.

Eriksen, C. W., & Brown, C. T. An experimental and theoretical analysis of perceptual defense. *Journal of Abnormal and Social Psychology,* 1956, **52,** 224–230.

Eriksen, C. W., & Collins, J. F. Sensory traces versus the psychological moment in the temporal organization of form. *Journal of Experimental Psychology,* 1968, **77,** 376–382.

Eriksen, C. W., Collins, J. F., & Greenspon, T. S. An analysis of certain factors responsible for nonmonotonic backward masking functions. *Journal of Experimental Psychology,* 1967, **75,** 500–507.

Eriksson, E. S. Distance perception and the ambiguity of visual stimulation: A theoretical note. *Perception and Psychophysics,* 1973, **13,** 379–381.

Evans, C. R., & Marsden, R. P. A study of the effect of perfect retinal stabilization on some well-known visual illusions, using after image as a method of compensating for eye movements. *British Journal of Physiological Optics,* 1966, **23,** 242–248.

Evans, R. M. *An introduction to color.* New York: Wiley, 1948.

Evans, S. H. Redundancy as a variable in pattern perception. *Psychological Bulletin,* 1967, **67,** 104–113.

Fantz, R. L. A method for studying depth perception in infants under six months of age. *Psychological Records.,* 1961, **11,** 27–32. (a)

Fantz, R. L. The origin of form perception. *Scientific American,* 1961, **204,** 66–72. (b)

Fantz, R. L. Visual perception and experience in early infancy: A look at the hidden side of behavior development. In H. W. Stevenson, E. H. Hess, & H. L. Rheingold

(Eds.), *Early behavior: Comparative and developmental approaches.* New York: Wiley, 1967.

Fantz, R. L., & Nevis, S. Pattern preferences and perceptual-cognitive development in early infancy. *Merrill-Palmer Quarterly*, 1967, **13**, 77–108.

Fechner, G. *Elements of psychophysics* (trans. H. E. Adler). New York: Holt, 1966.

Feddersen, W. E., Sandel, T. T., Teas, D. C., & Jeffress, L. A. Localization of high frequency tones. *Journal of the Acoustical Society of America.* 1957, **29**, 989–991.

Fehrer, E. V. An investigation of the learning of visually perceived forms. *American Journal of Psychology*, 1935, **47**, 187–221.

Fernberger, S. W. New phenomena of apparent visual movement. *American Journal of Psychology*, 1934, **46**, 309.

Festinger, L., Conen, S. & Reven, G. The effect of attention on brightness contrast and assimilation. *American Journal of Psychology*, 1970, **83**, 189–207.

Fieandt, von, K. Uber Sohen von Tiefengevilden bei wechselnder Beleuchtungsrichtung. *Psychological Abstracts*, 1939, **13**, 4524.

Fieandt, von, K., & Gibson, J. J. The sensitivity of the eye to two kinds of continuous transformation of a shadow pattern. *Journal of Experimental Psychology*, 1959, **57**, 344–347.

Fiedler, F. E. The psychological distance dimension in interpersonal relation. *Journal of Personality*, 1953, **22**, 142–150.

Fisher, G. H. Experimental and theoretical appraisal of the perspective size-constancy theory of illusion. *Quarterly Journal of Experimental Psychology*, 1970, **22**, 631–652.

Fitts, P. M., et al. Stimulus correlates of visual pattern recognition: A probability approach. *Journal of Experimental Psychology*, 1956, **51**, 1–11.

Fletcher, H., & Munson, W. A. Loudness, its definition, measurement and calculation. *Journal of the Acoustical Society of America*, 1933, **5**, 82–108.

Flock, H. R., & Freidberg, E. Perceived angle of incidence and achromatic surface color. *Perception and Psychophysics.* 1970, **8**, 251–256.

Flock, H. R., & Noguchi, K. An experimental test of Jameson and Hurvich's theory of brightness contrast. *Perception and Psychophysics*, 1970, **8**, 129–136.

Forgus, R. H. The effect of early perceptual learning on the behavior organization of adult rats. *Journal of Comparative Psychology*, 1954, **47**, 331–336.

Forgus, R. H. Early visual and motor experience as determiners of complex maze learning ability under rich and reduced stimulation. *Journal of Comparative Physiological Psychology*, 1955, **48**, 215–220. (a)

Forgus, R. H. Influence of early experience on maze learning with and without visual cues. *Canadian Journal of Psychology*, 1955, **9**, 231–238. (b)

Forgus, R. H. The effect of different kinds of form pre-exposure on form discrimination learning. *Journal of Comparative Physiological Psychology*, 1958, **51**, 75–78.

Forgus, R. H., & DeWolfe, A. S. Perceptual selective in hallucinatory schizophrenics. *Journal of Abnormal Psychology*, 1969, **74**, 288–292.

Forgus, R. H., & DeWolfe, A. S. Coding of cognitive input in delusional patients. *Journal of Abnormal Psychology*, 1974, Vol. **83**, No. 3, 278–284.

Forgus, R. H., & Schwartz, R. J. Efficient retention and transfer as affected by learning method. *Journal of Psychology*, 1957, **44**, 135–139.

Fraisse, P., & Elkin, E. H. Etude genetique de l'influence des modes de présentation sur le seuil de reconnaissance d'objets familiers. *L'Année Psychologie*, 1963, 1–12.

Francés, R. *Le développement perceptif.* Paris: Presses Univer., 1962.

Freedman, S. J. On the mechanisms of perceptual compensation. In S. J. Freedman

(Ed.), *The Neuropsychology of Spatially Oriented Behavior.* Homewood, Ill.: Dorsey, 1968. (a)

Freedman, S. J. Perceptual compensation and learning. In S. J. Freedman (Ed.), *The Neuropsychology of Spatially Oriented Behavior.* Homewood, Ill.: Dorsey, 1968. (b)

Freeman, G. L. An experimental study of the perception of objects. *Journal of Experimental Psychology,* 1929, **12**, 241–258.

Freeman, R. B. Contrast interpretations of brightness constancy. *Psychological Bulletin,* 1967, **67**, 165–187.

French, D. The relationship of anthropology to studies in perception and cognition. In S. Koch (Ed.), *Psychology: A study of a science.* Vol. 6. *Investigation of man as a socius.* New York: McGraw-Hill, 1963.

Frisby, J. P. Real and apparent movement—Same or different mechanisms? *Vision Research,* 1972, **12**, 1051–1056.

Fujiwara, K., & Obonai, T. The qualitative analysis of figural after-effects. II. Effects of inspection time and the intensity of light stimulus upon the amount of figural after-effects. *Japanese Journal of Psychology,* 1953, **24**, 114–120.

Fuster, J. M. Effects of stimulation of brain stem on tachistoscopic perception. *Science,* 1958, **127**, 150.

Gaito, J. An informational approach to problem solving and thinking behavior. *Dissertation Abstracts,* 1959, **20**, 388. (a)

Gaito, J. Visual discrimination of straight and curved lines. *American Journal of Psychology,* 1959, **72**, 236–242. (b)

Galambos, R., Schwartzkopff, J., & Rupert, A. Microelectrode study of superior olivary nuclei. *American Journal of Physiology,* 1959, **197**, 527–536.

Galanter, E., & Galanter, P. Range estimates of distant visual stimuli. *Perception and Psychophysics,* 1973, **14**, 301–306.

Ganz, L. Is figural after-effect an after-effect? A review of its intensity, onset, decay and transfer characteristics. *Psychological Bulletin,* 1966, **66**, 151–165. (a)

Ganz, L. Mechanism of the F. A. Es. *Psychological Review,* 1966, **73**, 128–150. (b)

Ganz, L. The role of selective receptive fields in visual perception. In *Perception and its disorders. Proceedings of the Association for Research in Nervous and Mental Disease,* 1970, **48**, 186–190. Baltimore: Williams & Wilkins.

Ganz, L., & Day, R. H. An analysis of the satiation-fatigue mechanism of figural after-effect. *American Journal of Psychology,* 1965, **78**, 345–361.

Gardner, M. B. Some monaural and binaural facets of median plane localization. *Journal of the Acoustical Society of America,* 1973, **54**, 1489–1495.

Gardner, M. B., & Gardner, R. S. Problem of localization in the median plane: Effect of pinnae cavity occlusion. *Journal of the Acoustical Society of America,* 1973, **53**, 400–408.

Gardner, R. W. Cognitive controls of attention deployment as determinants of visual illusions. *Journal of Abnormal and Social Psychology,* 1961, **62**, 120–127.

Gardner, R. W., & Long, R. I. Control defense and centration effect: A study of scanning behavior. *British Journal of Psychology,* 1962, **53**, 129–140. (a)

Gardner, R. W., & Long, R. I. Cognitive controls of attention and inhibition. *British Journal of Psychology,* 1962, **53**, 381–388. (b)

Garner, W. R. *Uncertainty and structure as psychological concepts.* New York: Wiley, 1962.

Garner, W. R. To perceive is to know. *American Psychologist,* 1966, **21**, 11–19.

Garner, W. R. Good patterns have few alternatives. *American Scientist,* 1970, **58**, 34–42. (a)

Garner, W. R. The stimulus in information processing. *American Psychologist,* 1970, **25,** 350–358. (b)

Gelb, A. Die Farbenkonstanz der sehdinge. *Handbook of Normal and Pathological Physiology,* 1929, **12** (I), 594–678.

Geldard, F. A. *The human senses.* New York: Wiley, 1972.

Gemelli, A., & Capellini, A. The influence of subjects' attitudes in perception. *Acta Psychologica,* 1958, **14,** 12–23.

Ghent, L. Recognition by children of realistic figures presented in various orientations. *Canadian Journal of Psychology,* 1960, **14,** 249–256.

Ghent, L., & Bernstein, L. Influence of the orientation of geometric forms on their recognition by children. *Perception and Motor Skills,* 1961, **12,** 95–101.

Gibson, E. J. Improvement in perceptual judgement as a function of controlled practice or training. *Psychological Bulletin,* 1953, **50,** 401–431.

Gibson, E. J. The effect of prior training with a scale of distance on absolute and relative judgements over ground. *Journal of Experimental Psychology,* 1955, **50,** 97–105.

Gibson, E. J. A re-examination of generalization. *Psychological Review,* 1959, **66,** 340–342.

Gibson, E. J. *Principles of perceptual learning and development.* New York: Appleton-Century-Crofts, 1969.

Gibson, E. J., Gibson, J. J., Pick, A. D., & Osser, H. A. A developmental study of the discrimination of letter like forms. *Journal of Comparative Physiological Psychology,* 1962, **55,** 897–906.

Gibson, E. J., & Olum, V. Experimental methods of studying perception in children. In P. H. Mussen (Ed.), *Handbook of Research in Child Development.* New York: Wiley, 1960.

Gibson, E. J., Schapiro, F., & Yonas, L. Confusion matrices for graphic patterns obtained with a latency measure. The analysis of reading skill: A program of basic and applied research. Final Rep. Project No. 5-12b, Cornell University and USOE, 1968, 76–96.

Gibson, E. J., Tighe, T. J., & Walk, R. D. Behavior of light and dark reared rats on a visual cliff. *Science,* 1957, **126,** 80–81.

Gibson, E. J., & Walk, R. D. The effect of prolonged exposure to visually presented patterns on learning to discriminate them. *Journal of Comparative Physiological Psychology,* 1956, **49,** 239–242.

Gibson, E. J., & Walk, R. D. The "visual cliff." *Scientific American,* 1960, **202**(4), 64–71.

Gibson, J. J. Adaptation, after effect, and contrast in the perception of curved lines. *Journal of Experimental Psychology,* 1933, **16,** 1–31.

Gibson, J. J. Adaptation, after-effect, and contrast in the perception of tilted lines. II. Simultaneous contrast and the area restriction of the after-effect. *Journal of Experimental Psychology.* 1937, **20,** 553–569. (a)

Gibson, J. J. Adaptation with negative after-effect. *Psychological Review,* 1937, **44,** 222–244. (b)

Gibson, J. J. The perception of the visual world. Boston: Houghton Mifflin, 1950.

Gibson, J. J. The relation between visual and postural determinants of the phenomenal vertical. *Psychological Review,* 1952, **59,** 370–375.

Gibson, J. J. The visual perception of objective motion and subjective movement. *Psychological Review,* 1954, **61,** 304–314.

Gibson, J. J. Optical motions and transformation as stimuli for visual perception. *Psychological Review,* 1957, **64,** 288–295.

Gibson, J. J. The information contained in light. *Acta Psychologica,* 1960, **17,** 23–30. (a)

Gibson, J. J. The concept of stimulus in psychology. *American Psychologist,* 1960, **15,** 694–703. (b)

Gibson, J. J. The useful dimensions of sensitivity. *American Psychologist,* 1963, **18,** 1–15.

Gibson, J. J. The senses considered as perceptual systems. Boston: Houghton Mifflin, 1966.

Gibson, J. J. What gives rise to the perception of motion. *Psychological Review,* 1968, **75,** 335–346.

Gibson, J. J., & Gibson, E. J. Perceptual learning: Differentiation or enrichment? *Psychological Review,* 1955, **62,** 32–41.

Gibson, J. J., & Gibson, E. J. Perceptual learning: Differentiation or enrichment? *Americana,* 1956, **2,** 83–94.

Gibson, J. J., & Gibson, E. J. Continuous perspective transformations and the perception of rigid motion. *Journal of Experimental Psychology,* 1957, **54,** 129–138.

Gibson, J. J., & Mowrer, O. H. Determinants of the perceived vertical and horizontal. *Psychological Review,* 1938, **45,** 300.

Gibson, J. J., & Radner, M. Adaptation, after-effect and contrast in the perception of tilted lines. I. Quantitative studies. *Journal of Experimental Psychology,* 1937, **20,** 453–467.

Gibson, R. H., & Tomko, D. L. The relation between category and magnitude estimates of tactile intensity. *Perception and Psychophysics,* 1972, **12,** 135–138.

Gilinsky, A. S. The effect of attitude on the perception of size. *American Journal of Psychology,* 1955, **68,** 173–192.

Gillam, B. Perceived common rotary motion of ambiguous stimuli as a criterion of perspective grouping. *Perception and Psychophysics,* 1972, **11,** 99–101.

Gilliland, A. R. The effect of practice with and without knowledge of results in grading handwriting. *Journal of Educational Psychology,* 1925, **16,** 532–536.

Glick, J. An experimental analysis of subject-object relationships in perception. In R. N. Haber (Ed.), *Contemporary research and theory on visual perception.* New York: Holt, 1968.

Gogel, W. C. The sensing of retinal size. *Vision Research* (Summarized by Lardner & Epstein.) 1969, 275.

Gogel, W. C. The adjacency principle and three-dimensional visual illusions. *Psychonomics Monograph Supplement,* 1970, **3,** (Whole No. 45), 153–160.

Gogel, W. C., & Koslow, M. The effect of perceived distance on induced movement. *Perception and Psychophysics,* 1971, **10,** 142–146.

Gogel, W. C., & Koslow, M. The adjacency principle and induced movement. *Perception and Psychophysics,* 1972, **11,** 309–314.

Gogel, W. C., & Sturm, R. C. A comparison of accomodative and fusional convergence as cues to distance. *Perception and Psychophysics,* 1972, **11,** 166–168.

Gogel, W. C., & Tietz, J. The effect of perceived distance on perceived movement. *Perception and Psychophysics,* 1974, **16,** 70–78.

Goldard, F. A. *The human senses* (2d ed.). New York: Wiley, 1972.

Goldberg, J. M., & Brown, P. B. Response of binaural neurons of dog superior olivary complex to dichotic tonal stimuli. Some physiological mechanisms of sound localization. *Journal of Neurophysiology,* 1969, **32,** 613–636.

Goldberg, J. J., Diamond, I. T., & Neff, W. D. Auditory discrimination after oblation of temporal and insular cortex in cat. *Federation Proceedings,* 1957, **16**, 47.

Goldiamond, I. Perception. In A. J. Bachrach (Ed.), *Experimental foundations of clinical psychology.* New York: Basic Books, 1962.

Goldiamond, I., & Hawkins, W. F. Vexierversuch: The log relationship between word frequency and recognition obtained in the absence of stimulus words. *Journal of Experimental Psychology,* 1958, **56**, 457–463.

Goldstein, M. J. A test of response probability theory of perceptual defense. *Journal of Experimental Psychology,* 1962, **63**, 23–28.

Gollin, E. Developmental studies of visual recognition of incomplete objects. *Perception and Motor Skills,* 1960, **11**, 289–298.

Gomrich, E. H. *Art and illusion.* London: Phaidon, 1962.

Gottschaldt, K. Uber den Einfluss der Erfahrung auf die Wahrnehmung von Figuren. I Uber den Einfluss gehaufter Einpragung von Figuren auf ihre Sicherheit in umfassen der Konfigurationen. *Psychologische Forschung,* 1926, **8**, 261–317.

Graham, C. H. *Vision and visual perception.* New York: Wiley, 1965.

Graham, C. H., & Hsia, Y. Color defect and color theory. *Science,* 1958, **127**, 675–682.

Green, D. M., & Swets, J. A. *Signal detection theory and psychophysics.* New York: Wiley, 1966.

Gregory, R. L. Human perception. *British Medical Bulletin,* 1964, **20**, 21–26.

Gregory, R. L. *Eye and brain.* London: Weidenfeld and Nicolson, 1966.

Gregory, R. L. Perceptual illusions on brain models. *Proceedings of the Royal Society,* 1968, **171**, 279–296. (a)

Gregory, R. L. Visual illusions. *Scientific American,* 1968, **219**, 66–76. (b)

Gregory, R. L. *The intelligent eye.* London: Weidenfeld and Nicolson, 1970.

Gregory, R. L., & Wallace, J. G. Recovery from early blindness. *Experimental Psychological Science Monographs,* 1963, No. 2.

Grim, K. Uber die Genauigheit der Wahrnehming und Ausführung von Augenbenregungen. *Zeitschrift für Sinnesphysiologie,* 1911, **45**, 9–26.

Gruber, H. E. The relation of perceived size to perceived distance. *American Journal of Psychology,* 1954, **67**, 411–426.

Gruber, H. E. The size-distance paradox: A reply to Gilensky. *American Journal of Psychology,* 1956, **69**, 469–476.

Gruber, H. E., Fink, C. D., & Damm, V. Effects of experience on perception of causality. *Journal of Experimental Psychology,* 1957, **53**, 89–93.

Guilford, J. P. *Psychometric methods.* New York: McGraw-Hill, 1954.

Gulick, W. L. *Hearing, physiology and psychophysics.* New York: Oxford University Press, 1971.

Gyr, J. W. Is a theory of direct visual perception adequate? *Psychological Bulletin,* 1972, **77**, 246–261.

Haber, R. N. Nature and the effect of set on perception. *Psychological Review,* 1966, **73**, 335–357.

Haber, R. N., & Hershenson, M. The effects of repeated brief exposures on the growth of a percept. *Journal of Experimental Psychology,* 1965, **69**, 40–46.

Haber, R. N., & Hershenson, M. *The psychology of visual perception.* New York: Holt, 1973.

Haber, R. N., & Nathanson, L. S. Processing of sequentially presented letters. *Perception and Psychophysics,* 1969, **5**, 359–361.

Haber, R. N., & Standing, L. G. Clarity and recognition of marked and degraded stimuli. *Psychonomic Science,* 1968, **13,** 43–54.

Haber, R. N., & Standing, L. G. Direct memory of short term visual storage. *Quarterly Journal of Experimental Psychology,* 1969, **21,** 43–54.

Hake, H. W. *Contributions of psychology to the study of pattern vision.* USAF WADC-TR-57-621, October, 1957.

Hall, K. R. L., Earle, A. E., & Crookes, T. G. A pendulum phenomenon in visual perception of apparent movement. *Quarterly Journal of Experimental Psychology,* 1952, **4,** 109–120.

Hallett, P. E., Marriott, F. H. C., & Rodger, F. C. The relationship of visual threshold to retinal position and area. *Journal of Physiology,* 1962, **160,** 364–373.

Hallowell, A. I. Cultural factors in the structuralization of perception. In J. H. Rohrer and M. Sherif (Eds.), *Social psychology at the crossroads.* New York: Harper, 1951, 164–195.

Hambacher, W. O. An experimental investigation of whiteness constancy with suggestions for an explanatory approach. *Dissertation Abstracts,* 1956.

Hammer, E. R. Temporal factors in figural after-effects. *American Journal of Psychology,* 1949, **62,** 337–354.

Hanawalt, E. M. Memory trace for figures in recall and recognition. *Archives of Psychology,* 1937, No. 216.

Hanawalt, N. G. The effect of practice upon the perception of simple designs masked by more complex designs. *Journal of Experimental Psychology,* 1942, **31,** 134–148.

Harlow, H. F. The formation of learning sets. *Psychological Review,* 1949, **56,** 51–65.

Harris, C. S. Adaptation to displaced vision; visual, motor or proprioceptive change. *Science,* 1963, **140,** 812–813.

Harris, C. S. Perceptual adaptation to inverted, reversed, and displaced vision. *Psychological Review,* 1965, **72,** 419–444.

Harris, G. G. Binaural interactions of impulsive stimuli and pure tones. *Journal of the Acoustical Society of America,* 1960, **32,** 685–692.

Harris, J. D. Pitch discrimination. *Journal of the Acoustical Society of America,* 1952, **24,** 750–755.

Harris, J. D. Loudness discrimination. *Journal of Speech and Hearing Disorders,* 1963, Monograph Suppl. No. 11, 1–63.

Harter, M. R., & Smitt, C. D. Visually-evoked cortical responses and pattern vision in the infant. *Psychonomic Science,* 1970, **18,** 235–237.

Harvey, L. O., & Leibowitz, H. W. Effects of exposure duration, cue reduction, and temporary monocularity on size matching at short distances. *Journal of the Optical Society of America,* 1967, **57,** 249–253.

Hastorf, A. H., & Way, L. Apparent size with and without distance cues. *Journal of General Psychology,* 1952, **47,** 181–188.

Hawkins, J. E., & Stevens, S. S. The masking of pure tones and of speech by white noise. *Journal of the Acoustical Society of America,* 1950, **22,** 6–13.

Hay, J. C., & Pick, H. L., Jr. Visual and proprioceptive adaptation to optical displacement of the visual stimulus. *Journal of Experimental Psychology,* 1966, **71,** 150–158. (a)

Hay, J. C., & Pick, H. L., Jr. Gaze-contingent prism adaptation: Optical and motor factors. *Journal of Experimental Psychology,* 1966, **72,** 640–648. (b)

Hay, J. C., Pick, H. C., & Ikeda, K. Visual capture produced by prism spectacle. *Psychonomic Science,* 1965, **2,** 215–216.

Hebb, D. O. The innate organization of visual activity. I. Perception of figures by rats reared in total darkness. *Journal of Comparative Psychology,* 1937, **24,** 277–299. (a)

Hebb, D. O. The innate organization of visual activity. II. Transfer of response in the discrimination of brightness and size by rats reared in total darkness. *Journal of Comparative Psychology,* 1937, **24,** 277–299. (b)

Hebb, D. O. Emotion in man and animal; an analysis of the intuitive processes of recognition. *Psychological Review,* 1946, **53,** 88–106.

Hebb, D. O. *The organization of behavior.* New York: Wiley, 1949.

Hebb, D. O. The American revolution. *American Psychologist,* 1960, **15,** 735–745.

Hebb, D. O. Concerning imagery. *Psychological Review,* 1968, **75,** 466–477.

Hebb, D. O., & Foord, E. N. Errors of visual recognition and the nature of the trace. *Journal of Experimental Psychology,* 1945, **35,** 335–348.

Hecht, S. Vision: II. The nature of the photoreceptor process. In C. Murchison (Ed.), *Handbook of general experimental psychology.* Worcester, Mass.: Clark University Press, 1934, 704–828.

Hecht, S., & Shlaer, S. Intermittent stimulation by light. V. The relation between intensity and critical frequency for different parts of the spectrum. *Journal of General Physiology,* 1936, **19,** 965–977.

Hecht, S., Shlaer, S., & Pirenne, M. H. Energy, quanta, and vision. *Journal of General Physiology,* 1942, **25,** 819–840.

Heider, F. *The psychology of interpersonal relations.* New York: Wiley, 1958.

Heider, F., & Simmel, M. L. An experimental study of apparent behavior. *American Journal of Psychology,* 1944, **57,** 243–249.

Heinemann, E. S. Simultaneous brightness induction as a function of inducing-and-test field brightness. *Journal of Experimental Psychology,* 1955, **50,** 89–96.

Held, R. Dissociation of visual functions by deprivation and rearrangement. *Psychologische Forschung.,* 1967, **31,** 338–348.

Held, R., & Hein, A. V. Adaptation of disarranged hand-eye coordination contingent upon reafferent stimulation. *Perception and Motor Skills,* 1958, **8,** 87–90.

Held, R. & Hein, A. Movement-produced stimulation in the development of visually guided behavior. *Journal of Comparative Physiological Psychology,* 1963, **56,** 872–876.

Helmholz, von, H. *Handidbuch der physiologischen Optik* (2d ed.). Hamburg and Leipzig: Voss, 1896.

Helson, H. Some factors and implications of color constancy. *Journal of the Optical Society of America,* 1943, **33,** 555–567.

Helson, H., & Feher, E. V. The role of form in perception. *American Journal of Psychology,* 1932, **44,** 79–102.

Henneman, R. H. A photometric study of the perception of object color. *Archives of Psychology,* 1935, No. **179,** 444.

Hering, E. Grundzuge den Lihre von Lichtsinn. In W. Engelmann (Ed.), *Handbook der gesammten Augenheilkunde,* Vol. 3, Chapter 13, 1905. 2d Ed. Leipzig: J. Springer, 1920.

Heron, W. The pathology of boredom. *Scientific American,* 1957, **196,** 52–56.

Heron, W. In Soloman et al. (Eds.), *Sensory deprivation.* Cambridge, Mass.: Harvard, 1961.

Heron, W., Doane, B. K. & Scott, T. H. Visual disturbances after prolonged perceptual isolation. *Canadian Journal of Psychology,* 1956, **10,** 13–18.

Hershenson, M. Development of the perception of form. *Psychological Bulletin,* 1967, **67,** 326–339.

Hess, E. H. Development of the chick's responses to light and shade cues of depth. *Journal of Comparative Physiological Psychology,* 1950, **43,** 112–122.

Hilgard, E. R., Edgren, R. D., & Whipple, J. E. Rote memorization, understanding and transfer: An extension of Katona's card-trick experiments. *Journal of Experimental Psychology,* 1953, **46,** 288–292.

Hirsch, H. V. B., & Spinelli, D. N. Visual experience modifies distribution of horizontally and vertically oriented receptive fields in cats. *Science,* 1970, **168,** 869–871.

Hirsch, I. J. The measurement of hearing. New York: McGraw-Hill, 1952.

Hochberg, J. E. The psychophysics of pictorial perception. *Audio-Visual Communications Review,* 1962, **10,** 22–54.

Hochberg, J. E. *Perception.* Englewood Cliffs, N.J.: Prentice-Hall, 1964.

Hochberg, J. E. In the mind's eye. In R. W. Haber (Ed.), *Contemporary theory and research in visual perception.* New York: Hall, Rinehart, Winston, 1968.

Hochberg, J. E. Attention, organization and consciousness. In D. I. Moskotsky (Ed.), *Attention: Contemporary theory and analysis.* New York: Appleton-Century-Crofts, 1970.

Hochberg, J. E. Perception: I. Color and shape, II. Space and movement. In J. W. Kling & L. A. Riggs (Eds.), *Woodworth and Schlossberg's Experimental Psychology,* 1971, Vol **1,** New York: Holt, Rinehart and Winston, 395–550.

Hochberg, J. E., & Beck, J. Apparent spatial arrangement and perceived brightness. *Journal of Experimental Psychology,* 1954, **47,** 263–266.

Hochberg, J. E., Gleitman, H., & MacBride, P. D. Visual thresholds as a function of simplicity of form. *American Journal of Psychology,* 1948, **60,** 341–342.

Hochberg, J. E., & Hardy, D. Brightness and proximity factors in grouping. *Perception and Motor Skills,* 1960, **10,** 22.

Hochberg, J. E., & McAlister, E. A quantitative approach to figural "goodness." *Journal of Experimental Psychology,* 1953, **46,** 361–364.

Hochberg, J. E., & Silverstein, A. A quantitative index of stimulus similarity: Proximity vs. differences in brightness. *American Journal of Psychology,* 1956, **69,** 456–458.

Hochberg, J. E., Triebel, W., & Seaman, G. Color adaptation under conditions of homogeneous visual stimulation (Ganzfeld). *Journal of Experimental Psychology,* 1951, **41,** 153–159.

Holst, von, E., Relations between the central nervous system and the peripheral organs. *British Journal of Animal Behavior,* 1954, **2,** 89–94.

Holst, von, E., & Mittelstaedt, H. Das Reaffenzprinzip (Wechselwirkungen zeischen-zentral Nervensystem und Peripherie). *Naturwissenschaften,* 1950, **37,** 464–476.

Holway, A. H., & Boring, E. G. Determinants of apparent visual size with distance variant. *American Journal of Psychology,* 1941, **54,** 21–37.

Holzman, P. S., & Gardner, R. W. Leveling and sharpening and memory organization. *Journal of Abnormal and Social Psychology,* 1960, **61,** 176–180.

Horowitz, M. W., & Kappauf, W. E. Aerial target range estimation. SRD report No. 5301, 1945, Publ. Bd. No. 15812, U.S. Dept. Commerce, 1946, 10–60.

Hotopf, W. H. N. The size constancy theory of visual illusions. *British Journal of Psychology,* 1966, **57,** 307–318.

Houssiadas, L. Effects of set and intellectual level on the perception of causality. *Acta Psychologica,* 1964, **22,** 155–161.

Howard, I. P. Displacing the optic array. In S. J. Freedman (Ed.), *The Neuropsychology of Spatially Oriented Behavior.* Homewood, Ill.: Dorsey, 1968.

Howard, I. P., Craske, B., & Templeton, W. B. Visuomotor adaptation to discordant exafferent stimulation. *Journal of Experimental Psychology,* 1965, **70,** 189–191.

Hsia, Y. Whiteness constancy as a function of difference in illumination. *Archives of Psychology,* N.Y., 1943, No. **284.**

Hubel, D. H., & Wiesel, T. N. Receptive fields of single neurons in the cat's striate cortex. *Journal of Physiology,* 1959, **148,** 574–591.

Hubel, D. H., & Wiesel, T. N. Receptive fields, binocular interaction and functional architecture in the cat's visual cortex. *Journal of Physiology,* 1962, **160,** 106–154.

Hubel, D. H., & Wiesel, T. N. Receptive fields of cells in striate cortex of very young, visually inexperienced kittens. *Journal of Neurophysiology,* 1963, **26,** 994–1002. (a)

Hubel, D. H., & Wiesel, T. N. Shape and arrangement of columns in cat's striate cortex. *Journal of Physiology,* 1963, **165,** 559–568. (b)

Hubel, D. H., & Wiesel, T. N. Receptive fields and functional architecture in two nonstriate visual areas (18 and 19) of the cat. *Journal of Neurophysiology,* 1965, **28,** 229–289.

Hubel, D. H., & Wiesel, T. N. Receptive fields and functional architecture of monkey striate cortex. *Journal of Physiology,* 1968, **195,** 215–243.

Humphrey, N. K., & Weiskrantz, L. Size constancy in monkeys with inferotemporal lesions. *Quarterly Journal of Experimental Psychology,* 1969, **21,** 225–238.

Hunt, W. A. Recent developments in the field of emotion. *Psychological Bulletin,* 1941, **38,** 249–276.

Hurvich, L. M., & Jameson, D. An opponent-process theory of color vision. *Psychological Review,* 1957, **64,** 384–404.

Hurvich, L. M., & Jameson, D. *The perception of brightness and darkness.* Boston: Allyn and Bacon, 1966.

Hurvich, L. M., & Jameson, D. Opponent processes as a model of neural organization. *American Psychologist,* 1974, **29,** 88–102.

Hyman, R., & Hake, H. W. *Form recognition as a function of the number of forms which can be presented for recognition.* USAF WADC-TR-54-164, May 1954.

Ikeda, H., & Obonai, T. The quantitative analysis of figural after-effects: I. The process of growth and decay of figural after-effects. *Japanese Journal of Psychology,* 1953, **23,** 246–260; **24,** 59–66.

Ikeda, H., & Obonai, J. Figural after-effect, retroactive effect and simultaneous illusion. *Japanese Journal of Psychology,* 1955, **26,** 235–246. (a)

Ikeda, H., & Obonai, J. The studies of figural after-effects: The contrast-confluence illusion of concentric circles and the figural after-effect. *Japanese Psychological Research,* 1955, **2,** 17–23. (b)

Jameson, D., & Hurvich, L. M. Complexities of perceived brightness. *Science,* 1961, **133,** 174–179.

Jameson, D., & Hurvich, L. M. Theory of brightness and color contrast in human vision. *Vision Research,* 1964, **4,** 135–154.

Jameson, D., & Hurvich, L. M. The perception of brightness and darkness. Boston: Allyn and Bacon, 1966.

Jameson, D., & Hurvich, L. Improvable, yes; insolvable, no: A reply to Flock. *Perception and Psychophysics,* 1970, **8,** 125–128.

Jenkin, N., & Hyman, R. Attitude and distance-estimation as variables in size-matching. *American Journal of Psychology,* 1959, **72,** 68–76.

Johannsen, G. *Configurations in event perception.* Uppsala, Sweden: Almquist and Wiksell, 1950.

Johannsen, G. Visual perception of biological motion and a model for its analysis. *Perception and Psychophysics,* 1973, **14,** 201–211.

Judd, C. H. Practice and its effects on the perception of illusions. *Psychological Review,* 1902, **9,** 27–39.

Julesz, B. Binocular depth perception with familiarty cues. *Science,* 1964, **145,** 356–362.

Julesz, B. *The cyclopean eye.* New York: Academic, 1970.

Jung, R., & Kornhuber, H. (Eds.) *The visual system: Neurophysiology and psychophysics.* Berlin: Springer-Verlag, 1961.

Kaas, J., Axelrod, S., & Diamond, I. T. An ablation study of the auditory cortex in the cat using binaural tonal patterns. *Journal of Neurophysiology,* 1967, **30,** 710–724.

Kagan, J. The growth or "face" schema: Theoretical significance and methodological issues. In J. Hellmuth (Ed.), *Exceptional infant,* Vol. **1.** *The normal infant.* Seattle: Spenal Child Publications, 1967.

Kagan, J. Attention and psychological change in the young child. *Science,* 1970, **170,** 826–832.

Kahneman, D. An onset-onset law for one case of apparent motion and metacontrast. *Perception and Psychophysics,* 1967, **2,** 577–584.

Kahneman, D. Method, findings and theory in studies of visual masking. *Psychological Bulletin,* 1968, **70,** 404–425.

Kahneman, R., & Wolman, R. E. Stroboscopic motion: Effects of duration and interval. *Perception and Psychophysics,* 1970, **8,** 161–164.

Karmel, B. Z. The effect of age, complexity, amount of contour on pattern preferences in human infants. *Journal of Experimental Child Psychology,* 1969, **7,** 339–354.

Karmel, B. Z., Hoffman, R. F., & Fegy, M. J. Processing of contour information by human infants evidenced by pattern-dependent evoked potentials. *Child Development,* 1974, **45,** 39–48.

Katona, G. Zur Analyse der Helligkeitskon-stanz. *Psychologische Forschung,* 1929, **12,** 94–126.

Katona, G. *Organizing and memorizing.* New York: Columbia, 1940.

Katsuki, Y. Neural mechanism of auditory sensation in cats. In W. A. Rosenblith (Ed.), *Sensory communication.* Cambridge: M.I.T.; New York: Wiley, 1961, pp. 561–584.

Katz, D. Die Erscheinungsweisen der Farben. *Zeitschrift für Psychologie,* 1911, **7,** 7–10.

Katz, D. (Ed.) *Der Aufbau der Farbenwelt.* Leipzig: Barth, 1930. (R. B. MacLeod & K. L. Fox, trans.) *The world of color.* London: Routledge, 1935. 7–7, 9.

Kaufman, L., & Rock, I. The moon illusion. *Scientific American,* 1962, **207,** 120–130.

Kendon, A. Some relationships between body motion and speech: An analysis of an example. In A. Siegman and B. Pope (Eds.), *Studies in Dyadic Communication.* London: Pergamon, 1972.

Kenkel, F. Untersuchungen über den Zusammenhang zwischen Erscheinungsegrösse und Erscheimungsbewegung bei einigen sogenannten optischen Tauschungen. *Zeitschrift für Psychologie,* 1913, **67,** 358–447.

Kiang, N. Y.-S. *Discharge patterns of single fibers in the cat's auditory nerve.* Cambridge: M.I.T., 1965.

Kilpatrick, F. P. *Explorations in transactional psychology.* New York University Press, 1961.

Kilpatrick, F. P., & Ittelson, W. H. The size-distance invariance hypothesis. *Psychological Review,* 1953, **60,** 223–231.

Kinchla, R. A. Visual movement perception: A comparison of absolute and relative movement discrimination. *Perception and Psychophysics,* 1971, **9,** 165–172.

Klein, G. S. Semantic power of words measured through the interference with color naming. *American Journal of Psychology,* 1964, **77,** 576–588.

Klimpfinger, S. See Brunswik, E. (Ed.), et al. Untersuchungen über Wahrnehmung Gegenstände. *Archiv für die Gesamte Psychologie,* 1933, **88,** 377–628.

Klimpfinger, S. Über den Einfluss von intentionaler Einstellung und Ubung auf die Gestaltkonstanz. *Archiv für die Gesamte Psychologie,* 1933, **88,** 551–598.

Kluckholm, C. Culture and behavior. In G. Lindzey (Ed.), *Handbook of social psychology,* Vol. **2,** Cambridge, Mass: Addison-Wesley, 1954, 921–976.

Koffka, K. *The principles of gestalt psychology.* New York: Harcourt, Brace & World, 1935.

Kohlberg, L. The cognitive-developmental approach to socialization. In D. A. Goslin (Ed.), *Handbook of socialization theory and research.* Chicago: Rand McNally, 1969.

Kohler, I. Uber Aufbau und Wandel lungen der Wahrnehmungswelt: Insbesonderc über "bedingte" Empfindungen. Vienna: Rudolph M. Rohrer, 1951.

Kohler, I. The formation and transformation of the perceptual world. *Psychological Issues,* 1964, **3,** 1–173.

Köhler, W. *Gestalt psychology.* New York: Liveright, 1929.

Köhler, W., & Emery, D. A. Figural after-effects in the third dimension of visual space. *American Journal of Psychology,* 1947, **60,** 159–201.

Köhler, W., & Fishback, J. The destruction of the Müller-Lyer illusion in repeated trials. *Journal of Experimental Psychology,* 1950, **40,** 267–281.

Köhler, W., & Wallach, H. Figural after-effects: An investigation of visual processes. *Proceedings of the American Philosophical Society,* 1944, **88,** 269–357.

Kolers, P. A. Intensity and contour effects in visual masking. *Vision Research,* 1962, **2,** 277–294.

Kolers, P. A. The illusion of movement. *Scientific American,* 1964, **211,** 98–106.

Kolers, P. A., & Rosner, B. S. On visual masking (metacontrast): Dichoptic observation. *American Journal of Psychology,* 1960, **73,** 1–21.

Kopferman, H. Psychologische Untersuchgen über die Wirkung zweidimensionaler Darstellungen korperlicher Gebilde. *Psychologische Forschung,* 1930, **13,** 203–364.

Korte, A. Kinematoskopische Untersuchungen. *Zeitschrift für Psychologie,* 1915, **72,** 193–296.

Krauskopf, J., Duryea, R. A., & Bitterman, M. E. Threshold for visual form: Further experiments. *American Journal of Psychology,* 1954, **67,** 427–440.

Kravitz, H., & Boehm, J. J. Rhythmic habit patterns in infancy: Their sequence, age of onset, and frequency. *Child Development,* 1971, **42,** 399–414.

Kristofferson, A. B. Attention and psychophysical time. *Acta Psychologica,* 1967, **27,** 93–100.

Kuffler, S. W. Discharge patterns and functional organization of mammalian retina. *Journal of Neurophysiology,* 1953, **16,** 37–68.

Künnapas, T. Scales for subjective distance. *Scandinavian Journal of Psychology,* 1960, **1,** 187–192.

Lacey, J. I., & Dallenbach, K. M. Acquisition by children of the cause-effect relationship. *American Journal of Psychology,* 1939, **52,** 103–110.

Ladd-Franklin, C. *Colour and colour theory.* New York: Harcourt, Brace Jovanovich, 1932.

Landauer, A. A., & Epstein, W. Does retinal size have a unique correlate in perceived size? *Perception and Psychophysics,* 1969, **6,** 273–275.

Landauer, A. A., & Rodger, R. S. Effect of "apparent" instructions on brightness judgement. *Journal of Experimental Psychology,* 1964, Vol. **68,** 80–84.

Langdon, J. The perception of changing shape. *Quarterly Journal of Experimental Psychology,* 1951, **3,** 157–165.

Langdon, J. Further studies in the perception of changing shape. *Quarterly Journal of Experimental Psychology,* 1953, **5,** 89–107.

Langdon, J. The perception of three-dimensional solids. *Quarterly Journal of Experimental Psychology,* 1955, **7,** 133–146. (a)

Langdon, J. The role of spatial stimuli in the perception of shape, Pt. I. *Quarterly Journal of Experimental Psychology,* 1955, **7,** 19–27. (b)

Langdon, J. The role of spatial stimuli in the perception of shape, Pt. II. *Quarterly Journal of Experimental Psychology,* 1955, **7,** 28–36. (c)

Langley, L. L. *Outline of physiology* (2d ed.). New York: McGraw-Hill, 1965.

Lappin, J. S. Attention in the identification of stimuli in complex visual displays. *Journal of Experimental Psychology,* 1967, **75,** 321–328.

Lashley, K. S. The mechanism of vision. XV. Preliminary studies on the rat's capacity for detail vision. *Journal of Genetic Psychology,* 1938, **18,** 123–193.

Lashley, K. S., Chow, K. L., & Semmes, J. An examination of the electrical field theory of cerebral integration. *Psychological Review,* 1951, **58,** 123–136.

Lawrence, D. H. Acquired distinctiveness of cues. I. Transfer between discrimination on the basis of familiarity with the stimulus. *Journal of Experimental Psychology,* 1949, **39,** 770–784.

Lawrence, D. H. Acquired distinctiveness of cues. II. Selective association in a constant stimulus situation. *Journal of Experimental Psychology,* 1950, **40,** 175–188.

Lawrence, D. H. Generalization gradients and transfer of a discrimination along a continuum. *Journal of Comparative Physiological Psychology,* 1952, **45,** 511–516.

Lawson, E. A. Decisions concerning the rejected channel. *Quarterly Journal of Experimental Psychology,* 1966, **18,** 260–265.

Lazarus, R. S. *Psychological stress and the coping process.* New York: McGraw-Hill, 1966.

Lazarus, R. S., Eriksen, C. H., & Fonda, C. P. Personality dynamics in auditory perceptual recognition. *Journal of Personality,* 1951, **19,** 471–482.

Lazarus, R. S., & McCleary, R. A. Autonomic discrimination without awareness: A study of subception. *Psychological Review,* 1951, **58,** 113–122.

Lefton, L. A. Metacontrast: A review. *Perception and Psychophysics,* 1973, **13,** 161–171.

Leibowitz, H. W. Effect of reference lines on the discriminating movement. *Journal of the Optical Society of America,* 1955, **45,** 829–830. (a)

Leibowitz, H. W. The relation between the rate threshold for the perception of movement and luminance for various durations of exposure. *Journal of Experimental Psychology,* 1955, **49,** 829–830. (b)

Leibowitz, H. W. Sensory, learned and cognitive mechanisms in size perception. *Annals of the New York Academy of Sciences,* Conference on Sensory Orientation, 1971, in press.

Leibowitz, H. W., Bussey, T., & McGuire, P. Shape and size constancy in photo-graphic reproductions. *Journal of the Optical Society of America,* 1957, **47,** 658–661.

Leibowitz, H., Chinetti, P., & Sidowski, J. Exposure duration as a variable in percep-tual constancy. *Science,* 1956, **123,** 668–669.

Leibowitz, H. W., & Harvey, L. O. Size matching as a function of instructions in a naturalistic environment. *Journal of Experimental Psychology,* 1967, **74,** 378–382.

Leibowitz, H. W., & Harvey, L. O., Jr. A comparison of experimental and nonexperi-mental approaches to size perception. *Bulletin de Psychologie,* 1968–1969, **276,** 22, 9–13.

Leibowitz, H. W., & Judisch, J. M. Size-constancy in older persons: A function of distance. *American Journal of Psychology,* 1967, **53,** 294–296.

Leibowitz, H., Mitchell, E., & Angrist, N. Exposure duration in the perception of shape. *Science,* 1954, **120,** 400.

Leibowitz, H., & Moore, D. Role of changes in accommodation and convergence in the perception of size. *Journal of the Optical Society of America,* 1966, **56,** 1120–1123.

Leibowitz, H. W., & Sacca, E. J. Comparison of watching and drawing in the percep-tion of shape at various intelligence levels. *Perception and Psychophysics,* 1971, **9,** 407–409.

Leibowitz, H. W., Shiina, K., & Hennesy, R. *Perception and Psychophysics,* 1972, **12,** 477–500.

Leibowitz, H., Waskow, I., Loeffler, N., & Glaser, F. Intelligence level as a variable in the perception of shape. *Quarterly Journal of Experimental Psychology,* 1959, **11,** 108–112.

Lettvin, J. V., Maturana, H. R., McCulloch, W. S., & Pitts, W. H. What the frog's eye tells the frog's brain. *Proceedings of the Institute of Radio Engineers,* 1959, **47,** 1940–1951.

Lindsay, P. H., & Norman, D. A. *Human information processing: An introduction to psychology.* New York: Academic, 1972.

Liss, P. Does backward masking by visual noise stop stimulus processing? *Perception and Psychophysics,* 1968, **4,** 328–330.

Lorenz, K. Z. The evolution of behavior. *Scientific American,* 1958, **199,** 67–83.

Lowenstein, W. R. Biological transducer. *Scientific American,* 1960, **203,** 98–104.

Luchins, A. S. Mechanization in problem solving. *Psychological Monographs,* 1942, **54,** No. 6, 1–95.

Luchins, A. S. The autokinetic effect and gradations of illumination of the visual field. *Journal of General Psychology,* 1954, **50,** 29–37.

Luneberg, R. Metric methods in binocular visual perception. In *Studies and Essays Presented to R. Courant.* New York: Interscience, 1948.

Mack, A., & Rock, I. A re-examination of the Stratton effect: Egocentric adaptation to a rotated visual image. *Perception and Psychophysics,* 1968, **4,** 57–62.

Mackavey, W. R. Spatial brightness changes in Koffka's ring. *Journal of Experimental Psychology,* 1969, **82,** 405–409.

Mackworth, J. F. The duration of the visual image. *Canadian Journal of Psychology,* 1963, **17,** 62–81.

Mackworth, W. H., & Morandi, A. S. The gaze selects informative details within pictures. *Perception and Psychophysics,* 1967, **2,** 547–552.

MacLeod, R. B. An experimental investigation of brightness constancy. *Archives of Psychology,* 1932, **135,** 7–20.

MacLeod, R. B. Brightness-constancy in unrecognized shadows. *Journal of Psychology*, 1940, **27**, 1–22.

MacLeod, R. B. The effects of "artificial penumbra" on the brightness of included areas. *In Miscellanea psychologica, Albert Michotte.* Paris: Librairie Philosophique, 1947.

MacNichol, E. J., & Svactichin, G. Electric responses from the isolated retinas of fishes. *American Journal of Ophthamology*, 1958, **46**, 26–40.

Maddi, S. The search for meaning. In W. J. Arnold & M. M. Page (Eds.), *Nebraska Symposium on Motivation*, 18, Lincoln: Univ. of Nebraska Press, 1970, 137–180.

Malhotra, M. K. Figural after-effects: An examination of Köhler's theory. *Acta Psychologica*, 1968, **14**, 161–199.

Mann, C. W. Visual factors in the perception of verticality. *Journal of Experimental Psychology*, 1952, **44**, 460–464.

Mann, C. W., et al. The perception of the vertical. I. Visual and non-labyrinthine cues. *Journal of Experimental Psychology*, 1949, **39**, 538–542.

Mann, C. W., & Boring, R. O. The role of instruction in experimental space perception. *Journal of Experimental Psychology*, 1953, **45**, 44–48.

Marks, W. B., Dobelle, W. H., & MacNichol, E. F. Visual pigments of single primate cones. *Science*, 1964, **143**, 1181–1183.

Marshall, H. A., & Talbot, S. A. Recent evidence for neural mechanisms in vision leading to a general theory of sensory acuity. In H. Klüver (Ed.), *Visual mechanisms*. Lancaster, Pa.: Jacques Cattell, 1942.

Masterton, R. B., & Diamond, I. T. Effects of auditory cortex ablation on discrimination of small binaural time differences. *Journal of Neurophysiology*, 1964, **27**, 15–36.

McCall, R. B., & Kagan, J. Stimulus-schema discrepancy and attention in the infant. *Journal of Experimental Child Psychology*, 1967, **5**, 381–390.

McCall, R. B., & Kagan, J. Individual differences in the infants distribution of attention to stimulus discrepancy. *Developmental Psychology*, 1970, **2**, 90–98.

McCall, R. B., & Melson, W. H. Attention in infants as a function of magnitude of discrepancy and habituation rate. *Psychonomic Science*, 1969, **17**, 317–327.

McCleary, R. A. Type of response as a factor to interocular transfer in the fish. *Journal of Comparative Physiological Psychology*, 1960, **53**, 311–321.

McCleary, R. A., & Longfellow, L. Interocular transfer of pattern discrimination without prior binocular experience. *Science*, 1961, **134**, 1418–1419.

McEwan, P. Figural after-effects, retinal size and apparent size. *British Journal of Psychology*, 1959, **50**, 4–7.

McGinnies, E. Emotionality and perceptual defense. *Psychological Review*, 1949, **56**, 244–251.

Mednick, S. A., & Lehtinen, L. E. Stimulus generalization as a function of age in children. *Journal of Experimental Psychology*, 1957, **53**, 180–183.

Mehrabian, A. Verbal betrayal of feeling. *Journal of Experimental Research in Personality*, 1971, **5**, 64–73.

Mehrabian, A. *Nonverbal communication*. Chicago: Aldine-Atherton, 1972.

Melamed, L. E., Halay, M., & Gildow, W. An examination of the role of task oriented attention in the use of active and passive movement in visual adaptation. *Journal of Experimental Psychology*, 1973, **98**, 125–201.

Melamed, L. E., & Moore, L. Visual re-adaptation produced by a proprioceptive task. Paper presented at Midwestern Psychological Association Meeting, May, 1973.

Melamed, L. E., & Thurlow, W. R. Analysis of contrast effects in loudness judgments. *Journal of Experimental Psychology,* 1971, **90,** 268–274.

Mershon, D. H., & Gogel, W. C. Effect of stereoscopic cues on perceived whiteness. *American Journal of Psychology,* 1970, **83,** 55–67.

Metzger, W. *Psychologische Forschung,* 1926, **8,** 114. (Quoted by M. D. Vernon, *A further study of visual perception.* London: Cambridge, 1954, 14–22.)

Metzger, W. Beobachtungen über phanomenale identität. *Psychologische Forschung,* 1934, **19,** 1–60.

Metzger, W. Gesetze des Schens. Frankfurt: Waldemar Kramer, 1953.

Meyers, B., & McCleary, R. A. Interocular transfer of a pattern discrimination in pattern deprived cats. *Journal of Comparative Physiological Psychology,* 1964, **57,** 16–21.

Michael, C. R. Retinal processing of visual images. *Scientific American,* May, 1969, **220,** 104–114.

Michaels, C. Personal communication, 1974.

Michaels, K. M., & Zusne, L. Metrics of visual form. *Psychological Bulletin,* 1965, **63,** 74–86.

Michotte, A. La perception de la causalité. *Louvain Institut supérieur de philosophie,* 1946.

Michotte, A. Lecture given at Oxford University, 1950. (Quoted by M. D. Vernon, *A further study of visual perception.* London: Cambridge, 1954.) (a)

Michotte, A. A propos de la permanence phénomènale: Faits et théories. *Acta Psychologica,* 1950, **7,** 298–322. (Quoted by M. D. Vernon, *A further study of visual perception.* London: Cambridge, 1954.) (b)

Michotte, A. The emotions regarded as functional connections. In M. L. Reyment (Ed.), *The international symposium on feelings and emotions,* New York: McGraw-Hill, 1958, 56–93.

Michotte, A. The perception of causality. New York: Basic Books, 1963.

Miller, G. A. What is information measurement? *American Psychologist,* 1953, **8,** 3–11.

Miller, G. A. Information and memory. *Scientific American,* 1956, **195,** 42–46. (a)

Miller, G. A. The magical number, seven, plus or minus two: Some limits on our capacity for processing information. *Psychological Review,* 1956, **63,** 81–97. (b)

Miller, R. J. Cross-cultural research in perception of pictorial materials. *Psychological Bulletin,* 1973, **80,** 135–150.

Mills, A. W. Auditory localization. In J. V. Tobias (Ed.), *Foundations of modern auditory theory,* Vol. **2,** New York: Academic, 1972, pp. 301–348.

Moed, G. Satiation-theory and the Müller-Lyer illusion. *American Journal of Psychology,* 1959, **72,** 609–611.

Molino, J. A. Psychophysical verification of predicted interaural differences in localizing distant sound sources. *Journal of the Acoustical Society of America,* 1974, **55,** 139–147.

Morant, R. B., & Mikaelin, H. M. Interfield tilt after-effects. *Perception and Motor Skills,* 1960, **10,** 95–98.

Moray, N. Attention in dichotic listening: Affective cues and the influence of institutions. *Quarterly Journal of Experimental Psychology,* 1959, **11,** 56–60.

Murdock, B. B., Jr. Perceptual defense and threshold measurements. *Journal of Personality,* 1954, **22,** 565–571.

Murphy, G. *An historical introduction to modern psychology.* New York: Harcourt, Brace & World, 1949.

Natsoulas, T. What are perceptual reports about? *Psychological Bulletin,* 1967, **67**, 249–272.

Neff, W. D., & Diamond, I. T. The neural basis of auditory discrimination. In H. F. Harlow & C. M. Woolsey (Eds.), *Biological and biochemical bases of behavior.* Madison: University of Wisconsin Press, 1958, pp. 101–126.

Neff, W. S. A critical investigation of the visual apprehension of movement. *American Journal of Psychology,* 1936, **48**, 1–42.

Neisser, U. *Cognitive psychology.* New York: Appleton, 1967.

Neisser, U. The processes of vision. *Scientific American,* 1968, **219**, 204–214.

Neuhaus, W. Experimentelle Untersuchung der Scheinbewegung. *Archiv für die Gesamte Psychologie,* 1930, **75**, 315–458.

Newhall, S. M., Nickerson, D., & Judd, D. Final report of the OSA subcommittee on the spacing of the Munsell colors. *Journal of the Optical Society of America,* 1943, **33**, 385–415.

Newman, C. V. The role of gradients of binocular disparity in Gibson's theory of space perception. *Perception and Psychophysics,* 1972, **12**, 237–238.

Newson, J. Some principles governing changes in the apparent lightness of test surfaces isolated from their normal backgrounds. *Quarterly Journal of Experimental Psychology,* 1958, **10**, 82–95.

Norman, D. A. *Memory and attention: An introduction to human information processing.* New York: Wiley, 1968.

Nothman, F. H. The influence of response conditions on recognition thresholds for tabu words. *Journal of Abnormal and Social Psychology,* 1962, **65**, 154–161.

Noton, D., & Stark, L. Scanpaths in eye movements during pattern recognition. *Science,* 1971, **171**, 308–311.

Novik, N. Parallel processing in a word-nonword classification task. *Journal of Experimental Psychology,* 1974, **102**, 1015–1020.

Obonai, T., & Suto, Y. Studies of figural after-effects by the inspection of short time. *Japanese Journal of Psychology,* 1952, **22**, 248. (Abstract)

Ogle, K. W. *Researches in binocular vision.* Philadelphia: Saunders, 1950.

Olsen, R. K., & Attneave, F. What variables determine similarity grouping. *American Journal of Psychology,* 1970, **83**, 1–21.

Olum, V. Developmental differences in the perception of causality. *American Journal of Psychology,* 1956, **69**, 417–423.

Ono, H. Apparent distance as a function of familiar size. *Journal of Experimental Psychology,* 1969, **79**, 109–115.

Oonishi, S., & Katsuki, Y. Functional organization and integrative mechanism of the auditory cortex of the cat. *Japanese Journal of Physiology,* 1965, **15**, 342–365.

Osgood, C. E. *Method and theory in experimental psychology.* Fair Lawn, N.J.: Oxford, 1953.

Osgood, C. E., & Heyer, A. W., Jr. A new interpretation of figural after-effects. *Psychological Review,* 1952, **59**, 98–118.

Oyama, T. Experimental studies of figural after-effects. Temporal factors. *Japanese Journal of Psychology,* 1953, **23**, 239–245.

Oyama, T. Temporal and spatial factors in figural after-effects. *Japanese Psychological Research,* 1956, **3**, 25–36.

Oyama, T. Perceived size and perceived distance in stereoscopic vision and an analysis of their causal relations. *Perception and Psychophysics,* 1974, **16**, 175–181.

Oyama, T., & Hsia, Y. Compensatory hue shift in simultaneous color contrast as a function of separation between inducing and test fields. *Journal of Experimental Psychology,* 1966, **71,** 405–413.

Pastore, N. Some remarks on the Ames oscillatory effect. *Psychological Review,* 1952, **59,** 319–323.

Pastore, N. Selective history of theories of visual perception; 1650–1950. New York: Oxford, 1971.

Pelton, L. H., & Solley, C. M. Acceleration of reversals of the Necker cube. *American Journal of Psychology,* 1968, **81,** 585–589.

Penn, R. D., & Hagins, W. A. Signal transmission along retinal rods and the origins of the electroretinographic a-wave. *Nature,* 1969, **223,** 201–205.

Petersen, L., & Petersen, M. Short-term retention of individual items. *Journal of Experimental Psychology,* 1959, **58,** 193–198.

Piaget, J. *The psychology of intelligence.* New York: Harcourt, Brace & World, 1950.

Piaget, J., & Inhelder, B. *La représentation de l'espace chez l'enfant.* Paris: Presses Univer. France, 1948.

Piaget, J., & Inhelder, B. *La genese de l'idee de hasard chez l'enfant.* Paris: Presses Univer. France, 1951.

Pick, A. D. Improvement of visual and tactual form discrimination. *Journal of Experimental Psychology,* 1965, **69,** 331–339.

Pick, H. L., & Hay, J. C. Gaze-contingent adaptation to prismatic spectacles. *American Journal of Psychology,* 1966, **79,** 443–450.

Posner, M. I. Abstraction and the process of recognition. In J. H. Bower & J. T. Spence (Eds.), *The psychology of learning and motivation.* New York: Academic, 1969, pp. 44–100.

Posner, M. I., & Keele, S. W. On the genesis of abstract ideas. *Journal of Experimental Psychology,* 1968, **77,** 353–363.

Posner, M. I., Goldsmith, R., & Welton, K. E. Perceived distance and the classification of distorted patterns. *Journal of Experimental Psychology,* 1967, **73,** 28–38.

Posner, M. I., & Mitchell, R. F. Chronometric analysis of classification. *Psychological Review,* 1967, **74,** 392–409.

Postman, L., Bruner, J. S., & McGinnies, E. Personal values as selective factors in perception. *Journal of Abnormal and Social Psychology,* 1948, **43,** 142–154.

Postman, L., & Soloman, R. L. Perceptual sensitivity to completed and incompleted tasks. *Journal of Personality,* 1950, **18,** 347–357.

Powesland, P. F. The effect of practice upon the perception of causality. *Canadian Journal of Psychology,* 1959, **13,** 155–168.

Pratt, C. C. Review of Le developpement perceptif by Robert Frances in *Contemporary Psychology,* 1963, **2,** 38–39.

Pritchard, R. M. Visual illusions viewed as stabilized retinal images. *Quarterly Journal of Experimental Psychology,* 1958, **10,** 77–82.

Pritchard, R. M., Heron, W., & Hebb, D. O. Visual perception approached by the method of stabilized images. *Canadian Journal of Psychology,* 1960, **14,** 67–77.

Purcell, D. G., Stewart, A. L., & Dember, W. N. Spatial effectiveness of the mask: Lateral inhibitions in visual backward masking. *Perception and Psychophysics,* 1968, **4,** 344–346.

Quastler, H. (Ed.) *Information theory in psychology: Problems and methods.* New York: Free Press, 1955.

Radner, M., & Gibson, J. J. Orientation in visual perception: The perception of tip character in form. *Psychological Monographs,* 1935, **46,** (210), 48–65.

Ranken, H. B. Personal communication and paper read at Eastern Psychological Association, Atlantic City, 1956.

Rappaport, M. The role of redundancy in the discrimination of visual forms. *Journal of Experimental Psychology,* 1957, **53,** 3–10.

Ratliff, F. The role of physiological nystagmus in monocular acuity. *Journal of Experimental Psychology,* 1952, **43,** 163–172.

Ratliff, F. *Machbands: Quantitative studies on neural networks in the retina.* New York: Holden-Day, 1965.

Ratliff, F., & Hartline, H. K. The responses of *limulus* optic nerve fibers to patterns of illuminations on the receptor mosaic. *Journal of General Physiology,* 1959, **42,** 1241.

Ratliff, F, Hartline, H. K., & Miller, W. H. Spatial and temporal aspects of retinal inhibitory interaction. *Journal of the Optical Society of America,* 1963, **53,** 110–120.

Reed, S. K. *Psychological processes in pattern recognition.* New York: Academic, 1973.

Reicher, G. M. Perceptual recognition as a function of meaningfulness of stimulus material. *Journal of Experimental Psychology,* 1969, **81,** 275–285.

Richards, W. Anomalous stereoscopic depth perception. *Journal of the Optical Society of America,* 1971, **61,** 410–414.

Riesen, A. H. The development of visual perception in man and chimpanzee. *Science,* 1947, **106,** 107–108.

Riesen, A. H. Plasticity of behavior: Psychological aspects. In H. F. Harlow & E. N. Woolsey (Eds.), *Biological and biochemical bases of behavior,* Madison: Univ. of Wisconsin Press, 1958, pp. 425–450.

Riesen, A. H. Stimulation as a requirement for growth and function in behavioral development. In D. W. Fiske & S. R. Maddi (Eds.), *Functions of varied experience,* Homewood, Ill.: Dorsey, 1961.

Riesen, A. H., & Aarons, L. Visual movement and intensity discrimination in cats after early deprivation of pattern vision. *Journal of Comparative Physiological Psychology,* 1959, **52,** 142–149.

Riess, B. F. Genetic changes in semantic conditioning. *Journal of Experimental Psychology,* 1946, **36,** 143–152.

Riesz, R. R. Differential intensity sensitivity of the ear for pure tones. *Physical Review,* 1928, **31,** 867–875.

Riggs, L. A. Electro physiology of vision. In C. H. Graham (Ed.), *Vision and visual perception.* New York: Wiley, 1965.

Riggs, L. A., Cornsweet, J. C., & Lewis, W. G. Effects of light on electrical excitation of the human eye. *Psychological Monographs,* 1957, **71,** No. 434, 12–14.

Rivers, W. H. R. Introduction and vision. In A. C. Haddor (Ed.), *Reports of the Cambridge anthropological expedition to the Torres Straits.* Vol. **2,** Pt. I. London: Cambridge, 1901.

Rivers, W. H. R. Introduction and vision. Observations on the senses of the Todas. *British Journal of Psychology,* 1905, **1,** 321–396.

Robinson, D. W., & Dadson, R. S. A re-determination of the equal loudness relations for pure tones. *British Journal of Applied Physics,* 1956, **7,** 166–181.

Robinson, J. O. *The psychology of visual illusions.* London: Hutchinson University Library, 1973.

Rock, I. *The nature of perceptual adaptation.* New York: Basic Books, 1966.

Rock, I. Toward a cognitive theory of perceptual constancy. In A. Gilgen (Ed.), *Contemporary scientific psychology.* New York: Academic, 1970.

Rock, I., & Ebenholtz, S. M. The relational determination of perceived size. *Psychological Review,* 1959, **66,** 387–40.

Rock, I., & Engelstein, P. A study of memory for visual form. *American Journal of Psychology,* 1958, 9–28.

Rock, I., & Harris, C. S. Vision and touch. *Scientific American,* 1967, **216,** 96–104.

Rock, I., Hill, A. L., & Fineman, M. Speed constancy as a function of size constancy. *Perception and Psychophysics,* 1968, **4,** 37–40.

Rock, I., & Kremen, I. A re-examination of Rubin's figural after-effect. *Journal of Experimental Psychology,* 1957, **53,** 23–30.

Rock, I., & McDermott, W. The perception of visual angle. *Acta Psychologica,* 1964, **22,** 119–134.

Rose, J. E., Brugge, J. F., Anderson, D. J., & Hind, J. E. Phase-locked response to low-frequency tones in single auditory nerve fibers of the squirrel monkey. *Journal of Neurophysiology,* 1967, **30,** 769–793.

Rose, J. E., Greenwood, D. D., Goldberg, J. M., & Hind, J. E. Some discharge characteristics of single neurons in the inferior colliculus of the cat. I. Tonotopical organization, relations of spike-counts to tone intensity, and firing patterns of single elements. *Journal of Neurophysiology,* 1963, **26,** 294–300.

Rose, J. E., Gross, N. B., Geisler, C. D., & Hind, J. E. Some neural mechanisms in the inferior colliculus of the cat which may be relevant to localization of a sound source. *Journal of Neurophysiology,* 1966, **29,** 288–314.

Royer, F. L., & Garner, W. R. Response uncertainty and perceptual difficulty of auditory temporal patterns. *Perception and Psychophysics,* 1966, **1,** 41–47.

Royer, F. L., & Garner, W. R. Perceptual organization of nine-element auditory temporal patterns. *Perception and Psychophysics,* 1970, **7,** 115–120.

Rubin, E. *Visuelle wahrgenommene Figuren.* Copenhagen: Gyldendalske, 1921.

Rule, S. J., & Markley, R. P. Subject differences in cross-modality matching. *Perception and Psychophysics,* 1971, **9,** 115–117.

Rush, G. P. Visual grouping in relation to age. *Archives of Psychology,* New York, 1937.

Rushton, W. A. H. The physical analysis of cone pigment in the living human eye. *Nature,* 1957, **179,** 571–573.

Rushton, W. A. H. Dark adaptation after exposing the eye to an instantaneous flash. *Nature,* 1963, **199,** 971–972.

Rushton, W. A. H. Bleached rhodopsin and visual adaptation. *Journal of Physiology,* 1965, **181,** 645–655.

Rushton, W. A., Campbell, F. W., Hagins, W. A., & Brindley, G. S. The bleaching and regeneration of rhodopsin in the living eye of the albino rabbit and of man. *Optica Acta,* 1955, **1,** 182–190.

Rutherford, W. A new theory of hearing. *Journal of Anatomy and Physiology,* 1886, **21,** 166–168.

Ryan, T. A., & Schwartz, C. B. Speed of perception as a function of mode of representations. *American Journal of Psychology,* 1965, **69,** 60–69.

Salapatek, P. Visual scanning of geometric figures by the human newborn. *Journal of Comparative Physiology,* 1968, **66,** 247–255.

Salapatek, P., & Kessen, W. Visual scanning of triangles by the human infant. *Journal of Experimental Child Psychology,* 1966, **3,** 155–167.

Sanders, A. The selective process in the functional visual field. Institute for Perception. RVU-TNO, Soesterberg, The Netherlands, 1963.

Schachter, S. The interaction of cognitive and physiological determinants of emotional states. In L. Benkonilly (Ed.), *Advances in experimental social psychology.* Vol. 1, New York: Academic, 1964.

Schachter, S., & Latané, W. Crime, cognition and the A.N.S. In D. Levine (Ed.), *Nebraska Symposium on Motivation,* 1964, 221–272.

Schachter, S., & Singer, J. E. Cognitive, social and physiological determinants of emotional state. *Psychological Review,* 1962, **69,** 221–272.

Scharf, B. Critical bands. In J. V. Tobias (Ed.), *Foundations of modern auditory theory,* Vol. 1. New York: Academic, 1970, pp. 157–202.

Schiffman, H. R. Size estimation of familiar objects under informative and reduced conditions of viewing. *American Journal of Psychology,* 1967, **80,** 229–235.

Schiller, P. H., & Smith, M. C. Monoptic and dichoptic metacontrast. *Perception and Psychophysics,* 1968, **3,** 237–239.

Schlosberg, H. Stereoscopic depth from single pictures. *American Journal of Psychology,* 1941, **54,** 601–605.

Secord, P. F., Bevan, W., & Katz, B. The negro stereotype and perceptual orientation. *Journal of Abnormal and Social Psychology,* 1956, **53,** 78–83.

Segall, M. H., Campbell, D. T., & Herskovitz, M. J. *The influence of culture on visual perception.* Indianapolis: Bobbs-Merrill, 1966.

Sekuler, R. W., & Ganz, L. Aftereffect of seen motion with a stabilized retinal image. *Science,* 1963, **139,** 419–420.

Seligman, D. G. The vision of the native of British Guinea. In A. C. Maddon (Ed.), Reports of the Cambridge anthropological expeditions to Torres Straits. Vol 2. London: Cambridge, 1901.

Senden, von, M. *Raum und Gestalt Auffassung bei opeuerten blindgeboren en vor und nach der Operation.* Leipzig: Barth, 1932.

Senden, von, M. *Space and sight: The perception of space and shape in the congenitally blind before and after operation.* (Trans. P. Heath.) London: Methuen, 1960.

Seward, J. P. The effect of practice on the visual perception of form. *Archives of Psychology,* N.Y., 1931, **20,** No. 130.

Sgro, F. J. Beta motion thresholds. *Journal of Experimental Psychology,* 1963, **66,** 281–285.

Shaffer, O., & Wallach, H. Extent of motion thresholds under subject-relative and object-relative conditions. *Perception and Psychophysics,* 1966, **1,** 447–451.

Shannon, C. E., & Weaver, W. *The mathematical theory of communication.* Urbana: The University of Illinois Press, 1949.

Sheehan, M. R. A study of individual consistency in phenomenal constancy. *Archives of Psychology,* 1938, No. 222 (Whole No. 438).

Sheppard, J. J. *Human color perception. A critical study of the experimental foundation.* New York: American Elsevier, 1968.

Shiffrin, R. M., & Geister, W. S. Visual recognition in a theory of information processing. In R. L. Solso (Ed.), *Contemporary issues in cognitive psychology.* Washington: Winston, 1973.

Shinar, D., & Owen, D. H. Effects of rotation on the speed of classification: The development of shape constancy. *Perception and Psychophysics,* 1973, **14,** 169–174.

Shipley, T., & Rawlings, S. C. The nonius horopter—I. History and theory. *Vision Research,* 1970, **10,** 1225–1262. (a)

Shipley, T., & Rawlings, S. C. The nonius horopter—II. An experimental report. *Vision Research,* 1970, **10,** 1263–1299. (b)

Shurley, J. T. The hydro-hypodynamic environment. *Proceedings of Third World Congress of Psychiatry,* 1963, **3,** 232–236. Toronto: University of Toronto Press.

Siegal, A. I. Deprivation of visual form definition in the ring dove. I. Discriminatory learning. *Journal of Comparative Physiological Psychology,* 1953, **46,** 115–119.

Smith, K. Attraction in figural after-effects. *American Journal of Psychology,* 1954, **67,** 174–176.

Smith, O. W., Impater, N., & Exner, Jr. J. E., Effects of practice on reversals of incomplete Necker cubes. *Perception and Motor Skills,* 1968, **27,** 951–954.

Soloman, R. L., et al. *Sensory deprivation.* Cambridge: Harvard, 1961.

Soloman, R. L., & Howes, D. Word frequency, personal values, and visual duration thresholds. *Psychological Review,* 1951, **58,** 256–270.

Solso, R. L. (Ed.) *Contemporary issues in cognitive psychology.* Washington: Winston, 1973, page X.

Somjen, G. *Sensory coding in the mammalian nervous system.* New York: Appleton-Century-Crofts, 1972.

Sommer, R. Small group ecology. *Psychological Bulletin,* 1967, **67,** 145–152.

Spence, D. P. A new look in vigilance and defense. *Journal of Abnormal Psychology,* 1957, **54,** 103–108. (a)

Spence, D. P. Success, failure, and recognition thresholds. *Journal of Personality,* 1957, **25,** 712–720. (b)

Spencer, T. J. Some effects of different masking stimuli on iconic storage. *Journal of Experimental Psychology,* 1969, **81,** 132–140.

Spencer, T. J., & Shuntich, R. Evidence for an interruption theory of backward masking. *Journal of Experimental Psychology,* 1970, **85,** 198–203.

Sperling, G. The information available in brief visual presentations. *Psychological Monographs,* 1960, **74,** No. 11 (Whole No. 498).

Sperling, G. A model for visual memory tasks. *Human Factors,* 1963, **5,** 19–31.

Sperling, G. Successive approximations to a model for short-term memory. *Acta Psychologica,* 1967, **27,** 285–292.

Spiegel, I. Relation of movement aftereffect duration to interpolated darkness intervals. *Life Science,* 1962, **6,** 239–242.

Spiegel, I. (Ed.) *Visually perceived movement.* New York: Harper & Row, 1965.

Stavrianos, B. K. The relation of shape perception to explicit judgements of inclination. *Archives of Psychology,* New York, 1945, No. 296 (Whole No. 487).

Stebbins, W. D., Miller, J. M., Johannsen, L-G, & Hawkins, J. E. Ototoxic hearing loss and cochlear pathology in the monkey. *Annals of Otology, Rhinology, and Laryngology,* 1969, **78,** 1007–1026.

Stein, K. B. Perceptual defense and perceptual sensitization under neutral and involved conditions. *Journal of Personality,* 1953, **21,** 467–478.

Steiner, I. D. Human interaction and interpersonal perception. *Sociometry,* 1959, **22,** 230–235. (a)

Steiner, I. D. Interpersonal orientation and assumed similarity between opposites. U.S. Public Health Service Grant M1774. Univer. of Ill., Dept. of Psychology, Group Effectiveness Res. Lab., 1959, pp. 1–11. (b)

Steinig, K. Untersuchungen über die Wahrnehmung der Bewegung durch das Auge: IV. *Zeitschrift für Psychologie,* 1929, **109,** 291–336.

Sternberg, S. Scanning a persisting visual image versus a memorized list. Paper presented at the meeting of the Eastern Psychological Association, Boston, April, 1967.

Sternberg, S. The discovery of processing stages: Extensions of Donders' method. *Acta Psychologica,* 1969, **30,** 273–315. (a)

Sternberg, S. Memory scanning: Mental processes revealed by reaction-time measurements. *American Scientist,* 1969, **57,** 421–457. (b)

Stevens, S. S. The relation of pitch to intensity. *Journal of the Acoustical Society of America,* 1935, **6,** 150–154.

Stevens, S. S. Mathematics, measurement, and psychophysics. In S. S. Stevens (Ed.), *Handbook of experimental psychology.* New York: Wiley, 1951, Chapter 1.

Stevens, S. S. The direct estimation of sensory magnitudes—Loudness. *American Journal of Psychology,* 1956, **69,** 1–25.

Stevens, S. S. On the psychophysical law. *Psychological Review,* 1957, **64,** 153–181.

Stevens, S. S. Ratio scales, partition scales, and confusion scales. In H. Gulliksen & S. Messick (Eds.), *Psychological scaling.* New York: Wiley, 1960, pp. 49–66.

Stevens, S. S. To honor Fechner and repeal his law. *Science,* 1961, **133,** 80–86.

Stevens, S. S. The surprising simplicity of sensory metrics. *American Psychologist,* 1962, **17,** 29–39.

Stevens, S. S. & Davis, H. *Hearing.* New York: Wiley, 1938.

Stewart, E. C. "The Gelb effect." *Journal of Experimental Psychology,* 1959, **57,** 235.

Stotler, W. A. An experimental study of the cells and connections of the superior olivary complex of the cat. *Journal of Comparative Neurology,* 1953, **98,** 401–432.

Stratton, G. M. Vision without inversion of the retinal image. *Psychological Review,* 1897, **4,** 341–360.

Stroud, J. The fine structure of psychological time. In H. Quastler (Ed.), *Information theory in psychology.* Glencoe, Ill.: Free Press, 1956.

Sutherland, N. S. Figural after-effects and apparent sizes. *Quarterly Journal of Experimental Psychology,* 1961, **13,** 222–228.

Sutherland, N. S. Outlines of a theory of visual pattern recognition in animals and man. *Proceedings of the Royal Society,* 1968, **171,** 297–317.

Sutherland, N. S. Object recognition. In E. C. Canterette & M. P. Friedman (Eds.), *Handbook of perception,* Vol. **3.** New York: Academic, 1973.

Sylvester, J. Apparent movement and the Brown-Voth experiment. *Quarterly Journal of Experimental Psychology,* 1960, **12,** 231–236.

Tagiuri, R. Movement as a cue in person perception. In H. P. David & J. C. Brengelmann (Eds.), *Perspectives in personality research.* New York: Springer, 1960.

Tagiuri, R. Person perception. In G. Lindzey and E. Aronson (Eds.), *The Handbook of social psychology,* Vol. **3,** pp. 395–449. Reading, Mass.: Addison-Wesley, 1969.

Tajfel, H. Value and the perceptive judgement of magnitude. *Psychological Review,* 1957, **64,** 192–204.

Tajfel, H. Social and cultural factors in perception. In G. Lindzey and E. Aronson (Eds.), *The handbook of social psychology,* Vol. **3,** Reading, Mass.: Addison-Wesley, 1969.

Tajfel, H., & Wilkes, A. L. Classification and quantitative judgement. *British Journal of Psychology,* 1963, **54,** 101–114.

Tanaka, Y., Uemura, Y., & Torif, S. Decrease and increase in test threshold luminance induced by a contiguous annular field. *Perception and Motor Skills,* 1967, **24,** 1319–1326.

Taylor, J. G. *The behavioral basis of perception.* New Haven, Conn.: Yale, 1962.

Tees, R. C. Effect of early restriction on later form discrimination in the rat. *Canadian Journal of Psychology,* 1968, **22,** 294–301.

Teghtsoonian, M., & Teghtsoonian, R. Scaling apparent distances in natural indoor setting. *Psychonomic Science,* 1969, **16,** 281–283.

Teghtsoonian, R., & Teghtsoonian, M. The effects of size and distance on magnitude estimations of apparent size. *American Journal of Psychology,* 1970, **83,** 601–612.

Templeton, W. B., Howard, I. P., & Wilkinson, D. A. Additivity of components of prismatic adaptation. *Perception and Psychophysics,* 1974, **15,** 249–275.

Ternus, J. The problem of phenomenal identity. *Psychologische Forschung,* 1926, **7,** 81.

Thorndike, E. L., & Lorge, I. *The teacher's word-book of 30,000 words.* New York: Columbia, Teachers College, 1944.

Thouless, R. H. Phenomenal regression to the real object. I. *British Journal of Psychology,* 1931, **21,** 339–359. (a)

Thouless, R. H. Phenomenal regression to the real object. II. *British Journal of Psychology,* 1931, **22,** 1–30. (b)

Thouless, R. H. Individual differences in phenomenal regression. *British Journal of Psychology,* 1932, **22,** 216–241.

Thouless, R. H. A racial difference in perception. *Journal of Social Psychology,* 1933, **4,** 330–339.

Thurlow, W. R., & Runge, P. S. Effect of induced head movements on localization of direction of sounds. *Journal of the Acoustical Society of America,* 1967, **42,** 480–488.

Tinbergen, N., & Perdeck, A. C. On the stimulus situation releasing the begging response in the newly hatched herring-gull chick. *Behavior,* 1950, **3,** 1–38.

Tomita, T. Electrophysiological study of the mechanisms subserving color coding in the fish retina. Cold Spring Harbor Symposium, 1965, **30,** 559–566.

Tomkins, S. S. *Affect, imagery, consciousness.* Vol. **1.** *The positive affects.* New York: Springer, 1963.

Tomkins, S. S., & McCarter, R. What and where are the primary affects? Some evidence for a theory. *Perception and Motor Skills,* 1964, **18,** 119–158.

Torgerson, W. S. Quantitative judgement scales. In H. Gulliksen and S. Messick (Eds.), *Psychological scaling.* New York: Wiley, 1960, pp. 21–31.

Treisman, A. Strategies and models of selective attention. *Psychological Review,* 1969, **76,** 282–299.

Treisman, A. M. The effect of irrelevant material on the efficiency of selective listening. *American Journal of Psychology,* 1964, **77,** 533–546.

Treisman, A. M., & Geffen, G. Selective attention: Perception or response? *Quarterly Journal of Experimental Psychology,* 1967, **19,** 1–17.

Treisman, A. M., & Riley, J. S. Is selective attention selective perception or selective response: A further test. *Journal of Experimental Psychology,* 1969, **79,** 27–34.

Triandis, H. C. Cultural influence upon cognitive processes. In L. Berkowitz (Ed.), *Advances in experimental social psychology,* Vol. **1.** New York: Academic, 1964.

Tronick, E. Stimulus control and the growth of the infant's effective visual field. *Perception and Psychophysics,* 1972, **11,** 373–376.

Uhlarik, J. J., & Cannon, L. K. Influence of concurrent and terminal exposure conditions on the nature of perceptual adaptation. *Journal of Experimental Psychology,* 1971, **91,** 233–239.

Uttal, W. R. Masking of alphabetic character recognition by dynamic visual noise. (DVN). *Perception and Psychophysics,* 1969, **6,** 121–128.

Uttal, W. R. *The psychology of sensory coding.* New York: Harper & Row, 1973.

Valins, S. Cognitive effects of false heart-rate feedback. *Journal of Personality and Social Psychology,* 1966, **4,** 400–408.

Valins, S. Persistent effects of information about internal reactions: Ineffectiveness of debriefing. In R. H. London & R. E. Nisbett (Eds.), *The cognitive alteration of feeling states.* Chicago: Aldine, 1972.

Valins, S., & Ray, A. A. Affects of cognitive desensitization on avoidance behavior. *Journal of Personality and Social Psychology,* 1967, **7,** 345–350.

Vernon, J. A., McGill, T. E., & Schiffman, H. Visual hallucinations during perceptual isolation. *Canadian Journal of Psychology,* 1958, **12,** 31–34.

Vernon, M. D. The perception of inclined lines. *British Journal of Psychology,* 1934, **25,** 186–196.

Vernon, M. D. *Perception through experience.* London: Methuen, 1970.

Vickers, D. Perceptual economy and the impression of visual depth. *Perception and Psychophysics,* 1971, **10,** 23–27.

Vogel, J., & Teghtsoonian, M. The effects of perspective alterations on apparent size and distance scales. *Perception and Psychophysics,* 1972, **11,** 294–298.

Wald, G. Photo-labile pigments of the chicken retina. *Nature,* 1937, **140,** 545–546.

Wald, G. Eye and camera. *Scientific American,* 1950, **183,** 32–41.

Wald, G., & Brown, P. K. Human color vision and color blindness. Cold Spring Harbor Symposium on Quantitative Biology, 1965, **30,** 345–361.

Wallach, H. On sound localization. *Journal of the Acoustical Society of America,* 1939, **10,** 270–274.

Wallach, H. The role of head movements and vestibular and visual cues in sound localization. *Journal of Experimental Psychology,* 1940, **27,** 339–368.

Wallach, H. Brightness constancy and the nature of achromatic colors. *Journal of Experimental Psychology,* 1948, **38,** 310–324.

Wallach, H. The perception of motion. *Scientific American,* 1959, **201,** 56–60.

Wallach, H. The perception of neutral colors. *Scientific American,* 1963, **208,** 107.

Wallach, H. *Visual perception of motion. The nature of art and motion.* New York: Brazilles, 1965.

Wallach, H., & Floor, L. The use of size matching to demonstrate the effectiveness of accommodation and convergence as cues for distance. *Perception and Psychophysics,* 1971, (Dec.), **10,** (6) 423–428.

Wallach, H., & Frey, K. J. Adaptation in distance perception based on oculomotor cues. *Perception and Psychophysics,* 1972, **11,** 77–83. (a)

Wallach, H., & Frey, K. J. On counteradaptation. *Perception and Psychophysics,* 1972, (Feb.), **11,** (2), 161–165. (b)

Wallach, H., Frey, K. J., & Bode, K. A. Adaptation in distance perception based on oculomotor cues. *Perception and Psychophysics,* 1972 (Jan.), **11**(1-B), 161–165. (a)

Wallach, H., Frey, K. J., & Bode, K. A. The nature of adaptation in distance perception based on oculomotor cues. *Perception and Psychophysics,* 1972, **11,** 110–116. (b)

Wallach, H., & Galloway, A. The constancy of colored objects in colored illumination. *Journal of Experimental Psychology,* 1946, **366,** 119–126.

Wallach, J., Kravitz, J. H., & Lindauer, J. A. A passive condition for rapid adaptation to displace visual direction. *American Journal of Psychology,* 1963, **76,** 568–578.

Wallach, H., & O'Connell, D. N. The kinetic depth effect. *Journal of Experimental Psychology,* 1953, **45,** 205–217.

Wallach, H., & Schaffer, O. Extent of motion thresholds under subject-relative and object-relative conditions. *Perception and Psychophysics,* 1966, **1,** 447–451.

Wapner, S., Werner, H., & Chandler, K. A. Experiments on the visual perception of verticality. *Journal of Experimental Psychology,* 1951, **42,** 351–357.

Ward, W. D. Musical perception. In J. V. Tobias (Ed.), *Foundations of modern auditory theory* (Vol. **1**). New York: Academic, 1970, pp. 405–447.

Warren, D. H., & Platt, B. B. Understanding prism adaptation: An individual-differences approach. *Perception and Psychophysics,* 1975, **17,** 337–345.

Weber, C. O., & Bicknall, N. The size-constancy phenomenon in stereoscopic space. *American Journal of Psychology,* 1935, **47,** 436–488.

Wegel, R. L., & Lane, C. E. The auditory masking of one pure tone by another and its probable relation to the dynamics of the inner ear. *Physical Review,* 1924, **23,** 266–285.

Weinstein, S., Serson, E. A., Fisher, L., & Weosinger, M. S. Is reafference necessary for visual adaptation? *Perception and Motor Skills,* 1964, **18,** 641–648.

Weintraub, D. J., & Gardner, G. T. Emmert's Laws: Size constancy vs. optical geometry. *American Journal of Psychology,* 1970, **83,** 40–51.

Weisstein, N. Backward masking and models of perceptual processing. *Journal of Experimental Psychology,* 1966, **72,** 232–240.

Weisstein, N. A Rashevsky-Landahl neural net: Simulation of metacontrast. *Psychological Review,* 1968, **75,** 494–521.

Weisstein, N., & Haber, R. N. A U-shaped backward masking function in vision. *Psychonomic Science,* 1965, **2,** 75–76.

Weitman, B. A figural after-effect produced by a phenomenal dichotomy in a uniform contour. *Journal of Experimental Psychology,* 1963, **66,** 195–200.

Welch, R. B., Choe, C. S., & Heimrich, D. R. Evidence for a three-component model of prism adaptation. *Journal of Experimental Psychology,* 1974, **103,** 700–705.

Werner, H. Studies on contour. *American Journal of Psychology,* 1935, **47,** 40–64.

Werner, H., & Wapner, S. Sensory-tonic field theory of perception. *Journal of Personality,* 1949, **18,** 88–107.

Werner, H., & Wapner, S. Toward a general theory of perception. *Psychological Review,* 1952, **59,** 324–338.

Werner, H., & Wapner, S. The Innsbruck studies on distorted visual field in relation to the organismic theory of perception. *Psychological Review,* 1955, **62,** 130–138.

Wertheimer, M. Experimentelle Studien über das Sehen von Bewegung. *Zeitschrift für Psychologie,* 1912, **61,** 161.

Wertheimer, M. Untersuchen zu Lehre von der Gestalt. I. *Psychologische Forschung,* 1923, **1,** 47–58; II. 1923, **4,** 301–350.

Wever, E. G. Figure and ground in the visual perception of form. *American Journal of Psychology,* 1927, **38,** 194–226.

Wever, E. G. *Theory of hearing.* New York: Wiley, 1949.

Wever, E. G., & Bray, C. W. Action currents in the auditory nerve in response to acoustic stimulation. *Proceedings of the National Academy of Sciences,* 1930, **16,** 344–350.

Wexler, D., Mendelson, J., Leiderman, P. H., & Solomon, P. Sensory deprivation. *Archives of Neurology and Psychiatry,* 1958, **79,** 225–233.

Wheeler, D. D. Processes in word recognition. *Cognitive Psychology,* 1970, **1,** 59–85.

White, B. L. *Human infants: Experience and psychological development*. Englewood Cliffs, N.J.: Prentice-Hall, 1971.

Whitfield, I. C. *The auditory pathway*. (Monographs of the Physiological Society, No. 17.) London: E. Arnold, 1967.

Wickens, D. D. Characteristics of word encoding. In A. W. Melton & E. Martin (Eds.), *Coding processes in human memory*. New York: Winston, 1972, pp. 191–216.

Wiesel, T. N., & Hubel, D. H. Single-cell responses in striate cortex of kittens deprived of vision in one eye. *Journal of Neurophysiology*, 1963, **26**, 1003–1017.

Wiesel, T. N., & Hubel, D. H. Comparisons of the effects of unilateral and bilateral eye closure on cortical unit responses in kittens. *Journal of Neurophysiology*, 1965, **28**, 1029–1040.

Wiesel, T. N., & Hubel, D. H. Spatial and chromatic interactions in the lateral geniculate body of the rhesus monkey. *Journal of Neurophysiology*, 1966, **29**, 1115–1156.

Wilkinson, D. A. Visual-motor control movement: A linear system? *Journal of Experimental Psychology*, 1971, **89**, 250–257.

Witkin, H. A. Individual differences in the ease of perception of embedded figures. *Journal of Personality*, 1950, **19**, 1–16 (a)

Witkin, H. A. Perception of the upright when the direction of the force acting on the body is changed. *Journal of Experimental Psychology*, 1950, **40**, 93–106. (b)

Witkin, H. A. The perception of the upright. *Scientific American*, 1959, **200**, 50–56.

Witkin, H. A., & Asch, S. E. Studies in space orientation. III. Perception of the upright in the absence of a visual field. *Journal of Experimental Psychology*, 1948, **38**, 603–614. (a)

Witkin, H. A., & Asch, S. E. Studies in space orientation. IV. Further experiments on perception of the upright with displaced visual fields. *Journal of Experimental Psychology*, 1948, **38**, 762–782. (b)

Witkin, H., Dyk, R. B. Faterson, H. F., Goodenough, D. R., and Karp, S. A. *Psychological differentiation*. New York: Wiley, 1962.

Wolford, G. L., Wessel, D. L., & Estes, W. K. Further evidence concerning scanning and sampling assumptions of visual detection models. *Perception and Psychophysics*, 1968, **3**, 439–444.

Woodruff, A. B., & Slovak, M. L. The effects of severely restricted visual experience on the perception of "Identity." *Psychonomic Science*, 1965, **2**, 41–42.

Woodworth, R. S., & Schlosberg, H. *Experimental Psychology*. New York: Holt, 1954.

Wright, W. D. *The measurement of color*. New York: Van Nostrand, 1964.

Wulf, F. Uber die Veränderung von Vorstellungen (Gedächtnis und Gestalt). *Psychologische Forschung*, 1922, **1**, 333–373.

Wyszecki, G., & Stiles, W. S. *Color science: Concepts and methods, quantitative data and formulas*. New York: Wiley, 1967.

Yarbus, A. L. *Eye movements and vision*, chap. 7. New York: Plenum, 1967.

Yonas, A., & Gibson, E. J. A developmental study of feature-processing strategies in letter discrimination. Paper presented at Einstein Psychological Association meeting, Boston, April, 1967.

Young, T. *A course of lectures on natural philosophy and the mechanical arts*. Vol. I. London: Taylor and Welton, 1845.

Zaidel, S. F., & Mehrabian, A. The ability to communicate and infer positive and negative attitudes facially and verbally. *Journal of Experimental Research in Personality*, 1969, **3**, 233–241.

Zegers, R. T. The reversal illusion of the Ames trapezoid. *Transactions of the New York Academy of Sciences,* 1965, **26,** 377–400.

Zeigler, H. P., and Leibowitz, H. Apparent visual size as a function of distance for children and adults. *American Journal of Psychology,* 1957, **70,** 8–11.

Zubek, J. P. (Ed.) *Sensory deprivation: Fifteen years of research.* New York: Appleton-Century-Crofts, 1969.

Zubek, J. P., Aftanas, M., Hasek, J., Sansom, W., Schludermann, E., Wilgosh, L. & Winocur, G. Intellectual and perceptual changes during prolonged perceptual deprivation. Low illumination and noise level. *Perception and Motor Skills,* 1962, **15,** 171–198.

Zubek, J. P., & MacNeill, M. Effects of immobilization: Behavioral and EEG changes. *Canadian Journal of Psychology,* 1966, **20,** 316–336.

Zubek, J. P., & MacNeill, M. Perceptual deprivation phenomena: Role of the recumbant position. *Journal of Abnormal Psychology,* 1967, **72,** 147–150.

Zubek, J. P., Pushkar, D., Sansom, W., & Gowing, J. Perceptual change after prolonged isolation (darkness and silence). *Canadian Journal of Psychology,* 1961, **15,** 83–100.

Zuckerman, M. Variables affecting deprivation results and hallucinations, reported sensations and images. In J. P. Zubek (Ed.), *Sensory deprivation,* New York: Appleton-Century-Crofts, 1969.

Zusne, L. *Visual perception of form.* New York: Academic, 1970.

Index